EXPLORING
LONG-TERM
SOLUTIONS FOR
LOUISIANA'S
TAX SYSTEM

I0109759

EXPLORING LONG-TERM SOLUTIONS FOR LOUISIANA'S TAX SYSTEM

James A. Richardson

Steven M. Sheffrin

James Alm

LOUISIANA STATE UNIVERSITY PRESS

BATON ROUGE

Published by Louisiana State University Press
Copyright © 2018 by Louisiana State University Press
All rights reserved
Manufactured in the United States of America
First printing

Designer: Laura Roubique Gleason
Typeface: Minion Pro
Printer and binder: Sheridan Books, Inc.

Maps by Mary Lee Eggart

Library of Congress Cataloging-in-Publication Data

Names: Richardson, James A., author. | Sheffrin, Steven M., author. | Alm, James, author.
Title: Exploring long-term solutions for Louisiana's tax system / James A. Richardson, Steven M. Sheffrin, and James Alm.
Description: Baton Rouge : Louisiana State University Press, 2018. | Includes bibliographical references and index.
Identifiers: LCCN 2018019075 | ISBN 978-0-8071-6991-9 (pbk. : alk. paper)
Subjects: LCSH: Taxation—Louisiana. | Budget deficits—Louisiana. | Finance, Public—Louisiana.
Classification: LCC HJ2409 .R53 2018 | DDC 336.2009763—dc23
LC record available at https://lccn.loc.gov/2018019075

The paper in this book meets the guidelines for permanence and durability of the Committee on Production Guidelines for Book Longevity of the Council on Library Resources. ∞

CONTENTS

FOREWORD

As Speaker of the Louisiana House of Representatives and President of the Louisiana Senate, we appreciate the importance of having accurate and objective information on which to make important public policy decisions. And this is especially true when it comes to tax policy. We acknowledge that the ultimate decisions about tax policy must benefit the state as a whole, and as leaders of the state it is our responsibility to gather the best information we can get regarding taxation. Members of the Louisiana legislature want to know about the stability of our current tax structure, the simplicity of our tax code, the effects of changes in tax policy on who ultimately pays the tax and the distributional effects of the tax, the impact of any changes on our business environment, and the comparison of Louisiana's tax policy to those in other states and localities.

In the 1980s, the state was going through a major economic downturn. The state relied heavily on revenues from oil and gas and had experienced a decade of unprecedented growth followed by a sudden decline in prices. As a result, the state experienced years of fiscal uncertainty. Louisiana State University, the state's flagship university, with the assistance of the Council for A Better Louisiana, asked Dr. Jim Richardson to gather a group of tax experts to examine Louisiana's tax structure. Dr. Richardson assembled a team of economists and other tax experts around the state and produced *Louisiana's Fiscal Alternatives: Finding Permanent Solutions to Recurring Budget Crises,* published by LSU Press in 1988.

Decades later, Louisiana is again experiencing fiscal instability due to declines in revenues. While not of the same magnitude or cause as the decline of revenues in the 1980s, the current fiscal instability leads to uncertainty in the viability of the state's support for public services, such as infrastructure and education, and in the predictability of the taxes levied by the state.

As a means of initiating a new discussion of the state's fiscal stability, we thought it was time for an updated independent study of the state's tax structure. We again turned to Dr. Richardson to take the lead in assembling a team of experts to examine the state's tax system. He, in turn, asked two noted public finance scholars at Tulane University to assist him. Dr.

Steven M. Sheffrin served as the Dean of the Division of Social Sciences at the University of California–Davis from 1998 to 2008 and is now the Director of the Murphy Institute and a faculty member in the Department of Economics at Tulane. Dr. James Alm served as Chair of the Department of Economics and Dean of the Andrew Young School of Public Policy at Georgia State University before becoming chair of the Department of Economics at Tulane University.

The following study provides the basic framework that we, as legislators, should consider as we make decisions in our role as representatives of the citizens of Louisiana. We have an obligation to gather the most accurate information and to review and understand the implications of making the tax system viable for another twenty-five years. The goal is a tax system that will provide the revenues necessary to fund the public services that the citizens consider important and necessary, maintain the economic competitiveness of Louisiana with other states as we compete for jobs and economic development, and make sure that the taxes are borne equitably among all taxpayers in the state.

This study gives the legislature and citizens of Louisiana information and options toward this goal. We appreciate the careful and thoughtful approach taken by Professors Richardson, Sheffrin, and Alm.

The Honorable Chuck Kleckley
Speaker of the Louisiana House of Representatives, 2015

The Honorable John Alario
President of the Louisiana Senate, 2015

ACKNOWLEDGMENTS

The authors wish to acknowledge the assistance that we received in completing this study from persons who work with the state legislature, the governor's office, and Louisiana State University and Tulane University. First, we note the support from the Speaker of the House of Representatives in 2014, the Honorable Chuck Kleckley, and the President of the Louisiana Senate in 2014, the Honorable John Alario. Speaker Kleckley and President Alario initiated the study and then provided funding for it along with very generous financial support from The Murphy Institute, Tulane University; the Department of Economics, Tulane University; and the Public Administration Institute, Louisiana State University.

We especially want to recognize the assistance of Mr. Greg Albrecht, the chief economist for the Louisiana Legislative Fiscal Office. He assisted in preparing the second chapter of the book, but he was most generous in providing his database on the collection of taxes over many years as well as making available his background and information in dealing with possible tax changes. The state is quite fortunate to have a person with Greg's professional ability and integrity. We needed the assistance of the Louisiana Department of Revenue, and we received its professional support under Secretary Tim Barfield (the Jindal Administration) and Secretary Kimberly Robinson (the Edwards Administration). We are very grateful for the assistance of Tim and Kim and their staffs. At the very beginning of this study, we asked Professor George R. Zodrow, the Allyn R. and Gladys M. Cline Chair of Economics at Rice University, and William F. Fox, the William B. Stokely Distinguished Professor of Business and the Director of the Boyd Center for Business & Economic Research at the University of Tennessee, to give us their impressions of the state and local tax structure in Louisiana. Both were very generous with their time, analysis, and observations. We appreciate their assistance.

Finally, we appreciate the assistance of students and faculty members at Tulane University and Louisiana State University who provided research support and technical assistance. We want to note the assistance of Ms. Jinyoung Park, Assistant Director of the Center for Public Policy Research at

The Murphy Institute, Tulane University; Grant Driessen, Rachel Butler, Gabriella Runnels, Dan Teles, and Bibek Adhikari, all students at Tulane University when they worked on this project; Dr. Roy Heidelberg, Assistant Professor of Public Administration, and Dr. Greg Upton, Assistant Professor in the Center for Energy Studies, at Louisiana State University; and Mr. Nathan Babb, a student at Louisiana State University when he worked on this project.

We acknowledge the difficult task of implementing fiscal reform in any state. Preparing a report is quite easy compared to implementing tax reforms. We enjoyed working with the Task Force on Structural Change in Budget and Tax Policy, a group of thirteen citizens who spent hours working through the various tax options available to the state and local governments. They used our study as a starting point and then discussed the difficult political choices involved and the simple reality of what might be doable. So we appreciate the many agonizing hours that Governor John Bel Edwards, members of the Louisiana House of Representatives, and members of the Louisiana Senate have devoted and will have to devote to solving the state's long-term fiscal problems.

We also acknowledge that tax laws can change quickly. The Louisiana sales tax rate was 4 percent when we did our first report to the State Legislature; it was 5 percent when we served on the Task Force on Structural Change in Budget and Tax Policy; and it is now 4.45 percent. The U.S. Supreme Court just made a significant ruling affecting the possible collection of state and local sales taxes from remote sellers. The federal government made changes in the individual income tax affecting Louisiana income tax collections. These changes are significant, but they do not create a sustainable tax structure for Louisiana. Long-term solutions will still need actions by public officials and the electorate. We hope that this book will help in this process.

1

AN INTRODUCTION TO TAX POLICY

James A. Richardson, Steven M. Sheffrin, and James Alm

The Louisiana legislature in 2014 asked us to prepare a report regarding the Louisiana tax structure, including an analysis of all revenue sources, all exemptions, deductions, and credits associated with the tax code, and the short- and long-term adequacy and stability of the overall Louisiana tax structure. We made a presentation to the House Committee on Ways and Means and the Senate Committee on Revenue and Fiscal Affairs in March 2015 on the major findings from the tax study. In that presentation, we provided a number of suggestions for improving the Louisiana tax structure in terms of increasing the long-term stability of the tax structure, maintaining its economic competitiveness, enhancing its horizontal and vertical equity, and simplifying the administration of the tax laws. These recommendations are laid out in this book, but we also appreciate that tax studies are just the first step in the process of actually making major revisions in any tax structure.

The 2015 presentation preceded four legislative sessions in which tax measures were seriously considered (the regular legislative session 2015; first extraordinary legislative session 2016; second extraordinary legislative session 2016; first extraordinary session 2017; and regular 2017 legislative session).[1] These sessions led to a number of temporary and permanent changes in the tax structure dealing with the following:

- Limiting exemptions and credits—mostly temporary at first and then made permanent
- Expanding the sales tax base—temporary
- Increasing the state sales tax rate from 4 percent to 5 percent—temporary
- Amending two income tax credits—permanent
- Improving the administration of the corporate income tax base—permanent

- Extending the corporate franchise tax definition—permanent
- Increasing excise taxes on tobacco, beer, and alcoholic beverages and wine—permanent.

Some of the changes were consistent with the suggested reforms as presented in our presentation to the Louisiana legislature, especially administrative changes in the corporate income tax, increases in the excise taxes on tobacco, beer, and alcoholic beverages and wine, expansion of the sales tax base, improvements in the application of the enterprise zone program, and several changes in individual income tax credits. Other changes were not in line with the recommendations of the legislative study, namely, increasing the sales tax rate and not considering substantial changes in the individual income tax. However, the sales tax changes were the only choices for the governor and legislature in the spring of 2016 to cover a deficit of over $1 billion in less than five months. The sales tax produces net new tax revenues quickly, and the state needed to cover its expenditures. This sales tax rate increase is scheduled to expire by the end of fiscal 2018, so the legislature will have an opportunity to reconsider this increase in the sales tax rate and the expansion of the sales tax base.

Several constitutional amendments put on the November 2016 ballot were fully consistent with the suggestions made in our 2015 presentation, including expanding the tax base for the corporate income tax and lowering its top marginal tax rate, and the use of mineral revenues to pay for public services. The proposed changes in the corporate income tax failed to gain the support of the Louisiana electorate.[2] The voters approved an enhanced Revenue Stabilization Fund, which directs revenues from mineral revenues and corporate taxes above a certain amount to be placed in the stabilization and not be used to fund recurring expenditures. This enhanced Revenue Stabilization Fund has several methods by which the legislature, with a super-majority vote, could overcome any restrictions that the amendment puts on the use of certain tax dollars.

Other changes were made to generate additional revenues since the state tax structure was not generating sufficient revenues to maintain and support the public programs the state legislature felt were in the best interest of the state. These changes were related to having sufficient political support as opposed to being consistent with the basic principles of an optimal tax structure. But this point also makes us aware of a basic fact in a democratic society: the proposed tax changes must be acceptable to the electorate since the electorate owns the tax structure.

The other provision placed in the tax changes in both 2015 and 2016 was a sunset provision. This means that many of the changes were temporary. In the first extraordinary legislative session of 2016, the state legislature passed House Concurrent Resolution 11, which created the Task Force on Structural Changes in Budget and Tax Policy. The authors of the Tax Study for the Legislature were members of this Task Force, which submitted its report and recommendations as of November 1, 2016. The purpose of the Task Force was to provide additional information to the legislature to make permanent changes in the Louisiana tax structure. The study was performed by academic tax experts with experience across many states. The Task Force included persons with tax experience who also represented many of the various parts of the Louisiana economy from business to labor to local governments.

A summary of the recommendations of the Task Force is included as an appendix to this study. These recommendations are in line with the principles and recommendations contained in our report to the legislature. The recommendations contained in our report to the state legislature and in the report of the HCR 11 Task Force envisioned creating a competitive, efficient, and equitable tax structure that is compatible with the acceptance of the electorate. The full report is available on the website of the Louisiana Department of Revenue.

We spent 2014 and 2015 completing the tax study for the state at the request of the state legislature; we testified before House and Senate committees; we participated in the meetings of the HCR 11 Task Force during 2016; and we shared our studies with decision makers in the state in 2015, 2016, and 2017. The studies and analysis by economists provide information and insight to policy makers and to the public as they work on developing a stable, equitable, and competitive tax structure. This study will be helpful in setting the stage for a thorough discussion of what makes a state's tax structure competitive and equitable during the debate in late 2017 and 2018 or, for that matter, regardless of what year we might be discussing.

We have offered recommendations given the 2014–2017 status of the federal individual and corporate income tax policies, since there are links between the state's administration of individual and corporate income taxes and the impact of federal policies on defining the tax base for Louisiana and ultimately the income tax collections. The US Congress made several major changes in the federal tax laws in 2017, with these changes affecting the Louisiana taxable income and ultimately Louisiana income tax collections. These changes range from reducing certain deductions, such as state and local taxes paid and mortgage interest on Schedule A in a person's federal individual income tax returns, to making a major realignment for corporate taxes with a reduction in the top marginal tax rate from 35 percent to 21 percent, a major change in the expensing of capital spending from allowing depreciation over a number of years to full expensing in the year of the capital spending, and a limit on interest expensing up to 30 percent of interest paid. Any tax bill numbers in the hundreds of pages, and certain sections of the bill may affect a particular industry in Louisiana. Some of the tax changes are permanent, while others expire within the next five to ten years. We are still examining the 2017 federal tax changes for implications for Louisiana state tax collections. As a general rule, federal tax reductions will positively affect Louisiana tax collections.

Public officials have an enormous responsibility to provide information to their constituents so the constituents can appreciate and understand all the conflicts and alternatives that the state faces in developing a long-term tax structure that is equitable, competitive, stable, and simple. Tax studies provide this information and will provide recommendations to the leadership of the state. However, at the end of the day, we appreciate and accept that the preferences of the electorate will take precedence over any findings in any study.

Notes

1. The regular session in 2016 is a nonfiscal session, so major changes in the tax structure were not on the table.

2. There was no formal opposition and no organized support for this amendment. Typically, to pass a tax amendment there would need to be some major support effort by local officials and other political and economic leaders.

2

DEVELOPMENT OF THE LOUISIANA TAX STRUCTURE

James A. Richardson

Introduction and Purpose

Every state and, for that matter, every local political subdivision has to come to grips with establishing *the appropriate level of public expenditures* in line with the political preferences of its electorate and with *a tax structure that is capable of funding* the desired state or local expenditures and, at the same time, *not deterring the economic development* of the state or local political subdivision *or unfairly imposing a disproportionately large and perhaps counterproductive tax burden* on any one segment of the community. The tax structure, while providing the financial support for public services at the state or local level, supporting economic development and growth, and creating a sense of fairness among all taxpayers, should also be as *simple and transparent as possible.* We want to minimize the resources required to both collect taxes and comply with the tax laws, and, equally important, we want to minimize unintended consequences of the tax laws.

From an economist's perspective, the guiding principles of constructing a state tax structure entail broad tax bases accompanied by low tax rates that contribute to the simplicity of the tax structure, equity among taxpayers, long-term stability of the tax system, minimization of unintended consequences, and adequacy of paying for the public services demanded by the electorate. These economic principles of taxation are sometimes amended by the political preferences of the electorate.

A state's tax structure reveals a great deal about a state's preferences and priorities, with these choices and decisions typically being made over a long period of time. In a democratic society the people of the state determine the state's tax structure through their elected public officials and through their voting on constitutional issues. The present Louisiana tax structure is based on constitutional and/or legislative limitations put in place at some point in the past. These choices and preferences suggest *more* than just the *type of taxes* to be utilized in funding state and local government and the *rates* that apply. The *exact definition of the tax base* or *any exclusion or exemption* of an economic activity is an important component of the discussion and decision. In fact, the erosion of the state and local tax base and tax capacity is represented by exemptions and exclusions, refundable and nonrefundable tax credits and tax rebates, and other tax advantages that apply to an industry, a special community, individuals, or other units as defined in the law.[1] Some of these exemptions and credits as embodied in the Louisiana tax structure are of long standing, while others are relatively new. All of these decisions, including the choice of the tax rate or rates, the general definition of the tax base, and any exclusions or exemptions from the base or special credit or rebates to reduce one's tax liability, are part of the administrative makeup of the state's tax structure. These constitutional and legislative decisions have economic and social consequences.

The tax structure in any state almost surely is influenced by the business and industrial structure of the economy. A state with minerals is apt to include minerals in its tax structure, and a state with a large tourism industry may find the sales tax attractive since tourists contribute to paying for public services, or at least it appears that they do. At the same time a state is taking advantage of its business and industrial structure, it is also looking at enhancing and expanding those businesses and possibly appealing to other industries. Many of the tax exemptions and credits will be related to the industries that are located in the state since the state may believe that certain tax breaks may be important to keeping the industry.

The state's tax structure matters. It provides the revenues necessary to fund public services deemed important, meaningful, and productive to the citizens and businesses of the state; it is one of the components of a state's business climate; it establishes who pays for public services within the state; it affects, at least at the margin, individual and business decisions[2]; and, certainly in Louisiana and typically in most states, the state has a major role in defining and limiting the ability of local governments to support local public services.

Purpose of Tax Study

Given the importance and role of the state's tax structure, it is important to review it from time to time to examine it on the grounds of adequacy and stability, economic competitiveness, fairness, and simplicity. Fluctuations in tax collections in the 1980s led a group of academic and professional tax experts, with the support of The Council for A Better Louisiana and Louisiana State University, to initiate a study of the Louisiana tax structure. The report was published as *Louisiana's Fiscal Alternatives: Finding Permanent Solutions to Recurring Budget Crises* in 1988 by the Louisiana State University Press.[3] The tax study in the 1980s was motivated by recurring fiscal issues that could only be resolved by deliberative action on the part of the state legislature and the governor.

The preface to the report stated:

> The state of Louisiana has experienced recurring fiscal problems throughout the 1980s. Major reductions in public expenditures and/or significant increases in taxes have been imposed in every year since 1982. Public agencies cannot accurately plan their activities. Private citizens and businesses cannot be sure of the public services that they may count on or the tax liabilities that they may incur. A major tax increase in 1984 did not prevent major budget cuts in 1985 and major budget cuts in 1985 did not eliminate the need for another tax increase in 1986. The fiscal crisis of the 1980s is fast becoming a 10-year war.

It has now been over twenty-five years since a major tax study was completed for the State of Louisiana, and certain tax reforms have been made, tax laws have been amended, and tax bases have changed due to changes in the economy or changes in the law; technology has augmented the choices that individuals and businesses have in terms of purchasing goods; the service industry has grown much more quickly than have other industries in Louisiana and the nation; the state's major industries have not necessarily changed in terms of what they do, but they have certainly changed in how they do it; and the state experienced major natural disasters, Hurricanes Katrina and Rita, within one month of each other in 2005. Perhaps even more significantly, the state is back to the issues of the 1980s, with a fundamental gap between what the state receives from its tax structure to support public services and what the state apparently wants to spend for these public services. During the 1980s, the problem centered around a long-lasting downturn due to the decline of the energy market in the 1980s and a tax structure that was dominated by oil and gas tax collections. Tax receipts declined because of economic conditions and the state's tax structure. State officials did not want to cut state spending similarly.

The state is facing similar issues presently, though not for the same reasons. As an example, in planning for fiscal year 2016 (July 2015 through June 2016), legislators had to deal with an estimated $1.2 to $1.6 billion gap between what the state wanted to spend based on previous commitments and what the state was projected to collect in taxes and fees. As soon as the budget for fiscal year 2016 was finalized, state budget analysts were anticipating another $1 billion gap for fiscal year 2017, and this gap eventually became a $1.6 to $2.0 billion gap. And there will be a fiscal shortfall of over $1 billion for fiscal year 2019, or what is now called the fiscal cliff.

There is a fundamental structural imbalance between what the tax system will yield and what the state apparently wants to spend. This structural imbalance is not due to an ongoing economic downturn. The national recession in 2008 certainly had a short-term impact on state tax collections, but Louisiana's employment had been growing since 2010 though the downturn in the oil market adversely affected employment growth in 2015 and 2016; employment growth has picked up in 2017.[4] The tax structure has not generated the growth in revenues consistent with the apparent demand for public expenditures. This is why the Speaker of the House and President of the Senate[5] asked a group of economists to closely examine Louisiana's tax structure, including the tax exemptions, deductions, credits, and rebates.[6] Speaker Chuck Kleckley, in announcing the study, noted that, "To compete for business, to provide a fair structure, to fund the needs of our citizens, and to fund the services consistent with growth and prosperity, we need a stable, easily understood, sufficient tax system. Now is the time to closely examine our taxing methods once again."

The purpose of this tax study is to provide an objective and analytical perspective of the Louisiana tax structure, knowing that a state's tax structure matters, and taxes can have an impact, both intended and unintended, on personal and business decisions. The findings and conclusions of any tax study should have a long shelf life since the political process typically spreads over several years.

The Louisiana Economy

The Louisiana economy has been built on its energy-based industries (oil and gas extraction, the processing and refining of this oil and gas, and industries supporting the oil and gas industries); its natural resources ranging from agricultural products to timber, including the production of these products and the manufacturing units associated with developing final products for consumers; its role in the transportation of goods throughout the state, nation, and globe given its six deep draft ports, nine coastal ports, and eighteen inland ports; and its tourism. The Louisiana economy is certainly sensitive to the energy markets; it is sensitive to the national and global economy, though typically with a lag; and it is obviously sensitive to natural disasters, though these natural disasters will vary in severity and the length of time that might be required for the recovery.

These fluctuations in the Louisiana economy are clearly illustrated by examining various time periods from the 1970s to the present. The years from 1975 to 1981 were heady ones for the Louisiana economy. The price of crude oil had risen from about $3 per barrel in 1973 to almost $40 per barrel in early 1981 (or approximately $100 per barrel in 2014 dollars). Employment in the oil and gas extraction sector rocketed up from about 50,000 in the early 1970s to just over 102,000 in 1981. Overall nonfarm employment boomed as well, rising at an average rate of 4.1 percent a year from 1975 to 1981. Louisiana has never matched the employment growth experienced in the 1970s.

Louisiana went through an extended recessionary period from 1982 through 1987 despite the fact that the US economy was moving forward. Nearly 150,000 jobs, or 9 percent of the workforce, were eliminated within the state. Plunging energy prices cut the extraction workforce in half as the state lost all of the jobs in the oil and gas extraction industry that it had gained in the 1970s. In the early 1980s the dollar appreciated quickly and substantially, and this appreciation adversely affected the export markets for the Louisiana chemical industry, prompting a substantial layoff of the workforce in an industry that dominates the manufacturing sector in the Louisiana economy. The industries that fed the boom in the 1970s led to the bust in the 1980s.

Louisiana in 1988 began its recovery. A primary driver behind this recovery was the chemical industry, just as this industry contributed to the downturn earlier in the 1980s. In 1985, a complete reversal in the trend of the exchange value of the dollar occurred. Global markets were observing US chemical prices declining dramatically due to a depreciation of the dollar relative to foreign currencies. The result was a very strong resurgence in the demand for Louisiana chemicals. Chemical firms began large-scale capital expansion projects, augmenting employment not only in chemicals but also in the industrial construction sector. Growth was occurring in other sectors as well, helping to diversify the economy and making it slightly less vulnerable to negative trends in any one industry. The transportation equipment industry, once heavily tied to oil- and gas-related activities, diversified into defense contracting and more general shipbuilding. The textile industry began a major expansion, led by Fruit of the Loom with state incentives, a firm which expanded so much that it was at one time the largest manufacturing firm in the state, as measured by employment. But Fruit of the Loom and other textile companies left the state in the early 2000s.

Health care also enjoyed a major expansion during this period due to a huge injection of federal Medicaid monies into the state. Medicaid dollars rose from under $1 billion in 1989 to over $3 billion by 1993. By 1993, the state had finally recovered all the jobs lost during the 1982–87 recession. Several industries contributed to this continued spurt of strong growth. After twelve years of employment declines, the oil and gas extraction sector began a recovery, even though oil prices were still relatively low compared to the prices in the 1970s. In 1993, there was no gaming industry in Louisiana. In the 1990s Louisiana allowed fifteen riverboat casinos to be created, with most of these being in Lake Charles and Shreveport; one land-based casino was created in New Orleans. It is always very difficult to distinguish between the transfer of dollars within the state and the actual increase in net new economic activity due to the creation of a gaming industry, but, due to the location of the riverboats in Lake Charles and Shreveport, it is reasonable to believe the gaming industry in Louisiana created net new jobs and did not just move them around. Perhaps most importantly, the Louisiana economy was supported throughout the 1990s by a growing national economy. The five years from 1994 to 1998 were especially good ones for the state.

From 2000 through 2006 Louisiana incurred ups and downs in the oil and gas extraction industry, a national recession and a slow national recovery through 2003, and then two monster hurricanes, Katrina and Rita, which occurred within a month of each other, in August and September 2005. Rita was a more typical hurricane, with severe damage being caused, but people were able to get back to their homes and businesses within a relatively short period of time and begin the process of restarting the local economies. Katrina was different for people living in the New Orleans area (especially the parishes of Orleans, St. Bernard, and Plaquemines)—it was not possible for everyone to get back to his or her home or job. Public facilities such as schools and hospitals could not quickly reopen. The colleges and universities in New Orleans had to find out-of-town alternatives for their students for the fall 2005 semester. Employment in the New Orleans Metropolitan Area[7] fell from approximately 620,000 in July 2005 to less than 500,000 overnight. From August 2005 to November 2005 the state of Louisiana saw employment decline by 165,100 jobs, or about 8.5 percent of the total workforce. From 2005 to 2006 Louisiana employment declined by about 65,000 jobs.

Disasters breed recoveries and Katrina/Rita was no exception. By 2007 the state had recovered almost all of the jobs lost in 2005 and 2006, with the recovery being led by a huge construction boom. Massive amounts of recovery monies were pumped into the Louisiana economy by both the federal government, with this spending ranging from public assistance to home construction to rebuilding the levee system to infrastructure repairs, and private insurance companies, with this spending ranging from rebuilding and restoring damaged properties to business interruption assistance. Gulf Opportunity Zone (Go-Zone) legislation was passed by Congress to further incentivize companies to make capital expenditures in the affected regions.[8] Go-Zone legislation provided either (1) an upfront 50 percent depreciation provision or (2) tax-exempt bonds for construction. A rough count showed over $20 billion in construction projects in the New Orleans area and $6.5 billion in the Baton Rouge MSA—construction figures that were eight to ten times larger than in normal years. A second boost came to Louisiana's oil and gas extraction sector due to very high oil and natural gas prices. These prices especially pumped up the energy-dependent Lafayette and Houma MSAs, two areas very connected to offshore exploration and production, and set the stage for the development of the Haynesville Shale in northwest Louisiana.

The national recession that started in December 2007 and ended in mid-2009, according to the National Bureau of Economic Research, did not show up in Louisiana until 2009, the first year in which employment declined in the state. In 2008 the Louisiana economy was still being bolstered by recovery spending and by increasing energy prices (oil prices peaked in July 2008 at over $140 per barrel) and extensive exploration for natural gas in northwest Louisiana due to the Haynesville Shale. In fact, in 2008 energy companies paid out approximately $3 billion in mineral lease payments to citizens and businesses in northwest Louisiana during the Haynesville Shale boom, and in 2009 they paid another $1.0 billion in mineral lease payments while incurring direct drilling expenditures of $1.2 billion in 2008 and $4.4 billion in 2009.[9]

Recovery spending gradually declined, and energy prices fell quickly from mid-2008 through the end of 2008, so Louisiana did not continue to have a buffer from the national recession. In 2009 and 2010 employment in Louisiana declined by over 52,500. The Louisiana economy had just started its employment loss as the national economy was beginning to experience employment gains for the first time in eighteen months. The decline in employment in Louisiana occurred statewide—no metropolitan area was spared. The New Orleans Metropolitan Area had the least decline in employment, while Houma-Thibodaux, Lafayette, and Lake Charles, three metropolitan areas with the largest concentration of the energy industry, including oil and gas exploration and extraction and the petrochemical industry, had the largest relative employment losses.

Louisiana started its recovery from the national recession in 2011 and by 2014 had surpassed its employment in 2008. This recovery has been spurred along by a very robust chemical industry due to low natural gas prices relative to oil prices, spending associated with the oil spill in 2010, offshore oil and gas activity, and efforts by state government to encourage business investment in Louisiana. But this economic recovery was interrupted by a reduction in oil prices, and so in 2015 fell to just less than a 0.5 percent growth rate and then a negative growth rate of 1.1 percent in 2016.

Fluctuations in state revenues and employment are compared in Figure 2.1 with both normalized to be 1 in 1974–75. It is no surprise that tax collections, including growth related to the growth of the economy and structural changes based on legislative acts, are much more volatile than employment. Employment and state tax collections have a correlation coefficient of 0.81, but the change in employment and the change in tax collections have a correlation coefficient of 0.37. Tax collections, starting in 1987, do not maintain the same ratio to 1975 tax collections that employment maintains to 1975 employment. The only variation in this ratio is during the post-Katrina years of 2007 and 2008. This increase in tax collections relative to its historical amount is related to increased activity due to disaster recovery efforts as well as the personal income tax collections being affected by a major change in the income tax effective as of 2003 and major changes in the federal income tax liability, which influenced income tax collections in Louisiana.

Industry Changes in the Louisiana Economy

Economies can and do change over time as illustrated in Figure 2.2. The most obvious change is the percentage of the labor force that is now in the service sector of the economy in 2016 as compared to 1988, a change that follows national trends.[10] The service sector of the economy and the wholesale and retail trade sector of the economy increased from about 56 percent of total employment in 1988 to 65 percent of total employment in 2016, and this compares to about 62 percent of the US labor force being classified in the service and trade sectors of the economy.[11] Manufacturing employment in Louisiana declined from just over 11 percent of total employment to 6.8 percent of total employment in 2016. For the US economy, manufacturing declined from just over 16 percent of total nonagricultural employment in 1988 to approximately 8.6 percent in 2016. Mining, which is predominately oil and gas in Louisiana, declined from 3.9 percent of total employment to less than 2 percent from 1988 to 2016. Nationwide, mining has declined from about 1 percent of total nonagricultural employment to about

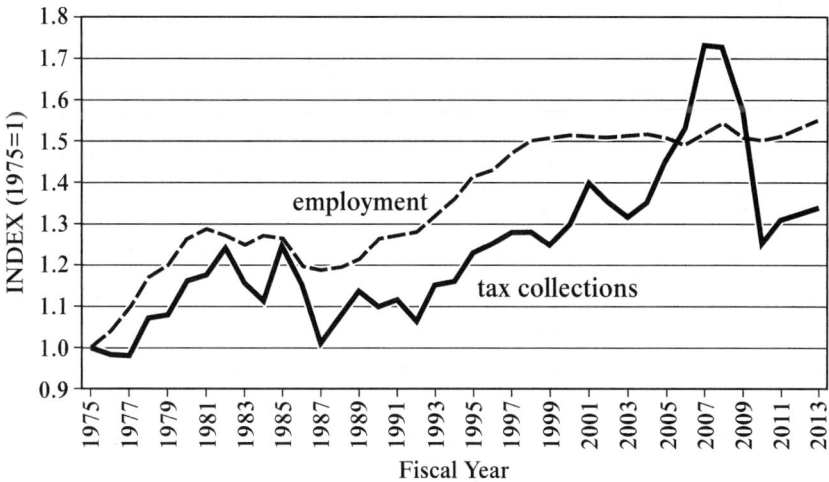

FIGURE 2.1. State Employment and State Tax Collections (1974–75 base)

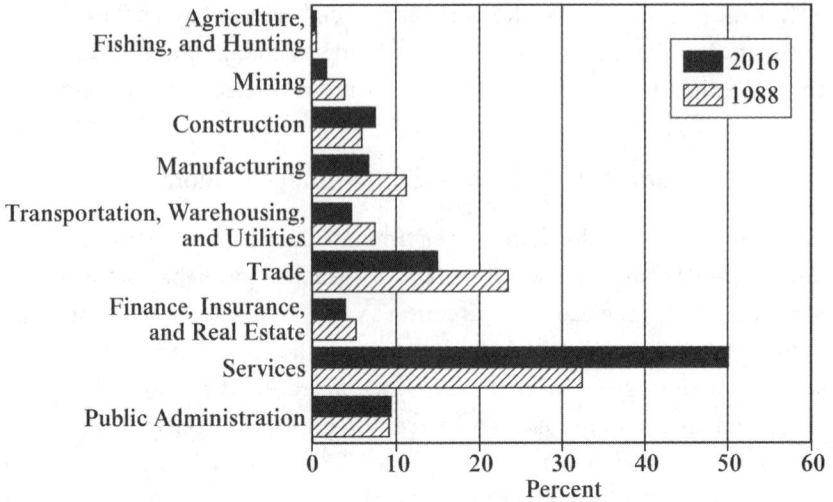

FIGURE 2.2. Employment by Industrial Sector, 1988 and 2016

0.5 percent. Trends in the Louisiana economy are in step with the trends nationally.

As we focus on the Louisiana economy and note that the relative size of the manufacturing sector is diminishing, we also need to ask if there are any major shifts within the manufacturing sector that might have implications for the state's economy or its tax base. Food and kindred products, paper and pulp, chemicals and related products, petroleum refining, and fabricated metals have been the major manufacturing sectors in Louisiana. These five manufacturing sectors in 1977 made up about 47 percent of all manufacturing employees and by 2007 represented almost 53 percent of all manufacturing employees; in 1977 these five groups made up 54 percent of manufacturing payroll while in 2007 they made up over 62 percent of manufacturing payroll in Louisiana; and, in terms of value-added, these five groups accounted for 68 percent in 1977 and just under 85 percent in 2007. Chemicals and petroleum refining accounted for about 20 percent of employees in both 1977 and 2007; 30 percent of total manufacturing payroll in 1977 and 35 percent in 2007; and 56 percent of value-added in 1977 and over 70 percent in 2007. In terms of payroll and value-added, the chemical industry and petroleum refining were dominant in 1977 and remain even more so in 2007. The manufacturing industry that has gained the most in terms of employees and payroll is fabricated metals, and these firms are connected primarily to offshore oil and gas activities. The Louisiana economy is still very much connected to the oil and gas industry, both upstream and downstream. Since around 2010 the focus in Louisiana has been major capital investment in LNG facilities. These are facilities that take natural gas, convert it to a liquid form, put it into a tanker, and then export it around the globe. These industries are very capital-intensive.

The service sector has grown substantially across the United States, and Louisiana is no exception. Within the service sector, health care and social assistance accounts for 30 percent of total service sector employment in 2016 and educational services account for approximately 17 percent of the service sector. Approximately 47 percent of all service-sector employment in 2016 is within the health care, social assistance, and educational sectors. Approximately 24 percent of the service sector employment is part of leisure and hospitality, a major part of the Louisiana tourism industry. The service sector is very labor-dominated, while the manufacturing sector and mining sector have become more capital-intensive. This has an important impact on possible tax policies and especially possible tax incentive programs.

Final Comments on Louisiana Economy

State and local tax collections are generated by the underlying economy and, as the economy transfigures itself, we have to be aware of the implications of the changes or possible changes in the collection of state and local taxes. State and local tax collections are also the product of the specific tax structure that a state has adopted at a point in time and its relationship to the prevailing economy. This specific tax structure in Louisiana is defined in the state's constitution and in revised statutes. Our analysis will focus on both possible constitutional changes that will improve the long-term viability of the Louisiana tax structure and changes that can be made by the Louisiana legislature without any constitutional changes.

Constitutional Guidelines for
State and Local Taxation in Louisiana

Louisiana's state and local tax structure is determined by provisions established in the state constitution as well as state revised statutes. The Louisiana Constitution specifically establishes guidelines for the personal income tax, the corporate income tax, state and local sales taxes, excise taxes, severance taxes, and property taxes. These provisions are summarized in Table 2.1. Louisiana is a state that is very constitutionally motivated in establishing its tax structure. Major tax changes have to be approved by the electorate.

The constitutional provisions establish limitations on the state legislature as it reviews and suggests changes in the state tax structure. The personal

TABLE 2.1. Foundations of Louisiana Tax Structure in State Constitution Taxes Source of Louisiana State and Local Tax Structure

General Tax Provisions	Power to tax is vested in state legislature. *Levy* of new tax, *increase* of existing tax, or *repeal* of existing tax exemption requires *super-majority* of state legislature.
Personal Income Tax	Income tax rates may be graduated but shall never exceed the rates and brackets as set forth as of January 1, 2003, for joint filers (single filers): 2% on first $25,000 ($12,500) of taxable income 4% on next $25,000 ($12,500) of taxable income 6% above $50,000 ($25,000) of taxable income Federal income taxes paid shall be allowed as a deductible item in computing state income taxes for the same period. Political subdivisions shall not levy an income tax.
Corporate Income Tax	Equal and uniform tax rates can be levied on net incomes, and those rates can be graduated. Federal income taxes paid shall be allowed as a deductible. Political subdivisions cannot levy a corporate income tax.
General Sales Tax	*State* sales tax does not apply to food for home consumption; natural gas, electricity, water sold directly to the consumer for residential use, and prescription drugs. Sales tax cannot be levied on gasoline and special fuels for use by vehicles. State sales taxes are collected by Louisiana Department of Revenue. *Local sales taxes are collected by the designated tax collector in each parish* as opposed to collection by multiple sales tax collectors in each parish, as was done prior to 1990. Political subdivisions can levy and collect a tax upon sale at retail; on the use, lease or rental, consumption, and storage for use as consumption of tangible personal property; and on sale of services as defined by state law. Local sales tax rate for all political subdivisions cannot exceed 3% unless approved by the State Legislature and approved by electors voting in a special election.

Excise Taxes	Political subdivisions shall not levy a tax on motor fuel.
	Cigarette tax rate shall not be less than the rate as set forth as of January 1, 2012.
Motor License Tax	License tax of no more than $1 per each $1,000 of actual value of automobile for private use, but the annual license fee cannot be less than $10 for automobile for private use. For other vehicles the legislature shall impose an annual license fee based on carrying capacity, horsepower, value, weight, or any of these parameters.
Severance Tax	Can be levied on natural resources severed from ground based on either quantity or value *at the time of severance from the ground.*
	No tax can be added to land because of the presence of oil and gas reserves on the property.
	Creation of Budget Stabilization Fund specifying that mineral revenues (including severance tax collections and other mineral revenues) greater than a certain amount will be directed to the Budget Stabilization Fund.
	Political subdivisions shall not levy a severance tax.
Property Tax	Taxation of property based on *assessed value,* which ispercentage of its fair market value with the assessment ratios being as follows: residential property 10% commercial and industrial 15% public service properties 25% Agricultural, horticultural, marsh, and timber land assessed at 10% of *use value* (not markeFair Market Value determined by *elected Tax Assessor* in each Parish. All property subject to taxation shall be reappraised at intervals of not more than 4 years.
	Property not taxable includes: cash and other financial assets; personal property used in home; agricultural products, machines, and equipment; commercial vessels used for gathering seafood; nonprofits; public buildings; oil and gas reserves; ships, oceangoing tugs, towboats, and barges;, artwork including sculptures, glassworks, paintings, drawings, and other artwork; and other such property listed in state constitution.
	Homestead exemption of *$7,500 of Assessed Value* applying to homestead not exceeding 160 acres, including mobile homes. Special assessment for persons 65 and older given certain income characteristics, members of armed forces, and/or disabilities.
	Industrial tax exemption for manufacturing facilities as approved by Louisiana Board of Commerce for up to 5 years with the possibility of a renewal for another 5 years. Exemption applies to entire local millage, including school districts.
	State has authority to tax up to 5.75 mills.
	Local subdivisions have constitutional millage levied for general purposes; other millage approved by voters with specific purpose/time.

TABLE 2.1. (*continued*)

Other Taxes/ Revenue Sources	No new tax or fee after November 30, 2011 is allowed upon the sale or transfer of immovable property, including documentary transaction taxes or fees. Fees for the cost or recordation, filing, or maintenance of documents, impact fees for development, annual parcel fees, and ad valorem taxes are not considered taxes or fees upon the sale or transfer of immovable property.
	Political subdivisions shall not levy an inheritance tax.
	Political subdivisions can levy an occupational license tax.
	The Louisiana Lottery was created constitutionally in 1990. Other gaming revenues, specifically video poker receipts, riverboats, and the land-based casino in New Orleans, were declared to be constitutional even though the Constitution declares that the state should "define and suppress gambling."

income tax has constitutionally defined limits on how high the marginal tax rates can be and on the definition of the tax brackets, while the corporate income tax merely indicates that graduated corporate tax rates are constitutionally acceptable. The Louisiana Constitution establishes the deductibility of federal tax liability for both personal and corporate income taxes. Local governments are prohibited from levying a personal or corporate income tax.

The state rate for the sales tax is not defined in the Louisiana Constitution but is left to the discretion of the state legislature. The state's sales tax base has limitations imposed by the state's constitution, namely, food for consumption at home, natural gas, electricity, and water sold directly to the consumer for residential use, and prescription drugs. Neither the state nor local sales tax rate can be applied to gasoline and special fuels for use by vehicles.

The severance tax has a constitutional definition stating that it must be applied to the quantity or value of the natural resource at the point of its severance from the ground. This definition creates some administrative issues in determining the market value of the resource at the point of its severance from the ground since most market transactions do not occur at this point. Hence, the taxable value of the resource must be determined by the establishment of its market value less any costs in transporting/processing the resource from the ground to the ultimate market transaction.

The property tax is specified in the Louisiana Constitution, with assessment ratios being specified for land and home improvements, public service property, and all other property (including business and industrial); with a homestead exemption for homeowners; with the option of an industrial tax exemption for five years and the option to renew for five additional years; and with a list of property not subject to the property tax, including religious and nonprofit property, public buildings, cash and financial instruments, personal property used in the home, agricultural products and machines and equipment, commercial vessels used for gathering seafood, oil and gas reserves, ships, oceangoing tugs, towboats, and barges, and artwork, including sculptures, glassworks, paintings, drawings, and other artwork.

The Louisiana Constitution establishes "hard" guidelines in changing the state and local tax structure without asking for the electorate to approve any proposed changes. Upon examination of the Louisiana tax structure, one has to note the tax changes that can be completed by the state legislature and governor by the appropriate vote (typically a supermajority if the legislation calls for raising a tax, but only a majority if the legislation calls for reducing a tax or providing a tax advantage to certain groups), and any tax changes that must be submitted to the people to be voted on with the proposed constitutional amendments taking a supermajority to even get to the vote of the people and then a simple majority of the electorate to approve the changes.

Any and all tax laws passed by the Louisiana legislature must comply with the Louisiana Constitution. As we evaluate the Louisiana tax structure we will refer to the legislation that has been passed and provide further definition to the Louisiana tax structure. As we make recommendations regarding possible changes in the Louisiana tax structure, we will distinguish between those that require a vote of the electorate and those that can be done by the Louisiana legislature by the appropriate vote.

Given the political process to implement changes in the state and local tax structure and given that it is not good tax policy to continuously change the state's tax code, it is vital to stress the importance and significance of any proposed tax changes to the long-term well-being of the state and local economy in terms of fiscal sustainability, long-term economic competitiveness, and basic fairness among different groups of taxpayers. A tax structure should be predictable and stable, both in terms of providing revenues to sustain the state's budgetary obligations over time and in terms of allowing individuals and businesses to plan their economic activities without any unexpected tax changes that can disrupt business plans. In one way, the Louisiana Constitution provides a very stable background for the state's tax structure, but one does not want to eliminate all discretion in designing a tax structure, especially given the multiple outcomes that we want the tax structure to accomplish. And it is not absolutely necessary to put tax provisions in the constitution in order to have a stable tax structure.

Notes

1. *Louisiana Department of Revenue, Tax Credits and Other Exemptions,* Louisiana Legislative Auditor, February 2012, provides a summary of tax credits and exemptions by tax and amount.

2. In a recent book published in 2014, *Abba: The Official Photo Book,* a member of the Swedish pop group Abba indicated that the group's flamboyant outfits were designed so as to count as a tax deduction according to the Swedish tax laws. The costumes had to be so outrageous that they would not be worn on the street in normal life: an interesting example of tax policy influencing real life decisions, but perhaps without great significance. This decision by the pop group is not monumental in terms of affecting the tax base or the local community, but it illustrates that personal and business decisions can be influenced by tax policy, either intentionally or unintentionally.

3. Contributors to the tax study were Professors James A. Richardson (LSU), William Oakland (Tulane), Tim Ryan (University of New Orleans), Loren Scott (LSU), and Tom Sale (Louisiana Tech). It should be noted that the major supporters of doing the tax study in the 1980s were Chancellor Jim Wharton of LSU; President Ed Stagg of the Council for A Better Louisiana; and Mr. David Conroy, an attorney with the Milling Law Firm in New Orleans and a major supporter of the Council for A Better Louisiana.

4. https://www.bls.gov/eag/eag.la.htm.

5. The Speaker of the Louisiana House in 2015 was Chuck Kleckley from Lake Charles and the President of the Louisiana Senate was John Alario from Westwego.

6. The group of economists will be led by Professors Jim Richardson, Director of the Public Administration Institute at Louisiana State University, Steven Sheffrin, Director of the Murphy Institute at Tulane University, and James Alm, Professor of Economics at Tulane University.

7. Including parishes of Jefferson, Orleans, Plaquemines, St. Bernard, St. Charles, St. John the Baptist, and St. Tammany in 2005.

8. The effectiveness of tax incentives, as a method of speeding up recovery from a natural disaster, is still being evaluated.

9. *Economic Impact of Haynesville Shale on Louisiana Economy, 2008 and 2009,* Loren C. Scott, with 2008 report done for Louisiana Department of Natural Resources and 2009 report completed for Louisiana Oil and Gas Association.

10. The year 1988 was used since this was the last year in which the Louisiana Workforce Commission provided employment by industrial sector. Definitions of industrial sectors in 1988 may vary slightly since the US Department of Labor changed its industrial classifications in 1990.

11. National employment is taken from *Economic Report of the President, 2017.* State employment is from the Louisiana Workforce Commission, *Annual Wage and Employment, 2016.*

3

LOUISIANA REVENUES
History and Trends

James A. Richardson, Gregory V. Albrecht, and Steven M. Sheffrin

Louisiana State Tax Collections, 1970–71 through 2014–15

The state's tax collections, in nominal and real terms, from the early 1970s through fiscal 2015 are illustrated in Figure 3.1. These charts indicate the growth of the tax collections from just over $1 billion in the early 1970s of just over $12 billion in 2007–08, and most recently in 2014–15 a decline of approximately $10.5 billion. In real dollars (1983–84 = 100), the state of Louisiana collected approximately $2.7 billion in 1970–71, peaked at $5.72 billion in 2006–07, and presently collects about $4.4 billion. The chart also indicates the volatility of the tax collections, with negative growth rates in four of the ten fiscal years between 1980 and 1989 and a major decline in taxes, licenses, and fees from 2007–08 through 2009–10. Many of the jumps in tax revenues were related to tax increases as illustrated by bumps in 1973–74, 1977–78, and 1984–85, while a tax cut in 1980 was partially responsible for the decline in tax revenues in 1981–82.

In 2003–04 a jump in tax collections occurred for a variety of reasons, one being an income tax/sales tax swap that, while revenue-neutral in the year in which it was implemented, certainly enhanced the growth potential of overall tax collections. This tax change also corresponded with significant growth in the Louisiana economy and changes in the federal tax code that automatically enhanced state income tax collections.[1] The dramatic decline in state taxes, licenses, and fees from just over $12 billion in 2007–08 in nominal dollars to less than $9 billion in 2009–10, a drop of just over 26 percent, was magnified by tax cuts in 2006–07 and 2007–08, among other state, national, and international events taking place. The reduction in state tax collections in real dollars was just over 28 percent from 2007–08 to 2009–10.

The Louisiana economy is divided by major events that had an espe-

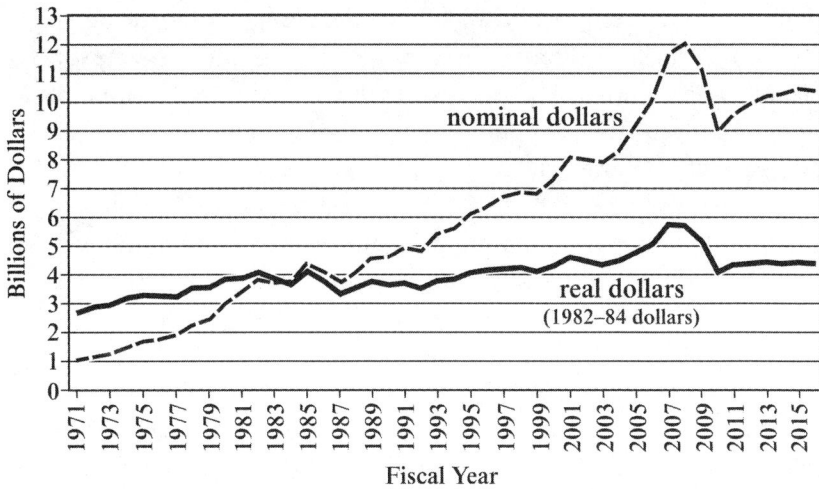

FIGURE 3.1. Louisiana Taxes, Licenses, and Fees, FY 1971 through FY 2016

cially large impact on it. The oil boom in the 1970s, followed by the oil bust in the 1980s, influenced the Louisiana economy in a number of directions. The state anticipated the oil boom in the early 1970s and significantly changed the method by which the state taxed oil. The state moved from a volume-based tax on oil to a value-based tax in a special session in 1973 and increased the volume-based tax on natural gas[2]—it was a strategic change that benefited the state significantly in terms of state collections. The state also chose to put more emphasis on mineral taxes as a means of financing ongoing state government and less on the more traditional methods of financing state government, namely, personal income taxes and/or sales taxes.[3] Both the sales tax and personal income tax were lowered in the special session in 1973, with food and drugs being removed from the sales tax base and the federal tax deductibility being reinstated as a deduction in determining Louisiana taxable income.[4] Everyone believed that the state had solved its financial woes forever or, at least, they acted as if the state had solved its financial woes forever. By 1977 the state was feeling pressed for money and significantly increased the corporate income tax rates, with the top rate going from 4 percent to 8 percent.

In 1980, just as the revenues were peaking, the governor proposed and the state legislature voted to reduce the state income tax. But other factors, such as the falling price of oil, greatly complicated the revenue outlook for

Louisiana. State revenues did not fall as dramatically during the oil bust as they rose during the oil boom because of major tax increases passed in a special session in the fall of 1983, essentially rescinding the income tax reductions of 1980. Then in another special session of the legislature during the spring of 1984, the state increased the sales tax rate from 3 percent to 4 percent, doubled the corporate franchise tax from $1.50 per $1,000 of equity and/or debt to $3.00 per $1,000, and made other tax increases, including on motor fuels, tobacco, and insurance premiums. In total during the 1984 Spring Special Session the state raised an estimated $790 million in taxes or close to 20 percent of overall state revenues.[5]

And these tax increases were followed by a temporary sales tax of 1 percent starting in fiscal 1986 and eventually 2 percent on all commodities that had been specifically exempted from the state sales tax. This included imposing a state sales tax on food purchased for home consumption, drugs, medical devices, and all other items that had been exempted by statute from the state's sales tax.

The 1990s illustrated, if not proved, that a growing economy is by far the best tonic for a state's fiscal structure. From fiscal 1989 to the start of the new century, state revenues doubled in nominal dollars from just over $4 billion to approximately $8 billion. During the oil boom of the 1970s, state revenues grew from just over $1 billion to almost $4 billion at the end of the 1970s. In the 1970s this growth was accelerated by conscious changes in the tax code, including the change in the taxation of oil accompanied by a substantial increase in the price of oil globally and the increase in the corporate income tax. During the 1990s the only revenue gains, other than growth in tax collections, came from the introduction of gaming into Louisiana communities. Gaming includes the Louisiana Lottery, riverboats, video poker, and the land-based casino in New Orleans. There were mild drops in Louisiana revenues in the pause of the US economy in 1991, a mild drop in fiscal 1999, and then a larger drop due to the national slowdown at the beginning of the new century. Overall, state revenues rose substantially during the decade of the 1990s.

Louisiana tax collections declined modestly from fiscal 2001 through fiscal 2003 by about 2 percent or $160 million. The national economy went through a mild downturn in 2001 and then had a relatively lethargic recovery for 2001 through 2003, motivating federal tax reductions in 2001 and again in 2003. Louisiana tax collections started to increase in 2003–04, related to the growth in the economy, the change in the Louisiana income tax produced by a constitutional amendment in 2002 (typically referred to as the Stelly Plan),[6] and the changes in the federal tax laws in 2001 and 2003[7] that automatically propelled an increase in Louisiana income tax collections.

In 2005 several major events struck Louisiana and other coastal states. Hurricanes Katrina and Rita hit the Gulf Coast states, causing significant damage to homes, businesses, public facilities, infrastructure, and all other structures. No one was spared. Such storms create a daunting recovery process and require substantial amounts of dollars to restore and rejuvenate the damaged areas. Private insurance assistance (estimated to be close to $40 billion in Louisiana) and federal assistance (estimated to be close to $110 billion from 2005 through 2009) unleashed sustained spending in the Louisiana economy for approximately four to five years.

State revenues rose substantially from fiscal 2005 through fiscal 2008. State revenues grew by approximately $4 billion from fiscal 2004 through fiscal 2008, or about 33 percent. This increase in revenue was propelled by a combination of events: the additional spending for the recovery, rising oil prices, the state income tax change in 2002, and federal tax changes that positively affected the Louisiana income tax base. The fiscal posture of the state changed dramatically at the end of fiscal 2008. Oil prices dropped within a relatively short period of time from over $140 per barrel in July 2008 to less than $40 per barrel by December 2008. The price had returned to the mid-$60s by mid-2009. Income tax reductions had been passed by the Louisiana legislature in the regular session of 2007 and were signed by Governor Kathleen Babineaux Blanco, and were passed in the regular session of 2008 and signed by Governor Bobby Jindal. Essentially, the state legislature overturned the income tax changes that had been approved in 2002. But the state legislature did not overturn the reduction in sales taxes that had been part of the tax plan accepted by the people in 2002. These income tax cuts were similar to the tax cuts in 1980—occurring at the peak of state tax collections—but different in the sense that the 2007 and 2008 tax cuts were maintained despite the fact that the state's revenues were in a major decline.

The additional spending for the recovery by the federal government and private insurance companies was winding down. The national economy confronted a major downturn that technically started in December

2007 and ended in mid-2009. Financial turmoil accompanied and perhaps caused the national recession. The Louisiana economy did not follow the lead of the national economy step for step, but employment in Louisiana did decline in 2009 and then again in 2010.

Another factor, namely, the use of exemptions, credits, and rebates, has accompanied the trends in tax collections in Louisiana. In 1998–99 Louisiana collected approximately $4.46 billion from sales tax collections, personal income taxes, corporate income and franchise tax collections, and severance taxes. The state granted $1.217 billion of exemptions and tax credits/rebates, or about 27 percent of the collection of these major taxes. By 2013–2014, the latest year with available data on exemptions, Louisiana's collection of these major taxes amounted to $6.893 billion, with $7.539 billion of exemptions and tax credits/rebates, or over 109 percent of these collections. Exemptions and credits had increased by a factor of 6 over this time period while actual tax collections increased by a factor of 1.5.[8]

The abrupt drop in revenues from fiscal 2008 through fiscal 2010, the escalating erosion of the tax bases, and the relatively modest growth in major taxes such as general sales and personal income taxes, and the actual decline in corporate income tax collections from 2008 through the present, created questions regarding the sustainability of the overall tax structure. The Revenue Study Committee, a fourteen-member study panel of legislative leaders chaired by Senator Jack Donahue, was created to review the estimated $4.4 billion in tax exemptions, rebates, and credits established by law to see if the state was getting the expected benefits from these tax provisions. A final report was issued but without an assessment of the various tax exemptions, rebates, and credits.[9] The report came to these conclusions:

1. The legal authority for most tax expenditures lacks any expectation as to specific justifiable benefits to be realized by state in relation to the cost to the taxpayer
2. Few data exist with respect to many tax expenditure programs, thereby preventing any real consideration of the actual outcome with respect to the public policy objective.
3. Future review and sunset should occur where feasible, providing for periodic data-based cost-benefit analyses.
4. Annual awareness is needed of the cost of the exemptions, credits, rebates, and other tax expenditures.

5. The committee had insufficient time to properly estimate projected costs of proposed tax expenditures.

Just as the Revenue Study Committee was meeting and trying to reach a consensus regarding what acceptable public fiscal policy was regarding the extent and magnitude of the exemptions and exclusions, tax credits, and rebates, Governor Jindal, in January 2013, introduced his own version of tax reform. Mainly this did away with the personal income tax and the corporate and franchise taxes and replaced them with alternative tax sources, mostly an increase in the state sales tax rate and an expansion of the tax base for the sales and use tax, with additional services being added to the base, using the services taxed in Texas as a model.

The Public Affairs Research Council of Louisiana (PAR) put together a panel of public finance economists, tax accountants, tax attorneys, and other experts to examine the governor's proposals. PAR put out a very concise report on the governor's plan and on basic principles that should guide the state in adopting changes to the state's tax structure.[10] The complications of the governor's plan with respect to replacing the revenues lost due to eliminating the personal income tax, corporate income tax, and franchise tax (approaching $3.3 billion) by increasing the sales tax rate and/or expanding the sales tax base, eventually led the governor to, in his words, "park" his proposal before the 2013 legislative session even started.[11]

Recent and Projected Revenue Trends

Total tax collections for each fiscal year since 1990 through the latest complete fiscal year (2014–15), and through the current forecast horizon (2017–18), are depicted in Figure 3.2. This depiction over time gives a sense of the underlying growth in the tax base, as well as changes to that base, both legislatively imposed and resulting from the business cycle and the dramatic natural disaster of Hurricanes Katrina and Rita in 2005.

A number of interesting things can be discerned from the chart. Aside from the years of fiscal 2006 through fiscal 2010, actual revenue collections tend to exhibit fairly modest cycling around a long-run growth path. This is evident in the years fiscal 2005 and fiscal 2015, albeit around a lower path in the years after fiscal 2010. The effects of the national recessions in 1990/91, 2000/01, and 2009/10 are reflected in dips below the long-run path.

These state revenue cycles are fairly modest because Louisiana does not have the degree of consumer and industrial durable goods production that the rest of the nation has, and because it is an energy-producing state with a state business cycle that is somewhat countercyclical to the national cycle. These characteristics work to moderate the effects of the national business cycle on the state, in both timing and severity. Obviously, national recessions catch up with the Louisiana economy. Louisiana does not manufacture many cars, but the petrochemical industry produces the plastic that goes into the cars, and eventually this shows up in activity in the chemical industry. Tourism and travel are affected by a national downturn, and this eventually shows up in a destination city such as New Orleans.

In addition, as an energy state, Louisiana can experience its own state level recessions as evident in the fiscal 1999 dip below trend as oil prices dropped to around $10/bbl in fiscal 1999. State revenue can also climb above trend as a result of energy prices, as evident in the large bubble over trend in fiscal 2008 due, in part, to the sharp runup in oil and natural gas prices that peaked in the summer of 2008 at nearly $150/bbl for oil and $10/mcf for natural gas.

The large bubble over trend in fiscal 2008 is due only in part to energy price spikes during those years, and is primarily the result of massive recovery spending after Hurricanes Katrina and Rita. Households and businesses across much of the southern segment of the state were replacing

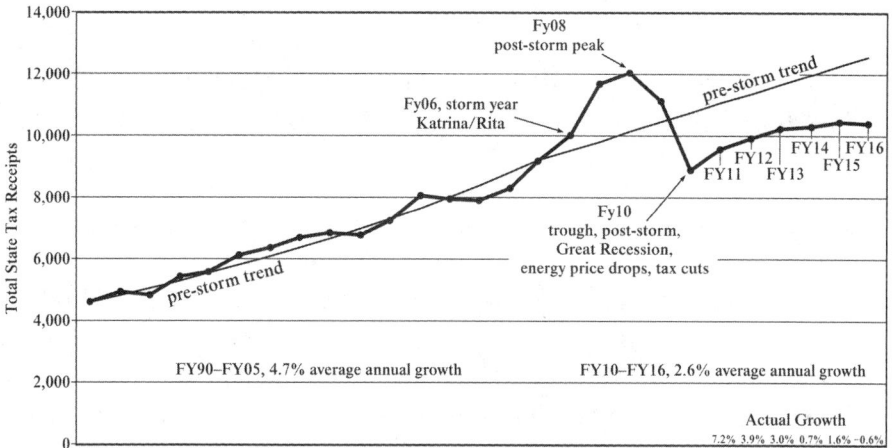

FIGURE 3.2. State Tax Receipts, 1990 through 2016 (millions of dollars)

possessions and rebuilding structures in the impacted areas. In addition, population shifting required new housing construction outside of the impacted areas, and public infrastructure repair was also occurring. This surge in spending was, to some extent, directly taxable and generated income that was taxable along with attracting in-migration of workers who generated taxable spending and income. This rebuilding spending continued through fiscal 2009 and 2010, and even into the current period, but was eventually overwhelmed by the effects of the national recession, the collapse of energy prices in the fall and winter of 2008, and tax reductions that especially impacted sales and income taxes. Consequently, state revenues from fiscal 2005 to fiscal 2008 rose by $2.801 billion, a 30 percent rise in three years, and then fell by $3.101 billion from fiscal 2008 to fiscal 2010, a 26 percent drop in just two years.

Since the revenue trough in fiscal 2010, recovery has occurred each year along a new, lower long-run growth path reflecting the new tax base permanently reduced by tax reductions that became fully effective with fiscal 2010 and subsequent years. In fiscal 2011, the first year of recovery, a strong bounceback in growth was experienced, with the following two years exhibiting positive growth as well. While a slowdown in growth in fiscal 2012 would be expected following the bounce-back year, of concern is the continued deceleration in fiscal 2013 and fiscal 2014, with only very modest growth occurring in fiscal 2015. As of fiscal 2015 actual collections, the new path is some $1.8 billion lower than the former time path, and it seems unlikely that future revenue growth will be sufficient to eliminate this gap. The future of the state's tax revenue growth path seems destined to be well below the path that existed prior to Hurricanes Katrina and Rita, the Great Recession, and the tax cuts implemented through fiscal 2010. These paths show the permanently diminished yield of the current state tax structure.

The state's major tax revenues, as a whole, now appear to be permanently below where they would likely be if the prestorm/recession tax base were still in place. In addition, the average growth rate of tax receipts appears materially lower between these two periods. The compound annual average growth in tax receipts from fiscal 1990 through fiscal 2005 was 4.7 percent, while the growth rate from fiscal 2010 through fiscal 2015 is only 3.3 percent. The lower growth in the latter period is, in part, influenced by current revenue forecasts, which will change each time a base forecast revision is adopted. However, the calculated average growth rate for this seven-year period is also influenced by three years of actual tax collections growth. Even if the new growth path ultimately parallels the former path, it will be permanently below the former path.

Composition of the State of Louisiana Tax Structure

For state government budgeting purposes, Louisiana monitors and forecasts its major state tax receipts through the Consensus Revenue Estimating Conference[12] (REC). Approximately forty different receipts are overseen, although only a few of these dominate the overall revenue base. The major receipts are the typical ones such as personal income tax, sales tax, corporate income and franchise taxes, motor fuels taxes, and for Louisiana the mineral revenues, which consist of severance tax collections (a true tax) and royalties (the state being a property owner), and gaming activities.

The importance of sales tax and personal income tax to the state's revenue base is obvious upon examination of the state's tax collections. These two revenue sources combined to $5.983 billion, over half the state's major tax revenue (58 percent) in fiscal 2015, and these two taxes now in fiscal 2017 made up over 62 percent of the state's revenue collections. Despite greatly weakened oil prices, the mineral revenue share was the next largest, at 10 percent and $1.057 billion in 2015, but now is around 3 to 4 percent of total state collections due to weak prices and a reduction in oil production within the boundaries of Louisiana; gaming activity contributed $887 million, or 8 percent, in 2015, and this amount is relatively predictable and is not a growth revenue source; and motor vehicle fuels tax brings in about $600 million, or 6 percent of all state revenues. Taxes on insurance premiums now bring in close to $1 billion, or a 5 percent share, a number that has grown over the last several years due to expanding the insurance premium tax on Medicaid insurance programs. Corporations and businesses contribute $350 to $400 million per year, or about a 3 to 4 percent share. Corporate income taxes are very volatile. Shares and amounts fall off to only 2 percent and $212 million from the personal excise taxes of tobacco and alcohol, and to only 1 percent and $155 million from vehicle licensing and titling taxes. Given its resource base, Louisiana was first able to substitute oil and gas revenue for more traditional tax sources such as sales and individual income taxes. In the 1990s, gaming revenue became the substitute for oil and gas revenue collections, but gaming revenue is not a long-term growth revenue, so since 2000 or so the state has had to rely on its sales and income tax collections to support public services.

Final Comments on Louisiana Fiscal Structure

In the 1980s Louisiana's fiscal issues revolved around an energy-intensive tax structure, and these fiscal issues were eventually accommodated by increasing other taxes and adjusting expenditures, and eventually by a growing economy. In 2015 the fiscal issues revolved around a dramatic growth in taxes up through 2008, followed by an abrupt and substantial decline in state revenues and a projected modest growth in revenues for the foreseeable future.

We have compared Louisiana's overall tax structure to that in other states, and generalizations can be made about how the Louisiana tax structure compares to those in its neighbor states. These differences may point us in the direction in which we should look for change, but there is no reason to believe that every state should have exactly the same tax structure. It is also known that a state's tax structure consists of a plethora of details that describe the tax bases, tax rates, and other dimensions of the tax structure. These details, as well as the overall performance of the system in generating the revenues to support worthy public programs, have to be evaluated from time to time. These details include examining exemptions, credits, and other tax issues and how they relate to the major sources of revenue. The study of a state's tax structure is about the specifics of each tax that is enacted as well as the trends associated with a set of state taxes. An excellent method of initiating a tax study is to have outside experts review a state's tax structure and, from their perspective, indicate what they might suggest to improve it in accordance with economic principles of taxation.

External Evaluation of Louisiana Tax Structure

As part of our review process, we solicited an analysis of the Louisiana tax system from two national experts in state taxation: Professor William F. Fox, the William B. Stokely Distinguished Professor of Business and the Director of the Center for Business and Economic Research at the University of Tennessee; and Professor George R. Zodrow, the Allyn R. and Gladys M. Cline Chair of Economics at Rice University and currently coeditor of the

National Tax Journal. Both Professors Fox and Zodrow are recipients of the prestigious Steven D. Gold award for significant contributions to state and local fiscal systems and bring a wealth of experience to this task. We provided them with a background paper written by James A. Richardson and Gregory V. Albrecht and asked them to draw on their extensive national and international experience in taxation as they analyzed the Louisiana tax system. Their full reports will be available from the authors, but here we summarize the key points of their analysis.

Both experts agreed upon a number of key points. The overall tax burden in Louisiana was below the national average but on par with those of southeastern states. They advocated reform of the sales tax, including changes to the tax base and to its administrative structure; noted that business taxes and especially the franchise tax applied to a narrow segment of business entities; noted that the existing corporation tax could be reformed and streamlined; and pointed out that Louisiana's extensive use of exemptions and exclusions from taxes has led to high nominal tax rates. Both urged a careful examination of all exemptions and exclusions. They also made specific recommendations for the major taxes used by the state.

Beginning with the *personal income tax,* both experts noted that rates could be lowered if the base were broadened. In particular, they recommended considering eliminating the deduction for federal tax liability, "excess" itemized deductions, and certain retirement exclusions in order to lower tax rates. These changes would both lead to a lower perceived tax burden and also begin to decouple Louisiana's revenue stream from the inevitable changes in federal taxation that will transpire in coming years.

With respect to the *sales and use tax,* they recommended expanding the tax base to include personal services, while avoiding increases in sales taxes for business purchasers. These changes could be used either to lower tax rates or to increase revenues. They noted that the differences in tax bases between state and local governments create significant administrative burdens for business. Moving towards an administrative structure consistent with the Streamlined Sales Tax Agreement—including a single collector and auditor and increased uniformity in tax bases—would improve administration and reduce the costs of compliance. Compliance with either the Streamlined Sales Tax Agreement or simplification along these lines could almost surely be required to allow Louisiana to tax remote sales if federal laws are changed.

Both experts noted that many *excise taxes* in Louisiana are below national levels and offered specific suggestions for changes. Excise taxes are potentially an important part of the overall tax structure and need to be examined carefully. Zodrow suggested looking carefully at increasing excise taxes on cigarettes, liquor, and wine. We might note that Zodrow made this suggestion prior to the 2015 legislative session. During that session cigarette taxes were increased from 36 cents per pack to 80 cents per pack, and in the first extraordinary session in 2016 cigarette taxes were raised to $1.08 per pack, and the tax on liquor, wine, and beer was increased.

Both experts had a number of suggestions for *franchise and corporation taxation.* Both recommended eliminating deductions for federal tax liability and carefully reviewing other deductions and credits. Zodrow also noted that the high statutory corporate tax rate in the state could lead corporations to find ways to report profits to other states, regardless of whether it was truly earned in the state.

Fox noted that the franchise tax only reaches corporate entities and does not extend to LLCs or partnerships doing business in Louisiana.[13] With respect to corporate taxation, Fox also expressed concern that Louisiana's separate-entity taxation was vulnerable to routine corporate tax planning, through the shifting of intangible income out of state. He recommended Louisiana consider enacting an "add-back" statute to ensure that intangible income is not shifted outside the state, or even consider a regime of combined reporting. Add-back statutes are common in the southeastern states that have single-entity taxation.

Both experts recommended that Louisiana streamline its *apportionment rules* and move more to single sales apportionment of business income. Not only is this in line with the trend in other states, but it also reduces the burden on in-state business by exporting the tax burden. Fox also suggested that in conjunction with this change, the apportionment rules for services should be changed to a destination basis, again in line with recent trends in the state.[14]

With respect to *mineral taxes,* Zodrow suggested a thorough review of alternative taxing mechanisms and suggested some specific alternatives. He recommended eliminating the horizontal drilling exemption, finding no principled justification for this exemption. He also suggested a careful examination of the severance tax as it is now implemented, since severance taxes distort business decisions regarding investment and production. He did not suggest forgoing the taxation of oil and gas production, but rather the way Louisiana taxes it.

The two experts also floated some more speculative proposals and made other specific observations. For example, Zodrow suggested potentially replacing the corporate tax with a general business tax, thereby reaching partnerships, LLCs, S-corporations, and sole proprietorships. This would allow the overall rate to be lowered, although it would differ from federal practice for pass-through entities. On the other hand, Fox suggested considering a gross receipts tax in lieu of a corporation tax, but Zodrow did not recommend this as an alternative. Fox noted that other external estimates suggested that business taxes were relatively high in Louisiana—partly due to sales taxes paid by business. Zodrow noted that state value-added taxes (VAT) could potentially deal with this problem, but that the experience in Michigan with a VAT was not encouraging for this development. Finally, in terms of equity, Fox concluded from a review of external studies that the Louisiana tax system was approximately proportional and in line with tax systems in other states. The generous homeowner exemption reduces property tax revenues collected from homeowners, shifting the burden to other property owners and to other taxes, such as the local sales tax.

Our experts also raised a few other general points. Zodrow advocated for a closer look at user charges in the state, to ensure that they are appropriate as taxing use and not simply disguised general taxes. User charges can be extremely useful in allocating resources for the public sector and deciding upon the mix for private and public provision of services, but they need to be true user charges. Fox noted that the tax structure in Louisiana was not stable—frequent law changes and amnesties have created an unstable tax environment. This suggests that the underlying foundation needs improvement.

In our own analysis of specific taxes, we have taken much of the advice of these experts. For example, in the following chapters, we advocate for extensive reform of the sales tax, broadening its base by including consumer services and streamlining the administration of the sales tax with a goal of having a structure in place consistent with the Streamlined Sales Tax Agreement. We advocate for increased excise taxes, to bring them up to regional standards. With respect to the personal income tax, we endorse their recommendations for removing federal deductibility and eliminating other deductions, with a goal to reducing personal tax rates. With respect to taxes on corporations, we also follow many of their suggestions. We suggest phasing out the franchise tax, which in our view entails reforming and tightening the corporate income tax. We suggest several alternatives to deal with the loss of passive income due to separate-entity taxation, including enacting legislation to include add-backs and, eventually, combined reporting.

In the subsequent chapters, we also provide specific suggestions for reforming many of the tax credit programs and advocate taking a fresh look at exemptions. We explore the property tax in detail, not only looking at the homeowners' exemption but also the equally large and growing industrial tax exemption. And we provide a thorough analysis of alternatives for mineral taxation in the state.

Notes

1. Federal tax liability is deductible from adjusted gross income in defining Louisiana Taxable Income, so changes in the federal tax code will automatically affect state income tax collections. In addition, the state starts with the federal definition of adjusted gross income.

2. In 1973 interstate natural gas prices were subject to federal price controls while intrastate natural gas prices responded to market forces. And since Louisiana companies were a major user of Louisiana natural gas, the state legislature did not want to relate the tax on natural gas to the value of natural gas.

3. One can question the long-term sustainability of funding permanent and ongoing obligations of the state with a revenue base being primarily supported by dollars from a finite resource; however, that was the political choice made in the early 1970s.

4. Federal tax liability deductibility had been eliminated in 1970 in order to raise revenues. This was politically unpopular, so it was reinstated in 1973.

5. Governor Edwin Edwards made the decision that he would not cut the budget, but rather he would support tax increases. He had suggested a tax increase of approximately $1.0 billion. He was able to raise almost $800 million of tax increases before the legislature was unwilling to support any further tax increases.

6. The tax proposal was authored and promoted by Representative Vic Stelly from the Lake Charles area. Representative Stelly traveled the state explaining the amendment to various constituencies prior to the statewide vote on the constitutional amendment.

7. The Bush tax cuts at the federal level automatically increases state income tax collections.

8. In the 1980s Governor Edwards did not want to cut any spending so he put all of his efforts into raising taxes; in 2008 through the present, Governor Bobby Jindal has made it clear that he will not raise taxes, and this meant he would not support any elimination of a tax credit or tax exemption. Any budget adjustments have to be reductions in expenditures or find alternative sources of funding to support state expenditures. Governors Roemer,

Foster, and Blanco did not make absolute statements about not cutting expenditures or not raising taxes. They considered both in proposing a state budget.

9. *Final Report of the Revenue Study Commission,* www.house.louisiana.gov/rc/.

10. *PAR Advisory Group Principles and Recommendations, January 2013,* Public Affairs Research Council of Louisiana.

11. The Louisiana Department of Revenue did a very thorough job of going through the services that would be taxed and the services that would not be taxed if the governor's proposal were to pass. Ernst & Young was retained to assist the Department of Revenue with this task and to provide an estimate of the sales tax revenues that might be collected.

12. The Revenue Estimating Conference was created in statute by Act 814 of the 1987 Regular Session and has been adopting official revenue estimates for state government budgeting purposes since FY 1988–89. The Conference was subsequently placed in the State Constitution with voter approval of Act 1096 of the 1990 Regular Session.

13. Starting with the 2017 franchise tax period, an LLC for Louisiana franchise tax purposes is treated and taxed in the same manner that it is treated and taxed for federal income tax purposes, Act 12 of the 2016 First Extraordinary Session.

14. In June 2016 Governor John Bel Edwards signed into law H.B. 20, 2016 Extraordinary Session with this law adopting single sales factor apportionment, market sourcing, and a throwout rule for purposes of the Corporation Income Tax. H.B. 20 follows the Multistate Tax Commission's model market sourcing statute.

4

CHALLENGES FOR
THE SALES TAX IN LOUISIANA

Steven M. Sheffrin

The general sales tax is the major source of revenue for the state of Louisiana and its local governments. Louisiana's reliance on the sales tax at the state level is on par with that in other states, but our local governments use the sales tax much more extensively. According to nationally standardized data from the Tax Policy Center, for 2015 Louisiana collected 30 percent of state tax revenue from the general sales tax and other gross receipts taxes, which is on par with national averages. However, if we look at total state *and* local collections, for fiscal year 2012, Louisiana governments collected 39.4 percent of their tax revenue from the sales tax as compared to only 22.6 percent nationally. This reliance on the sales tax will increase due to tax changes made in several extraordinary sessions of the Louisiana legislature in 2016. The state rate was increased from 4 percent to 5 percent and the sales tax base was expanded to include goods that had been exempted from the tax base. It is estimated that in fiscal year 2017 the sales tax will make up approximately 36 percent of total state tax revenues. Even with the higher state rate in Louisiana, the sales tax rate at the state level is comparable to an average of the rates in other states, but local rates in Louisiana are considerably higher.

In Louisiana, the sales tax is collected and administered at the state level as well as at the parish level. This dual level of administration is an anomaly in the United States. Only Arizona and part of Colorado have dual-level administration, and Arizona has enacted legislation to change its system to a single collector. Moreover, the base for the sales tax differs between the state and the parishes and among the parishes. This system creates many challenges, one of which is simply the accurate filing of taxes by the taxpayer. Another challenge involves collection, registration, and auditing. Lastly, as with other states, collecting the use tax for internet sales is a difficult challenge.

In this chapter, we first present an overview of the role that state and local sales taxes play in the Louisiana fiscal system. We then turn to explore the issues raised by the fact that Louisiana has a dual administrative structure and multiple tax bases, and we consider what changes will need to be made to reform the system so that it will conform to developing national standards. Meeting these standards may be necessary to ensure that Louisiana can collect revenue from sales over the internet. We then sketch out a political process to reform the sales tax and create a single administrative structure, while recognizing the key role of local governments.

In the next chapter, we continue our discussion of the sales tax and examine the possibility for increased taxation of personal services. To the extent that we can increase the sales tax base by including additional personal services, we can provide state and local governments with additional revenue or allow them to lower or not to increase rates. We provide some estimates of the scope for such expansion. The expansion of the sales tax base to services is an important issue since services are the fastest growing part of the national and Louisiana economy.

The Sales Tax in Louisiana's Fiscal System

Currently, the largest component of major state tax revenue is sales tax, composed of general and vehicle sales tax; it was 30 percent of total receipts in fiscal year 2015 and is estimated to be over 36 percent in 2017. Sales taxes are very important to the state budget because of the absolute size of these receipts and their share of total collections, and the fact that they broadly reflect economic activity in the economy, including spending by both households and businesses. In addition, the receipts are so large that small errors in forecasting can mean substantial amounts of excess or deficient revenue for budgeting purposes. In fiscal year 2015, a 1 percent difference in actual collections versus forecast would amount to $31 million.

The bulk of this slice of revenue is composed of general sales taxes, $2.700 billion in fiscal year 2015, with the balance being sales taxes on vehicle transactions of $396 million. While vehicle tax receipts can exhibit significant swings due to the durable good nature of vehicle purchases, for both households and businesses, the absolute size of the tax is such that it alone is not likely to materially endanger or enhance a budget. However, while general sales tax transactions are not subject to the degree of aggregate purchasing variation as vehicles can be, this portion of the tax is large enough to "make or break" a budget from unexpected surges or pullbacks in spending across the economy. For these reasons, the sales tax warrants considerable monitoring within the budget process.

The history of the sales tax reflects a tumultuous period encompassing major economic events as well as numerous legislative changes over the years, especially with regard to the base of transactions subject to tax levy. General tax rate changes have been relatively few; starting with a 1 percent rate in 1938 after Mississippi had introduced the first sales tax in the nation in 1932, increased it to 2 percent in 1948, and then to 3 percent in 1970. Only one other rate increase has occurred since then, an increase to 4 percent in 1984, in response to declining collections as the oil boom ended in the early 1980s. The statewide sales tax rate has remained at 4 percent ever since.[1]

To understand the sales tax, there is one key principle: *the tax applies to sale or use of any transfer of tangible personal property unless specifically excluded or exempted by state law; the tax rate applies to services only if the services are specifically included in the law.* Specifically, the sales tax applies to the sale of tangible personal property in the state; the use, consumption, distribution, or storage for consumption or use in the state; and the lease or rental of any item or article of tangible personal property. Presently, there are 191 tangible personal properties that are specifically exempted or excluded from the sales tax. If these exemptions did not exist, it is estimated that the state's sales tax collections would have expanded by $2.998 billion in fiscal year 2014, or just about 89 percent of what the state actually collected in sales taxes. The exemptions with the most dollars forgone by state government are listed in Table 4.1. Nineteen exemptions represent well over 70 percent of the sales taxes forgone due to the constitutional provision or revised statute that specifies that a particular commodity will not be taxed.

Specifically excluded from the sales tax base in the Louisiana constitution are food for home consumption, residential utilities, and prescription drugs. These constitutional limitations became effective in 2003; a constitutional limitation on gasoline and special fuels became effective in 1990, when the excise tax on gasoline was increased from 16 cents per gallon to 20 cents per gallon. The other exemptions are all statutory.

Almost 70 percent of the exemptions listed in Table 4.1 refer to food to be prepared and consumed at home, prescription drugs, the sale of electric power or electricity, and gasoline, ethanol, and diesel. If we add state and local government purchases, then that represents 80 percent of the exemptions listed in Table 4.1.

TABLE 4.1. Exemptions from Louisiana State Sales Tax

Select Exemptions as Defined in Louisiana Revised Statutes	Estimate of Sales Tax Collections Foregone	Percent of All Exemptions
Manufacturers' rebates on new motor vehicles	$18,234,000	0.6
Purchases of manufacturing machinery and equipment	$73,448,000	2.5
Purchases by state and local governments	$195,649,000	6.6
Purchases of tangible personal property for lease or rental	$8,542,000	0.3
Used manufactured homes and 54% of cost of new manufactured homes	$7,036,000	0.2
Sales of water—nonresidential	$8,558,000	0.3
Sales of electric power or energy—nonresidential	$403,401,000	13.6
Certain trucks and trailers used 80% in interstate commerce	$15,676,000	0.5
Annual Louisiana sales tax holidays (Back-to-School, Hurricane Preparedness, 2nd Amendment)	$4,062,000	0.1
Vendor's compensation	$25,648,000	0.9
Sales of gasoline, gasohol, and diesel	$365,837,000	12.3
Sales of food for preparation and consumption in the home	$392,543,000	13.2
Sales of electric power or energy to the consumer for residential use	$197,926,000	6.7
Drugs prescribed by physicians or dentists	$283,653,000	9.5
Subtotal	*$2,001,089,000*	*67.2*
Others	*$974,150,000*	*32.8*
Total Exemptions	*$2,974,363,000*	*100.0*

Source: Louisiana Department of Revenue

Louisiana also has three sales tax holidays: (1) the annual Louisiana sales tax holiday occurring in the month of August for back-to-school shopping, (2) the hurricane preparedness sales tax holiday occurring at the start of hurricane season, and (3) the second amendment sales tax holiday occurring just before the beginning of hunting season. These holidays are relatively inexpensive in terms of forgone sales tax collections, but increase the cost of collecting the sales tax.

Services that are subject to sales tax are the furnishing of sleeping rooms by hotels; the sale of admission to places of amusement and to athletic and recreational events; the furnishing of access to amusement, entertainment, athletic, or recreational facilities; the furnishing of storage or parking privileges by hotels and parking lots; the furnishing of printing and overprinting; the furnishing of laundry, cleaning, pressing, and dyeing services; the furnishing of cold storage space and the preparation of property for such storage; the furnishing of repairs to tangible personal property; and the furnishing of telecommunications services.

While the state tax rate has been only infrequently changed, the tax base has undergone many changes over the years, as can be expected if there are almost two hundred items that are specially exempted from the sales tax. Only the major base changes will be discussed here, but changes are made almost every year; in some years numerous changes are made, and almost all of these annual changes are reductions in the tax base.

After the 1984 tax rate increase, state tax collections continued to weaken as the oil price collapse bottomed out in the spring of 1985. With regard to the sales tax, the state began to suspend exemptions to various portions of the state levy, effectively expanding the tax base into a broad collection of transactions that had previously enjoyed exemption from taxation. Initially, virtually all transactions with explicit statutory exemption were subjected to a 1 percent state tax for a single year, fiscal year 1987.[2] The state has subjected selected exemptions to some portion of the state tax levy for every year since then. While almost all of this taxation finally expired at the end of fiscal year 2010, there is a group of transactions, exempt from tax prior to fiscal year 1987, that are still subject to a 1 percent state tax, but now on a permanent basis.

In fiscal year 1987, the first year of this "suspension" taxation, the state collected $142 million. In other years, depending on the specific exemptions being suspended to what level of tax rate, annual collections were in excess of $400 million. This taxation was implemented via numerous legislative instruments at varying tax bases and rates, even within a single fiscal year. Base erosion has been a continual feature of the sales tax, starting with federally funded spending such as low-income food supplement programs and sales in certain public facilities and enterprise zones, and ultimately extending to large components of this tax base such as gasoline and diesel fuel, medical prescriptions, ships and vessels, and various farm transactions. Eventually, a fairly stable set of transactions was settled upon, and annual collections depended primarily on the tax rate imposed, which was ultimately driven by the needs of the budget at the time. The primary components of this tax base became food for home consumption, residential and business electricity, natural gas, and water utilities, along with a variety of other largely business transactions.

By the early 2000s, the annual and then biennial ritual of suspending these exemptions to some portion of the 4 percent statewide sales tax was becoming politically tiresome. A major reduction in this sales tax base was implemented with adoption of what has come to be known as the Stelly Plan.[3] Starting with the year 2003, sales taxes on food for home consumption, prescription drugs, and residential utilities were made exempt from state sales tax in the State Constitution. The revenue loss from this was offset by an increase in the state personal income tax. In the initial period of full implementation, the tax swap was essentially revenue-neutral. In subsequent years, though, as planned, the losses in slower growing sales taxes were more than offset by the gains in the faster growing income tax. This left the bulk of the remaining "suspension" taxation from the mid-1980s being business utilities.

Legislation passed in 2004 and 2008 combined to completely eliminate the state sales tax on business utilities in fiscal year 2010.[4] The taxation of various other business transactions was reduced as well, but a 1 percent tax rate on these transactions was permanently retained, and is still in effect today. From the budget policy-making perspective, however, this finally ended the temporary taxation of formerly exempt transactions that began in 1986.

One of the recommendations from a 1988 tax study was that the sales tax on machinery and equipment used in manufacturing should be eliminated. It was finally initiated in 2005 with a gradual phaseout so that the state's economy would not see a major drop in sales tax revenues due to this legislative change. It was being phased out over a five-year time horizon. The phaseout was proposed and initiated during the Blanco administration; it was accelerated and completed under the Jindal administration. This exemption is reported to be worth about $49 million in 2013, just over $60 million in 2014, and over $73 million in 2015. A $73 million tax exemption for machinery and equipment implies capital improvements in the state worth approximately $1.8 billion.

The trend in state sales tax collections in Louisiana is illustrated in Figure 4.1. The trends reflect the economy, acts of the state legislature, and approval by the people of Louisiana of certain constitutional amendments that affected the tax base. In the early 2000s the economy faltered, so sales tax collections declined naturally; food and residential utilities were withdrawn from the sales tax base so the tax base was changed constitutionally; machinery and equipment was initiated as a sales tax exemption, further affecting the tax base as an act of the state legislature; among other factors affecting sales tax collections in Louisiana. Hurricanes Katrina and Rita created a major resurgence in the economy, so state revenues grew spectacularly and sales tax grew along with other taxes.

The sales tax as a percent of state revenues is presented in Figure 4.2. After averaging around 25 percent of total state revenue in the 1970s, the tax rate increase of 1984 brought the sales tax share to a peak at almost 35

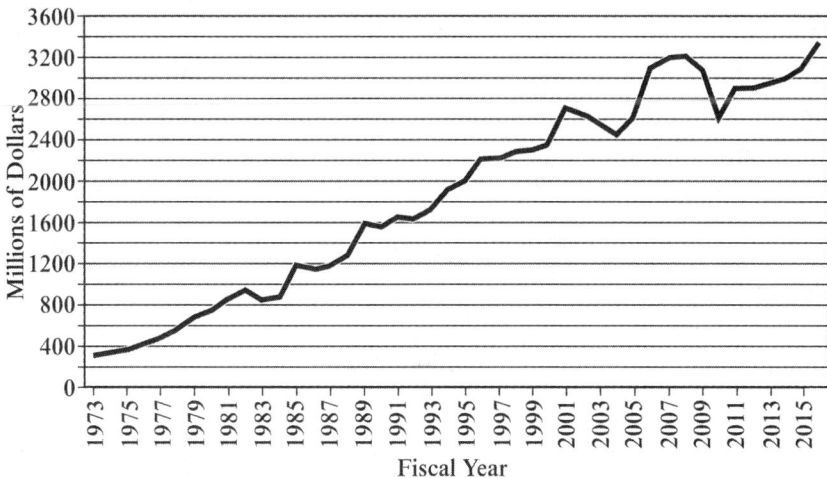

FIGURE 4.1. State Sales Tax Collections

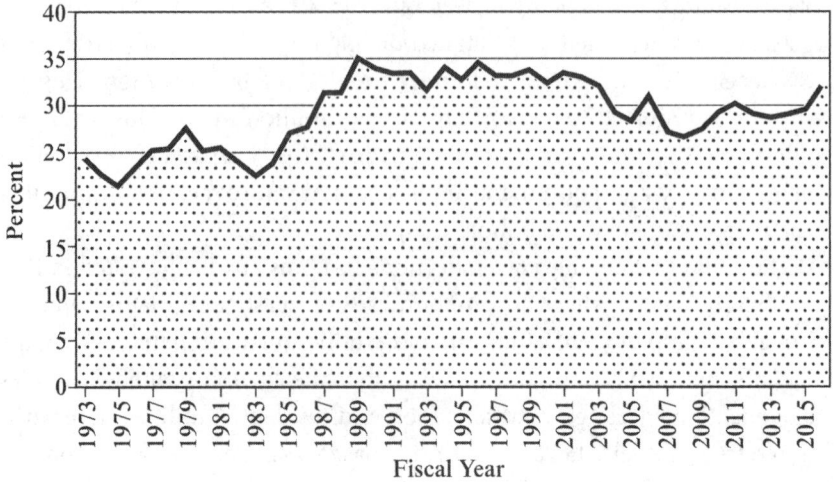

FIGURE 4.2. State Sales Tax as Share of Total State Tax Collections

percent of all state revenues in fiscal year 1989. In the 1990s sales tax collections stayed in a relatively stable range of 30 to 35 percent of all state revenues, as base expansion through suspensions of exemptions was balanced by the growth of income tax and new gaming revenues. Since 2000, sales tax collections as a percent of overall state tax collections have fallen off to a somewhat lower range of 25 to 30 percent, as gaming activity matured in the state, oil prices steadily rose and increased the mineral revenue share, and personal income tax grew more rapidly than other taxes. The 2009–10 slowdown in Louisiana, reduction in the sales tax base related to the general economy and legislative acts, and a lethargic economic recovery have worked to keep the sales tax share in that lower range for the time being.

The sales tax is a major revenue source for the state and local governments. The effective sales tax rate can approach 9–10 percent, including both state and local taxes. The state's Department of Revenue collects the sales tax for the state, while each parish has its own sales tax collector. The school board may collect the sales tax for every governmental subdivision in the parish, or it could be the sheriff or some other unit of government. The sales tax base can and does differ from the state to the parishes and even within a parish from one governmental unit to another. As we discuss below, the state does not tax machinery and equipment, but most parishes still tax business machinery and equipment. The state does not tax food for home consumption, but many governmental subdivisions do. But even within a parish some governmental subdivisions may tax food for home consumption while others may not. The local rates for each parish are contained in Table 4.2. Even though the state rate is relatively low by national

TABLE 4.2. Local Sales Tax Rates

Parish	Local Sales Tax Rates	Lowest (percent)	Highest (percent)
Acadia	5	4.250	5.500
Allen	3	4.700	6.000
Ascension	3	4.500	5.500
Assumption	1	5.000	5.000
Avoyelles	4	3.250	5.250
Beauregard	2	4.750	5.000
Bienville	4	3.000	5.500
Bossier	4	4.250	5.250
Caddo	6	3.350	6.350
Calcasieu	2	5.000	5.250
Caldwell	1	5.000	5.000
Cameron	0	0.000	0.000
Catahoula	1	6.000	6.000
Claiborne	3	3.125	4.500
Concordia	1	4.750	4.750
DeSoto	3	4.000	5.500
East Baton Rouge	2	5.000	5.500
East Carroll	2	5.000	7.000
East Feliciana	1	5.000	5.000
Evangeline	1	5.000	5.000
Franklin	3	4.000	6.000
Grant	3	4.000	6.000
Iberia	4	3.750	4.500
Iberville	2	5.000	5.670
Jackson	2	4.000	5.000
Jefferson	1	4.750	4.750
Jefferson Davis	2	4.500	5.000
Lafayette	6	4.000	6.000
Lafourche	4	4.000	5.200
LaSalle	2	3.500	4.500

TABLE 4.2. (*continued*)

Parish	Local Sales Tax Rates	Lowest (percent)	Highest (percent)
Lincoln	4	3.250	5.000
Livingston	6	4.000	6.500
Madison	3	3.500	5.500
Morehouse	4	3.500	6.000
Natchitoches	4	3.500	5.500
Orleans	1	5.000	5.000
Ouachita	6	4.600	6.000
Plaquemines	1	4.000	4.000
Pointe Coupee	2	4.000	5.000
Rapides	5	3.000	5.000
Red River	2	4.500	5.500
Richland	3	4.000	5.500
Sabine	3	4.625	6.625
St. Bernard	1	5.000	5.000
St. Charles	1	5.000	5.000
St. Helena	2	5.000	6.000
St. James	1	3.500	3.500
St. John the Baptist	1	5.000	5.000
St. Landry	7	3.550	5.750
St. Martin	4	3.500	6.000
St. Mary	2	4.000	4.300
St. Tammany	5	4.750	5.750
Tangipahoa	4	3.000	5.500
Tensas	3	5.250	6.250
Terrebonne	1	5.000	5.000
Union	3	4.000	6.000
Vermilion	7	3.750	6.000
Vernon	3	4.000	5.500
Washington	4	3.830	5.500
Webster	6	3.000	5.500
West Baton Rouge	1	5.000	5.000
West Carroll	2	5.000	6.000
West Feliciana	1	5.000	5.000
Winn	2	3.500	5.000

standards, the totals are very high—for example, state and local sales tax rates in Louisiana are as high as or higher than those in local jurisdictions in Los Angeles.

State and local sales taxes are compared to those in other southern states in Table 4.3. Among the southern states, Louisiana has the lowest state sales tax rate, along with Alabama, but local governments in Louisiana have a range of relatively high sales tax rates. The only states that appear to rely on the sales tax for financing local governments as much as Louisiana does are Alabama and Arkansas.

The sales tax in Louisiana becomes complex, not for the final consumer who merely pays the tax as it is posted on his or her bill, but for the stores and units collecting the tax and remitting it to the governmental units. The complexity of the sales tax system complicates efforts to encourage online stores to collect sales taxes for the state and local governments. The use tax on purchases made outside the state is determined according to a line on the personal income tax form on which one files his or her state income tax to declare purchases that are done online or through catalog shopping on

Table 4.3. Sales Tax Comparisons, State and Local, in Southern States

State	State Sales Tax Rate (%)	Has Local Sales Tax	Rates (%)	Total Sales Tax Jurisdictions*
AL	4.0	Yes	1.0 to 6.5	791
AR	6.5	Yes	1.0 to 5.5	370
FL	6.0	Yes	0.5 to 1.5	56
GA	4.0	Yes	2.0 to 4.0	162
KY	6.0	No	0	No local sales tax
LA	4.0	Yes	3 to 7	341
MS	7.0	Yes	0.25 to 1.0	3: State, Jackson, and Tupelo
NC	4.75	Yes	2.0 to 2.75	105
SC	6.0	Yes	1.0 to 3.0	41
TN	7.0	Yes	1.5 to 2.75	125
TX	6.25	Yes	0.5 to 2.0	1,515
VA	4.3	Yes	1.0 to 1.7	174
WV	6.0	Yes	0.5 to 1.0	11: Municipalities only

Source: Tax Foundation
* Note from Joseph Henchman of the Tax Foundation to Steven Sheffrin, Murphy Institute, Tulane University.

which tax has not been paid. Consistent with the experience of other states, this approach has not been overly successful in generating very much revenue and is extremely expensive to monitor effectively and fairly. As we discuss below, to effectively collect the use tax, Louisiana will likely have to make major changes in its sales tax system.

Conforming to National Standards on Administration

The fact that Louisiana parishes have their own collection systems and often have tax bases that differ from the state base creates many difficulties for taxpayers. For example, they may be audited by the state and one or more parishes on the same return. This contrasts with other states in which there is a single audit authority. In addition, businesses cannot assume that goods are either taxable or nontaxable throughout the state, as parishes typically have tax bases that differ from the state base and from each other.

It was precisely these complexities across the country that led the Supreme Court in two cases, first in *National Bellas Hess* and later in *Quill Corporation,* to require a seller to have physical presence within a state before a state could require it to collect the use tax from customers through its sales into a state. For example, if Amazon has a warehouse in California, then California can require Amazon to collect use tax on internet purchases from California residents. But without that warehouse or other physical presence, it could not.

This is primarily an issue for consumer purchases, not business purchases. Any business located within a state is expected to accrue use tax on its purchases, and sales tax auditors will check this in the regular course of their audits. However, consumers are not audited for sales taxes, and very few individual taxpayers remit use tax on their remote purchases on their tax returns. The only hope for states to collect use tax revenue from consumers is for businesses to be compelled to remit the use tax to them or use some similar mechanism. But in *National Bellas Hess* and *Quill,* the Supreme Court left that up to Congress under its Commerce Clause power. This standard changed in 2018 in the U.S. Supreme Court case *South Dakota v. Wayfair,* which eliminated the physical presence test and allowed increased scope for a rational system of taxation.

Congress has taken some steps in this direction. The Marketplace Fairness Act is proposed federal legislation that would grant states the authority to compel online sellers to collect use tax from out-of-state sellers. For the states to be granted the authority under the Market Place Fairness Act, they must simplify their sales tax laws, which is the trade-off with the business community for imposing use tax collection requirements. Under the proposed legislation, states must either join the Streamlined Sales and Use Tax Agreement (SSUTA) as a full member or meet five simplification mandates that are similar to the SSUTA.

The purpose of the Streamlined Sales and Use Tax Agreement is to simplify and modernize sales and use tax administration in order to substantially reduce the burden of tax compliance. The Agreement focuses on improving sales and use tax administration systems for all sellers and for all types of commerce through all of the following:

- State level administration of sales and use tax collections
- Uniformity in the state and local tax bases
- Uniformity of major tax base definitions
- Central, electronic registration system for all member states
- Simplification of state and local tax rates
- Uniform sourcing rules for all taxable transactions
- Simplified administration of exemptions
- Simplified tax returns
- Simplification of tax remittances
- Protection of consumer privacy

As of 2015, the SSUTA currently has twenty-four members, twenty-three of which are full members and one an associate member. A full member is in compliance with the SSUTA through all of its laws, rules, regulations, and policies, and an associate member is a state that has achieved substantial compliance with the terms of the Agreement taken as a whole, but not necessarily with each provision. The membership roster has grown over time—in October 2005, there were twelve full members and three associate members. Louisiana is not a member.

Under the Marketplace Fairness Act, if states do not wish to join the SSUTA, they must abide by the following five simplification mandates:

- Notify retailers in advance of any rate changes within the state
- Designate a single state organization to handle sales tax registrations, filings, and audits
- Establish a uniform sales tax base for use throughout the state
- Use destination sourcing to determine sales tax rates for out-of-state purchases
- Provide free software for managing sales tax compliance, and hold retailers harmless for any errors that result from relying on state-provided systems and data

In order to join SSUTA as a full member, Louisiana would need to make substantial changes to its sales tax laws, including changes in collection and administration, and removing the disparity between state and local tax bases.

As we discussed above, the Louisiana sales tax law is governed by the state constitution and a long list of statutory exemptions. In addition to the constitutional restrictions on taxing food consumed at home, residential utilities, prescription drugs, and gasoline, the state has an extensive array of various exemptions and exclusions set forth in the Louisiana revised statutes. Some of these exemptions appear on Schedule A of the tax form, but the taxpayer is responsible for identifying the rest of the exemptions.

The sales tax at the local level is constrained by the Louisiana Uniform Local Sales Tax Code. Each political subdivision that is authorized to levy and impose a sales and use tax must have a local ordinance by which it imposes levies, and administers and collects the tax. The Uniform Local Sales Tax Code lists exemptions at the state level that also apply to all local governments, as well as exemptions that are optional. The local taxing authorities have the ability to decide whether or not to extend the optional exemptions to their respective local governments.

The provisions of the SSUTA *do* allow a state to have a zero rate for food for home consumption and prescription drugs while having them subject to tax at local jurisdictions. However, there must be one local tax rate within each political jurisdiction.

To determine how exemptions varied across local governments and whether there are single local rates, we examined the top ten parishes in terms of population and compared them to the state in the three key exemption categories: food for home consumption, prescription drugs, and

TABLE 4.4. Differences in Sales Tax Exemption among Local Governments

	Tax Rate (%)	Food for Home Consumption and Prescription Drugs	Manufacturing Machinery and Equipment
State	4	Exempt	Exempt
East Baton Rouge	5–5.5	Reduced rate of 3%–4.5%, depending on jurisdiction (1%–2% exemption)	No reduction/exemption
Jefferson	4.75	Reduced rate of 3.5%	Exempt with parish-issued exemption certificate
Orleans	5	Reduced rate of 4.5%	Exempt (Sec 150–580 (2) in ordinance)
Caddo	3.35–6.35	No reduction/exemption	2.75% exemption only in Shreveport
St. Tammany	4.75–5.75	No reduction/exemption	No reduction/exemption
Lafayette	4–5.50	Reduced rate of 2%–4.5%, depending on jurisdiction (1%–2% exemption)	No reduction/exemption
Calcasieu	5–5.25	1% exemption for unincorporated areas only, including Ward 1	2.5% exemption valid only in Lake Charles
Ouachita	4.6–6	1% exemption in Monroe only	2% exemption in East and West Ouachita Parish
Rapides	3–5	No reduction/exemption	No reduction/exemption
Livingston	4–6	No reduction/exemption	No reduction/exemption

Note: Information from Parish websites

machinery and equipment used in manufacturing. As mentioned above, the exemptions for food and prescription drugs are part of the state constitution. The exemption for machinery, while not in the constitution, is included in the Revised Statues 47:301 of the state legislature. Tax exemptions for all of these three categories are optional for the local governments. The differences between the state and local bases are identified in Table 4.4.

None of the top ten parishes has complete exemption for food and drugs. Many have reduced rates, with most parishes reducing the local rate by 1–2 percent for these two categories. Four parishes do not have any reduction of the sales tax for food and drugs. As for the machinery exemption, some parishes have complete exemption, some have reduced rates in certain locations within the parishes, and the remainder do not have any exemption or reduction.

With just these three key exemptions, there are already many differences across the parishes. However, many more differences exist as a result of the long list of optional exemptions. As an illustration, Jefferson Parish provides a table of its sales tax exemptions, comparing them with the state exemptions. The exemptions that are not applicable or only partially applicable to Jefferson Parish sales tax are listed in a table that can be found on their website at: https://www.jpso.com/DocumentCenter/View/232.

For Jefferson Parish, food for home consumption, prescription drugs, and some medical devices are subject to a lower rate of 3.5 percent local sales tax. The rest of the categories in the referenced table are not exempt and are subject to taxation at the full rate. For example, the sales of materials, supplies, equipment, fuel, and related items other than vessels used in the production and harvesting of crawfish are exempt from state sales tax, but not from the Jefferson Parish sales tax. The same is true for the sale or use of storm shutter devices, and many more categories, as listed in the table. This list with all of its detail is only for one of the parishes in Louisiana. Each parish could decide whether or not to extend any of the optional exemptions, which results in many minor differences in the sales tax base across the parishes.

To conform to the sales tax base provisions of the SSUTA, Louisiana would have to revise its laws to promote uniformity (except for food for home consumption and prescription drugs) between the state and local governments and also require that each local jurisdiction could only impose a single rate. One consideration in making any changes to the tax base for local governments is that they or their subdivisions may rely on sales tax revenue for borrowing. Thus, it is important that any changes to the sales tax provide sufficient funding for local governments to meet their debt covenant obligations. Requiring local governments to exempt more categories of goods in the name of conformity could thus be problematic unless there were sufficient other sources of sales tax revenues available, for example, from increased taxes on services or increased use taxes.

To achieve uniformity without compromising local tax bases, we suggest that the state phase out the optional exemptions over time and continue to allow local jurisdictions to tax food at home and prescription drugs. This would tend to preserve local revenues. One difficult issue for uniformity would be deciding upon the manufacturing machinery and equipment exemption—eliminating the ability for local governments to tax these sales. These issues will need to be addressed through a political process that includes local governments. The key issue of moving towards a single administration structure would also have to be addressed through this process.

It is worth noting that federal law prohibits the imposition of sales tax on food purchased under the food stamp program (officially renamed the Supplemental Nutrition Assistance Program in 2008) or under the Women, Infants, and Children (WIC) program. As of November 2013, 19.3 percent of Louisiana residents participate in the food stamp program, whereas 18.7 percent of Louisiana residents live below the poverty level. Thus, a strong case can be made that the poor and near-poor are already exempt from sales taxes on food for home consumption. Requiring a single tax rate at the local level may thus not have severe distributional consequences

The Future of Taxation on Remote Sales

The Marketplace Fairness Act was reintroduced in the Senate in 2015. In the past session of Congress, it passed the Senate but not the House. States have adopted other strategies to collect use taxes and after the Wayfair decision will accelerate such efforts.

More than half of the states that have sales tax (twenty-four out of forty-five) are using a "click-through nexus" or "affiliate-nexus" strategy to attempt to require out-of-state retailers to collect the use tax. This policy started in a 2008 New York law and quickly spread to other states. Often referred to as the "Amazon law," click-through nexus allows a state to compel sellers who do not have physical nexus in the state to collect use tax for sales made to the state's residents, if the sellers have an affiliate within the state who is compensated for purchases made through a link on the affiliate's website. These policies have not been without controversy. Some states have had extensive litigation over whether their laws were consistent with the requirement in *Quill*. In other cases, retailers have simply disbanded their affiliate programs. There are also questions about its constitutionality.[5] In the last session, the legislature passed an affiliate-nexus bill. It was vetoed by Governor Jindal, who cited constitutional grounds.

Colorado initiated a different strategy based on requiring remote sellers to provide information to the state and consumers for all Colorado purchasers. In 2010, they amended their laws to impose the following obligations to remote sellers:

- *Transactional Notice:* notify Colorado purchasers that sales or use tax is due on certain purchases made from the retailer and that the state of Colorado requires the purchaser to file a sales or use tax return
- *Annual Purchase Summary:* send notification to all Colorado purchasers each year informing them of their purchases in the previous calendar year, obligation to pay use tax, and obligation of companies to give their names and purchase lists to the Colorado Department of Revenue
- *Customer Information Report:* file an annual statement for each purchaser to Department of Revenue with information from the Annual Purchase Summary

This law has been hotly debated since its enactment. A District Court granted partial summary judgment to a direct marketing organization that protested the law and enjoined Colorado from enforcing it. The US Court of Appeals for the Tenth Circuit then ruled that federal courts did not have jurisdiction under the Tax Injunction Act to hear the case, but the United States Supreme Court reversed their ruling and sent it back to the Appeals Court to decide on its further disposition. After review, the Appeals Court let the law stand. Colorado is now enforcing the law.

Louisiana adopted Colorado's approach effective July 1, 2017. Reporting requirements apply to remote sellers that have cumulative Louisiana sales of $50,000 per calendar year. There are requirements to notify the purchaser at the time of sale and the end of the calendar year and also provide the information to the Department of Revenue. It is too early to determine how the law has functioned.

In the *South Dakota v. Wayfair* decision, the U.S. Supreme Court abolished the physical presence test but still required that any use tax collection regime not unduly burden interstate commerce. To meet these requirements, Louisiana will be creating a separate system for collection of use tax on remote sales to run in parallel with the current system. The Louisiana Sales and Use Tax Commission for Remote Sales will be developing the new system. It will feature a single collector and be designed to ease the process for remote sellers. It will remain to be seen whether this new strategy for Louisiana will satisfy the requirements under the new legal regime.

A Political Process to Reform

As we have discussed, unlike in many other states, local governments in Louisiana heavily rely on the sales tax to fund their operations. It is essential, therefore, both for political and policy reasons to ensure that the interests are represented in any reform process. In that spirit, we propose the following steps in establishing a uniform method of collecting state and local sales taxes:

- As part of the tax reform effort, eliminate optional sales tax exemptions for any future legislative activity.
- Create a Local Sales Tax Commission (with members appointed by the Police Jury Association, the Louisiana Sheriffs Association, the Louisiana School Boards Association, the Louisiana Municipal Association, the Mayors Council, and the governor, Speaker of the House of Representatives, and President of the Senate) to initiate a process by which *local* taxes can be collected uniformly and appropriate auditing processes can be established.
- Once the Local Sales Tax Commission is working, have the state join the Local Sales Tax Commission to create a uniform process of state and local sales tax administration (collections and auditing).
- Initiate a Study Panel on State and Local Sales Tax Bases to estimate the variation in the tax bases among the state and localities and among the local governments themselves and to map out a reasonable way to gradually eliminate the variation and minimize the cost of such changes. This study should be completed in two years.

As we have discussed, unifying the state and local sales tax base is an important challenge for Louisiana in meeting the criteria for the SSUTA. To bring forth the desired uniformity, the SSUTA allows local governments to include food for home consumption and prescription drugs in the base even if they are exempt—as they are in Louisiana—at the state level. We would allow this practice to continue. Second, local optional exemptions from the sales tax should be eliminated by state legislation. Finally, legislation should eliminate other state exemptions to insure uniformity in tax bases.

The uniform collection of state and local sales taxes should be completed in a three-to-five-year window. The establishment of a uniform sales tax collection process is important to both the state and local governmental units. Current revenues are at stake, and even more future revenues are potentially at stake, especially if the sales tax is expanded to include services, which we discuss in the next chapter.

This proposal is submitted with the greatest respect for local governments and with the understanding of the absolute importance of including local governments in every step of the process in establishing a uniform method of state and local sales tax collection. The administration of sales tax collections is not just a state issue; it is a state-local issue.

Notes

1. Technically, since fiscal year 1991 and as authorized by Act 1038 of the 1990 Regular Session, the state sales tax rate has been reduced to 3.97 percent, and a levy of 0.03 percent has been imposed by the Tourism Promotion District. The District is a local political subdivision whose boundaries are coterminous with the state and whose tax base is the same as the state's tax base. The District's tax is collected by the State Department of Revenue along with the state tax, and taxpayers are generally unaware of the distinction. Revenue collected for the District is treated as typical dedication of state resources in the state government budgeting process.

2. HCR 55 of the 1986 Regular Session suspended all exemptions to 1 percent of state tax levy from July 1, 1986, to June 30, 1987.

3. Act 88 of the 2002 Regular Session prohibited state sales tax on purchases of food for home consumption and residential utilities as of July 1, 2003. State sales tax on medical prescriptions was also prohibited, but these purchases had already been statutorily returned to exempt status several years earlier. The plan also expanded the personal income tax via Act 51 of the same year. The legislation implementing these changes has been commonly referred to as the Stelly Plan, after its legislative author, Rep. Vic Stelly.

4. Act 4 of the 2004 First Extraordinary Session extended the taxation of business utilities at a 3.8 percent tax rate, but scheduled the elimination of 2.8 percent of this tax rate for fiscal year 2010. Act 1 of the 2008 Second Extraordinary Session eliminated a 1 percent tax rate as of fiscal year 2009. Thus, by the beginning of fiscal year 2010, business utilities were no longer subject to a state sales tax.

5. See Erika K. Lunder and Carol A. Petit, "'Amazon Laws' and Taxation of Internet Sales: Constitutional Analysis," Congressional Research Service, April 9, 2015, available at https://www.fas.org/sgp/crs/misc/R42629.pdf.

5

EXPANDING THE LOUISIANA SALES TAX TO SERVICES

James Alm and Grant Driessen

Introduction

The largest component of Louisiana state tax revenue is the sales and use tax, composed of the general sales tax and the vehicle sales tax (referred to as the "sales tax" for simplicity). In fiscal year 2015, 30 percent of total state receipts were generated by the sales tax, of which the bulk comes from general sales taxes ($2.700 billion in fiscal 2015), with the balance coming from sales taxes on vehicle transactions ($396 million). The sales tax is projected to contribute close to 36 percent of total state revenues in fiscal 2017 due to the increase in the state tax rate from 4 percent to 5 percent through fiscal year 2018. Over most recent history, sales tax collections demonstrated relatively stable long run growth. Even so, the sales tax has a turbulent record, with revenues affected by specific economic events and by many legislative changes in the base of taxation. In contrast, there have been few changes in the sales tax rate since 1938 with the rate going to 3 percent in 1970, 4 percent in 1984, temporarily to 5 percent in 2016 and now to 4.45 percent in 2018.

Louisiana is one of 45 states that impose a sales tax. The sales tax applies to the sale of tangible personal property in the state, the use, consumption, distribution, or storage for consumption or use in the state, and the lease or rental of any item or article of tangible personal property. Importantly, the tax rate applies to services only if the services are specifically included in the relevant law. Consumers pay the sales tax on the price of a good (and select services) at the point of sale, and the sales tax is remitted to the state by a seller that qualifies under Louisiana law as a "dealer." All businesses with a physical presence (e.g., offices, branches, warehouses, employees) have established "nexus" and are responsible for the collection and remittance of state and local sales tax. A use tax generally applies to a good if the good was purchased outside of Louisiana and brought into the state, or if the good was purchased on the internet and the sales tax was not paid.

Louisiana law also authorizes local governments to impose the sales tax at the local level, as permitted by the Louisiana Constitution. Local rates can vary, but are limited by the Constitution to 3 percent. An increase beyond 3 percent requires legislative approval and a vote of the people. The base of each local sales tax can deviate from the state tax base, as approved by the Legislature. There are at present 493 sales tax jurisdictions, and a business that operates in different parishes needs to know the rates within these parishes and local sales tax jurisdictions. While the state sales tax of 4 percent and 5 percent with the temporary tax passed in 2016 is relatively low compared to most states, the average local option sales tax is 4.85 percent, the highest in the nation. Overall, Louisiana has the third highest combined state and local option sales tax (9.85 percent) in the country.

There are at present 191 tangible personal properties that are specifically exempted or excluded from the sales tax. It is estimated that these exemptions lead to lost revenues of $2.998 billion in fiscal year 2015, or about 89 percent of actual (estimated) state collections. Of these exemptions, nineteen exemptions account for over 70 percent of foregone sales collections, generally due to the constitutional provision or revised statute that specifies that the specific delineated commodity will not be taxed. These exemptions are discussed in detail in Chapter 10.

Importantly, the tax rate applies to services only if the services are specifically included in the relevant law. It is this issue that is examined here; that is, what would be the effects of expanding the base of the sales tax to include services. The issue of exemptions, both for the sales tax and for other taxes as well, is examined in a separate report.

State sales taxes are typically applied to a wide range of goods but only to a limited range of services. The notion of expanding the sales tax to cover a broad range of services is intriguing for two reasons. First, such a plan has the potential to raise a large amount of revenue, given the importance of sales taxes for most states together with the size of non-taxed services. Second, there are indications that sales tax expansion is among the more feasible tax reform options available to state governments. In the past 15 years, an expansion of the sales tax to cover services has been proposed by the tax reform committees in ten states. However, these proposals have produced varying degrees of success: only one of these proposals was signed into law.

A similar proposal offered by Governor Jindal in March 2013 was eventually withdrawn from consideration.

However, debate over the merits of expanding the sales tax base to include services is often contentious. Advocates for sales tax expansion argue that it makes the tax system fairer, less sensitive to business cycle shocks, and easier to administer than the existing sales tax. Opponents often raise concerns about its potential to decrease progressivity of the tax system, to generate opposition from businesses, and to treat differently the various categories of services like internet sales.

It should be noted that proposals in other states to expand the sales tax to cover services have produced mixed results in the past few decades. Perhaps the most prominent example of a failure to enact service sales tax legislation occurred in Florida in 1987. The state legislature passed a proposal that instituted a sales and use tax on a wide range of services, which was then signed by the governor. However, after protests over the law's fairness and constitutionality, the proposal was put on the ballot and repealed later that year, with the executive branch turning on the tax in its last months. Subsequent research into the process in Florida attributes the downfall of the proposal to political circumstances, while other studies mention pyramiding and out-of-state vendors that were affected as other sources of the proposal's failure.[1]

A similar process, albeit on a smaller scale, took place in Massachusetts in 2013, where the state repealed the sales and use tax on computer services after public unrest.[2] At the recommendation of a state-appointed tax commission, the sales tax was expanded to cover a select group of services beginning in 2009, only to be placed on a referendum and repealed by voters in 2010.[3]

Legislation that expanded sales taxation to cover services has also experienced success in recent years. In 2014, the government in Washington, D.C. passed tax reform legislation that included sales tax expansion to car wash, health club and tanning, and carpet and upholstery cleaning services.[4] It should be noted that this reform included a smaller range of taxed services than previous efforts, and was accompanied by reductions in income and business taxes and an expanded low-income tax credit, which have traditionally garnered more robust public approval.

Finally, in the past 15 years ten of the seventeen tax reform committees appointed by state legislators around the country have recommended expanding the sales tax to cover services. Many of the remaining states either already tax many services (such as Hawaii) or have already tried and failed to pass such legislation (such as Florida and Maine).

This chapter examines the effects of expanding the sales tax to cover economic services on the Louisiana economy. First, we observe the general economic and practical arguments for and against such legislation. We then summarize the current tax setup in Louisiana and discuss the particular aspects of the system that make the effect of sales tax expansion different from those in a "typical" state. Finally, we estimate the revenue and behavioral implications of a sales tax expansion into services, including an analysis of the distributional effects of the expansion. These analyses lead to our recommendation that the Louisiana sales tax should be expanded to include services in the tax base.

The Pros and Cons of Expanding the Sales Tax to Services

Currently, 45 states impose some form of a sales tax. Most of these taxes are imposed primarily on goods and not services, since the typical sales tax legislation is written so that goods are taxed unless they are specifically excluded, while services are not taxed unless they are explicitly included in law.[5] This tax treatment has stimulated debate in many places over whether it is appropriate to expand the sales tax to cover service activity.

ARGUMENTS IN FAVOR OF INCLUDING SERVICES

Perhaps the most obvious benefit of expanding the sales tax to the service sector is the additional revenue generated. Mazerov estimates that the nationwide annual yield from taxing services would be $87 billion, with a maximum estimate of $856 million for Louisiana. For example, the 2013 proposal by Governor Jindal expanded the sales tax to service but not as broadly as suggested by Mazerov.[6]

Proponents of sales tax expansion also argue that taxing services promotes "horizontal equity," allowing more equal treatment of individuals and firms in otherwise equal economic situations. Taxing goods and not services can result in treatment of certain types of activity that is viewed by some as inconsistent, and so unfair. For example, say that a household is looking to purchase a remedy for a computer virus, and is considering two options: buying a computer cleaning program from Firm A, or hiring a computer programming expert from Firm B to address the issue. Under the typical sales tax policy described above, a program bought from Firm A would be subject to a sales tax, while the service provided by Firm B would not be subject to sales taxation, even though each alternative is addressing the same problem. This inconsistency violates the principle of horizontal equity.

A related aspect is that taxing services may improve economic efficiency. Continuing with the above example, the failure to tax the service provided by Firm B could distort consumer choices between the two firms, generating inefficiency. Merriman and Skidmore found that imposing sales taxes on goods and not services was responsible for one-eighth of the growth in the service sector in the 1980s and 1990s.[7]

There is also evidence that inconsistent sales tax treatment has led to other types of market distortions. Excluding services from sales taxation may be advantageous to larger firms over smaller ones, as bigger companies are more likely to hire in-house accountants and lawyers with services that would be exempt from the typical sales tax. Additionally, the California Budget Project asserts that this was responsible for favoring "big box" retailers that would pay sales taxes in local land decisions over other types of businesses.[8] Expanding the sales tax to services would eliminate such inconsistencies and increase the level of tax neutrality present in the system.

Finally, service tax expansion would increase government reliance on the sales tax, which has a number of features often deemed attractive. A sales tax on goods and services is a type of consumption tax, and therefore does not discourage savings and investment in the manner of a tax on capital gains or a tax on property. The tendency of individuals to smooth consumption levels across business cycles leads the sales tax to be a relatively stable source of revenues, particularly when compared to personal income taxation.[9] Sales taxes also have minimal compliance costs, especially for the consumer.[10] Furthermore, since expanding the tax to cover services would result in the sales tax being applied to almost all types of economic activity, such a tax would also carry low amounts of costs associated with evasion (the illegal refusal to pay taxes) and avoidance (legal maneuvering to reduce or eliminate tax payments).

ARGUMENTS AGAINST INCLUDING SERVICES

The regressivity of sales taxes is often cited as a key reason to forgo service tax expansion. Sales taxes are uniformly imposed at a flat rate, and thus the tax rates do not vary with household ability to pay like a tax with a more progressive structure, such as the federal tax on personal income. Moreover, households with lower levels of income tend to devote a higher percentage of their income to consumption, which means that lower income households tend to bear a relatively larger sales tax burden relative to their income than higher income households. Proponents of service tax expansion have countered this argument with proposals that link sales tax reform with a low-income tax credit in order to increase the progressivity of such a change, and with exemptions for educational, health, and other services deemed "essential."[11]

Critics also argue that subjecting services to the sales tax will increase the level of "pyramiding" in the tax system, or the imposition of multiple levels of taxes imposed on the production of a single good or service. This argument is derived from the fact that the more activity a sales tax covers, the more taxes are imposed on goods and services that are inputs to a final good rather than outputs and that are all reflected in the price of the final good. Pyramiding implies that goods that go through multiple stages of production may be subject to more taxation than their "simpler" counterparts. Some people in favor of service taxation have responded to this criticism by incorporating a ban on "business-to-business" service taxation to eliminate such pyramiding: however, such a policy would make the sales tax more complex and thus increase costs associated with compliance.

Another concern with expanding the sales tax to cover services is the effect of such a policy on a jurisdiction's business environment. A sizeable and growing literature has found significant evidence of tax competition between governments; that is, jurisdictions compete over how attractive their tax environments are to individuals and firms, who respond through their mobility and consumption decisions.[12] Applying the sales tax to services represents an effective increase in the tax rate for both businesses and individuals, and thus may provide a less favorable environment for potential entrants into a jurisdiction, thereby weakening an area's relative attractiveness.

Finally, issues have been raised with the implementation of a sales tax expansion. It is not clear how a sales tax on services would be applied to re-mote vendors who work outside of the relevant jurisdiction (e.g., online tu-torial services). Policies would likely need cross-jurisdictional agreements to resolve this issue. Otherwise, a sales tax that included services tax would favor remote and online vendors over local businesses. Additionally, there is concern that services will impose the greatest administrative burden on small businesses, which are less likely to have easily identifiable avenues to achieve tax compliance.

Some Relevant Features of the Louisiana Tax System

There are several characteristics of the Louisiana tax system that should be acknowledged when considering service tax expansion. As noted ear-lier, Louisiana's current combined state and local sales tax rate is approach-ing 10 percent, which is now the highest rate in the U.S. (Tax Foundation 2017). This high rate results in Louisiana's government revenue stream being much more reliant on sales tax receipts than the average state, as discussed in Chapter 2. The fact that Louisiana has a high sales tax rate means that it has more potential for revenue growth through service expansion than the average state, which can be used to fund budget deficits or finance expen-diture projects. The high sales tax rates also means that the potential for increased revenue stability offered by applying the sales tax to services is smaller, since the state already develops a significant amount of its revenue from the sales tax on goods.

Another unique feature of the Louisiana tax system is the allowance for localities to impose their own sales tax on goods. The Louisiana sales tax rate attributable to the *state* government is roughly in-line with the national average, with the *local* option the driver of the relatively high sales tax in the state. While the potential revenue benefits are equally beneficial to local governments, this division in control over sales tax policy means that the state may have less power to exercise sales tax reform than governments without a local sales tax. For example, reform by the state government that expands the sales tax base to cover services but lowers the sales tax rate on all activity could be undermined by local policymakers, who could respond by increasing their local sales taxes, despite state restrictions on the local sales tax rate.

Also, Louisiana offers its citizens three sales tax holidays: a holiday near the beginning of hurricane season to purchase storm-preparedness items, a holiday in the beginning of August on all items intended to help with back-to-school purchases (for only the state sales tax), and a holiday at the beginning of hunting season for firearms, ammunition, and hunting supplies. These holidays are designed to encourage consumption and stimulate the economy, although their effects are unclear. Should such holidays also apply to relevant services with a tax expansion, their effects are also likely to be unclear, potentially driving down collections from an expansion. Moreover, since services tend to be required less frequently than certain goods, the level of avoidance through service purchases may exceed that of goods. For instance, one may expect the increase in the requests for air conditioner repair to exceed the increase in food at home purchases for the sales tax holiday in early August, since the former is needed only occasionally (and thus can be planned around a holiday).

Currently, Louisiana is somewhere in the middle of the state efforts in taxing services. The Federation of Tax Administrators has periodically conducted a survey asking whether or not states tax 168 types of service categories. The last of these surveys was conducted in 2007, and reported that 55 such services were taxed in Louisiana, which was exactly equal to the median nationwide value and very close to the mean value of 55.8 (Federation of Tax Administrators 2008). More specifically, the survey breaks out the services into eight main categories. Of these, Louisiana taxes more than half of the possible services in the "Utilities," "Admissions/Amusements," and "Fabrication, Repair & Installation" categories, and under 20 percent of the services in the "Business Services," "Professional Services," and "Other" sections. Although in line with national averages, Louisiana's service coverage is among the lowest in the Southeast, as nearby states such as Texas, Tennessee, Mississippi, and Florida all report a greater number of services taxed.

Mazerov decomposes the survey from the Federation of Tax Administrators, and compiles a list of 40 taxes deemed to be "feasible," including services outside health care, housing, education, legal, banking, public transit, insurance, and funeral service sectors.[13] This list also places Louisiana toward the center of the taxation spectrum, with the state's 19 "feasibly-taxed" services ranking just ahead of the mean value of 17 items. States with the most comprehensive service coverage (or those with at least 10 percent more services taxed than Louisiana in each list) are not characterized by any obvious population-based, regional, or size trends. This group includes Washington, D.C., Hawaii, Kansas, Minnesota, Nebraska, New Jersey, New Mexico, South Dakota, Tennessee, Texas, Utah, West Virginia, and Wisconsin.

Some Effects of Expanding the Louisiana Sales Tax to Services

We conduct two types of empirical analysis to clarify the implications of expanding the sales tax to services in Louisiana. We first examine the distributional effects of including services. We then estimate the revenue effects of three plausible types of service expansion.

DISTRIBUTIONAL EFFECTS

Data. We use the 2012 Consumer Expenditure Survey (CEX) to empirically analyze the distributional effects of expanding Louisiana's sales tax to a broader array of services. The CEX contains data on total household income and spending, allowing us to rank household wealth by either metric. It offers rich detail on household expenditures; for example, it breaks down spending on household operations into several categories that include expenditures on child care, home maintenance, and appliance and labor charge value of equipment purchases. This level of detail allows us to separate household purchases into those on goods and those on services, and, more importantly, into those that are taxed and untaxed in the state of Louisiana.

Note that the full 2012 CEX sample contains over 10,000 households, and provides weights that are designed to be nationally representative. However, comprehensive representation is not assured for samples in individual states. It is possible to use the nationwide sample to make judgments about Louisiana, although this runs the risk of missing patterns unique to Louisiana due to state differences in demographics.

Accordingly, we conduct the incidence analysis on two separate subsamples of the complete CEX sample. The first subsample is comprised of 275 households in the CEX that are representative of Louisiana. The second subsample is comprised of all respondents defined as living in the South by the Bureau of Labor Statistics; this region is composed of the 17 states bounded to the north and east by Maryland and Delaware and to the north and west by Oklahoma and Texas. The 4591 households included in this group provide more desirable large-sample properties not available in the first subsample. Population weights provided by the CEX are applied to all households in each of our samples.

Methodology. Throughout, we make the standard assumption that consumers bear the full burden of any tax on services or consumption item.[14] Also, in constructing our measure of incidence, we define economic status using two metrics, total income and total consumption. Income is the most common metric used in incidence analysis, as it captures all of the resources flowing into a household. We use total after-tax income in this analysis, which includes revenues from pensions, tax refunds, and alimony payments. In addition, some studies have argued that consumption is a better measure of economic status because it captures expected income changes in transitory households, such as students who may undergo large increases in income after matriculation and senior citizens who are more likely to spend down accrued savings.[15] Therefore, we also rank households by consumption levels to test for differences in our findings across these measures.

The list of expenditures in the CEX does not match precisely the list of services as defined in Louisiana state law. We therefore make a series of judgments about how the bundle of services captured in each survey answer corresponds to services as defined in the Louisiana tax code. Services are placed in three categories: items that are entirely taxed, items that are exclusively untaxed, and items with partial or unclear taxation statuses. Large differences in the partial taxation category would suggest that CEX may be missing tax information that a dataset tailored more specifically to service expenditures might capture.

We sort households into deciles (determined by income and consumption). Then, for a given service the percentage of the total consumption attributable to each group is compared with those values for other groups, and with analogous observations for other services. For instance, consider a scenario where the lowest decile generates 8 percent of total consumption, while the highest decile generates 35 percent. Suppose also that the lowest decile generates 10 percent of total childcare service consumption, while the highest decile has 45 percent of total child care service consumption (with a consistently rising consumption pattern across deciles for both total consumption and child care service consumption). Then we would say that a childcare service tax is less progressive than a sales tax levied on all types of consumption. Accordingly, we focus on consumption patterns across deciles.

We complement measures of relative consumption with graphs that show the regression results of service consumption across household rank. One criticism of standard incidence work is that if income and consumption categories are sufficiently broad that merely comparing consumption levels across groups may fail to capture interesting distributional developments that occur within the groups themselves. Use of these regressions addresses that concern. We use the Epanechnikov kernel-weighted local polynomial regression in our analysis. This sort of regression is attractive because it assigns an exponential form that bests fits the observed data, which eliminates the possibility of biasing results because, say, a linear relationship is assumed when a second-order polynomial function would be more appropriate. All regression results are smoothed to convey the overall trends in the data without undue influence from outlier observations.

Note that we are not able to capture any behavioral effects that might stem from the imposition of a sales tax on services. Taxes on services taxes will increase the price of services relative to other goods, which will in turn reduce the quantity demanded of services. However, our analysis does not include such a behavioral response. If lower income households reduce their quantity demanded for services more than higher income households as a result of the sales tax expansion, then their consumption of services after the imposition of a tax will be lower than our estimates suggest, which would in turn make more progressive the taxation of services than suggested by our estimates. However, we expect any behavioral responses to be small, given the low level of sales taxes in Louisiana.

Results. Table 5.1 summarizes the results of the standard incidence analysis across deciles across all measures of service consumption in the CEX for the subsample of Louisiana households only. For this and all subsequent tables, households are ranked according to total consumption or total income deciles.

While each service is broadly increasing in consumption, there is notable heterogeneity in the rate of increase across deciles. For instance, households in the highest two deciles consumed more than 70 percent of the spending on entertainment fees, a luxury good. In contrast, those households were responsible for less than 45 percent of total spending on vehicle maintenance. This variation holds across the distribution. While the lowest decile spent virtually nothing (0.0 percent) on home repairs (likely due to the large portion of renters among that group), the lowest decile accounted

TABLE 5.1: Louisiana State Services Consumption Burden by Consumption and Income Decile, Selected Items

	Decile									
	1 (Lowest)	2	3	4	5	6	7	8	9	10 (Highest)
Measures										
Total consumption	2.2%	3.4%	6.0%	7.6%	8.8%	9.0%	9.4%	11.4%	18.5%	23.7%
Total disposable income	1.9%	3.2%	4.9%	6.7%	8.5%	10.0%	12.2%	12.4%	17.0%	23.1%
Entirely Taxed Services	0.6%	1.6%	3.2%	4.8%	7.2%	9.7%	11.4%	10.7%	17.9%	33.0%
Home maintenance	0.0%	1.3%	4.4%	4.7%	8.6%	12.9%	8.5%	10.5%	14.4%	34.7%
Vehicle maintenance	1.1%	1.5%	1.4%	6.7%	6.9%	5.0%	22.9%	10.9%	17.7%	25.8%
Entertainment fees	1.8%	2.7%	1.2%	2.3%	2.1%	5.1%	2.7%	11.6%	31.9%	38.7%
Partially Taxed Services	2.2%	1.8%	4.9%	4.7%	4.2%	11.5%	8.3%	12.8%	15.0%	34.6%
Other entertainment	2.7%	4.2%	0.5%	4.4%	2.4%	12.5%	2.0%	10.1%	17.7%	43.6%
Personal care	1.9%	0.2%	7.8%	4.9%	5.4%	10.8%	12.6%	14.7%	13.2%	28.5%
Untaxed Services	1.4%	2.9%	4.0%	5.7%	5.9%	8.7%	9.0%	17.2%	22.6%	22.5%
Miscellaneous	0.4%	0.8%	2.4%	9.0%	3.0%	6.0%	2.6%	50.2%	9.3%	16.3%
Food away from home	1.9%	3.1%	6.6%	6.2%	8.7%	12.6%	10.8%	12.1%	17.4%	20.7%
Domestic services	2.4%	5.0%	5.2%	12.1%	4.6%	6.1%	4.8%	9.2%	20.5%	30.1%
Child care	3.9%	2.6%	0.0%	9.5%	5.6%	4.9%	13.8%	11.4%	19.3%	29.0%
Other household expenses	1.9%	3.2%	3.5%	5.7%	8.5%	12.4%	12.5%	14.8%	18.9%	18.5%
Public transportation	2.5%	1.9%	0.7%	2.2%	0.3%	2.3%	7.9%	19.2%	9.0%	53.9%
Medical services	0.5%	6.0%	2.5%	3.5%	4.0%	6.9%	10.3%	5.1%	32.1%	29.2%
Educational services	0.0%	0.2%	0.1%	0.7%	1.5%	0.9%	4.1%	22.9%	58.5%	11.0%

Note: Percentages represent the share of the overall consumption level attributable to the decile, based on sample of 275 households.

for almost 4 percent of total spending on child care. These patterns illustrate that, if legislators were to selectively expand the sales tax to services, the distributional effects of the policy would be highly dependent upon the types of activities to which the tax was applied.

Although consumption of services, broadly defined, increased across deciles, this increase was not monotonic across all services. For some of these cases, there is no clear economic explanation, including for lower deciles other entertainment and in middle deciles medical services and home and vehicle maintenance. This variation may well be due to the size of the Louisiana sample; with less than 30 households in each decile, outliers have stronger statistical power than they would in the Southern sample. Miscellaneous spending is spread much more evenly across deciles than the other categories, with a large jump in the eighth decile. Other cases seem unlikely to be attributable to the number of observations. Public transportation consumption decreased at both the lower and upper end of the spectrum; since this category includes spending on subways, buses, and public transportation, it may be that lower- and higher-deciles households use such methods more due to reduced vehicle ownership. Notably, educational service spending undergoes a significant increase from decile eight to nine, with an even larger increase to the top decile, perhaps due to the charter school presence in Louisiana, particularly in New Orleans.

The overall distribution of services consumption was slightly more progressive than consumption and income measures, with the share of consumption in each service category exceeding that of income and consumption in the upper two deciles and falling short of income and consumption in the lowest two deciles. This pattern suggests that on the whole the bundle of services consumed by the Louisiana population is closer to a luxury set of purchases that the analogous bundle of goods consumed. Of some importance, this pattern also indicates that expansion of the sales tax to all services would increase the overall progressivity of the sales tax. Within the service sector, taxed services appear to be more progressive than untaxed services. Given that sales taxes are among the most regressive of tax policies, the lack of significant separation between service and total consumption means that such an expansion would likely make the tax system as a whole more regressive.

Table 5.2 displays the result of the distributional consumption shares for the subsample of CEX respondents living in the South. The broad hetero-

TABLE 5.2. Southern States Services Consumption Burden by Consumption and Income Decile, Selected Items

Measures	Decile									
	1 (Highest)	2	3	4	5	6	7	8	9	10 (Lowest)
Total consumption	2.1%	3.6%	4.9%	6.3%	7.5%	9.0%	10.5%	12.2%	16.8%	27.1%
Total disposable income	2.2%	3.5%	4.7%	6.2%	7.3%	9.2%	10.6%	12.7%	17.1%	26.6%
Entirely Taxed Services	1.1%	2.2%	3.0%	4.7%	6.0%	8.0%	9.1%	13.0%	17.4%	35.4%
Home maintenance	1.4%	2.2%	3.5%	4.6%	5.2%	7.9%	8.0%	13.8%	15.0%	38.4%
Vehicle maintenance	1.2%	3.0%	3.3%	6.1%	9.0%	10.2%	12.5%	12.9%	17.0%	24.8%
Entertainment fees	0.3%	1.2%	1.5%	3.0%	3.9%	5.4%	6.9%	11.4%	23.2%	43.0%
Partially Taxed Services	1.0%	1.7%	2.9%	4.7%	4.8%	10.1%	9.1%	17.1%	16.7%	31.9%
Other entertainment	0.4%	0.7%	1.2%	2.7%	2.0%	10.2%	6.6%	22.5%	16.5%	37.3%
Personal care	1.5%	2.6%	4.5%	6.5%	7.3%	10.0%	11.3%	12.4%	16.9%	27.1%
Untaxed Services	1.1%	2.1%	3.6%	4.5%	6.0%	7.6%	9.6%	12.7%	17.5%	35.2%
Miscellaneous	0.6%	1.6%	2.5%	2.7%	5.0%	5.2%	10.7%	11.3%	15.8%	44.6%
Food away from home	1.7%	2.9%	5.3%	6.1%	7.6%	9.6%	10.6%	13.4%	16.3%	26.4%
Domestic services	1.2%	2.9%	3.2%	4.1%	7.3%	3.6%	5.5%	11.4%	17.5%	43.4%
Child care	0.3%	1.6%	2.9%	2.9%	6.9%	5.8%	10.8%	13.2%	18.4%	37.2%
Other household expenses	1.7%	2.8%	5.3%	7.2%	7.7%	9.3%	10.0%	13.1%	17.4%	25.6%
Public transportation	0.8%	1.6%	1.5%	3.3%	3.9%	5.2%	8.3%	14.0%	18.3%	43.0%
Medical services	0.7%	1.5%	3.0%	4.5%	5.2%	10.0%	9.9%	13.4%	21.7%	30.1%
Educational services	0.3%	0.7%	0.6%	0.7%	1.9%	3.9%	6.8%	10.5%	18.1%	56.4%

Note: Percentages represent the share of the overall consumption level attributable to the decile, based on a sample of 4,591 households.

geneity of incidence across services is sustained in the larger sample, indi-cating that the patterns in Table 5.1 were not the result of a small sample or a phenomenon unique to Louisiana residents. Indeed, the main pattern is a strong and steady increase in consumption shares across deciles for most all categories of services consumption. The large-sample properties of the Southern analysis confirm the Louisiana results. Notably, however, the rise and decline of consumption in educational services among the upper deciles in Louisiana is not present among this subsample, suggesting that the previous result could be a product of the charter school system.

The increased progressivity of service bundles relative to total consump-tion and income that was found earlier is also present for this sample, sug-gesting that services as a whole are more progressive in their consumption distribution across deciles than are bundles of goods. However, unlike in the Louisiana sample, there is no detectable difference in the progressivity of services by taxation status, as untaxed services have a strikingly simi-lar incidence as taxed activities. Again, the underlying regressivity of sales taxes relative to other taxation types would therefore suggest that an expan-sion of the sales tax onto services would make the entire tax system more regressive.

Finally, Figures 5.1 and 5.2 show the result of regressions of relative ser-vice spending by tax status across levels of consumption. Each figure exhib-its much greater consumption of untaxed services than those of entirely and

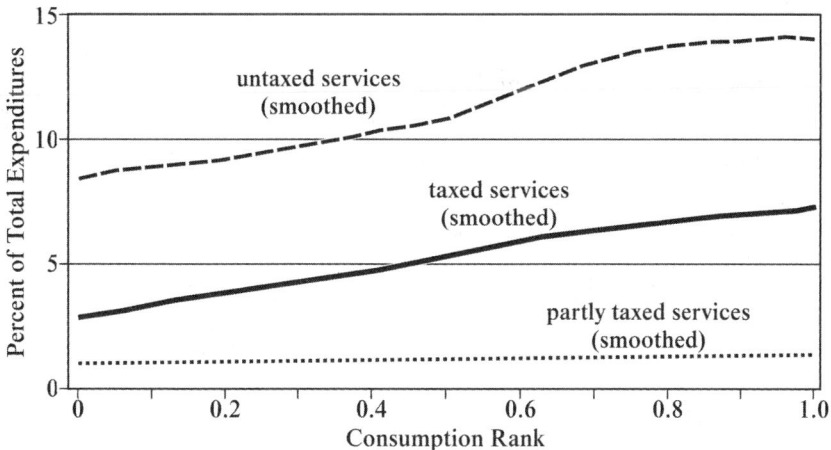

FIGURE 5.1. Service Spending Levels by Total Consumption Rank (LA)

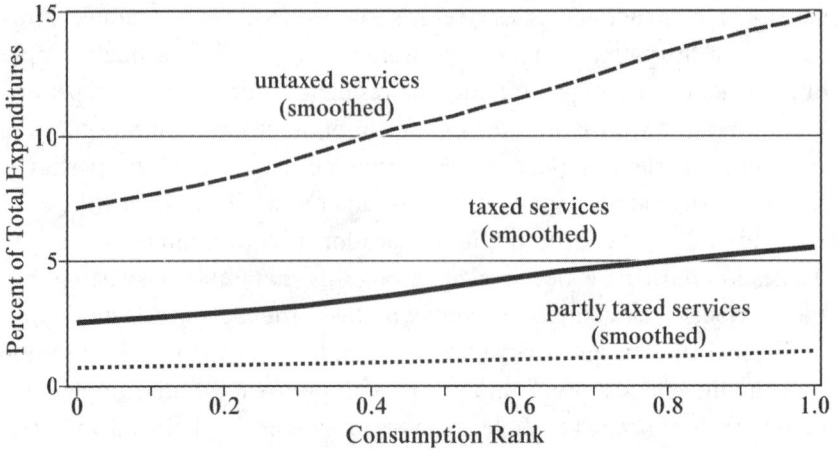

FIGURE 5.2. Service Spending Levels by Total Consumption Rank (Southern States)

partly taxed activities, indicating the small percentage of services that are taxed in Louisiana (and the potential revenues that could stem from taxing those activities). The increased slope of the untaxed service regression, particularly in the Southern subsample, suggests that observing within-decile variation produces a larger difference in the incidence of services that are taxed and untaxed than was indicated by the standard analysis.

REVENUE EFFECTS

Methodology. Our revenue projections are based upon the consumption estimates provided by the Jindal administration[16] for their revenue estimates. We update these consumption estimates from 2013 to 2015 using Louisiana GDP growth over this period. See Table 5.6 (at end of chapter) for a list of items under various scenarios discussed in 2013.

In order to get a sense for the type of revenue gains that might result from an expansion of the sales tax to cover services, we develop revenue estimates for several different scenarios. The first two scenarios are variants of the proposal offered by the Jindal administration in 2013. The first scenario expands the sales tax only to services that were in the Jindal proposal and that deal with personal (non-business) activity only. The second scenario taxes services that are either strictly personal or serve both households and businesses, so that strictly business activity is excluded. Business service activity was excluded from these scenarios in response to the double taxation criticisms that have been levied at such an expansion, regarding services that are also subject to the corporate income tax. The third scenario expands the sales tax to cover the range of "feasible" services identified by Mazerov that are not taxed by Louisiana but are taxed by Tennessee and Texas, two of the southern states that levy sales taxes on services more aggressively.

Revenue estimates were generated through a three-step process. First, each service was assigned a tax base that corresponded to the 2013 estimates from the Jindal proposal. For the first two scenarios this mapping was straightforward, as the service language in the proposal and the scenarios were identical. For the third scenario, this involved compiling a list of services that represented the "personal care" services proposed by the Jindal administration. Second, we assumed a sales tax of 4 percent (e.g., the current rate) on the given tax base. Many of the arguments to expand sales taxes to services have explicitly argued for such a uniform tax rate across goods and services, as that would promote tax equity and ease the costs of

TABLE 5.3. Scenario #1: "Personal" Services from Jindal 2013 Plan

Included Items	Jindal Tax Base Estimate	21013 Tax Estimate (at 4%)	Adjustment for CY2015
Scenic and sightseeing transportation services and support activities for transportation	$1,080,872,150	$43,234,886	$47,329,167
Veterinary services	$207,122,851	$8,284,914	$9,069,484
Cable and other subscription services	$221,854,739	$8,874,190	$9,714,563
Performing arts	$44,550,187	$1,782,007	$1,950,761
Promotional services for performing arts and sports and public figures	$229,732,279	$9,189,291	$10,059,504
Independent artists, writers, and performers	$57,663,899	$2,306,556	$2,524,983
Museum, heritage, zoo, and recreational services	$169,553,541	$6,782,141	$7,424,400
Personal care services	$631,267,683	$25,250,707	$27,641,913
Other personal services	$663,683,918	$26,547,356	$29,061,353
Total	$3,306,301,247	$132,252,050	$144,776,127

compliance and evasion. Third, as noted, we updated our estimates of services by GDP growth to represent consumption in 2015, given that the estimates from the Jindal proposal were produced in 2013. Accordingly, our estimates reflect a passage of sales tax expansion effective in the beginning of calendar year 2015.

Results. The results of each scenario may be found in Tables 5.3 through 5.5. The expansion to only personal services from the Jindal plan is estimated to raise $145 million in 2015. That estimate includes expanding services to all entertainment services as well as veterinary and other personal care activities. The second scenario further expands the tax base to cover services for all types of activity, such as accounting, transportation, and data processing services. This expansion would significantly add to the revenue

TABLE 5.4. Scenario #2: "Personal" and "All" Services from Jindal 2013 Plan

Included Items	Jindal Tax Base Estimate	21013 Tax Estimate (at 4%)	Adjustment for CY2015
From Scenario #1	$3,306,301,247	$132,252,050	$144,776,127
"All" services:			
Transit and ground passenger transportation services	$367,811,060	$14,712,442	$16,105,689
Couriers and messenger services	$707,881,040	$28,315,242	$30,996,654
Accounting, tax preparation, bookkeeping, and payroll services	$1,577,445,934	$63,097,837	$69,073,111
Architectural, engineering, and related services	$3,455,246,566	$138,209,863	$151,298,136
Photographic services	$70,201,160	$2,808,046	$3,073,964
All other miscellaneous professional, scientific, and technical services	$827,151,371	$33,086,055	$36,219,257
Data processing-hosting-ISP-web search portals	$555,398,097	$22,215,924	$24,319,740
Other information services	$81,956,833	$3,278,273	$3,588,721
Insurance-related support services	$338,513,160	$13,540,527	$14,822,795
Total	*$11,287,906,468*	*$451,516,259*	*$494,2/4,194*

TABLE 5.5. Scenario #3: All Service Items on Mazerov List Not Taxed in LA but Taxed in TX/TN

Included Items	Comparable Item (Jindal)	Jindal Tax Base Estimate	2013 Tax Estimate (at 4%)	Adjustment for CY2015
Pet grooming	Personal care services and other personal services	$1,294,951,601	$51,798,064	$56,703,266
Landscaping/lawn care	Personal care services and other personal services	$1,294,951,601	$51,798,064	$56,703,266
Swimming pool cleaning		$151,093,676	$6,043,747	$6,616,081
Cable TV	Facilities support services			
Health clubs				
Auto road services				
Parimutuel racing				
Exterminating				
Labor charges and remodeling	Architectural, engineering, and related services	$3,455,246,566	$138,209,863	$151,298,136
Marina services	Museum, heritage, zoo, and recreational services	$169,553,541	$6,782,142	$7,424,400
Total		*$5,070,845,384*	*$202,833,815*	*$222,041,884*

windfall, to an estimated $494 million. Scenario 3 considers expanding to only services covered by Texas and Tennessee, which would help alleviate concerns about the effects of tax competition. This scenario is estimated to produce $222 million in additional 2015 state revenue. The distributional effects of these various scenarios are indicated by our previous analysis.

Conclusions

Expanding the sales tax to cover services activity is an idea with significant potential benefits and costs, each highly dependent on context and existing legislation. Our analysis indicates that the high sales tax rate in Louisiana offers the particular appeal of strong revenue gains. Also, our analysis

TABLE 5.6 List of Services Taxed and Not Taxed Under 2013 Jindal Plan

NAICS Code	Service Category	Major Services	Estimated Tax Base	Estimated Revenue (at 5.88%)	P (personal), B (business), and A (all)
213133+	Mining		$34,361,692	$2,020,468	B
	Total Mining		$34,361,692	$2,020,468	
	Transportation	Transit and ground passenger transportation services	$367,811,060	$21,627,290	A
487 + 488	Transportation	Scenic and sightseeing transportation services and support activities for transportation	$1,080,872,150	$63,555,282	P
492	Transportation	Couriers and messenger services	$707,881,040	$41,623,405	A
	Total Transportation		$2,156,564,250	$126,805,978	
5412	Professional Services	Accounting, tax preparation, bookkeeping, and payroll services	$1,577,445,934	$92,753,821	A
5413	Professional Services	Architectural, engineering, and related services	$3,455,246,566	$203,168,498	A
5414	Professional Services	Specialized design services	$239,087,660	$14,058,354	B
541511	Professional Services	Custom computer programming services	$841,176,476	$49,461,177	B
541512	Professional Services	Computer systems design services	$373,045,402	$21,935,070	B
541513	Professional Services	Other computer-related services, including facilities management	$712,594,053	$41,900,530	B
54161	Professional Services	Management, scientific, and technical consulting services	$1,568,510,106	$92,228,394	B
54162	Professional Services	Environmental and other technical consulting services	$203,395,442	$11,959,652	B
5417	Professional Services	Scientific research and development services	$1,301,411,751	$76,523,011	B
54192	Professional Services	Advertising related services	$615,000,000	$36,162,000	B
54192	Professional Services	Photographic services	$70,201,160	$4,127,828	A
54194	Professional Services	Veterinary services	$207,122,851	$12,178,824	P
54199	Professional Services	All other miscellaneous professional, scientific and technical services	$827,151,371	$48,636,501	A
	Total Professional Services		$11,991,388,770	$705,093,660	

Code	Category	Description			
5613	Business Services	Employment services	$1,515,012,321	$89,082,724	B
5615	Business Services	Travel arrangement and reservation services	$253,313,737	$14,894,848	B
5611	Business Services	Office administration services	$570,934,026	$33,570,921	B
5612	Business Services	Facilities support services	$151,093,676	$8,884,308	B
5614	Business Services	Business support services	$685,835,915	$40,327,152	B
5616	Business Services	Investigation and security services	$387,069,010	$22,759,658	B
5617	Business Services	Services to buildings and dwellings	$1,738,417,195	$102,218,931	B
5619	Business Services	Other support services	$400,129,846	$23,527,635	B
562	Business Services	Waste management and remediation services	$1,127,985,136	$66,325,526	B
	Total Business Services		*$6,829,790,863*	*$401,591,703*	
5152	Information	Cable and other subscription services	$221,854,739	$13,045,059	P
518	Information	Data processing-hosting-ISP-web search portals	$555,398,097	$32,657,408	A
519	Information	Other information services	$81,956,833	$4,819,062	A
	Total Information Services		$859,209,669	$50,521,529	
52429	Financial Services	Insurance-related support services	$338,513,160	$19,904,574	A
	Total Financial Services		*$338,513,160*	*$19,904,574*	
7111	Entertainment	Performing arts	$44,550,187	$2,619,551	P
7113	Entertainment	Promotional services for performing arts and sports and public figures	$229,732,279	$13,508,258	P
7115	Entertainment	Independent artists, writers, and performers	$57,663,899	$3,390,637	P
712	Entertainment	Museum, heritage, zoo, and recreational services	$169,553,541	$9,969,748	P
	Total Entertainment		$501,499,907	$29,488,195	
8121	Personal Services	Personal care services	$631,267,683	$37,118,540	P
8129	Personal Services	Other personal services	$663,683,918	$39,024,614	P
	Total Personal Services		$1,294,951,602	$76,143,154	
	All Taxable Services		$24,006,279,913	$1,411,569,259	

TABLE 5.6. (*continued*)

Nontaxable Services

NAICS Code	Category	NAICS Code	Name of Services	P (Personal), B (Business), and A (all)
22	Utilities	221	Utilities	A
		22122	Electric power distribution	A
		221210	Natural gas distribution	A
		22133o	Steam and air-conditioning supply	A
23	Construction	236	Construction of buildings	B
		236118	Residential remodelers	P
		236220	Commercial and institutional building construction	B
		237	Heavy and civil engineering construction	B
		23713o	Power and communication line and related structures construction	B
		237210	Land subdivision	B
		23731o	Highway, street, and bridge construction	B
		23799o	Other heavy and civil engineering construction	B
		238	Specialty trade contractors	A
		238190	Other foundation, structure, and building exterior contractors	A
		238290	Other building equipment contractors	A
		238390	Other building finishing contractors	A
		23899o	All other specialty trade contractors	A
52	Finance and Insurance	521	Monetary authorities—Central bank	B
		52111o	Monetary authorities—Central bank	B

		Code	Description	
		522	Credit intermediation and related activities	A
		522190	Other depository credit intermediation	A
		522298	Securities, commodity contracts, and other financial assets	A
		522390	Other activities related to credit intermediation	A
		523	Securities, commodity contracts, and other financial investments and related activities	A
		523140	Commodity contracts brokerage	A
		523210	Securities and commodity exchanges	A
		523999	Miscellaneous financial investment activities	A
		524	Insurance carriers and related activities	A
		525	Funds, trusts, and other financial vehicles	A
		525190	Other insurance funds	A
		525990	Other financial vehicles	A
55	Management of Companies and Enterprise	551	Management of companies and enterprises	B
		551114	Corporate, subsidiary, and regional managing offices	B
61	Educational Services	611	Educational services	P
		611110	Elementary and secondary schools	P
		611210	Junior colleges	P
		611430	Professional and management development training	P
		611519	Other technical and trade schools	P
		611699	All other miscellaneous schools and instruction	P
		611710	Educational support services	P

TABLE 5.6. (*continued*)

NAICS Code	Category	NAICS Code	Name of Services	P (Personal), B (Business), and A (all)
		621112	Offices of physicians, mental health specialists	P
		621210	Offices of dentists	P
		621399	Offices of all other miscellaneous health practitioners	P
		621498	All other outpatient care centers	P
		621512	Diagnostic imaging centers	P
		621610	Home health care services	P
		621999	All other miscellaneous ambulatory health care services	P
		622	Hospitals	P
		622110	General medical and surgical hospitals	P
		622210	Psychiatric and substance abuse hospitals	P
		622310	Specialty (except psychiatric and substance abuse) hospitals	P
		623	Nursing and residential care facilities	P
		623110	Nursing care facilities	P
		623220	Residential mental health and substance abuse facilities	P
		623312	Homes for the elderly	P
		623990	Other residential care facilities	P
		624	Social assistance	P
		624190	Other individual and family services	P

Category	Code	Description	Type
	624230	Emergency and other relief services	P
	624310	Vocational rehabilitation services	P
	624440	Child day care services	P
481		Air Transportation	
	48112	Scheduled freight air transportation	A
	481219	Other nonscheduled air transportation	A
482		Rail Transportation	
	482112	Short line railroads	A
483		Water Transportation	
	483114	Coastal and great lakes passenger transportation	A
	483212	Inland water passenger transportation	A
484		Truck Transportation	
	484122	General freight trucking, long-distance, less than truckload	B
	484230	specialized freight (except used goods) trucking, long-distance, long-distance	B
486		Pipeline Transportation	
	486110	pipeline transportation of crude oil	B
	486210	Pipeline transportation of natural gas	B
	486990	All other pipeline transportation	B
491		Postal Service	
	491110	Postal service	A
531		Real Estate	
	531190	Lessors of other real estate property	A
	531210	Offices of real estate agents and brokers	A
	531390	Other activities related to real estate	A
	531395	Reinsurance carriers	A
813		Religious, Grantmaking, Civic, Professional, and Similar Organizations	
	813110	Religious organizations	P
	813219	Other grantmaking and giving services	P
	813319	Other social advocacy organizations	P

TABLE 5.6. (*continued*)

NAICS Code	Category	NAICS Code	Name of Services	P (Personal), B (Business), and A (all)
8139	Business, Professional, Labor, Political, and Similar Organizations	81391	Business associations	B
		813920	Professional organizations	B
		81393	Labor unions and similar labor organizations	B
		813940	Political organizations	B
		81399	Other Similar organizations (except business, professional, labor, and political organizations)	B
51993	Internet Publishing and Broadcasting and Web Search Portals	519130	Internet publishing and broadcasting and Web search portals	B
213112	Support Activities for Oil and Gas Operations			A
5411	Legal Services	54111	Offices of lawyers	A
		541120	Offices of notaries	P
		54119	Other legal services	A
		541191	Title abstract and settlement offices	A
		541199	All other legal services	A
8122	Death Care Services	81221	Funeral homes and funeral services	P
		812220	Cemeteries and crematories	P
	Advertising			A

confirms evidence that taxation of services is likely to increase in the progressivity of sales taxation, given the pattern of services consumption across income and consumption deciles. Of course, expanding the sales tax to services would increase the administrative complexity of the Louisiana sales tax. Overall, efforts to expand the sales tax to cover services should consider the lessons learned from past proposals across the nation, but should focus on the specific institutional features of Louisiana. Even so, our analyses lead to our recommendation that the Louisiana sales tax should be expanded to include services in the tax base.

Notes

1. Francis, J. (1988). The Florida Sales Tax on Services: What Really Went Wrong? In *The Unfinished Agenda for State Tax Reform*. Denver, CO: National Conference of State Legislatures, 129–149.

2. Michaelis, R., G. Sutton, J. C. Yesnowitz, P. Drennen, C. Jones, and L. Stolly (2013). Massachusetts Repeals Sales Tax on Computer and Software Services. *Grant Thornton*. Available online at http://www.mondaq.com/unitedstates/x/268280/sales+taxes+-VAT+GST/Massachusetts+Repeals+Sales+Tax+on+Computer+and+Software.

3. Bourdeaux, C. (2010). A Review of State Tax Reform Efforts. *Fiscal Research Center Report No. 216*. Atlanta, GA: Andrew Young School of Policy Studies, Georgia State University.

4. Bourdeaux, C. (2010). A Review of State Tax Reform Efforts. *Fiscal Research Center Report No. 216*. Atlanta, GA: Andrew Young School of Policy Studies, Georgia State University.

5. Fox, W. F. (2003). History and Economic Impact of the Sales Tax. In *Sales Taxation*. Atlanta, GA: Institute for Professionals in Taxation.

6. Mazerov, M. (2009). Expanding Sales Taxation of Services: Options and Issues. Washington, D.C.: Center on Budget and Policy Priorities. The 2013 Jindal Proposal also suggested using the expanded sales tax to replace the personal and corporate income tax. Given the magnitude of this change in the tax structure, the proposal did not get any traction and was pulled from the legislative agenda immediately.

7. Merriman, D. and M. Skidmore (2000). Did Distortionary Sales Taxation Contribute to the Growth of the Service Sector? *National Tax Journal, 55* (1), 125–142.

8. California Budget Project (2011). Should California Extend the Sales Tax to Services? *Budget Backgrounder*. Sacramento, CA: California Budget Project.

9. Zodrow, G. R. (2014). The Louisiana Tax System: Potential Directions for Reform. Unpublished manuscript. Houston, TX: Rice University.

10. Ibid.

11. Mazerov, M. (2009). Expanding Sales Taxation of Services: Options and Issues. Washington, D.C.: Center on Budget and Policy Priorities.

12. Wilson, J. D. (1986). A Theory of Interregional Tax Competition. *Journal of Urban*

Economics, 19 (3), 296–315; Slemrod, J. (2004). Are Corporate Tax Rates, or Countries, Converging? *Journal of Public Economics,* 88 (6), 1169–1186; Mintz, J. and M. Smart (2004). Income Shifting, Investment, and Tax Competition: Theory and Evidence from Provincial Taxation in Canada. *Journal of Public Economics,* 88 (6), 1149–1168.

13. Federation of Tax Administrators (2008). Survey of Services Taxation—Update. Available online at https://www.taxadmin.org/fta/pub/services/btn/0708.html; Mazerov, M. (2009). Expanding Sales Taxation of Services: Options and Issues. Washington, D.C.: Center on Budget and Policy Priorities.

14. Alm, J., E. Sennoga, and M. Skidmore (2009). Perfect Competition, Urbanization, and Tax Incidence in the Retail Gasoline Market. *Economic Inquiry,* 47 (1), 118–134.

15. Poterba, J. M. (1991). Is the Gasoline Tax Regressive? In *Tax Policy and the Economy, Volume 5,* J. M. Poterba (Ed.). Cambridge, MA: The MIT Press and National Bureau of Economic Research, 145–164; Metcalf, G. E. (1998). A Distributional Analysis of an Environmental Tax Shift. NBER Working Paper 6546. Boston, MA: National Bureau of Economic Research; Chernick, H. and A. Reschovsky (1997). Who Pays the Gasoline Tax? *National Tax Journal,* 50 (2), 233–259.

16. In 2013 the Jindal Administration suggested that the state eliminate the income tax and expand the use of the sales tax by substantially increasing the tax base, including services. Ernst & Young was hired to assist the administration in estimating the revenues that might be collected if the state expanded the sales tax base to include different combinations of services.

6

THE LOUISIANA INDIVIDUAL INCOME TAX

James A. Richardson

In Louisiana the individual income tax is a primary source of revenue that has grown in importance over the past few decades. In 1981, the individual income tax accounted for only 5 percent of Louisiana's overall revenue collections, while mineral revenues constituted over 40 percent of state revenues, and the sales tax constituted just over 20 percent. By 2015, however, the individual income tax was comparable to the sales tax in terms of dollars generated to support state services, comprising nearly 28 percent of total receipts. The reasons for the growth in the income tax as a part of the overall revenue structure are manifold. Part of the growth is due to the dilution of other revenue sources, such as oil and gas. Some of the growth is due to the connection between the Louisiana income tax and the federal income tax, which have a generally inverse relationship.[1] The overall growth in the economy, together with several changes imposed by popular vote (subsequently reversed by acts of the Louisiana legislature), have also affected the proportionality of the individual income tax. But even with this greater reliance on the individual income tax, Louisiana still lags other states in its overall reliance on individual income tax for total receipts; other states that use the income tax rely upon it on average to account for 37 percent of their overall revenues.[2]

The individual income tax has become essential to the state budget due to its share of total collections, its growth potential, and its broad reflection of economic activity. Its receipts are also large enough so that small errors in forecasting can mean substantial amounts of excess or deficient revenue for budgeting purposes. In fiscal 2014, a 1 percent difference in actual versus forecast collections would amount to about $30 million. This tax, like other taxes, is also important from the perspective that it can affect personal decision making regarding work, investment, and location decisions. The individual income tax is a common method of raising revenues to support public programs, as evidenced by the fact that forty-one states have a personal income tax,[3] but it is also a tax that can create reactions or changes in economic behavior from individual taxpayers.[4]

This chapter focuses on individual income tax and begins with a description of the individual income tax in Louisiana, its development over time, and the distributional effects of the current income tax structure. This description is then complemented with a consideration of the modifications of the income tax by the state legislature, either by exemptions, deductions, or credits, to affect equity, investment, and other economic decisions. These characteristics of the Louisiana personal income tax are then compared with income taxes in other states. The final analysis considers alternative income tax structures for Louisiana, with an analysis of the distribution of the tax burden and the potential growth of the tax collections over time. Questions swirling around any discussion of the income tax include (1) how much of the state's revenues should come from the personal income tax, (2) whether any group of taxpayers, such as retirees, should be exempt, either fully or partially, from paying the Louisiana individual income tax, (3) whether any type or types of income, such as capital appreciation of Louisiana-based investments, should be protected, either partially or fully, from the state individual income tax, and (4) whether the state should use the individual income tax to encourage or promote certain behaviors or certain social policies. Or should the individual income tax be focused solely on providing revenues to support public services that must be paid for by the state?

Ultimately, these choices will be influenced by the economic analysis, but it is not correct to say that the economic analysis will provide an absolute answer to every choice. The primary focus of the individual income tax in any state is to raise money to support public services, but the state still has to identify the parameters of the income tax. And this includes making decisions regarding the rates, brackets, and exemptions, deductions, and tax credits. As other social policies are also being considered, then the rates, brackets, and exemptions, deductions, and credits will have to be carefully analyzed and evaluated, given the fact that the primary mission of the individual income tax is to fund state services, but also the recognition that there are other objectives the state might want to pursue. At the end of the day, the choices about the use of the individual income tax will represent the consensus of the Louisiana electorate, either directly through voting on constitutional amendments or indirectly by voicing their opinions to their elected representatives.

Development of the Current Louisiana Income Tax Structure

Annual collections of the individual income tax as a whole and as a share of total state taxes are depicted in Figures 6.1 and 6.2. Personal income tax collections are composed of four components:

- Withholdings: tax payments taken from a worker's paycheck by his or her employer and remitted to the state
- Payments with returns: payments made as the taxpayer reconciles his or her payments over the year with the final tax liability
- Declarations of estimated taxes: payments made quarterly by taxpayers that may earn income in which withholdings are not made; typically, these declarations come from taxpayers with investment income, interest income, earnings from single proprietorships or partnerships, or other such income sources
- Fiduciary income: estates and trusts earning income from Louisiana sources

The most important mode of paying the income tax is withholdings since it involves much of the employment and compensation in the economy, with as much as 70 percent of annual receipts being collected through this mechanism. Payments with returns occur all year long, but are especially relevant in the spring filing season, reflecting the net reconciliation of calculated annual liabilities and payments already made, largely through withholdings, but also made by quarterly declarations of estimated taxes due. Withholdings, declarations of estimated taxes, payments and/or refunds to reconcile what is owed at the end of the tax year versus what has been paid during the tax year, and fiduciary payments are mechanisms for remitting taxes to the state. They are embedded in tax collections in every year and are especially important in contributing to a consistent cash flow for the state. The growth and dynamics of the increases and decreases in taxes collected in any one year are related to the condition of the economy, changes

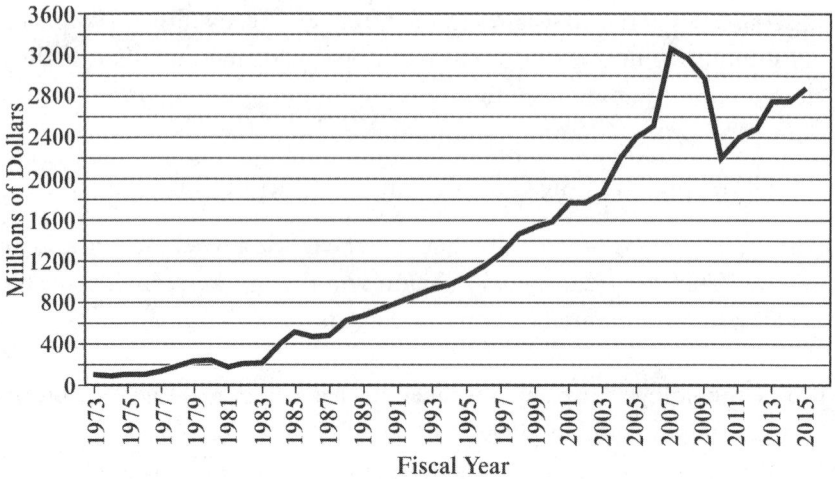

FIGURE 6.1. Individual Income Tax Collections

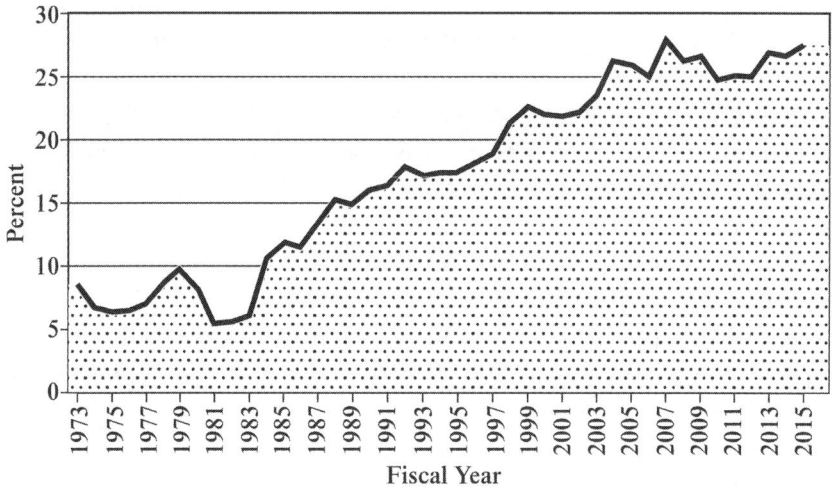

FIGURE 6.2. Individual Income Tax as Share of Total State Tax Collections

in factors outside of Louisiana such as changes in federal tax policy that affect collections in Louisiana, and any changes in tax policy passed by the legislature and signed by the governor.

Figure 6.1 displays actual personal income tax collections, while Figure 6.2 shows the percentage of total state revenues supported by the individual income tax. As income tax collections grew from the 1970s through the first decade of the 2000s, the fraction of the state budget supported by the income tax increased. In fiscal 1982 Louisiana collected about $200 million in individual income taxes, representing about 5 percent of the state's revenues, while in fiscal 2016, Louisiana collected approximately $2.9 billion through the individual income tax, representing about 28 percent of overall state revenues collected.

Income tax collections can be summarized by visualizing the decades of the 1970s to the 2010s. In the 1970s mineral revenues dominated the state's budget, so individual income taxes were a relatively small part of the overall budget, as noted in Figure 6.2, though the tax provisions (rates, brackets, and major exemptions and deductions) were basically the same as the state has presently. During the 1980s the Louisiana economy went into a major downturn, mainly due to a drastic reduction in oil prices, so mineral revenues went way down, and automatically other revenue sources, such as the income tax, made up a larger portion of the state's budget. But during the 1980s the federal government made major changes in federal tax law that affected Louisiana income tax collections because of how the Louisiana individual income tax provisions are constructed. The federal tax changes and the continued growth in the state's economy made income tax collections grow in the 1990s and early 2000s. In 2002 the state made significant changes in its tax provisions (the Stelly Plan), which, along with major federal changes in federal income tax and a growth spurt driven by major disasters, all contributed to a definite increase in individual income tax collections. But by 2008 this growth turned around due to legislative changes in the income tax and a slowdown in the national economy, which affected the state's economy. These decade-by-decade changes are examined more closely in the following sections.

The 1970s, 1980s, and 1990s

In order to understand the trends illustrated in Figures 6.1 and 6.2, one must examine the status of the Louisiana economy, the vitality of the global energy markets, changes in federal income tax policy, and legislative and constitutional changes in the Louisiana income tax structure. The Louisiana economy benefited from the energy dynamics of the 1970s. Substantial increases in the price of oil, as well as a major change in the taxation of oil and gas in 1973, created a surge in state tax collections based primarily on mineral revenues. At the same time that the state garnered higher revenues from oil and gas production, the 1974 Louisiana Constitution mandated that a Louisiana taxpayer's federal tax liability be deducted from adjusted gross income, thereby reducing the tax base and, consequently, overall individual and corporate income tax receipts. Income tax collections as a percentage of total state revenues fluctuated between 5 percent and 10 percent during the 1970s, with these fluctuations due to a variety of factors, such as the increase in energy prices and the increase in corporate tax collections starting in 1978. Income tax collections, as part of the overall state revenue structure, increased until 1978–79, when the collections declined and then stayed relatively stagnant until 1983–84. This decline in the early 1980s can be traced to the slowing down of the Louisiana economy and an income tax reduction in 1980.

Income tax collections began to rise again in 1983, despite the fact that the energy markets were still in the process of collapsing. This increase is related not to the growth of the economy, but rather to the fact that the newly elected Governor Edwin W. Edwards, and lame-duck Governor David Treen, persuaded the state legislature to repeal the tax cut made in 1980 during a special legislative session in the fall of 1983. Despite the legislative increase in income taxes beginning in 1984, individual income tax collections were still declining in 1985–86 due to the status of the Louisiana economy. Statutory increases in the income tax could not keep pace with the structural issues in the Louisiana economy and the impact of the state's economic downturn on overall revenue collections. The state lost about 150,000 jobs from 1982 through 1987.

By 1987–88 personal income tax collections started to increase more quickly than the growth in the economy.[5] Part of this increase was due to the estimated elasticity of 1.3 to 1.4 of the Louisiana personal income tax, meaning that as the economy grew by 1 percent, personal income tax collections increased by about 1.3 percent to 1.4 percent.[6]

An even more important explanation of this growth in Louisiana has to do with effects from the Federal Tax Reform Act of 1986, which expanded the definition of adjusted gross income, the starting point in defining Louisiana taxable income, thereby increasing the tax base in Louisiana. It also reduced itemized deductions on Schedule A of the federal income tax forms by allowing medical expenses that exceeded 7.5 percent of adjusted gross income, as opposed to 5 percent, as a deduction; eliminating interest paid on credit cards, auto loans, and other consumer borrowing as an itemized deduction; eliminating the deduction of sales taxes paid to state and local governments; and making miscellaneous deductions and employee business expenses deductible only if they exceeded 2 percent of adjusted gross income.[7] At the time, Louisiana taxpayers could deduct excess itemized deductions from their adjusted gross income to arrive at Louisiana taxable income. Thus, any federal changes to itemized deductions had a direct effect on Louisiana revenue. Reducing or eliminating federal itemized deductions would generate additional income tax collections in Louisiana by reducing excess itemized deductions that served as a deduction of Louisiana taxable income. Additionally, in the 1986 tax reform package the federal government reduced personal tax liability. This also enhanced Louisiana tax collections, since Louisiana allows each taxpayer unit to subtract his or her federal tax liability from his or her adjusted gross income, so lowering federal taxes actually increases the Louisiana income tax base. The 1986 tax reform program enhanced the collection of individual income taxes in Louisiana. The state legislature and Louisiana's governor did not have to execute any changes to accelerate the growth of the personal income tax.

The federal government did make several changes in the federal individual income tax in the 1990s under the Clinton administration. First, the top rate for citizens earning more than $115,000 was raised from 28 percent to 36 percent, and a 10 percent surcharge was attached to those earning more than $250,000. This had a negative impact on Louisiana income tax collections since federal taxes being paid increased. Second, the earned income tax credit was expanded in the 1990s, which had a positive effect on the state's income tax collections since it reduced federal income taxes paid. The growth of Louisiana's income tax collections continued through the 1990s, given the national economic growth and Louisiana's economic growth, overshadowing any possible negative impact of federal tax policy on the collections of Louisiana individual income taxes.

The income tax had become a major part of the Louisiana state budget during the 1980s and 1990s. But this was not a result of acts of the legislature or of constitutional changes by the electorate. Rather, it occurred because of the rather tight connection between the federal tax code and the Louisiana tax laws and the fact that the economy grew consistently from the late 1980s to the year 2000, and because mineral revenues were not returning as a major source of the state's revenue base.

Individual Income Taxes After 2000 and the Stelly Plan

Starting in 2000 there was a special effort to make fundamental changes in the Louisiana individual income tax. In 2000, at the urging of Representative Vic Stelly, the state legislature put a very ambitious proposal on the ballot as a constitutional amendment to eliminate federal tax liability and excess itemized deductions as exemptions on the Louisiana tax return.[8] Eliminating the federal tax liability as a deduction was a constitutional issue, since this specific deduction was part of the 1974 Louisiana Constitution. At the same time, the proposal also suggested changing tax brackets to 2 percent on the first $5,000, 3 percent on the next $5,000, 4 percent on the next $40,000, and then 5 percent on any taxable income above $50,000. These suggested changes would have increased everyone's income tax payments, but, at the same time, there was a proposal to lower the sales tax, eliminating the state's sales tax on food used at home as well as on natural gas, electricity, and water paid for by individuals and businesses. This swap between the income tax and sales tax was designed to generate about $200 million in state revenues for teacher pay raises. This plan was defeated by the voters. The vote of the electorate did not stop the interest in making better use of the individual income tax in paying for public services, given the recognition that mineral revenues were not likely to support the state's budget in the 2000s as it had in the 1970s.

In 2002 the Louisiana legislature put the revised Stelly Plan[9] on the ballot for the voters to consider. This plan constitutionally prevented the state from taxing food for home consumption, prescription drugs, and residential utilities, changed the income brackets associated with the individual income tax, and eliminated excess itemized deductions as an exemption on the state income tax. Changing the tax brackets was a constitutional issue since the tax brackets had been specifically defined in the 1974 Louisiana Constitution. This fundamental change in the individual income tax structure was based on a study completed in the 1980s regarding the Louisiana fiscal structure.[10] For single and joint filers, the brackets were changed in such a way that taxes generally went up for higher income earners, as illustrated in Table 6.1. The tax brackets for the income tax were also changed, with the brackets for the lowest income taxpayers being widened from $0–$20,000 to $0–$25,000, a measure that made the income tax slightly more progressive. The brackets for taxpayers making more than $25,000 in taxable income were reduced in size, as shown in Table 6.1. Both of these changes made the Louisiana income tax slightly more progressive.

The tax changes also eliminated the deduction of excess itemized deductions, defined as the state's standard deduction less the itemized deductions as generated from Schedule A for the federal income tax form 1040. This deduction is slanted in the direction of higher income taxpayers, though it applied to some low- to middle-income families buying their first home who itemized on their federal tax returns. The people voted on November 5, 2002, to approve these major changes in the state sales tax and the state individual income tax.

The Stelly plan made a fundamental change in the overall progressivity

TABLE 6.1. Income Tax Rates and Brackets and Excess Itemized Deductions in Louisiana, Pre-2000, 2002 through 2008, and Post-2008

	Rates and Brackets					
	Pre-Stelly, 2002 and Before		Stelly Plan, 2002–2008		Post-Repeal of Stelly, 2008–Present	
Filing Status	Rates and Deductions	Taxable Income	Rates	Taxable Income	Rates	Taxable Income
Single Filers	2%	$0 to $10,000	2%	$0 to $12,500	2%	$0 to $12,500
	4%	$10,001 to $50,000	4%	$12,501 to $25,000	4%	$12,501 to $50,000
	6%	Over $50,000	6%	Over $25,000	6%	Over $50,000
Joint Filers	2%	$0 to $20,000	2%	$0 to $25,000	2%	$0 to $25,000
	4%	$20,001 to $100,000	4%	$25,001 to $50,000	4%	$25,001 to $100,000
	6%	Over $100,000	6%	Over $50,000	6%	Over $100,000
	Excess Itemized Deductions					
Single and Joint Filers	57.5% deduction from taxable income		No deduction from taxable income		100% deduction from taxable income	

of the state income tax structure and attempted to improve the progressivity of the state's sales tax structure by eliminating sales taxes on food for home consumption, prescription drugs, and residential utilities.[11] The 2002 Stelly plan was not focused on raising more revenues immediately, but rather, it was focused on accomplishing a more growth-oriented income tax structure and a slightly more progressive overall state tax structure.

Reversing the Stelly Plan

Income taxes rose substantially from 2000–01 to 2007–08. Some of this growth can be attributed to the passage of the Stelly plan. Other factors, such as the federal tax cuts in 2001 and 2003 and the economic infusion into the Louisiana economy caused by redevelopment activity after Hurricanes Katrina and Rita, also contributed to the growth in income tax collections. Income tax collections exceeded sales tax collections only in fiscal year 2007, as both income and sales taxes were surging in the reconstruction aftermath of hurricanes Katrina and Rita in 2005.[12] During the post-Katrina revenue surge, the Louisiana legislature decided to reverse the income tax changes approved by the voters in 2002. In the 2007 legislative session under Governor Kathleen Blanco, the state reinstated the deduction of excess itemized deductions,[13] and in the 2008 legislative session under Governor Bobby Jindal, the state expanded the tax brackets closely in line with the pre-2002 tax brackets, as illustrated in Table 6.1.[14] Again, both in 2007 and 2008 the state had sufficient dollars to support public services, and the general argument was that the state could reduce taxes without affecting state public services. No one anticipated the US financial meltdown in 2008 and the continuing national recession in 2009, just as no one anticipated the plunge in energy prices in 2008 from over $140 per barrel in July 2008 to the mid-$30s by the end of 2008. These abrupt and substantial changes in the US economy and the energy markets created a financial shortfall in Louisiana just after the state had substantially reduced individual income taxes.

The onset of the 2007–09 national recession and its impact on the Louisiana economy,[15] combined with moderation of spending on Katrina reconstruction projects and the enactment of the substantial reductions in the individual income tax, led to absolute drops in income tax collections in fiscal 2008, 2009, and 2010. The individual income tax base has been permanently reduced as a result of reinstating excess itemized deductions and the expansion of tax brackets. As illustrated in Figure 6.1, individual income tax collections dropped by $400 to $500 million from fiscal 2008 to fiscal 2015, or a reduction of almost 15 percent.

Despite this cut in individual income tax base and rates, the personal income tax has retained its position as a significant share of state tax revenue. From shares between 5 percent and 10 percent in the 1970s and early 1980s, its relative significance rose to over 25 percent by the early 2000s and has remained in the 25 percent to 30 percent range. The individual income tax will remain as one of the top revenue sources to fund state government in Louisiana unless there are major changes in the Louisiana tax structure. There are simply no alternatives.[16]

One of the decisions the state of Louisiana has to make is exactly how the state should use the individual income tax in paying for state services. Namely, how much of the state's budget should the individual income tax support, and what should the exact parameters of the individual income tax be?

Income Tax Collections Per Capita: Another Way of Viewing Income Taxes

Income tax collections per capita in both nominal and real terms are shown in Figure 6.3. In 1981–82 income tax collections per capita in nominal and real terms were $50 and in 1986–87 income tax collections per person were $186 in nominal terms and $139 in real terms. By 1993–94 income tax collections per person had jumped to $230 in nominal terms, but slipped back to $133 in real terms. By 2000–01 nominal income tax collections per person had risen to $400 and real collections per person had risen to $196. The state had not made any change in the basic income tax structure, except for possible exemptions or credits being added during this time period,[17] and these were usually to diminish the tax base and total tax liability. The growth from 1986–87 to 2000–01 came from the overall growth in the Louisiana economy and the changes in the federal tax laws that benefited income tax collections in Louisiana. The increases in income taxes per capita are also related to the progressivity of the rate structure, which applies higher marginal tax rates on higher incomes—2 percent, 4 percent, 6 percent—but with relatively wide brackets.

In 2007–08 nominal income tax collections per capita jumped to $713 and real collections per capita rose to $293. This significant increase in col-lections per capita certainly is related to the constitutional changes made in the individual income tax in 2002, and the reductions in nominal and real income tax collections per capita in 2012–13 and 2015–16 reflect the legis-lative changes in 2007 and 2008 and the dip in the economy in 2015 and 2016.[18] These income tax reductions show up as a reduction in nominal and real income taxes collected per capita in 2013 and 2016 as illustrated in Fig-ure 6.3, though some of the downward movement in income taxes per cap-ita in 2016 is also due to the economic condition of the state.

Income Tax Incidence and Distribution

The person bearing the burden of the individual income tax is typically the person on whom the tax is levied. That is, the person paying the individual income tax has few options to pass the tax to another individual or busi-ness. Other taxes, such as business taxes, may be passed around to other economic participants such as consumers, workers, input providers, sup-pliers of raw materials, and so on. Sales tax is paid at the point of purchase, but a store could lower prices if the sales tax made the price of a good too high, or pass the tax along to other inputs in making the product. Taxes are

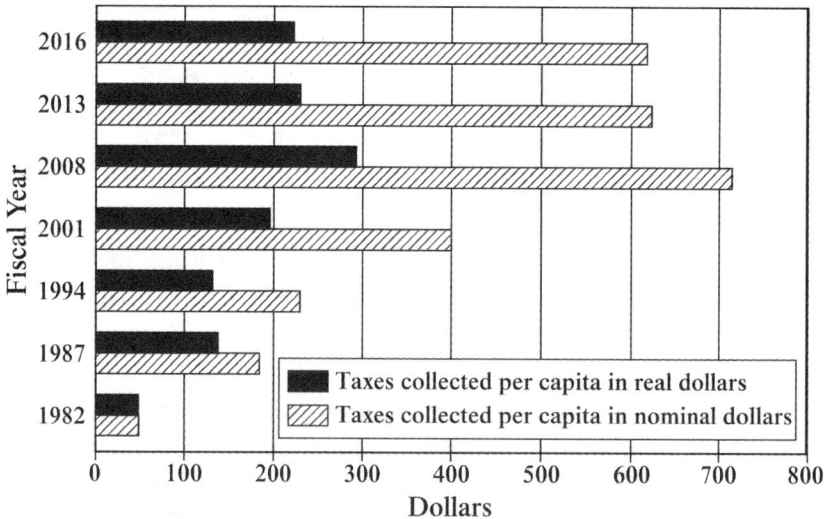

FIGURE 6.3. Individual Income Tax Collections Per Capita in Selected Years

ultimately paid by someone, but it is not simple to identify the person bearing the ultimate burden of the tax by government as the same person who has the responsibility to remit the tax to the government. However, the individual income tax typically stays put with the person on whom it is levied. This fact about the incidence of the individual income tax makes any political choices about it particularly sensitive. It also suggests that the incidence of the individual income tax can be derived from the distribution of the income tax.

Figure 6.4 illustrates the distribution of the Louisiana income tax. Almost 40 percent of Louisiana's 1.745 million taxpayers reported federal adjusted gross income of less than $25,000 in 2014. The federal adjusted gross income of this group of taxpayers made up about 9 percent of total federal adjusted gross income earned by all Louisiana taxpayers and translated into about 4 percent of all income taxes paid to the state of Louisiana. Approximately 24.2 percent of all taxpayers reported federal adjusted gross income between $25,000 and $50,000; they earned 14.4 percent of all federal adjusted gross income in the state, and paid just over 11 percent of all Louisiana individual income taxes. Taxpayers earning between $50,000 and $100,000 made up just over 20 percent of all taxpayers; they earned 25 percent of taxable income, and paid about 24 percent of all income taxes paid.

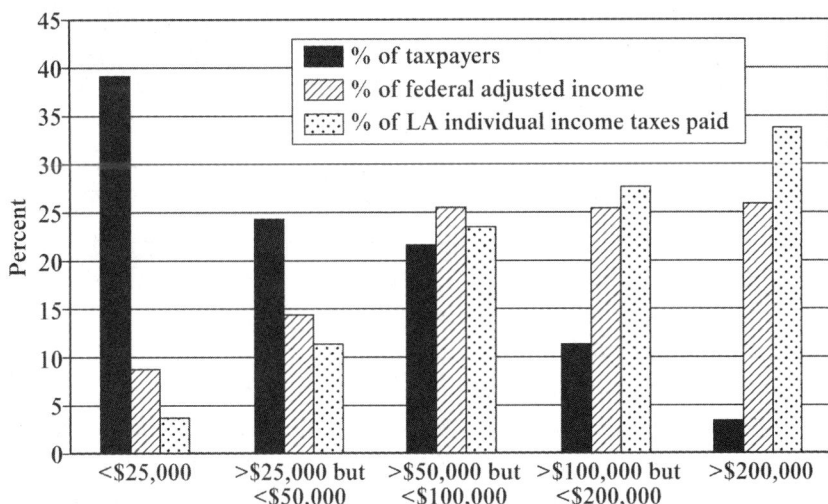

FIGURE 6.4. Louisiana's Income Distribution and Distribution of Income Taxes Paid, FY 2014

Taxpayers earning from $100,000 to $200,000 made up just over 10 percent of all Louisiana taxpayers; they earned 25 percent of all taxable income, and paid about 27 percent of all income taxes paid. Taxpayers earning over $200,000 of federal adjusted gross income represented 3.4 percent of all Louisiana taxpayers, but their income represented 25.9 percent of all federal adjusted gross income reported by Louisiana taxpayers, and the taxes paid by these taxpayers represented just over 33 percent of all individual income taxes paid.

The structure of the Louisiana individual income tax is modestly progressive, with marginal tax rates of 2 percent, 4 percent, and 6 percent, and with a relatively generous standard deduction. The outcome of the actual collection of the income tax in Louisiana is also modestly progressive, with the highest-earning citizens representing 3.4 percent of the taxpayers and 26 percent of federal adjusted gross income, but providing over one-third of all income tax collections. Any proposed changes in the Louisiana income tax should be analyzed with respect to the impact it has on the distribution of the income tax.

Defining the Income Tax Base and Income Tax Liability: Exemptions, Deductions, and Credits

Personal income tax obligations are determined by income, filing status (single or joint), and the rate structure, as well as by exemptions, deductions, and credits (EDCs). EDCs are in practice alterations to the base of the tax itself or to the tax liability associated with the income tax base. Exemptions and deductions reduce the tax base, thereby reducing a taxpayer's tax liability by the size of the exemption/deduction times the marginal tax rate, while a tax credit reduces a taxpayer's tax liability dollar for dollar. All EDCs alter the distribution of who pays the income tax in the state and reduce how much the state receives in income tax collections. Over time, these EDCs have grown to be substantial interventions into the income tax base. In fiscal 2015 individual income tax collections amounted to $2.89 billion, while EDCs associated with the income tax were estimated to be $2.43 billion. Put differently, the amount excepted from income tax is equivalent to 84 percent of actual collections. This proportion has grown substantially since fiscal 2008, when individual income tax collections amounted to $3.2 billion while EDCs totaled an estimated $1.4 billion, or about 44 percent of actual collections. EDCs have grown by 74 percent from 2008 to 2015, while income tax collections have declined by about 10 percent. The reasons for EDC growth include the general growth in value of specific exemptions, deductions, and credits because of increased activity; the addition of new exemptions and deductions meant to improve the overall economy; and the reinstatement of excess itemized deductions for individual income taxes due to the repeal of the Stelly Plan.

These EDCs deserve close consideration in any examination or evaluation of a state's income tax structure. There are tradeoffs that accompany the use of EDCs. In practice, EDCs are used in order to alter or at least influence the behavior of taxpayers, typically in a positive sense. What this means is that the state legislature has determined that more of an activity is desirable, and so this activity is encouraged to increase through the exceptions provided in the income tax structure. This is an inverse of the use of a tax as a penalty for behavior that is considered undesirable, such as a so-called sin tax. But EDCs function as an opportunity cost to the state. Thus, in order to make up for the loss of income from EDCs, rates must be generally higher, given that spending is constant or that some other tax is not being asked to take up the slack. EDCs focus on a particular economic issue. Conversely, rates could be lower and produce the same amount of revenue if the state decided that lower rates were more economically and socially efficient throughout the economy than the behavior encouraged, supported, or subsidized by the EDCs.

The EDCs that are now part of the Louisiana income tax structure are fully represented in Figure 6.4, which becomes the benchmark in evaluating whether any proposed income tax changes are more or less progressive. They are critical parts of the current income tax structure that have been put in place for a specific reason, so any reconsideration of EDCs must be done with attention to the intended effects of the specific exemption, credit, or deduction.

Evaluating Current Exemptions, Deductions, and Credits

The first stage of the process is to define Louisiana taxable income, which starts with federal adjusted gross income as computed on a taxpayer's 1040 tax form. Louisiana is thus sensitive to any changes the federal government may make defining adjusted gross income. Most states begin with federal adjusted gross income (AGI) since it is administratively more efficient for the taxpayer and the tax administrator in any state. Congressional changes in federal adjusted gross income tend to be minor. There have been suggestions to make substantial changes in the method of raising money for the federal government, such as adopting a value-added tax, but such suggestions have not garnered much political support. The bottom line is that the formal definition of AGI is not volatile, and so it is not likely to have much effect on the Louisiana income tax as a definition in itself.

However, the calculation of income tax liability in Louisiana is strongly connected to federal tax liability and excess itemized deductions, both of which are more commonly subject to major congressional changes. Federal tax increases or decreases are likely to be responses to either national economic conditions, thereby leading to an increase or reduction in federal taxes for stabilization purposes, or to a need to pay for additional federal spending such as defense necessities, reducing the imbalance between federal spending and federal tax collections, or investing in infrastructure. Federal taxes are changed for a variety of reasons, and these changes will affect Louisiana taxable income, either positively or negatively. Excess itemized deductions will also be affected by changes in federal tax policy, though these changes tend to occur only during major tax reform efforts, such as the aforementioned Tax Reform Act of 1986. Major changes in itemized deductions were suggested most recently in 2005 by The President's Advisory Panel on Federal Tax Reform, but the suggestions did not spur any action.[19] Suggestions from this panel did include changes in itemized deductions at the federal level. It is certainly predictable that any major federal tax reform in 2017 and 2018 will include changes in itemized deductions.

The exemptions for federal tax liability and excess itemized deductions reduced gross income tax liabilities in Louisiana by over $1.25 billion in 2015. These two exemptions accounted for over 55 percent of the opportunity cost of EDCs. The third major exemption is the personal exemption/ standard deduction/dependent exemption. The personal exemption/standard deduction is standard in almost all states, though the amount varies, and some states use a tax credit in lieu of an exemption or deduction that is subtracted from a person's adjusted gross income. The standard deduction and personal exemption serve as a threshold before anyone has to pay any Louisiana income tax.

The magnitude of all exemptions and credits is presented in Table 6.2 for fiscal years 2014 and 2015. Federal tax liability, excess itemized deductions, and the personal exemption and standard deduction together account for 65 percent of total EDCs in 2015, with the federal tax liability standing out as being the largest deduction in computing a person's income tax in Louisiana.

Table 6.2. Estimated Dollar Value of Exemptions/Credits for Individual Income Tax, Fiscal 2014 and 2015

Exemptions/Credits	Exemptions/ Credits, 2014		Exemptions/ Credits, 2015		Changes in 2015 and/or 2016
	Amount	% of Total	Amount	% of Total	
Federal tax liability	$812.3	38.7%	$912.7	40.4%	None
Excess itemized deductions	$345.8	16.5%	$351.8	15.6%	None
Personal exemption/ standard deduction	$247.8	11.8%	$249.1	11.0%	None
Retirement exclusions, including social security	$171.9	8.2%	$183.4	8.1%	None
Film program tax credits	$114.2	5.4%	$135.8	6.0%	Backdoor cap at $180 million*
Net income taxes paid to other states	$86.2	4.1%	$108.9	4.8%	Adjusted so credit cannot exceed LA taxes
Deductions for net capital gains	$57.3	2.7%	$51.8	2.3%	Modified to relate exemption to time in business
Earned income tax credit	$47.8	2.3%	$47.5	2.1%	None
Louisiana Citizens Property Insurance	$41.3	2.0%	$40.6	1.8%	Now 25% of assessment
Wind and solar credit	$31.8	1.5%	$38.1	1.7%	Capped; expires as of 2018
Rehabilitation of historic structures	$26.4	1.3%	$38.4	1.7%	Sunsets as of December 2021
Child care expenses	$18.6	0.9%	$17.8	0.8%	None
Others	$97.7	4.6%	$82.0	3.6%	
Total exemptions, credits, and rebates	$2,099.1	100%	$2,257.9	100.0%	

Source: Louisiana Department of Revenue
*This has been changed to a front door cap.

Federal tax liability and excess itemized deductions are exemptions that provide more tax relief to the higher income taxpayers since the federal individual income tax is progressive in its makeup, and higher income taxpayers typically have more expenditures that can be itemized on the federal tax return. The magnitude of the deduction for federal taxes paid and excess itemized deductions means that if the state wants to reduce the income tax rates, it has to eliminate or, at the very least, scale back these two exemptions. Or, if the state wants to increase dollars received from the individual income tax without increasing marginal tax rates, then it has to eliminate or modify these deductions. The one tax credit that is tailored to provide income tax relief to lower income taxpayers is the earned income tax credit. The federal tax liability deduction, the excess itemized deduction, and the earned income tax credit are all discussed in the following sections.

Federal Tax Liability

The deduction of federal income tax liability from a person's adjusted gross income for state income tax purposes is currently available in unrestricted form in only three states: Alabama, Iowa, and Louisiana. Alabama and Iowa are substantially different in terms of the highest marginal tax rate and when the highest rate becomes effective. In Alabama the highest marginal rate is 5 percent but it is effective once a joint filer's taxable income reaches $6,000. In Iowa the highest marginal tax rate is 8.98 percent and it is effective when the joint filer's taxable income reaches $68,175. Three other states put limits on the deductibility of federal tax liability. Both Missouri and Montana limit the deduction to $5,000 for single filers and $10,000 for joint filers. Oregon limits the federal deductibility to $5,950.

The impact by the level of income of the Louisiana taxpayer of eliminating the federal tax deductibility is illustrated in Figure 6.5. The average tax rate for a taxpayer making over $200,000 in Louisiana taxable income would increase from around 3.3 percent to just over 4 percent, while the average tax rate for the taxpayer making around $100,000 would go up by 0.5 percent, or from about 2.5 percent of their income being taxed to about 3 percent of their income being taxed. Every taxpayer would incur a larger individual income tax payment in the state, but the removal of the federal tax deduction would improve the progressivity of the Louisiana income tax structure and, by extension, the entire Louisiana tax structure, given that the income tax makes up over 25 percent of all state revenues and assuming no other tax changes were imposed.

Federal tax liability will further affect income tax collections in Louisiana, given the federal tax changes in late 2017. A reduction in federal tax liability will augment Louisiana taxable income since there will be less for individual taxpayers to pay. However, a change in the pass-through income and income for single proprietors is predicted to negatively affect Louisiana taxable income since Louisiana initiates its tax return with the adjusted gross income as determined by federal law. The 20 percent rule for single proprietors and partners will affect federal adjusted income in a downward fashion and will affect Louisiana taxable income as well.

Excess Itemized Deductions

Figure 6.6 presents excess itemized deductions by income range. The excess itemized deduction varies from around a $10,000 average at the lower income categories to over $160,000 at the highest income category. Overall, 24 percent of all Louisiana taxpayers itemize on their federal tax returns. About 16 percent of taxpayers in Louisiana making $100,000 or less itemize on their federal tax returns, whereas almost 70 percent of Louisiana tax-

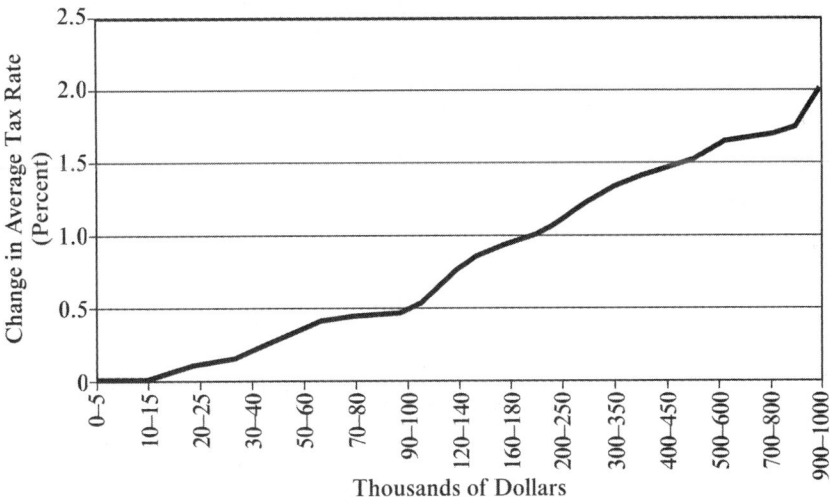

FIGURE 6.5. Change in Average Tax Rate Paid by Individual Taxpayers if Federal Tax Deduction Is Eliminated

payers making over $100,000 itemize at the federal level, and 90 percent of taxpayers making $200,000 or more in Louisiana taxable income itemize on their federal tax returns.

Itemized deductions are determined by federal law, and changes in these deductions are typically discussed if there is any discussion of federal tax reform. This was the case in 1986, when the federal government made several major tax reforms, and again in 2005, when the Bush administration initiated a major study, but no action was taken. This is very predictable since tax reform at the federal level, just as at the state level, is typically about lower rates and a broader tax base, so the focus is on getting rid of exemptions and deductions. Indeed, in the 2017 federal tax changes, major revisions in itemized deductions at the federal level will affect the tax base for Louisiana.

Earned Income Tax Credit

The one tax exemption/credit that does focus on lower income individuals is the earned income tax credit (EITC). The federal government created the EITC in 1975 and then enhanced it in 1986, 1990, 1993, 2001, and 2009. This credit is a refundable tax credit for low to moderate income families and individuals. The amount of the credit depends on a taxpayer's income

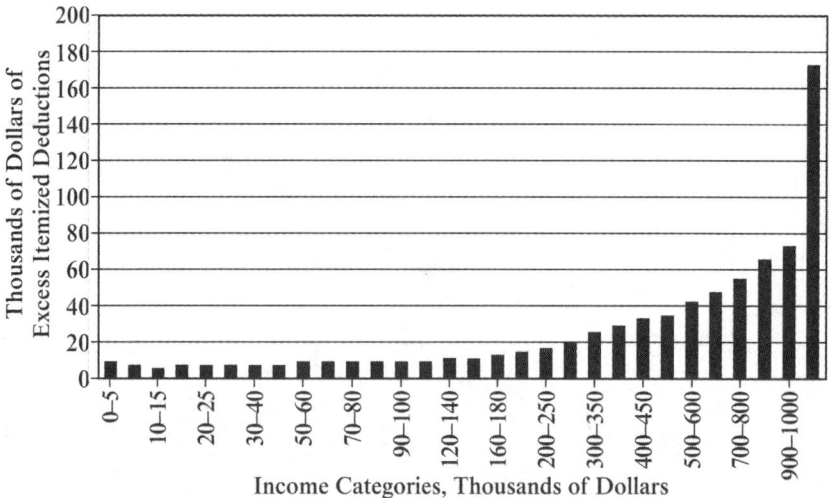

FIGURE 6.6. Tax Reduction Due to Excess Itemized Deductions by Income

and the number of dependent children claimed. In 2016 the federal EITC was as high as $6,269 for a joint filer with three or more children and with an income between $13,900 and $23,750; $5,572 for a joint filer with two children and an income between $13,900 and $23,750; $3,373 for a joint filer with one child and an income between $10,000 and $23,750; and $506 for a joint filer with no children and an income between $9,200 and $13,850. This credit gradually increases to the maximum credit as a person's income rises to $13,900 in the case of a joint filer with two children, and then it gradually diminishes once the person's income reaches $23,750, and it goes away completely once the person's income reaches $48,800. The cost of the program to the federal government is about $60 billion.

In Louisiana 506,000 taxpayers made use of the federal EITC, getting an average tax credit of $2,862 per taxpayer, or an estimate of $1.4 billion in federal tax credits for Louisiana citizens. This means that these Louisiana taxpayers reduced their federal tax liability by $1.4 billion. Twenty-six states have added an EITC to their income tax provisions, with Louisiana adding such a tax credit in 2007 effective as of 2008. The average EITC by states is 16.4 percent, and Louisiana's EITC is 3.5 percent. Louisiana's tax credit is fully refundable, while four states have EITCs that are not refundable. Louisiana is the only state in the South to have an EITC. This tax credit reduced the state's income tax collections by about $25 to $50 million.

The earned income tax credit affects Louisiana tax collections in two ways. First, the US earned income tax credit reduces a person's federal tax liability, so it adds to the Louisiana taxable income base from that perspective since federal tax liability is an exemption in Louisiana. Second, the Louisiana earned income tax credit is a direct reduction in Louisiana income tax payments since it is a refundable tax credit.

Other Exemptions, Deductions, and Credits

Other major EDCs include the standard deduction and personal exemption as well as exemptions on retirement income (social security, state and local retirement incomes, and federal retirement incomes). The standard deduction and personal exemption is a typical benchmark of how much income should be totally tax-free for any citizen. Most states make such a statement. State, local, and federal retirement income, including social security, is not taxed. Retirement exemptions remove an estimated $8.7 billion from Louisiana income tax, accounting for an estimated $200 million reduction in income tax revenues. Given the age distribution of the population, the retirement exemptions will most likely continue to increase over time. This becomes one of the sensitive issues the state has to deal with, given the changing age distribution of the population and the need to maintain certain public services.

Some tax credits may have nothing to do with the income tax structure per se, but income tax obligations are merely used as a method of supporting a certain type of spending done by the private or nonprofit sector. The motion picture tax credit is a perfect example. The purpose of this credit is to promote the development of the motion picture industry in Louisiana. An evaluation of this credit has nothing to do with evaluating the income tax specifically. Rather, the focus should be on the role of the motion picture tax credit in developing the motion picture industry in Louisiana, its expense, and its return on investment. In this case, the income tax is a useful method of funding this tax credit, especially since the tax credits can be marketable financial securities, so that one person's investment in the motion picture industry may become another person's tax credit, and this person will have a tax liability in Louisiana.

Economists are almost unanimous in stressing the importance of having a broad tax base with low rates—the tax structure that minimizes distortions in the marketplace, maintains neutrality in decision making, and establishes equity and simplicity in the tax structure at least as much as is possible. If a state is to meet these objectives of a broad tax base and low tax rates, then the state has to examine each and every tax exemption, deduction, and credit.

Comparing Louisiana's Income Tax to Individual Income Taxes in Other States

In this section we compare the parameters of the Louisiana income tax to that of southeastern and neighboring states. In Table 6.3 Louisiana is compared to other states in the Southeast and all neighboring states for joint filers.[20] North Carolina has a true flat tax. This tax plan was instituted in 2014 with a flat rate of 5.8 percent instead of the state rates of 6 percent, 7 percent, and 7.75 percent in effect prior to 2014.[21] By 2015 the single rate had dropped to 5.75 percent, and it is expected to remain there. The income tax in North Carolina represents about 50 percent of all state revenues, generating about $13 billion in tax revenues.[22]

Georgia, South Carolina, and Virginia also depend heavily on the individual income tax for funding state services. Income taxes in Georgia represented 53.2 percent of all state tax collections; in South Carolina, income taxes represented just over 45 percent of all state tax collections; and in Virginia, income tax collections represented over 60 percent of all state tax collections. Georgia has six tax brackets, with a top marginal rate of 6 percent, which goes into effect at $10,000 of taxable income. South Carolina has five tax brackets, with a top rate of 7 percent starting at $14,650 of taxable income. Virginia has four tax brackets, with the top rate of 5.75 percent starting at $17,000 of taxable income. All of these states make much more use of the income tax to pay for public services than Louisiana does, and all of these states initiate their top marginal tax rate at a much lower income threshold than Louisiana does.

For states that have an income tax, Louisiana's income tax structure is more favorable in terms of rates, and especially when the highest marginal tax rate becomes effective. Georgia, North Carolina, South Carolina, and Virginia rely more heavily on the income tax than Louisiana does, but with a top bracket going into effect at such generally low incomes ($10,000 to $17,000 for joint filers), these states appear to have not put a high priority on progressivity in the income tax. And, to a certain extent, states are careful in terms of making their income tax system highly progressive, since a highly progressive income tax structure could cause higher income individuals and households to locate in other states or to rearrange their asset holdings. It has been of concern that high income filers, capital income, and retirees could be more mobile and could react to higher income taxes.[23] The results have not been conclusive; in fact, other factors such as state spending on education and health care also have an impact on migration into a state.

Louisiana, just like other southern states, has to compete with states that have no income taxes or a very limited income tax. Florida and Texas both have no individual income tax, but they both have more substantial state sales taxes and local property taxes. Tennessee does not have an income tax, but does have a 6 percent tax on interest income and dividends. Tennessee also has a high state sales tax rate of 7 percent, which is comparable to the state sales tax rate in Indiana, Mississippi, New Jersey, and Rhode Island, but lower than California's state sales tax rate of 7.5 percent. None of these states, though, relies so heavily on the sales tax at the local level as Louisiana does. Even as we discuss the individual income tax, we keep referring to other taxes as well, since if a state chooses not to use the individual income tax, then it must select another tax to fund public services.

No single tax defines a state, nor does a tax structure, but each tax has its own peculiarities and its own impacts on individuals and businesses in the state. The income tax has been chosen to support public services by eleven out of fourteen states in the southeastern part of the country and nearby

TABLE 6.3. Income Tax Comparison with Neighboring and Nearby States, 2016 (for Joint Filers)

State	Standard Deduction and Personal Exemption	Number of Marginal Tax Rates	Lowest Rate	Bracket for Lowest Rate	Highest Rate	Incom Level When Highest Rate Begins
Alabama	$10,500	3	2.00%	$0 to $1,000	5.0%	$6,000
Arkansas	$4,400	6	0.90%	$0 to $4,299	6.90%	$35,100
Florida	No income tax					
Georgia	$10,400	6	1.00%	$0 to $1,000	6.00%	$10,000
Kentucky	$2,480	6	2.00%	$0 to $3,000	6.00%	$75,000
Louisiana	$11,000	3	2.00%	$0 to $25,000	6.00%	$100,000
Mississippi	$16,600	3	3.00%	$0 to $5,000	5.00%	$10,000
North Carolina	$17,500	1	5.499%		5.499%	
Oklahoma	$14,700	6	0.50%	$0 to $2,000	5.00%	$12,200
South Carolina	$20,800	5	3.00%	>$2,930	7.00%	$14,650
Tennessee	No income tax, except on income received from stocks, bonds, and notes receivable					
Texas	No income tax					
Virginia	$7,860	4	2.00%	$0 to $3,000	5.75%	$17,000
West Virginia	$4,000	5	3.00%	$0 to $10,000	6.50%	$60,000

Source: Tax Foundation

to Louisiana. The income tax is a common method of supporting a state's budget.

Summary Comments on Individual Income Tax

A state, either through a vote of the people or through the persons representing the people in the state legislature and the office of the governor, has to make a choice about its overall tax structure and about the role of the individual income tax in paying for state services. The income tax has a number of strengths: (1) it provides a degree of progressivity in a state's tax structure, and this progressivity can be structured by the tax laws, (2) the income tax provides a growth tax to maintain support of public services over time and will offset taxes that may not grow in accordance with the economy, (3) the incidence of the tax is predictable, and (4) its administration is tied to the federal income tax.

To make decisions we have to have information about the projected impacts of various tax scenarios on the state's budget and on taxpayers. We have the tools to present simulations of the impact of different income tax alternatives. We can compare different scenarios to the current tax structure for a joint filer: 2 percent on the first $25,000 of taxable income, 4 percent on the next $75,000 of taxable income, and 6 percent on taxable income above $100,000, and all of the current exemptions, deductions, and credits. For example, we can eliminate the two major exemptions of federal tax liability and excess itemized deductions, but we lower the rates to 1 percent on the first $25,000, 3 percent on the next $75,000, and 5 percent on taxable income in excess of $100,000, and estimate what it means by income categories and what it means in terms of providing revenue for the state. We can estimate what it means for persons and families in different income categories. From the perspective of the economist, we have expanded the tax base and lowered the tax rates.

There are numerous income tax alternatives. We can illustrate the impact of lowering the marginal tax rates but eliminating the largest tax deduction and the impact of narrowing the tax brackets and eliminating excess itemized deductions. We could examine imposing a flat rate with major changes in the tax exemptions and tax deductions, but we need to project the impact on each set of taxpayers so the political leaders and the electorate will be able to assess the impact of such tax changes on the population. This is why the income tax from one perspective is a very good method of raising money to pay for state services—we can assess fairly precisely exactly who will be paying for these services. For the same reason this attribute makes it a more controversial tax since each taxpayer will know fairly precisely how much he or she will be paying.

Notes

The author appreciates the assistance of Dr. Roy Heidelberg for his careful reading, editing, and suggestions.

1. Changes in federal tax policy can also contribute negatively to individual income tax collections in Louisiana. Most of the changes in the past forty years have contributed positively.

2. Tax Foundation, *State Individual Income Tax Rates and Brackets for 2016,* Nicole Kaeding, February 2016.

3. Tax Foundation, *Fiscal Fact No. 500: State Individual Income Tax Rates and Brackets for 2016.* Two additional states, New Hampshire and Tennessee, tax interest and dividend income only.

4. "Effects of Income Tax Changes on Economic Growth," William G. Gale and Andrew A. Samwick, in *Economic Studies at Brookings,* September 2014; Martin Feldstein, "Effects of taxes on economic behavior," *National Tax Journal,* 2008.

5. Louisiana's economy is discussed in Chapter 2.

6. Based on estimates by the author in projecting income tax estimates in the 1980s.

7. "The Tax Bill of 1986: Nuts and Bolts of New System: Step-by-Step Instructions for Calculating the Changes," Gary Klott, Special to the *New York Times,* August 19, 1986. The federal income tax changes were very much in line with the economist's perspective of creating a large tax base and keeping the rates low.

8. Public Affairs Research Council, "The 'Stelly Plan': A Proposed Income/Sales Tax Swap," September 2002. Vic Stelly was a Republican member of the Louisiana House of Representatives from the Lake Charles area. Representative Stelly developed Stelly 1, the 2000 tax reform amendment, and Stelly 2, the 2002 tax reform amendment.

9. Representative Stelly won the 2002 vote with 534,989 in favor (51 percent) and 506,938 opposed (49 percent).

10. *Louisiana's Fiscal Alternatives: Finding Permanent Solutions to Recurring Budget Crises,* ed. James A. Richardson (Baton Rouge and London: LSU Press, 1988).

11. The fact that everyone benefits from the elimination of taxes on food for home consumption and prescription drugs diminishes some of the improvement in the progressivity of not taxing food. In addition, lower income individuals who receive WIC payments or SNAPs will automatically not pay a sales tax on food, so many of the lower income persons are already exempt from paying taxes on their food. And the higher sales tax rate will apply to other purchases such as clothes for their children, cosmetics, and so on.

12. We compare the state's use of the sales tax and the individual income tax since these

taxes now make up over 60 percent of all tax collections and, if the state were in need of revenues, it would almost have to turn to one of these two taxes.

13. The deduction of excess itemized deductions was phased in over a three-year period with 57.5 percent deduction being allowed in 2007, 65 percent in 2008, and 100 percent in 2009 and thereafter. We should note that Governor Blanco did not actively push this tax change, but she signed the legislation into law.

14. The legislation kept the expanded bracket for the 2 percent rate as approved in 2002, but increased the tax brackets for the 4 percent and 6 percent rates back to the pre-2002 rate/bracket structure. Governor Jindal did not push for this tax change, but once it gained momentum in the legislature, he did make it part of his tax program.

15. The Louisiana economy lost over 50,000 jobs from 2008 through 2010 as a result of the national recession and the sharp drop in oil prices in 2008.

16. Governor Jindal initiated a plan in 2013 to eliminate the individual and corporate income taxes, but these plans were, using his terminology, "parked" since there was no way to make up the loss in state revenues.

17. As one example, the state had allowed for retirement income for state employees to be exempt from the state income tax as of the late 1940s. After 1989 Louisiana had to allow, if the exemption for state retirement was to be retained, federal retirement income to also be exempt from the state income tax, based on the ruling of the US Supreme Court in Paul S. Davis v. Michigan Department of Treasury, 489 U.S. 803, March 28, 1989.

18. *Louisiana Economic Outlook,* 2016.

19. *Simple, Fair, and Pro-Growth: Proposals to Fix America's Tax System,* November 2005. The panel was composed of a bipartisan group of economists and tax experts. One of the cochairs was a Republican, Senator Connie Mack of Florida, and the other was a Democrat, Senator John Breaux of Louisiana.

20. Florida, Tennessee, and Texas do not have an income tax.

21. North Carolina Department of Revenue.

22. US Census Bureau, "2016 Annual Survey of State Government Tax Collections by Category."

23. "Base Mobility and State Personal Income Taxes," Donald Bruce, William F. Fox, and Zhou Yang, report for Federation of Tax Administrators, September 2010.

7

REFORMING THE CORPORATION INCOME AND FRANCHISE TAX

Steven M. Sheffrin

Introduction

Louisiana has two taxes specifically levied on corporations, the franchise tax and the corporation income tax. Although these taxes in recent years have together only provided 4–5 percent of own-source revenue, they are nonetheless an important part of the tax structure of the state. Both depend on highly complex tax and accounting rules. The franchise tax is effectively a tax on a corporation's equity capital, while the corporation income tax is based on corporate income. For multistate corporations, the tax is allocated or apportioned to Louisiana by formula.

From an economic and public finance point of view, the intellectual case for state taxation of corporations is often depicted as surprisingly weak. Since states are relatively small relative to the entire country (or the world), corporations have many options of where to locate or expand their production. To the extent that taxes on corporations provide incentives for firms to invest outside of the state, a state's stock of productive capital will be reduced. This will reduce wages within the state and make the state less productive. Moreover, by moving its activities outside a state with high corporate taxes, a corporation will reduce its tax burden, thus shifting the burden of taxation to those who cannot as easily move—workers, land, and immobile capital.

However, this picture is perhaps too bleak. While corporations are sensitive to tax burdens, they compare the overall tax burden in one state to overall burdens in other states. By that metric, what matters is the level of tax rates and structure of taxation on corporations relative to those in other competing states. As we discuss below, the specific structure of corporate taxes can have an important effect on corporate incentives independent of the actual rates. Moreover, corporate taxes are only part of the total tax burden facing corporations. Depending on the state, they may also pay extensive sales and property taxes. Thus, a state has room to design an effective tax on business and not necessarily make it uncompetitive on the national stage.

There is also an important political dimension to taxes on corporations. The corporation income tax was introduced in Louisiana in 1934 as part of the same legislation introducing income taxation. The franchise tax was introduced even earlier, in 1932. In all the states, the introduction of taxes on corporations was closely tied to the introduction of taxes on individuals. This historical connection also has a deep psychological connection. In the popular mind, these taxes are viewed as sharing the burden between individuals and corporations. Regardless of the economic merit of this view, simply abolishing all taxes on corporations would seem unfair as long as individuals pay taxes directly.

Nonetheless, there are important ways to reform the taxation of corporations in Louisiana. However, corporate taxation is a particularly complicated subject matter, and before we proceed to specific recommendations, we need to set the appropriate background. We begin with an overview of the revenue raised from corporate taxation and then proceed to an analysis of structural reform.

Corporate Taxes and Revenues

Corporate taxes are composed of a variety of taxes remitted directly by businesses as a result of their operations in the state. These taxes include provider fees paid by health care units, hazardous waste taxes, natural gas franchise tax, a Public Service Commission tax, and several others, but business taxes are dominated by two major taxes, the corporate income tax and the corporate franchise tax. Corporate income and franchise taxes flow entirely to the state general fund, and they have exhibited a high degree of volatility over the years. The following discussion focuses on the income and franchise tax as a combined total. While the two taxes have distinct tax base and rate structures, they are filed on a combined return that culminates in a single liability figure. Thus, for the purposes of this section, they are treated as a single combined tax.

The tax rate schedules for the corporate and franchise taxes are:

Corporate Income Tax Rates	Net Income
$1–$25,000	4%
Next $25,000	5%
Next $50,000	6%
Next $100,000	7%
Over $200,000	8%

Corporate Franchise (Total Equity-Based Capital Stock, Surplus, and Undivided Profits)

$0–$300,000	$1.50 per $1,000
Over $300,000	$3.00 per $1,000

The corporate income tax is imposed only upon that part of net income that is derived from sources within Louisiana. Corporations provide schedules for the apportionment and allocation of net income. We discuss the methods that are used to determine the share of corporate income from Louisiana sources below.

Figure 7.1 displays their combined collections history. Receipts climbed in the 1970s, being augmented by a corporate income tax increase in 1977, and then were bounded between $400 million and $600 million per year for much of the 1980s, the 1990s, and into the early 2000s, again being augmented by an increase in the corporate franchise tax in 1984. Collections dramatically exceeded that norm for the rest of the 2000s, peaking in fiscal year 2007 at $1.052 billion before falling off to a contemporary low of $175

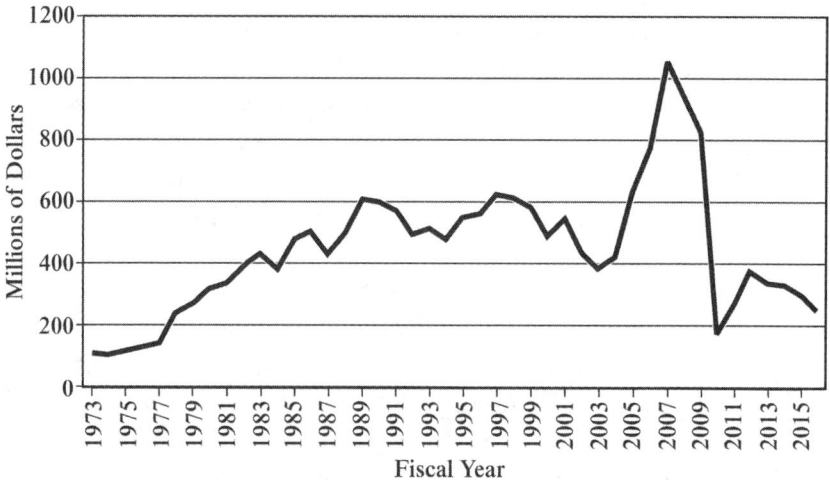

FIGURE 7.1. Corporate Income and Franchise Tax Collections

million in fiscal year 2010. Collections are up from that level since then, but have not achieved even the norm exhibited in the 1980s and '90s. There are two likely reasons why that norm has not been achieved: the completion of the phaseout of borrowed capital from the franchise tax base, and the effects of tax amnesties.

A significant portion of the franchise tax base, the applicability of the tax to borrowed capital, began to be phased out with the 2006 tax year, with completion by tax year 2011. At the time of enactment of this phaseout, the revenue loss at completion was estimated to be some $161 million. While estimates of tax loss or gain from any changes to the corporate tax base are highly uncertain, and much of this phaseout occurred in a period of rapidly rising corporate collections overall as energy prices rose and the US and world economies approached the top of the last economic expansion, simply adding that dollar amount back to the actual collections in the latter part of the collections history would place the combined tax solidly within the norm experienced in the 1980s and '90s.

In addition, the state implemented a tax amnesty program in the fall of 2009. The performance of a tax amnesty is understood to largely reflect the acceleration of tax receipts that would otherwise be collected in subsequent periods, and is typically dominated by corporate collections, as a large stock of disputed corporate tax liabilities is a normal course of business for large corporate taxpayers as a whole. Thus, nominal fiscal year 2010 collections were over $500 million, but two-thirds of that total was amnesty collections, the receipt of which in fiscal year 2010 appears, to some extent, to have been at the expense of receipts in the following fiscal years. This amnesty was implemented during a period of national and state economic slowdown. Disentangling amnesty effects on corporate collections from general economic conditions is impossible to do with any high degree of confidence, but these events did occur and do provide a plausible explanation for some of the collections pattern of the tax.

Causal evidence of an amnesty effect may also be found in an earlier amnesty offered in the fall of 2001. Collections in the three fiscal years following this earlier amnesty program also fell off from the levels prior to the amnesty. As with the 2009 amnesty program, this earlier program occurred during a period of national and state economic slowdown, making it difficult to disentangle amnesty effects from general economic conditions. Finally, along these same lines, a third amnesty program was offered in the fall of 2013. While fiscal year 2014 was not complete and was not included in the collections history depicted above, corporate amnesty payments were substantial. In the absence of those amnesty payments, corporate collections so far in fiscal year 2014 are well behind collections in the same period of the prior fiscal year, and revenue forecasts for corporate collections in fiscal year 2014 through fiscal year 2018 were downgraded substantially in anticipation of an amnesty effect suppressing future collections.

Looking back into the earlier history of corporate collections, there have been a number of significant tax rate and/or base changes and other events that have influenced these receipts. The rise of collections until the mid-1980s generally reflects the rise of oil prices and associated industries. Oil prices took their first material dip in 1982, stopping the steady increase in corporate collections, and then a dramatic price collapse occurred in 1986, resulting in a severe contraction of the Louisiana economy centered on oil and gas and associated industries. To counter the downward pressure on corporate taxes, the franchise tax component was essentially doubled in 1984. For much of the 1980s and through the early 2000s, however, no strong trending occurred as these two taxes bounced in the $400 million to $600 million per year range, averaging around $500 million per year. For corporate taxes, this 25 percent swing around the average constitutes relative stability. This is actually fairly remarkable in light of the various significant changes to these taxes that occurred during this period.

Examples of these significant changes include net operating loss deductions, which were made applicable to five subsequent profitable tax years and three prior profitable years; this carry-back provision resulted in refunds from taxes being paid in a current year. Corporations organized under Subchapter S of the Internal Revenue Code were allowed to pass income through to their resident individuals for taxation at personal income tax rates rather than at higher corporate income tax rates.

Other than the turmoil related to the end of rising oil prices in the early 1980s and then their collapse in 1986, the most significant changes to the level of collections during this period likely resulted from the implementation of refundable tax credits allowed for certain local property taxes paid by eligible businesses. Starting in 1992, the state began a five-year phase-in of a reimbursement of local property taxes paid by businesses on the assessed value of inventory property. The reimbursement was provided by a refundable credit against the income tax (both corporate and personal) and the franchise tax. This was instituted as a means of being more competitive with other states by not taxing inventories. But inventory taxation was a local tax. The state absorbed the burden of the inventory ad valorem tax by allowing a refundable credit against state taxes. Similar reimbursements for property tax paid on offshore vessels were added in 1994, on public service property of landline telephone companies in 2000, and on stored natural gas in 2005. Together, these credits reduced total tax collections by some $500 million per year, with three-quarters of that attributable to the inventory component and, most of all, the reduction in corporate taxes. In addition, numerous other tax credits and reimbursements for various targeted expenditures have been allowed against corporate taxes, some of which have grown to material size, and all of which work to reduce collections below what they would otherwise be. They also likely contribute to the inherent high degree of volatility of corporate taxes in general.

There are fifty-two exemptions, credits, and rebates associated with corporate income and franchise taxes. Five of these exemptions make up approximately 95 percent of the dollars forgone, given the definition and administration of the exemptions. These five exemptions are noted in Table 7.1. The only constitutional exemption is the federal income tax liability, and it is worth about $211 million in 2013.

Finally, Figure 7.2 depicts the share over time of total state tax receipts comprised of corporate income and franchise tax.

This share was generally rising until the mid- to late 1980s, peaking at just over 13 percent in fiscal year 1990. Greater reliance on other revenue sources, such as sales tax, personal income tax, and gaming taxes, along with the proliferation of credits and charges allowed against corporate taxes

TABLE 7.1. Corporate Tax Exemptions, 2013

Corporate Exemptions	Value of Exemptions	Percent
Subchapter S corporation	$483,130,000	26.9
Net Louisiana operating loss	$330,359,000	18.4
Insurance company premium tax	$302,503,000	16.8
Inventory tax/ad valorem tax credit	$378,068,000	21.0
Federal income tax deduction	$207,100,000	11.5
Total Department of Revenue	*$1,701,160,000*	*100.0*

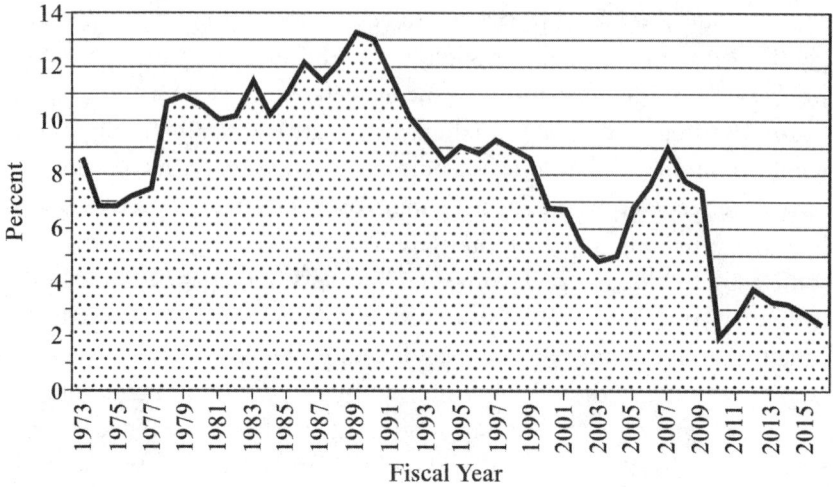

FIGURE 7.2. Corporate Taxes as Share of Total State Tax Collections

and the development of tax planning/avoidance strategies at the state level, have worked to reduce the corporate tax share in the state's tax revenue mix since that peak period at the beginning of the 1990s. These influences have been so strong that even at the peak of corporate tax receipts in fiscal year 2008 at over a billion dollars, well above any prior period's collections, the corporate share rose to barely the 9 percent level, before dropping back to just over 3 percent in the latest complete year. While the corporate income and franchise tax have dwindled as a share of total tax receipts, they are still important in their absolute level, and in the fact that they are among the very few taxes that largely or entirely flow to the state general fund, helping to support nearly one-third of total state expenditures.

Analysis of the Corporate Franchise Tax

The franchise tax law is contained in Louisiana Revised Statutes 47: 601 et seq. The taxable base for the tax is defined as the issued and outstanding capital stock, surplus, and undivided profits. While these terms all have very specific meanings and are defined in detail by statutes, regulations, and court rulings, the sum of the three items in the taxable base can loosely be construed as the amount paid for shares of a corporation plus its retained earnings. The rates that are applied to this taxable base are $1.50 per $1,000 up to $300,000, and $3.00 per $1,000 of taxable base above that. For corporations that operate across state lines, revenues and property within and without the state are utilized to determine the fraction of the total base subject to tax in Louisiana; for manufacturing, only the revenue factor is used. Since 2011, borrowed capital has been excluded from the tax base, effectively converting the franchise tax to a tax on equity capital.

An important recent Louisiana Court of Appeals Case in 2011 had also changed the scope of the franchise tax. In UTELCOM, Inc. and UCOM, Inc. v. Bridges ("UTELCOM"), the court ruled that out-of-state corporations that were limited partners in a partnership doing business in Louisiana were not subject to the franchise tax. The Louisiana Supreme Court declined to review the case, thereby making the Appeals Court ruling final. Prior to this case, the Department of Revenue would "look through" the partnership to subject the corporations investing in it to the franchise tax, even if they were limited partners. The court reasoned that once the limited corporate partners had made their investments, they were no longer conducting business in Louisiana in "corporate form" and thus were not subject to the tax.

The UTELCOM ruling had several important implications. First, a corporation could avoid the franchise tax by doing business through a partnership as long as they are limited partners. This considerably reduced the reach of the franchise tax. Second, combined with the exclusion of debt from the franchise tax base, the revenue potential of the franchise tax would be limited in the future. In recent years, it has brought in less than $100 million for the state, although these estimates are subject to much uncertainty as credits are taken jointly against the corporation income tax and franchise tax.

During the 2016 Special Session, the Louisiana legislature changed the law to offset this court decision. They passed a bill that had two parts. First, it defined a corporation for Louisiana tax purposes as any entity that "checked the box" to be taxed as a corporation for federal purposes. Second, it expanded the base to include corporations that own property in the state, either directly or indirectly, through other related business entities including partnerships, joint ventures, or any other business organizations, including subsidiaries. This had the effect of overturning the provisions in UTELCOM. The franchise tax is now applied more evenly to the use of equity capital in Louisiana.

As its history in Louisiana suggests, nationally the franchise tax is an old tax, in many cases predating the corporate income tax. Its underlying philosophy is that a state can tax a corporation for the privilege of doing business in its state, with a base that is best measured by financial accounting measures based on some notion of capital or net worth. Only sixteen states currently have franchise taxes similar in spirit to Louisiana's, and one of these states, Missouri, is phasing out its tax. The states that have a franchise tax are primarily in the South and Midwest, along with a few eastern states. Bases for these taxes do differ across the states, with North Carolina's taxable base being closest to Louisiana's. The states that are leaders in corporate income taxation—California, New York, and even Texas with its margin tax—do not have franchise taxes in the spirit of Louisiana's. For historical and other reasons, some states with corporate income taxes still use the franchise tax nomenclature or impose a minimum tax called a franchise tax. But these taxes are not based on measures of capital or net worth. Other states do subject certain industries (e.g., financial services) to franchise taxes rather than income taxes. Franchise taxes are taxes of the past, not the future; neither of the major national tax administration organizations, the Federation of Tax Administrators and the Multistate Tax Commission (MTC), have ever focused their efforts on the franchise tax.

Today in Louisiana, the franchise tax serves as a pure tax on equity capital for corporations in the state. This tax creates a direct incentive for corporations to avoid the tax by either changing their form (for example, by operating as partnerships or LLCs and not checking the box to be taxed as a corporation) or by retaining their corporate structure but reducing capital used in Louisiana and expanding outside the state.

For corporations operating solely within Louisiana, the franchise tax directly impacts their incentives for future expansion. For multistate corporations, their incentives are also affected by the allocation factors applied to the total taxable base of the corporation. For nonmanufacturing corporations, the franchise tax is based on an average of their share of revenues and share of property within the state, while for manufacturing firms it is only based on the share of revenues within the state. As public finance economists have noted, this creates an effective "excise tax" for any corporation selling into the state or using property in the state, as their franchise tax burden will increase with additional in-state sales or the use of in-state property. The tax on selling into a state is similar in spirit to a sales tax. A corporation may be able to shift part of the burden of this additional tax by raising prices to the ultimate purchaser in Louisiana. To the extent the corporation successfully shifts its burdens to others, the additional tax arising from sales will not be a deterrent to expansion within the state. On the other hand, this is less likely with property; using property in the state will increase its franchise tax burden and discourage further use.

Assuming the legislature wishes to retain the tax, it could improve business incentives by changing the allocation factors so that all corporations—not just manufacturers—could use a single revenue factor. This would have two consequences. First, it would reduce the tax burden on using property within Louisiana, as that would no longer have any consequences for the franchise tax burden. Second, it would shift some of the burden to corporations that are located outside the state and that sell into the state of Louisiana. Both outcomes would be beneficial for the state. Changing allocation factors could either increase or decrease revenues; the Department of Revenue should be able to provide estimates of these changes. Nonetheless, even if there are minor revenue losses from moving to a single revenue allocation factor, the positive economic incentives would still justify such a policy change.

However, we believe that it is time for Louisiana to move on from this source of taxation. Since the primary effect of the franchise tax is to reduce the use of equity capital in the state, our recommendation is to *phase out the franchise tax in a fiscally responsible manner.* To avoid fiscal disruption and to avoid shifting the tax burden to other types of taxes, it is important to find a palatable alternative. One alternative would be to cap the franchise tax at a level consistent with revenue needs. An alternative would be to reform the corporate tax system. We believe that reforms to the corporate income tax could not only improve its efficiency but also could raise revenue to offset the loss of revenue from the eventual phasing out of the franchise tax.

Analysis of the Corporate Income Tax

The corporation tax in Louisiana is governed by Louisiana Revised Statutes 47.287.2 et seq. All corporations and entities taxed as corporations for federal income tax purposes deriving income from Louisiana sources, whether or not they have any net income, must file an income tax return. The Louisiana corporate income tax is calculated on what is known as a "separate entity" basis. The tax for each corporation is calculated separately, regardless of its corporate affiliations or whether they are part of a consolidated return for federal tax purposes. As in most states, the starting point is federal gross income as reported on the federal corporate return. There are then a series of state adjustments. Unlike most states, Louisiana allows a deduction for federal taxes.

Certain items of the tax base (e.g., rents or royalties) are specifically allocated to Louisiana or to other states. The remainder of the tax base is apportioned to Louisiana, using specified apportionment factors. Air, pipeline, and other transportation all have their own apportionment factors. Manufacturing and merchandising corporations apportion income to Louisiana using a single factor determined by the fraction of sales into Louisiana over total sales. Service corporations use the average of a sales and payroll factor. All other corporations use a three-factor formula based on the average of the Louisiana share of payroll, property, and sales. However, under a 2012 law the Louisiana Department of Economic Development can provide the option for a single sales factor to corporations that sell more than 50 percent outside the state and meet certain other criteria.

The top corporate tax rate is 8 percent, which exceeds the top personal tax rate of 6 percent. By national standards this is a high headline or nominal rate—of states with corporate income taxes, it ties with Massachusetts for the fifteenth highest rate. While the deductibility of federal taxes reduces the effective tax rate on some new investments, the high nominal rate does have important effects in discouraging economic activity. First, there simply is the fact that the high nominal rate may deter businesses who do not carefully analyze all the provisions of the Louisiana corporation tax before making their economic decisions. They may be deterred by the appearance of a high rate. Second, the high nominal rate discourages companies from shifting some existing economic activity to Louisiana from another state. For example, corporations can rearrange their affairs to shift income from existing activity from one state to another (e.g., income from intangibles). In this case, the high nominal tax rate may also become a high effective rate, depending on the federal taxes paid on that income. Conversely, corporations have an incentive to shift income away from Louisiana to other states to take advantage of their low corporate rates.

These considerations lead to our second recommendation—*eliminate the deduction for federal taxes and lower the rates for corporate taxation.* Not only will this address the perception and income-shifting problems, but it will also make Louisiana's revenue structure less vulnerable to changes in the federal taxation that, through deductibility, would affect Louisiana tax collections. Finally, eliminating deductibility would also simplify reporting and auditing for corporate taxation. Corporations who file as part of a federal consolidated group must develop specific measures for each corporation's federal taxes, which is often the subject of audits and adjustments and adds to the complexity of the tax. Eliminating federal deductibility for either corporate or individual taxpayers would require a constitutional amendment. This might be feasible if coupled with a foreseeable rate reduction for taxpayers.

Corporations that have negative taxable income are sometimes allowed by states to "carryback" those losses to offset tax liability in prior years. This is a form of "income averaging" for corporations. In the 2015 session, Louisiana changed a prior statute that allowed a three year carryback period for corporate losses. Only two other states have three-year carryback periods; all others have shorter periods, while a large number of states disallow carrybacks altogether. The new legislation removes all carrybacks but extends the carry forward period to twenty years. We recommend maintaining this provision into the future.

Facing the Challenges of Separate-Entity Corporate Taxation

Separate-entity corporation taxes like Louisiana's face particular challenges in dealing with appropriately taxing income from intangibles and other passive income that is truly earned within the state but reported elsewhere for tax purposes. To understand this issue, it is useful to consider an example. Suppose a national retailer has a trademark (e.g., a giraffe) that is used in all its stores, including Louisiana. The retailer sets up a corporation in Delaware to hold this trademark and charges royalties to all its stores nationwide for the use of this trademark. A store in Louisiana will deduct these royalty payments from its revenues and reduce its tax base. The royalty payment will be received in Delaware, which by its law does not tax these receipts. From the point of view of the taxpayer, total state tax payments are reduced, but the state with the stores will have a reduction in their corporate tax base.

Louisiana would contend, however, that the royalty payments from sales in stores located in the state are Louisiana source income and should be taxed by the state. The intangible asset (the giraffe trademark) is being exploited within the state, regardless of where its formal ownership lies. This argument is precisely the same one that the US government uses for sourcing royalty or trademark payments—the source is where the intangible is exploited for commercial purposes. However, given Louisiana's separate-entity corporate tax structure, which respects corporate boundaries, how can it reach this royalty income, or other passive income, which is reported and booked within a separate entity in another state?

These challenges appear to be significant for Louisiana. In 2015, the Louisiana Department of Revenue issued a report from its "LDR Audit Intelligence" unit that analyzed corporate tax returns for 2011 and 2012. Their findings suggested that Louisiana revenues may suffer from its separate entity approach. For example, in 2012, their analysis indicated that "only 25 percent of the largest companies in Louisiana reported taxable income even though 96 percent of those affiliated with groups that publically report financial information are profitable."[1] These findings are far from definitive. Financial reporting and tax reporting can differ substantially, and it also appears that the analysis looked at corporations after they had taken their allowable credits, for example, the inventory credit. Nonetheless, the Department of Revenue research does suggest that there may be severe difficulties with Louisiana's separate-entity approach to corporate taxation.

There are three solutions that separate-entity states can adopt to avoid the depletion of their tax base through the loss of passive income to out-of-state entities. The first approach, which Louisiana historically had taken, was to assert a theory of "economic nexus" and claim jurisdiction to tax the out-of-state passive investment company. This is the strategy first adopted in South Carolina in the *Geoffrey* case to deal with precisely the facts outlined above: the giraffe trademark belonged to Toys "R" Us, it was held in a Delaware company, and royalty payments were deducted from the Toys "R" Us stores in South Carolina. The state asserted that it had nexus over the holding company and could tax the royalty income, despite the minimal physical presence the trademark had in the state. It prevailed in court. The taxpayers in this case and many similar ones have tried to have them adjudicated by the US Supreme Court, but the Supreme Court has repeatedly chosen not to hear these types of cases. The Supreme Court has effectively taken a different standard for income taxes versus sales taxes. In the sales tax context, the Supreme Court in its *Quill* ruling required physical presence of a taxpayer as a prerequisite for a state requiring that it collect use tax from out-of-state vendors. However, in the income tax arena, the Supreme Court has been silent on this issue.

Louisiana had followed this model and had been successful in its economic nexus claims in its own courts. It prevailed in a similar *Geoffrey* case in 2008, in *Gap (Apparel)* in 2004, and also with respect to Real Estate Investment Trusts (REITs) with *AutoZone Properties* in 2004. In all these cases, the state has asserted that intangibles used within the state generate Louisiana source income and are subject to the Louisiana corporation tax.

Other separate-entity states, particularly in the Southeast, use "add-back statutes" to address the passive investment issue. In the Special Session in 2016, the Louisiana legislature enacted its own add-back statute effective for 2017. Add-backs are statutes that essentially eliminate intercompany transactions as deductions from the corporate tax base within a state. Although states differ in their precise rules, the most extensive add-backs include royalties, intangible-related interest, intercompany interest, and management fees. Currently twelve states have statutes at least this broad, and many more have narrower statutes.[2] The MTC has developed a model add-back statute for state use.

The advantages of using add-back statutes over simply asserting economic nexus are twofold. First, add-back statutes provide more stability for the taxpayer and the state. Since add-back statutes are explicit laws that often have accompanying regulations, taxpayers can more effectively anticipate their tax liabilities. Since the Louisiana law (47:287.480) allows the secretary broad authority to reallocate income among related entities to "clearly reflect income," a statute and accompanying regulations would bring more certainty to taxpayers. The state, moreover, can provide better guidance to its auditors and not risk its tax base on the outcome of unpredictable judicial decisions. Second, from the state's point of view, add-back statutes can be designed to reach new and evolving types of passive income, whereas assertion of economic nexus will often require an extensive litigation process and will be subject to the particularities of the cases that are examined.

There are naturally complex issues involved in managing and administering add-back statutes, but this is true of virtually all corporate tax statutes. Even tax lawyers who find the statutes in many cases to be ambiguous have noted the paucity of legal challenges to them.[3]

The most ambitious way to deal with passive investment issues is to adopt combined reporting. Under combined reporting statutes, corporations are taxed based on their apportioned share of income of their "unitary group." Corporations are combined into a unitary group under a variety of criteria, including common ownership, common management, and operating in the same line of business. Combined reporting solves the "Geoffrey problem" because the holding company and the operating companies are part of a unitary group in which intercompany transactions are eliminated. A state will apportion the entire unitary group, using a combined return to determine its share of its tax base.

Combined reporting has long been used in states with strong affiliations to the MTC, such as California, and this method now covers roughly half of the states. It is employed less frequently in the southeastern states which, as noted, tend to use add-back statutes instead of combined reporting. Combined reporting has been recommended and discussed specifically for Louisiana.[4] The primary advantage of moving towards combined reporting is that it automatically handles the issues addressed in add-back statutes without having to anticipate them in specific situations. It is generally acknowledged as being the best backstop or safeguard for a state against corporate tax strategies to shift income to other locations.

The primary drawback for combined reporting is that it increases administrative costs and complexities. Louisiana would have to train an entire generation of auditors to understand the mechanics and complexities of combined reporting, as well as the difficult issues involved in determining a unitary group. While there are resources available for this training and the required enhanced education, there is no question that it would entail a major reorientation of the audit department. There are also many technical issues that need to be addressed with combined reporting. Even states that have used it consistently must deal with thorny issues, such as defining the scope of a unitary business or the nature of the apportionment factors in diverse businesses. It would also make Louisiana stand out among its southeastern counterparts, who generally do not have combined reporting regimes. The one primary exception is Texas, which uses combined reporting for its margin tax.

In the long run, we believe that Louisiana should transition to combined reporting. This may take several years to implement. In the short run, Louisiana has taken a step in the right direction by enacting the add-back statute effective in 2017. This leads to our third recommendation: *plan to implement combined reporting while using the existing add-back statute during the interim period.* We recommend that the Department of Revenue begin to prepare a plan for implementing combined reporting, including research into its fiscal impact. In the long run, there is really no substitute for combined reporting.

Apportionment Issues

The next set of issues for the corporate income tax deal with apportionment. Under the law in effect through 2016, single factor sales apportionment was available to manufacturing and merchandising corporations as well as corporations with out-of-state sales exceeding 50 percent, meeting certain other criteria, and receiving the approval of the Louisiana Department of Development. However, in the 2016 Second Special Session the legislature extended the single sales factor to all industries except for oil and gas, which now has a four-factor formula.

As we discussed with respect to the franchise tax, a corporation effectively pays a tax on its factors—for example, using additional property in the state has the effect of a tax on property. We do not want to discourage the use of labor or property within the state, and removing them from the apportionment formula would prevent this. Furthermore, this change to a single sales tax factor has two additional benefits for businesses operating in Louisiana. First, some of the burden of a tax on the sales factor may be shifted to ultimate consumers; second, it shifts some of the tax burden to corporations operating outside of Louisiana.

Taxation of services under the state corporate income tax in the United States faces special challenges and is undergoing significant change. The key issue has to do with how the sales factor for apportionment is defined and measured. Under the rules in the Uniform Division for Income Tax Purposes (UDITPA), which were adopted by many states, the sales factor was defined differently for tangible personal property than for services. For sales of tangible personal property, sales were assigned to the destination state, where the goods were delivered. For services, however, sales were assigned to states based on "cost of performance" or where the majority of the costs were incurred to produce the service. This is an "origin" as opposed to a "destination" method of assigning sales and is inconsistent with the notion of the sales factor reflecting the contribution of the "market state."

Many states, however, have now moved away from cost of performance to what has been called the "market sourcing" of sales, using a destination principle. For example, consider a national credit card company that has cards circulating inside the state but has its computers and operations located outside the state. Its cost of performance would be outside the state, but under market sourcing rules, there could be sales assigned to the state on the basis of the credit cards utilized for transactions within the state. For example, the share of total sales attributable to a state may be calculated by the fraction of total credit card transactions that are conducted within the state. There has been an active and ongoing debate in national organizations and among tax professionals about shifting towards market sourcing for services.[5] In some cases, there are complicated measurement issues. Nonetheless, the spirit of market sourcing seems most natural with the idea of using a sales factor to capture the contributions of the market state, as well as with trends in the increased use of the sales factor in corporate income taxation generally.

In the 2016 Second Special Session, the Louisiana legislature adopted market sourcing as part of the bill that implemented a single sales factor. Louisiana now joins a variety of states that in recent years have moved to market sourcing for services and have gone on to develop statutes and regulations. For example, Alabama adopted its statute effective in 2011 and promulgated regulations in 2013. In Massachusetts, market sourcing was implemented in 2014, and the state has also developed extensive regulations. The approach taken by Alabama and Massachusetts focuses on where a service is delivered. The MTC in 2014 adopted a market sourcing statute and is currently in the process of developing their own regulations, also focusing on where services are delivered. California has taken a slightly different approach, which focuses on where the benefits from a service are received. While Louisiana could adopt either approach in its regulation, we suggest that the Alabama-Massachusetts-MTC framework would be the easiest to implement.

Louisiana could adopt or modify the regulations used in other states and begin to implement market sourcing for services on an expedited basis. Having a clear regulatory framework is crucial for taxpayer understanding and compliance, particularly for complex business transactions. Our fourth major recommendation is for Louisiana to *move forward rapidly with regulations for market sourcing of services for the sales factor in the spirit of the MTC.*

Alternative Tax Bases?

Some tax experts have suggested that the base of the corporate tax should be expanded to other entities, with the goal of reducing the level of rates. The Louisiana corporate tax does not effectively impose taxation on S-Corporations or LLCs. S-Corporations are subject to the corporate income tax but are allowed to exclude a fraction of their income from taxation. This fraction of Louisiana net income that is excluded is based on the ratio of the shares owned by Louisiana residents over total outstanding shares. This provision was designed to provide pass-through treatment to Louisiana shareholders, mirroring the federal pass-through treatment for S-Corporations. As a practical matter, nonresident shareholders would typically choose to file as Louisiana residents to avoid the additional entity level tax. While the S-Corporation exclusion is labeled a "tax exemption" in official documents, it essentially provides federal pass-through treatment for these corporations, mirroring their federal treatment.

One alternative that has been suggested by some tax scholars is to recognize that all corporations and business entities use state services and so all exploit the economic base of the state for their profits.[6] These considerations would suggest moving to a statewide business tax. It would have the advantages of a broader tax base and would not discriminate against businesses based on their organizational form. With the federal check-the-box rules, many businesses have the flexibility to choose whether to be taxed as a corporation or a pass-through entity. Thus there are no hard-and-fast economic lines separating these entities.

A less extreme proposal than implementing a uniform business tax would be to tax pass-through entities at a lower rate. This tax would capture the benefits the state provides to the pass-through organizations but subject them to lower levels of taxation. This might be justified because shareholders of C-Corporations only pay personal taxes when dividends are paid or shares are sold, while owners of pass-through entities are taxed as income is earned.

Despite the potential merits of such proposals, it would put Louisiana out of line with its competitors. While some states impose fees for the use of LLCs or S-Corporations, full-blown taxation of these entities is rare. Moreover, the basic premise of such a tax—that business entities use state services so should pay taxes—is hard to quantify, particularly as businesses pay other taxes, including property taxes. Since adoption of entity-level taxation for pass-through entities would be a relatively large structural change for the Louisiana tax system and make the state an outlier, we do not believe they would be viable options at this time.

Credits Taken against the Corporate and Franchise Taxes

As we discussed earlier in this chapter, one of the reasons that revenue raised from the corporate sector through the franchise tax and corporate tax is so low is the credits that can be taken against these taxes. While there are numerous credits, here we focus on the inventory tax credit and the motion picture tax credit. The latter is often taken against personal income taxes or simply paid back to the taxpayer, albeit at some cost for the transaction.

INVENTORY TAX CREDIT

The inventory tax credit is one of the largest state tax credits, totaling $427 billion for 2013. The credit was originally introduced as an alternative to exempting inventory from the property tax base. By law, inventories are considered a form of personal property, and so their value is included in the property tax base at 15 percent of market value, the same rate as other personal property and commercial improvements. For competitive reasons, the legislature wished to eliminate the tax burden on inventory. Since a state requirement to remove inventories from parish tax rolls would lead to a significant reduction in local property tax revenue, the legislature decided to allow local governments to continue to include inventory in the property tax base, but allow businesses to take a full dollar-for-dollar credit against any payments made for property taxes levied on inventories.

According to the Tax Foundation, only eleven states, mostly in the South, include inventories in their property tax base. Despite its inventory tax credit, Louisiana is counted by the Tax Foundation as taxing inventories. While inventories contribute to personal property and so are, in principle, subject to property taxation, the majority of states do exempt them from the property tax base. Broadly, states exempt inventories for economic development reasons and to encourage retail outlets and warehousing, although in Louisiana large refinery and manufacturing operations report very large inventories. In principle, there are legitimate economic reasons for phasing out inventories from the property tax base. However, with the other exemptions from the property tax base—the homestead and industrial property tax exemptions—many local governments would suffer significant revenue losses from excluding inventories from their property tax base, or other properties would have to pick up a larger share of the local tax burden.

One difficulty with the current system is that local government and business taxpayers have a common interest in classifying property as inventory, and business has no reason to contest the valuation of its inventories. There is no effective monitoring of the classification or valuation of inventory. If a local government classifies personal property as inventory, it will collect additional revenue (as inventories are not subject to depreciation), while business taxpayers will experience a reduction in their total tax bill because of the inventory credit. This reduction in the total tax bill comes at the expense of the State of Louisiana. Further, business taxpayers in a local jurisdiction are not hurt if their local governments overvalue their inventory. In that case, taxpayers are held harmless as the increase in their property tax is offset by the inventory credit, but local governments gain revenue from higher valuations. As a natural consequence of these incentives, the value of inventories tends to grow over time faster than dictated by normal economic growth. It is the State of Louisiana that bears the revenue loss from the inventory tax credit.

Recognizing this fact and also seeking a source of short-term revenue, the Louisiana legislature in 2015 enacted a law that reduced the refundable nature of the inventory tax credit by 25 percent for those businesses with an aggregate inventory tax liability to all political subdivisions equal to or in excess of $10,000. The remaining 75 percent of the credit that exceeds the taxpayer's liability for the taxable year is refundable. The nonrefundable 25 percent of the credit may be carried forward for up to five years. Further changes on refundability were put into effect in legislative sessions in 2016.

In the interim, we believe this is a reasonable approach. However, this approach also effectively imposes taxes on inventories, which ideally should not be taxed. A better approach would be to find an alternative revenue source for local governments and eliminate the taxes on inventories altogether. We discuss some alternative approaches in Chapter 10 on property taxation.

MOTION PICTURE TAX CREDIT

Until this Legislative session, Louisiana's motion picture investor tax credit (film credit) provided a 30 percent transferable tax credit on total in-state expenditures, including resident and nonresident labor, with no cap, subject to a $300,000 minimum expenditure. The credits can offset personal or corporate tax liability, be sold or transferred to third parties, or be sold back to the state for 85 percent of face value. For productions using in-state labor, there is an additional 5 percent payroll tax credit. In 2013, Louisiana awarded approximately $250 million in credits.

Facing a revenue shortfall and recognizing that the program needed some limits, the legislature enacted some limitation on the credit, beginning July 1, 2015. It is now capped at $180 million annually. Any single state-certified production cannot claim credits greater than $30 million. Since these limitations have been enacted very recently, it is too early to assess their impacts.

There have been a number of formal and informal analyses of the motion picture investment credit, including those commissioned by the Louisiana Economic Development Agency. A fair reading of this literature suggests the following four points:

1. *The credit has been successful in attracting production of films to Louisiana and generating local economic activity.* Louisiana has become a leader in film production. While the benefits of this job creation have accrued to many areas of the states, it is highly concentrated in a few areas, such as New Orleans.
2. *The credit has cost the state considerable revenue, even after allowing for offsets due to the generation of new economic activity.* The most recent study from the Louisiana Economic Development Agency pegged the budgetary cost for 2012 at approximately $170 million,

while allowing for roughly a 33 percent offset from increased activity. We do not typically measure these types of offsets for regular state spending programs, such as those on infrastructure, education, or health. Moreover, there are no effective limits on the budgetary cost to the state—it is totally dependent on the utilization of the credit.

3. *There is no natural ending point to the subsidization of the film industry.* While there has been some infrastructure development, most observers believe that the level of film production we have witnessed in Louisiana is contingent upon the program continuing. These same observers expect that North Carolina, which recently sharply restricted its program, will experience a much lower level of production activity. The film credit cannot be justified as an "infant industry" that will no longer need subsidies in the future.

4. *Although the program is structured as providing tax credits, it really has nothing to do with taxes and is effectively a subsidy program to the industry.* Film production is not deterred from locating in Louisiana because of high personal or corporate tax rates. Tax credits are simply a vehicle to transfer benefits. Fully transferable tax credits are effectively equivalent to a subsidy program. The only difference is that there may be some transaction costs in selling the credits to third parties or receiving a reduced amount by returning them to the state.

These four points can be summarized simply. *The film tax credit should be viewed as an ongoing spending program that provides some benefits to the state.* As such, it should be treated by the legislature on par with other spending programs.

Viewing the film program as a spending program means explicitly weighing its benefits and costs against other worthwhile state programs. How does spending an additional dollar attracting production of films to Louisiana compare to spending an additional dollar on infrastructure or education? It also means applying the same type of analysis to the film tax credit as to other programs. When the legislature considers a major infrastructure program, it does not reduce its budgetary cost by "offsets" from the additional job creation or sales that the program would generate. That is not to say that increased infrastructure spending does not produce more jobs and eventually more revenue for the state. However, it is not appropriate to use one measuring rod for traditional spending programs and another, more favorable one for spending programs in the guise of tax incentives.

The second component to our proposal is to place caps on the expenditures for the program and not leave it as an open-ended entitlement. We believe that this is an irresponsible budgeting practice for the state. In 2015, the legislature did put limits in place for several years. However, the backlog of past claims will still cost the same revenue over for the next several years. In future years, the legislature can determine how much activity it wants to subsidize and, if resources become limited, what types of activity it wishes to subsidize. It will require careful thought to structure a program that the state can afford and that meets the broader needs of its residents. This is an appropriate role for the legislature.

Summary of Recommendations

We have made a number of important recommendations for the franchise and corporate tax. Here is a brief summary of our key points:

1. Phase out the franchise tax in a fiscally responsible manner. This will involve reforming and tightening the rules for corporate taxation.
2. Eliminate the deduction for federal taxes and lower the rates for corporate taxation. While this will require a constitutional change, it will provide stability to Louisiana revenue streams and improve our competitive posture.
3. Plan to implement combined reporting while relying on the newly enacted add-back statute during the interim period. Louisiana needs to transition from its current separate-entity corporate tax system, which is vulnerable to tax planning.
4. Now that Louisiana has adopted market sourcing for the sales factor for services, it should quickly move forward with developing regulations along the lines of Alabama, Massachusetts, and the MTC with the focus on where services are delivered. Once this is in place, Louisiana will be able to obtain its fair share of corporate income from service companies.

In addition, we recommend that the legislature continue its focus on credits taken against corporate and personal taxes. With respect to the inventory tax, the current 25 percent suspension of refundability and other changes give the legislature time to craft a new solution that ideally would eliminate the local property tax on inventory and find a suitable substitute for local governments. The current limitations on the movie credit will need to be evaluated and adjusted in light of the budget and desires for economic development. Careful thought must be given to developing a program with limited costs that is also effective.

Notes

1. LDR Audit Intelligence, CIFT Analysis of Top Corporations by Revenue, 2015, p. 3. Document available from the authors.

2. William Fox, "Comments on Louisiana Fiscal Structure, 2014," p. 11.

3. Borens, Michele, and Jessica Kerner, "20 Years of Ambiguity in Addback Statutes," *State Tax Notes*, October 28, 2013, pp. 263–67.

4. McIntyre, Michael, Paull Mines, and Richard Pomp, "Designing a Combined Reporting Regime for a State Corporate Income Tax: A Case Study of Louisiana," 61 *Louisiana Law Review* 699 (2001).

5. See, for example, Richard Pomp, "Report of the Hearing Officer, Multistate Tax Compact IV (UDITPA), Proposed Amendments," October 25, 2013.

6. See, for example, Zodrow, "The Louisiana Tax System: Potential Directions for Reform," June 2014.

8

MINERAL REVENUES IN LOUISIANA

Greg Upton

Introduction

For much of Louisiana's history, mineral revenues have made up a significant share of the state's income. This chapter provides an overview of how these mineral revenues are generated in Louisiana, with a focus on severance taxes and royalty receipts. It also describes the history of mineral revenues and the importance of these revenues in funding state government. Finally, it proposes alternative ways of collecting mineral revenues and makes recommendations on future policies.

In 1981 mineral revenues, meaning severance taxes on oil and natural gas and royalties from state-owned lands, made up close to 45 percent of revenues received by the state of Louisiana. By 2015, mineral revenues made up about 10 percent of the state's revenue collections and varied dramatically with the movement of oil and natural gas prices. During the current low price environment, fiscal year 2017 mineral revenues are projected to make up less than 5 percent of total state revenues.

Mineral revenue is primarily composed of severance taxes and royalty receipts from the extraction of crude oil and natural gas from private and public lands and water bottoms in the state's jurisdiction. Thus, production in federal waters, roughly greater than three miles from shore, is not considered in the state's taxing jurisdiction and does not directly generate revenue for the state based on severance tax collections or royalties and lease payments.[1] Royalty receipts are not actually tax receipts but are the value of the state's share of production from lands and water bottoms that the state owns, less any severance taxes to be paid by the private producer on the state's share of the production. Likewise, relatively small amounts of bonus payments paid to obtain the rights to drill on state lands and water bottoms, and lease payments made to maintain those rights, are included as mineral revenue but are not actually tax receipts.

Production from privately and publically owned lands and water bot-toms is subject to the state severance tax, and in fiscal year 2016 made up 65 percent of total mineral revenue, with royalty receipts and other lease payments making up just over 33 percent of mineral revenues. A relatively small amount of severance tax, about 2 percent, is generated from timber production and from various other natural resources, such as lignite, shell, and gravel. The story of mineral revenue in Louisiana, therefore, is the story of oil and natural gas production trends and energy price movements.

Overview of Current Mineral Revenue Structure

When a company wants to drill on state lands or in state waters, the com-pany must initiate a contract with the state in order to obtain the rights to do so. At the onset of the contract, a bonus payment is made to compensate the state for the right to drill on the land. This payment will occur regard-less of whether any oil or gas is ever extracted from the land. If production occurs in the future, then the state will collect a prenegotiated percentage of the value of the production. This is known as mineral royalty payments and is negotiated on a contract-by-contract basis. These royalty rates will vary with the short-term and long-term energy markets and may vary with other dimensions of the contractual offer, such as the size of the bonus.[2] Royalty payments are adjusted by the weighted severance tax associated with the state's share of the production. If no drilling occurs on the land within a specified amount of time, rental payments will be made to the state. Bo-nuses and rental payments make up a very small share of the state's mineral revenues and are therefore not the focus of this study.

Severance tax in Louisiana on crude oil is 12.5 percent of the value of the oil as it leaves the ground for most oil wells;[3] oil wells that are defined as in-capable wells, i.e., those unable to produce on average more than 25 barrels per day during the entire month and also those producing at least 50 per-cent salt water per day, are taxed at 6.250 percent, and oil wells defined as stripper wells (producing on average less that 10 barrels per day) are taxed at 3.125 percent.[4] The average tax rate is approximately 12 percent. These tax rates were instituted in 1974.[5] Prior to 1974, oil severance taxes were based on a volumetric charge that did not systematically vary with changes in the price of crude oil.[6] Figure 8.1 shows an overview of major changes to sever-ance tax rates for oil and gas over Louisiana's history.

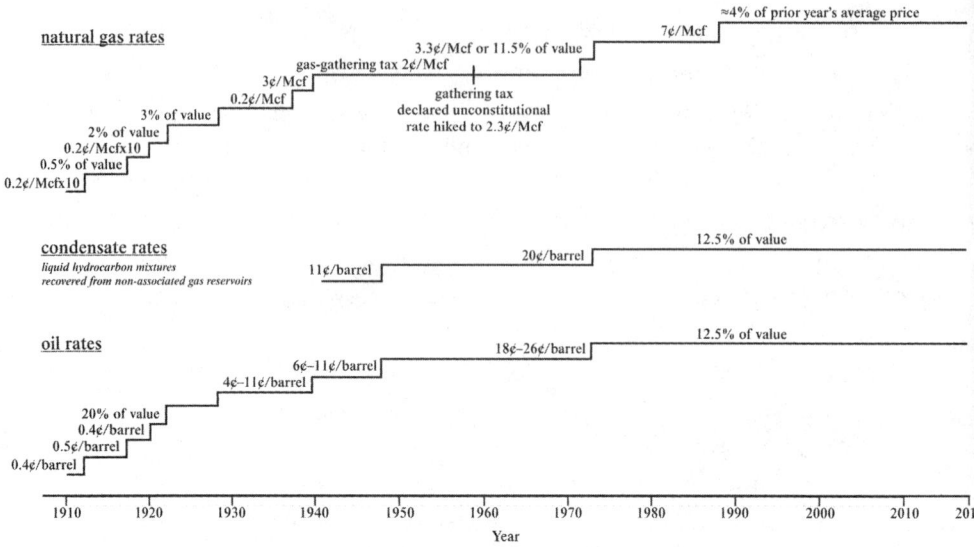

FIGURE 8.1. Louisiana Severance Tax Rates: 1910–2017

Natural gas is taxed on a volume basis but with the tax rate indexed to changes in the price of natural gas. The tax on natural gas was 7 cents per thousand cubic feet (Mcf) from 1974 through 1989—this volumetric tax was not a function of the price of natural gas. It was then indexed to the price of natural gas in 1990, and the tax rate has moved with the price of natural gas, though with a lag. The actual tax rate per year is illustrated in Table 7.1 since the change in the natural gas tax structure in 1990. The rate peaked in 2006 at 37.3 cents per Mcf, dropped to between 25 and 30 cents per Mcf from 2007 to 2008, and then peaked again in 2009 when it jumped to over 30 cents per Mcf. The natural gas tax rate then fell quite dramatically to almost half of its 2009 value in 2010 to 2012. The natural gas rate from July 1, 2015, through June 30, 2016, was set at 15.8 cents per Mcf, slightly higher than the 15.5 cents per Mcf from July 2014 through June 2015.[7] This rate dropped in fiscal year 2017 to 9.8 cents per Mcf and is projected to be 11.7 cents per Mcf in fiscal years 2018 and 2019.[8]

As can be seen in Figure 8.2, the severance tax rate itself varies from year to year, as the price changes in real time, but the tax rate is based on the previous year's price level. Therefore, in years where large changes in the price of natural gas are observed, this leads to large changes in the tax rate the following year. While the average natural gas tax rate since 1991 was 3.98 per-

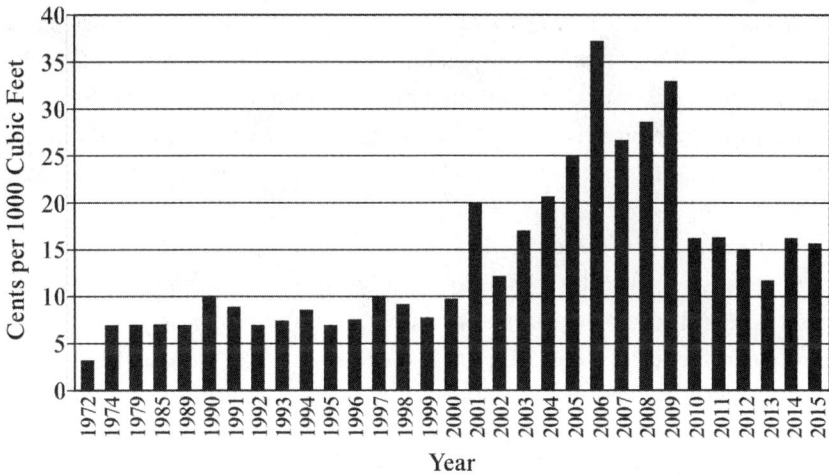

FIGURE 8.2. Natural Gas Tax Rates

cent, the tax rate varied from less than 2.5 percent to more than 8 percent.

Also noticeable is the difference in the tax rate between crude oil and natural gas. Crude oil is taxed at 12.5 percent, while natural gas is taxed at a much lower rate—averaging 3.98 percent over this time period. As is discussed later, this is not common, as many other major oil- and gas-producing states tax oil and natural gas at the same rate. In contrast, Texas taxes natural gas at a higher rate than crude oil, 7.5 percent for the market value of natural gas, compared to 4.6 percent for the market value of oil. Louisiana established its current oil and gas structure in 1974, with a minor adjustment in 1990. In the 1970s the federal government imposed price controls where oil and natural gas prices were constrained by the federal government for interstate gas but not for intrastate gas. The Louisiana tax policy tried to accommodate for the different federal policy with respect to oil and gas pricing. The adjustment in the taxation of natural gas came in 1990 after oil and natural gas prices had been deregulated.

History of Mineral Revenues in Louisiana

Severance tax and royalty receipts for Louisiana are provided in Figure 8.3. Mineral revenues have exhibited considerable variation since fiscal year 1973, when revenues amounted to $400 million. They steadily increased and maintained an average of approximately $650 million through fiscal year 1980, before increasing dramatically to $1.4 billion in fiscal year 1982. Mineral revenues began a consistent decline through fiscal year 1987 before maintaining a relatively more stable figure between $600 and $800 million. Starting in fiscal year 1999, mineral revenues began to increase from around $400 million to a peak of $1.8 billion in fiscal year 2007. Similar to the 1980s, revenues quickly dropped, and for the time period between fiscal year 2008 and fiscal year 2014 this revenue figure averaged $1.3 billion. In fiscal year 2016 mineral revenues dropped to $568.8 million or only 45 percent of the average mineral revenues from fiscal year 2008 through fiscal year 2014.

Through the present, mineral revenues have continued their downward trend, with the price of oil dropping from an average of $73.15 per barrel in fiscal 2015 to an average of less than $50 per barrel in fiscal 2016, and projections for 2017 range from $50 to $60 per barrel. While some analysis projects that oil prices will climb back toward the $60 to $70 per barrel benchmark,[9] the price projections are still quite soft. Specific events have pushed the price upward, such as a fire in Canada that slowed down production in that region of the world; potential disruptions in Nigeria; continued uncertainty about production in Iran and Iraq; and the efforts of OPEC to establish control over oil production. The success of shale production in the United States, though, has seemed to outweigh any of these factors in the intermediate term. There will always be unexpected developments, such as

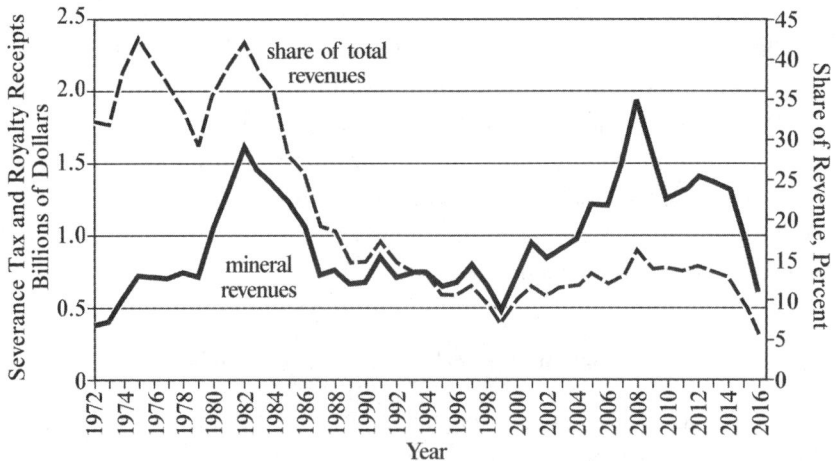

FIGURE 8.3. Severance Tax and Royalty Receipts: Collections and Share of State Revenues

the fire in a major field in Canada that may affect the price of oil and gas in the short run, but, in the long run, the price will be subject to market forces.

Variation in mineral revenues is largely associated with variation in the price of oil and natural gas. Production tends to follow well-known patterns of rapid rise as fields are exploited to extract the easiest volumes first, and then a peak production point, followed by a long secular decline reflecting a mature production region. Dramatic reversals of this typical production pattern can occur as a result of new technologies, such as what the combination of 3-D seismic, horizontal drilling, and hydraulic fracturing has done for natural gas production in Louisiana in recent years, and for oil and gas production in other areas of the country. As an example, natural gas production from horizontal drilling within the Haynesville Shale created a boom in natural gas production but did not create a demonstrable increase in state revenues, since the companies had a legislative act passed in 1994 that sheltered their receipts for the full cost of the drilling of the well or until two years had elapsed.

Figure 8.3 also shows mineral revenues as a percentage of total state revenue. During the revenue history discussed here, production has been on a long secular decline, with the exception of the horizontal gas boom since 2008. Thus, the variation in mineral revenue share is mainly due to the variation in mineral prices, largely oil prices, but also natural gas prices related to production on state-owned lands, over this history. High and volatile prices in the 1970s were associated with large and volatile mineral revenue shares. Then the oil price collapses of the 1980s and fairly low prices all through the 1990s dramatically reduced the mineral share, ultimately to a low of about 9 percent by the end of the decade. As prices began to climb again, especially from around 2003 to mid-2008, the mineral revenue share grew as well, peaking at 15 percent in 2008 as prices spiked to nearly $150/bbl for oil and $10/Mcf for gas. Since then, the share was relatively stable at 12–13 percent, reflecting stable oil and gas prices and the flatter tail end of the taxable production curve, until 2015 and thereafter given the major drop in oil prices.

At this point it is warranted to point out that since the summer of 2014 oil prices have dropped dramatically, from the $100/bbl range to the mid-$40s/bbl as of the late summer and early fall of 2015. And as we entered 2016 oil prices were below $30 per barrel before coming back up to around $40 per barrel near mid-2016, having a substantial impact on mineral revenues and affecting employment in the oil and gas industry in Louisiana. In 2017 oil prices had bounced back and stayed near the mid-$40 range. Natural gas prices have also fallen from the $3.50/Mcf–$4.00/Mcf range to $2.50/Mcf–$3.00/Mcf range. This has resulted in the sharp drop in total mineral revenue receipts and share of total revenue that is depicted at the far right end of Figures 8.3 and 8.4, and further underscores the dominance of price in determining the state's mineral revenue receipts.

Increased production will occur if new technology enhances production in the Tuscaloosa Marine Shale (TMS) or new methods of increasing production from aging wells become effective.[10] So far, the oil production volumes from the TMS formation have been very small, typically less than 1 percent of total state oil production in any month. Thus, for the foreseeable future, prices are likely to be the driver in terms of increases and decreases in oil and gas revenues. And with the lower prices, activity in the TMS formation is likely to be slow. Shale production in northwest Louisiana created a boom in the production of natural gas; however, there is no reason to expect a similar boom in the production of oil given current prices.

In order to understand the underlying reasons for these changes in revenues, next we examine the trends in both production as well as crude oil and natural gas prices. Figure 8.4 illustrates state production of both crude oil and natural gas since 1945. Oil and gas production experienced steady

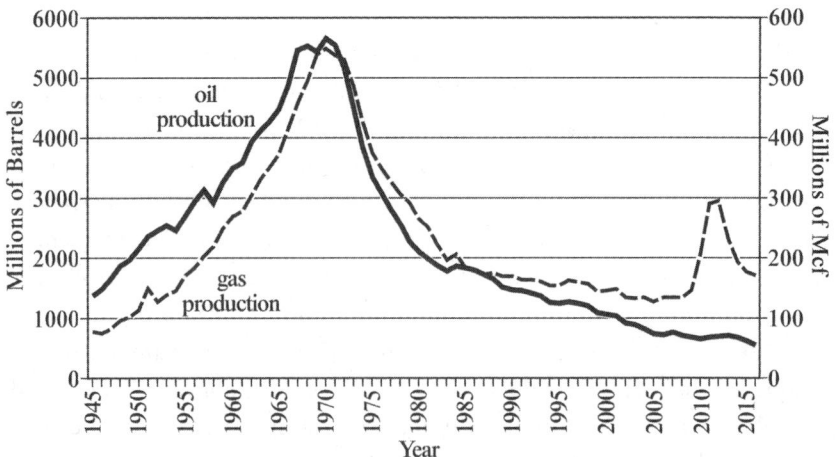

FIGURE 8.4. Louisiana Oil and Natural Gas Production

increases for more than a quarter of a century—from 1945 to the early 1970s. These steady increases ended in 1970—the year that Louisiana saw its highest levels of both crude oil and natural gas production in the state's history. For the next three-plus decades, this trend reversed itself, and both crude oil and gas production declined steadily. This steady decline is a common characteristic of a maturing basin and has been observed in other oil- and gas-producing states.

Comparing production in Figure 8.4 to the historic mineral revenues presented in Figure 8.3, it is apparent that the two do not track each other closely. The large increase in mineral revenues observed from 1979 to 1982 was associated with a decrease in both oil and gas production each year during this time period. By the time mineral revenues peaked in 1982 at more than $1.4 billion, crude oil and natural gas production was approximately 60 percent below the peak production experienced in 1970. We observed a similar pattern in the early 2000s. From 2000 to 2010, mineral revenues were up more than 75 percent, while crude oil production was down more than 35 percent, and natural gas production was relatively flat.

This comparison of oil and gas production also illustrates how technology can dramatically alter production. Oil and gas production in Louisiana followed a very similar trend for the past half century—both increasing steadily in the 1940s to 1960s, peaking in the early 1970s, and declining steadily since. This changed in 2009 when natural gas production increased drastically, while oil production continued along its past trend. This increase in natural gas production is due to the horizontal drilling activity in the Haynesville Shale formation of north Louisiana.[11] The Haynesville Shale is located in northwestern Louisiana, and essentially all of the increase in natural gas production seen in the state since 2008 is a result of this shale play. The Haynesville Shale, as well as other shale formations in Louisiana and Texas, is illustrated in Map 8.1.[12]

The early ramp-up of this new shale activity was accompanied by a more than doubling of gas prices from 2007 to mid-2008, which undoubtedly encouraged the leasing and initial drilling. Thus, it was a combination of sharp price increases occurring simultaneously with technological innovation that pushed natural gas production in Louisiana above its steady decline observed since the early 1970s.

Figure 8.5 shows the price of both oil and natural gas since the mid-1960s. As with state production of oil and gas, prices of oil and gas moved in

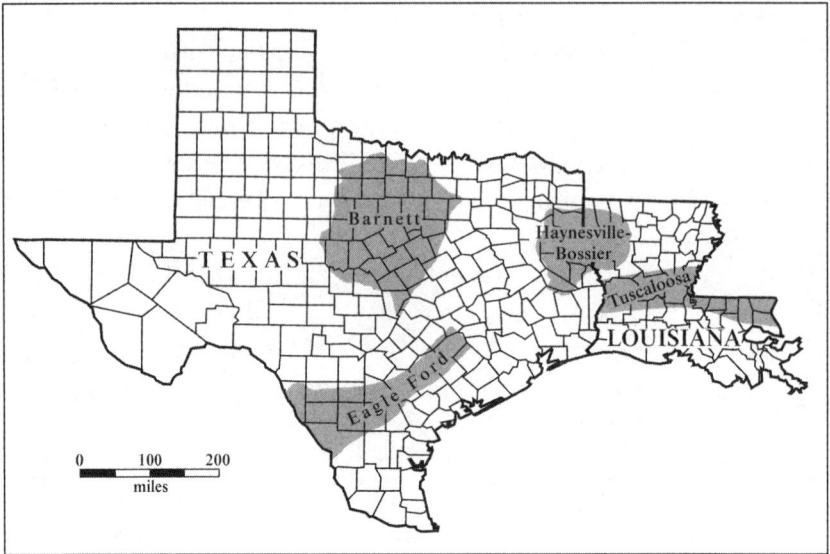

MAP 8.1. Louisiana and Texas Shale Plays

tandem over the past half-century. Prices for both oil and gas ultimately fell sharply as the 2008 recession took hold, but in 2009 a divergence of oil and gas prices was observed for the first time in history. This divergence is likely due to horizontal drilling technology that allowed for increases in natural gas production—not just in Louisiana—but also in other shale plays across the United States. By 2011 and 2012 production in Louisiana had peaked, and it has since fallen off some 22 percent from that peak point, likely due to the drop in natural gas prices. Up until 2008 the price of a barrel of oil was about 6 times the price of 1,000 cubic feet of natural gas. Since 2008 this ratio has changed dramatically being as high as the price of oil being 20 or more times the price of natural gas. This ratio is declining as the price of oil has dropped more substantially than the price of natural gas.

Interestingly, the dramatic increase in gas production observed over the past five years as illustrated in Figure 8.4 does not appear to have contributed much to direct state mineral revenue.[13] This production increase is the result of horizontal drilling techniques, which enjoyed a complete severance tax exemption for up to two years of their initial production.[14] While production experienced significant increase around 2010–2012, most of this increase was exempt from severance taxes. Whereas this tax exemption was

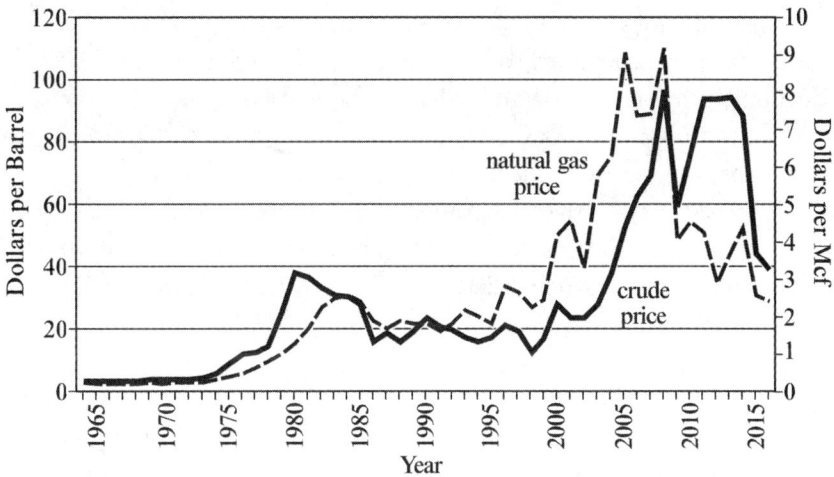

FIGURE 8.5. Oil and Natural Gas Prices

first enacted in 1994,[15] it finally became meaningful nearly fifteen years later, as drilling technology and rising gas prices combined to bring the Haynesville Shale formation online in a big way. There is a debate about the value of the exemption in terms of motivating the natural gas activity in northwest Louisiana, given the high price of natural gas in 2007 and 2008, but the horizontal exemption existed and it resulted in a reduction in severance tax revenues of over $1.1 billion from 2010 through 2014, assuming the exemption was not necessary to motivate the horizontal drilling activity.[16]

Wells in the Haynesville Shale formation deplete a large share of their total production early in their production lives, benefiting from a complete severance tax exemption during this early period. Once they are beyond their first twenty-four months of production they are subject to severance tax, but the state has foregone all severance tax value during the most prolific period of production. The severance tax value of the formation as a whole relies on the accumulation of many wells that are beyond their exemption period. This will occur over time, but is slowed down by the near halt in new drilling activity and reduced production levels likely caused by low gas prices over the past few years.

Figure 8.6 shows natural gas production alongside severance-taxed natural gas production. The amount of total production and the volume of gas that was subject to severance taxes tracked each other very closely over the past three decades until 2009, when the series began to diverge. This historic divergence coincided with the same time period when US shale production (including the Haynesville Shale here in Louisiana) was ramping up. For technical reasons, oil and gas producers gained the technology to extract natural gas economically from shale formations several years before crude oil (due to the relative density of the two hydrocarbons). Thus, when shale gas flooded the market, this produced a significant price drop both in absolute terms, as well as relative to oil. While oil markets experienced a similar phenomenon, the production-induced price drop lagged by several years.

Historically, the prices of crude oil and natural gas have been the major drivers in mineral revenues for the state. While prices will always play an important role, another major uncertainty is also on the horizon. For the last several decades, forecasting future production in Louisiana was a straightforward process, as production consistently followed a very smooth decline curve. As new shale technologies continue to improve, though, there is more uncertainty about future production in the state. If the price of natural gas increases and the cost of drilling horizontal wells continues to decline, will we again see a boom of natural gas production in the Haynesville Shale formation? Will the primarily oil shale play—the Tuscaloosa Marine

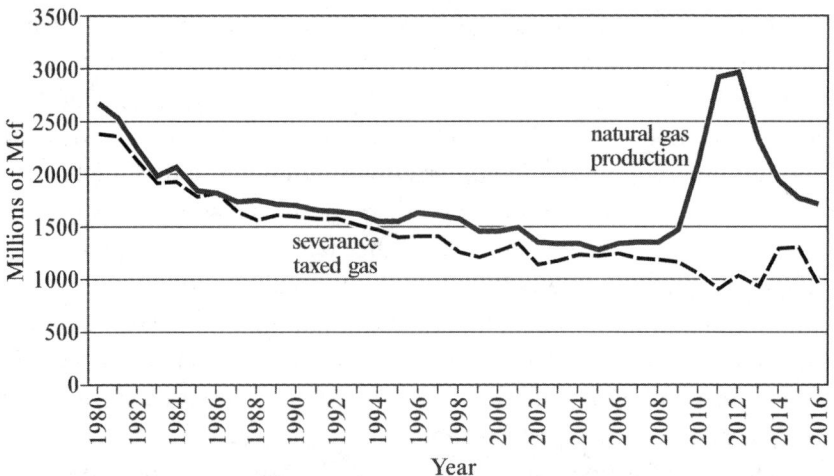

FIGURE 8.6. Natural Gas Production: Severance-Taxed Gas and Total Natural Gas Production

Shale—in central Louisiana and through southeast Louisiana see a similar boom once this resource is better understood?

Absent a breakthrough in technology that allows for the economic extraction of the Tuscaloosa Marine Shale, or significant increases in oil and natural gas prices, Louisiana oil and gas production will likely continue a downward to flat production trajectory in coming years. Further, as production from shale formations continues to experience cost reductions and new areas are discovered, prices are also expected to be relatively flat in coming years. While state policy makers might hope for a windfall in coming years, the reality is that mineral revenues cannot be counted on to provide the lion's share of the state's revenues as they did in the 1970s and early 1980s, nor can they be expected to assist the state in overcoming its revenue shortfalls in fiscal 2018 and beyond. To a certain extent, the question now is: Does a state oil and gas tax structure introduced in the 1970s under very different economic circumstances than we have today remain viable in the current time period?

While mineral tax policies have been largely consistent over time, as mentioned previously in this chapter, the most recent significant adjustment made was the creation of a tax exemption for horizontal drilling in 1994, an exemption that was not really used until 2008. This horizontal tax exemption is maintained as long as the price of oil is at or below $70 per barrel and the price of natural gas is at or below $4.50 per million BTU. From there the exemption decreases on a sliding scale until it disappears as the price of oil exceeds $110 per barrel and the price of natural gas exceeds $7.00 per million BTU. Given the current market for oil and gas, the projection is that the horizontal drilling exemption will continue at 100 percent in upcoming years.

This question of a total review of how oil and gas is taxed and possibly how it is used in funding the state budget requires an understanding of what other states are doing and what changes these states have made, if any, in the last several years.

Overview of Taxes in Other States

Thirty-six states impose some type of severance tax with thirty-one states levying a tax on the extraction of oil and gas from the ground.[17] The following six states received from 10.5 percent to 74.3 percent of their total state tax revenues from severance taxes: Alaska, Montana, New Mexico, North Dakota, Oklahoma, and Wyoming.[18] Severance taxation is not limited to the states that are typically defined as major producers of oil and gas. Combined horizontal drilling and sequential hydraulic fracturing in shale geological formations is now being carried out in a number of states that until recently have not been major oil and gas producers, with Pennsylvania at the forefront.

An overview of severance taxes and mineral rates in selected states is shown in Table 8.1. Every state, with the exception of California, has a severance tax on oil that is based on the value of the oil extracted from the ground. Severance taxes range from values as low as 2 percent to 15 percent in Alaska (and can be higher than 15 percent based on certain economic limit formulae). Louisiana has a high severance tax rate on oil at 12.5 percent, and it has a reduced rate for incapable wells and stripper wells that many other states do not enjoy. Also, Louisiana is a state that does not have an ad valorem tax on oil, just like Oklahoma and North Dakota.

Many of the states, including Alabama, California, Kansas, New Mexico, Oklahoma, and Wyoming, have the same severance tax rate for both crude oil and natural gas. Only two states have different rates for oil and gas—Texas and Louisiana. Texas taxes oil at a lower rate than natural gas, 4.6 percent and 7.5 percent, respectively. Louisiana, on the other hand, has a volumetric charge for gas that is based on the previous year's average natural gas price. As discussed previously, this rate averages to approximately 5 percent. Louisiana is the only state to tax natural gas at a lower rate than crude oil. Louisiana's severance tax structure was mainly created in the 1970s, in an entirely different economic environment (price controls on oil and interstate natural gas) than exists today.

As we compare severance tax rates across states, we see a rather significant variation, except that all of these states do levy a tax on oil and natural gas. A number of states have introduced special exemptions for horizontal drilling. Other states have not. Most states treat oil and natural gas similarly in terms of taxation, but Louisiana, Texas, and Alaska do not. Louisiana and Alaska tax oil more than they do natural gas, while Texas taxes natural gas more than it does oil. Some states, with Texas perhaps the most prominent, levy an ad valorem tax on oil and gas reserves, while many states, such as Louisiana, North Dakota, and Oklahoma, count the severance tax as an alternative to any ad valorem tax.

Revenues from oil and gas certainly are related to the tax rates, but perhaps more significantly to the natural endowment of oil and gas reserves in particular geographic areas and to the technology available to capture these reserves in a manner that is competitive in today's energy markets.

Louisiana is a mature oil and gas production area, and it does not have shale oil and gas exploration areas to the extent of the shale-rich areas in our neighbor, Texas. US oil production was less than 7 million barrels per day in 2007 just as the shale boom began. By 2013 US oil production was approaching 10 million barrels per day.[19] Louisiana's production in 2016 was 155,077 barrels of oil per day, not including the Gulf of Mexico Outer Continental Shelf (OCS). Production from the OCS was 1,503,234 barrels per day. In 1970 oil production in Louisiana was 1,408,402 barrels per day, while the Gulf of Mexico OCS production was 913,456 barrels per day.[20]

Other Potential Sources of Mineral Tax Revenues: Property Taxes and Salt Caverns

Louisiana's constitution explicitly forbids the state government or any local entity, including parishes or municipalities, from taxing underground oil and gas reserves as property. While property taxes are a significant source of revenue for parishes and municipalities in Louisiana, the state government does not collect any property taxes. Parishes and municipalities collect property tax, not only on the value of the land, but also the value of the assets on that land. Thus, some have made the argument that proved oil and gas reserves are also an asset associated with land and therefore should be treated as such for property tax purposes. While this is explicitly not allowed by the Louisiana constitution, this is also not a common practice in other states. In fact, there are only two states—Texas and California—that allow for oil and gas reserves to be taxed as property. While this does not raise tax revenues for the state per se, it does allow for an additional tool for revenue generation at the local level.

Potentially one of the reasons why very few states apply property taxes to oil and gas reserves is that it can incentivize producers to extract a resource at a faster rate.[21] If there is a known reserve in the ground that is being assessed a property tax based on the value of that reserve, then the firm is incentivized to extract the reserve as quickly as possible to avoid the tax. The impact of this activity on revenues will likely be positive in the short run,

TABLE 8.1. Comparison of Severance Taxes in Selected States

| State | Severance Tax Rate | | | Ad Valorem Tax on Oil and Gas Reserves |
	Oil	Natural Gas	Variation	
Alabama	3 to 10%	3 to 10%	Based on production of each well or depth or location	N.A.
Alaska	12.25% to 15.0% of value at point of production with economic limit factor	10.0% of gross value at point of production with economic limit factor	Economic limit factor leading to low tax rates for small, low productivity fields and higher rates for large, high productivity fields	20 mills on the appraised value of all oil and gas production and tangible property
California	$ per barrel of oil	$ per Mcf	Based on funds to support Division of Oil and Gas	Cities can levy severance tax
Kansas	4.33% of value	4.33% of value		3.37% rate for ad valorem taxes
Louisiana	12.5% of value of oil at wellhead except for smaller producing wells	$ per Mcf determined by changes in price of natural gas, but not less than 7 cents per Mcf	Horizontal drilling exemption for first two years of production or until cost of drilling has been covered whichever is less	No
New Mexico	3.75%	3.75%	Incentives for stripper wells; tax rate of 3.15% for oil and 4% for natural gas for schools	Tax is levied monthly on sale of all oil and natural gas
North Dakota	5% of gross value and oil extraction tax	$0.0555 per Mcf, varies with price of natural gas		Severance tax in lieu of property tax on oil and gas
Oklahoma	7%	7%	Horizontal wells get 2% tax rate for three years	Severance tax in lieu of ad valorem tax
Texas	4.6%	7.5%	Exemptions for enhanced oil recovery or high-cost gas wells	Ad valorem tax on oil and gas reserves
Wyoming	6%	6%		Varies by county

as faster extraction leads to increases in severance taxes in the short run in addition to the taxes that would be collected on the reserves. But in the long run, this might be detrimental to the state as (a) companies will have decreased incentives to search for oil and gas reserves, as this would lead to a tax liability before any benefit is received, and (b) the state's finite oil and gas resource will be depleted more quickly—and possibly less efficiently— thus having negative consequences in the long run.

The welfare effects of severance taxes and property taxes have been compared in the academic literature. Deadweight loss has been estimated to compare severance taxes to property taxes on exhaustible natural resources. Property taxes have been found to result in more than two times the deadweight loss than a severance tax.[22]

Louisiana is home to a number of large salt domes under the Earth's surface. These salt domes are naturally occurring and are the result of shallow seas that existed for more than tens of thousands of years. Salt domes are used commercially primarily through two means. First, a well can be drilled into the salt dome and fresh water pumped into the well. The salt dissolves into the water and a very high salt content water, called brine, is produced. This process is known as solution mining, and the brine extracted from this process is sold primarily for industrial uses. After the brine is mined from the salt dome, a salt cavern is left. There are currently more than four hundred salt caverns in twenty-eight salt domes in Louisiana.

The salt cavern left after the solution mining is completed can then be used to store natural gas. Natural gas usage is very seasonal in the United States, while production is relatively constant year round. During the summer, the extraction and refining of usable natural gas exceeds the demand by consumers, but during the winter, when natural gas is used for home heating, the natural gas demand exceeds the rate of production and refining. Therefore, storage of natural gas is necessary in order to meet customers' needs in the winter. The salt caverns can be used to store large quantities of natural gas during the summer, and then the gas is extracted when needed during the winter months.

In recent years, there has been controversy about the tax liability associated with owning land with a salt dome. In particular, two controversies have arisen: first, there is a distinction on ad valorem property taxes between "land" and "other property." Specifically, land is assessed at 10 percent of its market value, while property is assessed at 15 percent.[23] Tax assessors have argued that these salt caverns should be treated as an improvement for tax purposes and therefore be assessed at 15 percent of market value, while landowners have argued that the caverns are inseparable from the land, and therefore should be assessed at 10 percent of the market value.[24] The appropriate way to assess salt caverns is still being debated in Louisiana courtrooms.

The second controversy with taxing salt caverns has to do with taxing the well itself. Currently, only 40 percent of the cost of an oil and gas well is used as the assessed value for the purpose of ad valorem taxes, while 100 percent of the value is used to assess a "general business asset."[25] While historically the wells used to drill salt caverns have been assessed the same as any other oil and gas well, the appropriate assessment of these wells is also still being debated in Louisiana courtrooms.[26]

Both of these decisions will directly impact taxes associated with salt caverns at the local level and will potentially have an indirect impact on mineral taxes at the state level. Increased taxes on salt caverns can lead to a decrease in solution mining—which can lead to a decrease in mineral taxes at the state level. More importantly, though, the uncertainty associated with future tax liability on oil and gas activities in Louisiana can only serve as a deterrent to future investments in this state. Therefore, regardless of the outcome from these cases, the state will be better served to clarify the appropriate way to tax these salt caverns, and the wells associated with them, so as to remove uncertainty about taxes associated with future activities.

Conclusions and Recommendations

There is great uncertainty about the future of mineral revenues in Louisiana. While state production and mineral revenues as a percentage of total state revenues have declined over the past half-century, with the emergence of new technologies and new oil and gas frontiers, the potential for new revenues in Louisiana is significant. In order to take advantage of these potential new resources, Louisiana legislators need to tread lightly and smartly when addressing tax policies. That does not mean, though, that there is no potential for changing policies that can simultaneously benefit the state's budget, Louisiana citizens, and the oil and gas industry in the state.

The first item that should be addressed is the outdated method of valuing natural gas for tax purposes. As discussed, the severance tax on gas is based on the average price from the previous year, not the current market rate for natural gas. In years with large swings in natural gas prices, this can impact the effective tax rate substantially, as was seen from 2008 to 2009 when the tax rate doubled in just one year.

The second, and potentially controversial, recommendation is that the difference in the tax rate between oil and natural gas should be examined. Due to the discrepancy in severance tax rates, the emergence of an oil-based play can potentially have a substantial impact on future tax revenues, while the increases in natural gas production are estimated to have much smaller effects. Because the state has such a large differential in tax rates, its mineral revenues are more dependent on oil production than gas. A more diversified approach would be to level the tax rate to achieve revenue neutrality, while not favoring the production of one hydrocarbon over another. This would reduce volatility of revenues that occur with large changes in the respective production and prices of oil and gas.

Thirdly, the horizontal well exemption should be reconsidered. In 1994, when this exemption was passed through the legislature, horizontal drilling technology was in its infancy, and the purpose of the exemption was to provide an incentive for investment in new technologies. Today, horizontal drilling is not a new technology, and in fact, is the standard in all shale plays across the United States. By subsidizing horizontal drilling, the state is incentivizing the production of oil and gas from shale plays, while providing no incentive for drilling new, conventional, nonhorizontal wells, which have been the bread and butter of the oil and gas industry in south Louisiana for the past century. While an argument might be made for a subsidy on a new emerging technology, once the technology is developed, there is little need for continuation of the subsidy.

As previously discussed, however, the removal of the horizontal well exemption could have a potentially detrimental impact on drilling in Louisiana. For this reason, the potential impact of a complete removal of the exemption without any other changes in mineral revenues could actually be negative if effective increases in taxes prohibit the future production in Haynesville and the TMS. Thus, the removal of the horizontal drilling exemption and the leveling of oil and gas severance taxes should be considered in tandem. This would allow for a decrease in overall tax rates and a removal of exemptions that could lead to revenue neutrality for the state and end the incentives for producing gas over oil and for drilling horizontal wells over conventional wells.

Legislators should also consider clarifying the state's tax laws to explicitly state which assets can be subject to ad valorem taxes and which cannot in order to end the legal disputes over the taxation of salt domes. Finally, the state should continue its policy of not taxing oil and gas reserves—keeping the constitutional provision that forbids this at the state level all the way down to the local level.

The future of oil and gas production and, as a result, mineral revenues in Louisiana is uncertain. While there is potential for an upside in coming years, the current economics do not predict a significant increase in mineral revenues in the upcoming year. Tax policies that do not favor one technology or one hydrocarbon over another will better position Louisiana to be ready for the future, whatever it might hold. Even the world's utmost experts on oil and gas do not know what the economic and technological landscape of oil and gas development will be in future decades. Policy makers should not try to "guess" what tax policies will maximize revenues in the near future, but should instead focus on a diversified and long-term strategy that will allow the state's rich mineral resources to provide a livelihood for generations of Louisianans to come.

There are many uncertainties about long-term oil and gas production and pricing; however, there are several items that are not uncertain. First, mineral taxes imposed in Louisiana will not be easily passed along to consumers or producers in other parts of the world. Any tax imposed on oil and gas in Louisiana will be paid by someone in Louisiana—it may be the owner of the oil and gas resources or the company doing the production or the persons working on the project receiving lower compensation. Louisiana producers simply cannot pass it along to someone in another state or country because oil and gas operations are conducted worldwide.

Second, the basic rationale for taxing natural resources is that they are a finite resource, and therefore the state should share the fruits of this resource with future generations as well as the present generation. In other words, mineral resources should not be used solely to fund current governmental obligations. Many states with mineral revenues have initiated permanent trust funds with very specific ways in which the trust fund can be used. Louisiana created a Revenue Stabilization Trust Fund in 1991, but it is limited in the dedication of mineral revenues to long-term objectives. As envisioned in the 1990s, this trust fund was the equivalent of a rainy day fund that limited the use of oil and gas revenues until a certain amount of money was put into the trust fund. After the rainy day trust fund was fully funded, then the oil and gas revenues could be used at the discretion of the state legislature. In November 2016 the state passed a constitutional amendment limiting the use of dollars from mineral revenues and corporate tax revenues for recurring purposes, and the remainder will go into a special trust fund that can be used for special purposes such as transportation infrastructure projects or paying down the unfunded state retirement debt. Due to the inherently volatile nature of commodity prices, the use of mineral revenues to support recurring state expenditures will continue to be a challenge in forecasting and planning for the following year's revenues, whereas the depositing of mineral revenues in a permanent trust fund will allow the state to have a predictable fiscal outlook as well as to meet long-term obligations benefiting current and future generations.

Notes

1. There are exceptions to this revenue derived in a three-mile zone of federal waters abutting state waters. First, the federal government shares its royalty receipts from production in that zone with the state (commonly referred to as the 8(g) zone for the section of federal law laying out the revenue sharing provisions). Second, in 2006 the Gulf of Mexico Energy Security Act was passed, and it shared leasing revenues with Alabama, Louisiana, Mississippi, and Texas, with these funds to be used for coastal restoration.

2. Louisiana's mineral arrangements for drilling on state-owned lands and water bottoms differ from the federal government's process. The federal government maintains a definite royalty rate of 12.5 percent but allows companies to focus on the bonus payments in competing with each other, though the federal government could charge a higher rate. The goal of this system is to allow the government to compare a bonus offered by one applicant to a bonus offered by other applicants without having to translate a high royalty rate and a low bonus payment into a lower royalty rate and a higher bonus payment. There is pressure for the federal government to raise its royalty rate. "Royally Shortchanged," *U.S. News & World Report*, Economic Intelligence, June 24, 2015.

3. Louisiana Department of Revenue.

4. LA RS 47:633.

5. *Louisiana Severance Tax*. Department of Natural Resources. Technology Assessment Division.

6. *Louisiana Severance Tax*. Department of Natural Resources. Technology Assessment Division.

7. Louisiana Department of Revenue, Revenue Information Bulletin No. 15–007, March 20, 2015.

8. Greg Albrecht, *State Revenue Outlook,* May 16, 2017, Legislative Fiscal Office.

9. Christopher K. Coombs, David E. Dismukes, Dek Terrell, and Gregory B. Upton, *Gulf Coast Energy Outlook.* Spring 2017. LSU Center for Energy Studies and Economics & Policy Research Group.

10. A preliminary evaluation in 1997 indicated the Tuscaloosa marine shale could contain a potential reserve of 7 billion barrels of oil, according to *An Unproven Unconventional Seven Billion Barrel Oil Resource—The Tuscaloosa Marine Shale.* Chacko J. John, Bobby L. Jones, James E. Moncreif, Reed Bourgeois, and Brian J. Harder, Basin Research Institute, Louisiana State University. This estimate has not been updated.

11. M. J. Kaiser and Y. Yu, Louisiana Haynesville Shale 1: Characteristics, Production Potential of Haynesville Shale Wells Described. *Oil & Gas Journal* 109 (19): 68–79, 109; M. J. Kaiser and Y. Yu, Louisiana Haynesville Shale 2: Economic Operating Envelopes Characterized for Haynesville Shale. *Oil & Gas Journal* 110 (1A): 70–74, 87; M. J. Kaiser and Y. Yu, Shale 3 (conclusion): Operating Envelope of Haynesville Shale Wells' Profitability Described. *Oil & Gas Journal* 110 (2): 60–67.

12. A new shale play, called the Tuscaloosa Marine Shale (TMS), is the next potential source of revenues for the state and is discussed subsequently.

13. A distinction is made here with respect to direct state mineral revenue, primarily severance tax and royalty receipts. State revenue collections certainly benefited from the increased drilling and associated activities, primarily through sales tax and income taxes. These benefits surely contributed to the peak and near-peak overall state tax revenue collections of fiscal year 2007 through fiscal year 2009. However, with the exception of a spike in bonus receipts from leasing state lands in fiscal years 2008 and 2009, it is not apparent that large increases in natural gas production have added significantly to state severance and royalty receipts.

14. LA RS 47:633. 7(c)(ii)(bb).

15. Horizontal Well Severance Tax Investment, 1994.

16. Report by the Legislative Auditor, Severance Tax Suspension for Horizontal Wells, August 19, 2015.

17. Melissa Braybrooks, Julio Ruiz, and Elizabeth Accetta, State Government Tax Collections Summary Report: 2010, March 2011.

18. Melissa Braybrooks, Julio Ruiz, and Elizabeth Accetta, State Government Tax Collections Summary Report: 2010, March 2011.

19. BP Statistical Review of World Energy, 2014.

20. Louisiana Department of Natural Resources, Louisiana and GOM Central Crude Oil and Condensate Production.

21. Harold Hotelling, "The economics of exhaustible resources," *Journal of Political Economy,* 1983, 11 (3), 279–83; H. Stuart Burness, "On the Taxation of Nonreplinishable Natural Resources," *Journal of Environmental Economics and Management,* 1976 (3), 289–311; Robert F. Conrad and R. Bryce Hool, "Optimal Extraction with Grade Variation and Endogenous Reserves," *Resources and Energy,* December 1984, 6 (4), 331–38.

22. Robert F. Conrad and R. Bryce Hool, "Optimal Extraction with Grade Variation and Endogenous Reserves," *Resources and Energy,* December 1984, 6 (4), 331–38; Villamore Gamponia and Robert Mendelsohn, "The Taxation of Exhaustible Resources," *Quarterly Journal of Economics,* February 1985, 100 (1), 165–81.

23. Jesse R. Adams, Partner, Jones Walker LLP. *A Salty Situation: Recent Developments in Louisiana Ad Valorem Property Tax Treatment of Salt Dome Caverns and Wells. In Focus,* http://www.infocusmagazine.org/8.2/env_desalination.html.

24. Huval v. Jefferson Island Storage & Hub, LLC, No. 114,559 (16th J.D.C., Iberia Parish); Pine Prairie Energy Center, LLC v. Soileau, 14–5 c/w 13–1300 & 13–142 (La. App. 3 Cir. 06/11/2014).

25. Jesse R. Adams, Partner, Jones Walker LLP. *A Salty Situation: Recent Developments in Louisiana Ad Valorem Property Tax Treatment of Salt Dome Caverns and Wells. In Focus,* http://www.infocusmagazine.org/8.2/env_desalination.html.

26. In Re: Protest/Appeal of Jefferson Island Storage & Hub, LLC, Nos. 06–22045–003, 07–22045–001, and 08–22045–001 (La. Tax Commission 06/02/09).

9

THE USE OF EXCISE TAXES IN LOUISIANA

James Alm and Grant Driessen

Introduction

The State of Louisiana levies excise taxes on the sale of alcoholic beverages, tobacco products, and motor fuels. The power to levy excise taxes is largely vested in the state: the Louisiana Constitution prohibits political subdivisions from levying a tax on motor fuel (Louisiana Constitutional Amendment VII, §4). The administration of local excise taxes on tobacco and alcoholic beverages requires approval first by the state legislature and then by voters. However, parish and municipalities may impose a tax on beer and beverages of low alcohol content.

These taxes are administered by the Louisiana Department of Revenue (LDR) and collected at the wholesale level. Historically, these taxes have been an important source of revenue for the state in funding public services. According to the 2011 Census of Governments, selective sales tax revenue accounted for approximately 16 percent of government expenditures in Louisiana, compared to the national average of 12 percent.

In this chapter we first discuss the practice of excise taxes in Louisiana, focusing mainly on administrative issues. We then present estimates of the revenue and distributional effects of an increase in excise taxes. We have made in presentations to the Louisiana legislature the following recommendation: "At present, Louisiana excise taxes are lower, and in some cases significantly lower than regional or national average excise taxes. *We recommend that in all cases the Louisiana excise taxes be aligned to national or regional averages.*" In our summary, we note that the state legislature has accepted these recommendations for excise taxes over the last two years, and we conclude with further recommendations for reform. Our analysis begins with the excise taxes that were levied prior to 2015, and then we discuss the changes in these excise taxes in 2015 and 2016.

Louisiana's excise taxes, including for beer, wine, alcoholic beverages, tobacco, and gasoline and diesel fuel, are compared to those of other states in the nation in Table 9.11 at the end of the chapter, using information from the Federation of Tax Administrators.

Excise Taxes on Alcoholic Beverages

Louisiana taxes alcoholic beverages on a volumetric basis at the wholesale level. The tax is organized into a low alcohol content beverage tax (beer and malts) and a high alcohol content beverage tax (liquor and wine). In fiscal year 2013, receipts from alcoholic beverages totaled approximately $57 million, a slight increase from the previous year. At the time, beer and malts were taxed at a rate of $10.00 per 31-gallon barrel, or $0.32/gallon. This rate was relatively low compared to states in the southern region; nevertheless, it was slightly higher than the national average of $0.28/gallon. Note that the rate on beer was increased to $12.50 per 31-gallon barrel in 2016. See Table 9.1 for the Louisiana excise taxes on alcoholic beverages.

At $34.9 million in fiscal year 2013, beer receipts in Louisiana accounted for a majority of total alcoholic beverage revenue, despite its leveling growth patterns. Thus, growth in alcohol revenue can be attributed to liquor and wine sales.

Prior to 2016, liquor and wine were taxed at a rate of $0.66/liter ($2.50/gallon) and $0.03/liter ($0.11/gallon), respectively. Louisiana's liquor excise rate fell well below the national average, while the wine excise was the lowest in the United States. In addition, the state imposes a graduated tax on wine of higher alcohol content. The revenue collections from liquor and wine sales totaled $22.1 million for fiscal year 2013. Note that the tax rate on high alcoholic content was increased to $0.80/liter in 2016.

TABLE 9.1. Alcoholic Beverage Excise Taxes in Louisiana

Product	Excise Tax ($/gallon)	Revenue, FY 2012 ($)	Revenue, FY 2013 ($)
Beer	$0.32	$35,404.645	$34,889,371
Liquor	2.50	20,274,497	21,031,095
Low alcohol content wine	0.11	897,948	919,096
High alcohol content wine	0.23	127,707	129,437
Sparkling wine	1.59	763,517	811,911

Louisiana offers ten different tax exemptions and discounts, six of which are federally imposed, on the sale of alcoholic beverages. Tax exemptions and discounts are granted for interstate shipping and timely and accurate filing. In fiscal year 2013, Louisiana lost approximately $2.6 million in revenue after these exemptions. The economic impact of these exemptions is expected to increase in the coming fiscal years.

Under Title 26, local governments may "impose a tax on beverages of low alcoholic content of not more than one dollar and fifty cents per standard barrel of thirty-one gallons" (LA R.S. 26:492–3). This tax is paid at the wholesale level. In fiscal year 2013, the parish and municipal beer tax generated approximately $5.1 million in revenue.

Excise Taxes on Tobacco Products

Tobacco excise revenue makes up a significant portion of total excise receipts in Louisiana. Tobacco receipts have leveled after a period of steady decline. In fiscal year 2013, tobacco products generated approximately $135.6 million in revenue. There are two components of the tobacco tax: a cigarette tax and a tax on noncigarette tobacco. Prior to the tax changes in 2015 and 2016, Louisiana levied a tax of $0.36 per pack on cigarettes, which was at the time one of the lowest rates in the country despite four tax increases since 1970. The tax changes instituted in 2015 and 2016 raised the tax on cigarettes to $1.08 per pack. There are also taxes on cigars, smokeless tobacco, and smoking tobacco. The tobacco excise taxes are noted in Table 9.2.

TABLE 9.2. Tobacco Excise Taxes in Louisiana as of January 1, 2015

Product	Excise Rate	Measurement	Revenue, FY 2012 ($)	Revenue, FY 2013 ($)
Cigarettes	$0.36/pack	Dollars per pack	112,162,543	116,038,066
Cigars	8–20%	Percentage of manufacturer's price	27,816,197*	28,901,620*
Smokeless tobacco	20%	Percentage of manufacturer's price	—	—
Smoking tobacco	33%	Percentage of manufacturer's price	—	—

*These values represent the total revenue collected from all tobacco products classified as "other."

Table 9.A1 uses information from the Federation of Tax Administrators to compare cigarette excise rates across all states. The tobacco tax is collected on the sale of stamps for cigarettes and on monthly reports on cigars and other tobacco products. Cigarette receipts make up a large share of tobacco excise revenue. In fiscal year 2013, cigarettes generated approximately $116 million in revenue before refunds and discounts. However, their share has declined over time with the implementation of taxes on other tobacco products.

The state also taxes noncigarette products, including cigars, snuff, and smoking tobacco. Unlike cigarettes, these products are taxed as a percentage of the manufacturer's price. Cigars are taxed at a tiered rate of 8 percent and 20 percent based on price. Smokeless tobacco and smoking tobacco are taxed at 20 percent and 33 percent, respectively. In recent years, the revenue share of noncigarette products has increased. In fiscal year 2013, revenue from cigars and other tobacco products increased from $27.8 million to $28.9 million, before refunds and discounts.

Louisiana grants seven various tax exemptions and discounts, two of which are federally imposed, on the sale of tobacco products. Bulk sale, timely and accurate filing, and interstate shipments are all entitled to discounts or exemptions. The revenue lost from these exemptions totaled nearly $76 million, compared to the $135.6 million collected in fiscal year 2013.

Excise Taxes on Petroleum Products

Motor fuel comprises the largest source of excise revenue in Louisiana. In fiscal year 2013, motor fuel excise receipts totaled approximately $587.3 million. Gasoline and diesel sales generated $446.3 million and $136.6 million in revenue, respectively. As of 2006, these taxes are collected before distribution at the terminal rack (LA RS 47:818.13). Both gasoline and diesel fuel are taxed at a rate of $0.20 per gallon. Louisiana imposes an additional inspection fee of 0.125 cents per gallon for both diesel fuel and gasoline. See Table 9.3.

Louisiana's excise rates on motor fuel are similar to those of states in the southern region; however, they are relatively low compared to the national average gasoline and diesel excise rates of $0.2347 per gallon and $0.24 per gallon, respectively as noted in Appendix Table 9.A1.

TABLE 9.3. Motor Fuel Excise Taxes in Louisiana as of January 2015

Product	Excise Rate ($/gallon)	Revenue, FY 2012 ($)	Revenue, FY 2013 ($)
Gasoline/gasohol	$0.20/gallon	$440,635,891	$446,377,777
Diesel	0.20	134,427,241	136,647,595
Inspection fee	0.00125	4,337,114	4,356,761

Despite its large share of revenue, motor fuel is the most volatile excise tax source. Typically, there is significant variation each year in revenue; however, this variation may be due to the volatility in the price of motor fuel. Petroleum products comprise one of the largest tax exemptions in Louisiana. Louisiana offers fifteen tax exemptions, including refunds and discounts, on the sale of petroleum products. Two of these exemptions are federally imposed. These exemptions are offered for exports and interstate shipments; fuel used for commercial fishing, aviation, and agriculture; and timely filing. In fiscal year 2013, lost motor fuel excise revenue totaled approximately $73.3 million. Lost revenue is projected to increase in the next fiscal year.

The Effects of Increasing Louisiana Excise Tax Rates

The excise taxes on the sale of alcoholic beverages, tobacco products, and motor fuels have historically been an important source of revenue for the state in funding public services. For example, revenues from motor fuels excise taxes were $583 million in 2013, or about 6 percent of state revenues. However, revenues from alcohol and tobacco excises have been growing very little in recent years, and so their relative importance has declined significantly over time. In 2013, revenues from excise taxes on alcohol and tobacco products totaled $193 million (roughly two-thirds of which comes from tobacco excises). These revenues are less than 2 percent of state revenues, down from 7 percent of state revenues in the 1970s.

This decline is due largely to the low taxes that are imposed on alcohol, motor fuels, and tobacco, both in absolute levels and in levels relative to neighboring states. As is standard in other states, cigarettes are assessed as a unit tax (e.g., dollars per pack of cigarettes), and alcohol products are assessed on a volume basis (e.g., dollars per volume, differentiated according to alcoholic content). Cigarette taxes in Louisiana were, prior to 2015, 36 cents per pack, and alcohol taxes, prior to 2015, were $2.50 per gallon for liquor, $0.11 per gallon for wine, and $0.32 per gallon for beer. These taxes in Louisiana are in most cases significantly lower than regional and national values. Louisiana's cigarette tax ($0.36 per pack) ranked Louisiana forty-eighth among all states (including the District of Columbia), relative to a regional average cigarette tax of $0.71 per pack (Alabama, Arkansas, Florida, Georgia, Kentucky, Mississippi, North Carolina, South Carolina, Tennessee, Texas, Virginia, and West Virginia) and a median US tax of $1.36 per pack. Taxes on alcohol in Louisiana are also significantly lower than regional and national averages. Louisiana's tax on wine ($0.11 per gallon) is the lowest among all states, relative to a regional average of $1.07 per gallon and a national median of $0.81 per gallon. Louisiana's liquor tax rate does not rank the state as low as its cigarette and wine taxes do, but it is still somewhat lower than regional and national levels. (Louisiana's tax rate on beer is currently above the median value for all states.) Louisiana's motor fuels taxes ($0.20 per gallon on gasoline, diesel fuel, and gasohol) are also lower than regional ($0.23 per gallon) and national ($0.24) averages, but not by significant amounts.

There are several reasons for imposing excise taxes on tobacco and alcohol consumption (e.g., "sin taxes"). One reason is to generate revenues. A second reason is to compensate the state for public health care costs and the other "external costs" associated with alcohol-related car accidents or with tobacco-related illnesses. A third reason is simply to reduce smoking and alcohol consumption, especially among the young, whose demands for these products are likely to be more responsive. A fourth and related reason for excise taxes on tobacco and alcohol is to help individuals consider more fully the long-run effects of their current actions on their long-run welfare. There is always a tradeoff for the state in terms of wanting a tax that will generate revenues as opposed to a tax that might actually encourage a certain type of behavior. A state also has to appreciate the mobility of persons who want to smoke.

Similarly, taxes on motor fuels are justified by the revenues that they generate and by their ability to deal with pollution and other external costs associated with consumption of carbon products. Taxes on motor fuels can also be used to fund transportation infrastructure as a dedicated revenue source.

Given these considerations, we examine the effects of increasing the excise tax rates on motor fuel, alcohol, and tobacco. We include two types of estimates to offer insight into the fiscal impact of increasing Louisiana excise tax rates. We first estimate the distributional effects of increasing the rate of those taxes to the national average. We then examine the annual revenue effects of such legislation.

DISTRIBUTIONAL EFFECTS

Louisiana uses a specific tax structure—where each tax is set at a fixed dollar amount per unit consumed—for its excise taxation. Household financial surveys typically measure activity by the amount spent on products rather than the quantity consumed. This complicates our ability to analyze the distributional effects of excise tax increases, since a household's disposable income level may change the average price of excise-related goods it purchases (i.e., whether the wine bought for dinner costs $100 or $10). For goods with no or low price differentiation—as is the case with motor fuels—data on expenditures can be used to impute consumption levels and engage in distributional analysis.[1] However, the significant amount of price differentiation inherent in the markets for alcohol and tobacco products prevents us from calculating household consumption levels exclusively with expenditure data. Therefore, we complement this information with quantity consumption data to provide distributional estimates of excise tax increases on those products.

Data. We use the 2012 Consumer Expenditure Survey (CEX) to empirically analyze the distributional effects of increasing Louisiana's tax on motor fuels, and to highlight the financial burden of all excise-related goods across household consumption levels. The CEX contains data on total household income and spending, allowing us to rank households by either metric. It offers rich detail on household expenditures, including specific spending levels on motor fuel used for transportation, alcohol, and tobacco products.

The full 2012 CEX sample contains over 10,000 households, and provides weights that are designed to be nationally representative. However, comprehensive representation is not assured for samples in individual states. It is possible to use the nationwide sample to make judgments about Louisiana, although this runs the risk of missing patterns unique to Louisiana due to state differences in demographics.

Accordingly, we conduct the incidence analysis on two separate subsamples of the complete CEX dataset. The first subsample is comprised of 275 households in the CEX that are representative of Louisiana. The second subsample is comprised of all respondents defined as living in the South by the Bureau of Labor Statistics; this region is composed of the seventeen states bounded to the north and east by Maryland and Delaware and to the north and west by Oklahoma and Texas. The 4,591 households included in this group provide more desirable large-sample properties not available in the first subsample. Population weights provided by the CEX are applied to all households in each of our samples.

The 2013 Vital and Health Statistics Report produced by the Centers for Disease Control (CDC) is used to provide distributional estimates for taxes on alcohol and tobacco products. This survey studies how drug and alcohol consumption changes across a wide range of demographic factors from 2008 to 2010, including by the value of household income relative to the poverty level. Although geographic variables are included, distributional estimates of consumption across income measures are available only for the entire United States. Therefore, in this portion of the analysis we assume that the distributional drinking patterns for Louisiana residents match those of the American population at large.

Effective tax rate estimation requires data on the average price of each product, which we obtained from a few sources. Fuel price estimates were taken from the Energy Information Administration,[2] which provides annual price data for gasoline and diesel fuel and region of the country. We incorporated the difference between Louisiana tax rates on each product and the regional average to ensure that the resulting quantities were as reflective of actual state prices as possible. Finally, we weighted each value with state-level relative consumption data for each product published by the Federal Highway Administration to obtain a composite price that accurately represented Louisiana's motor fuel activity in 2014. Price data for tobacco products was taken directly from Kulwin, a survey that measures the annual value and change in each state's tobacco prices. Data on alcohol prices are less prevalent than those on motor fuel and tobacco.[3] For estimates of the price of wine, spirits, and beer, we took national estimates from Young, updated with historical price data for alcohol products from the Bureau of Economic Analysis and adjusted those estimates with the tax differential of Louisiana rates and the national average to obtain state-specific values.[4]

Methodology. Throughout, we make the standard assumption that consumers bear the full burden of any tax on services or consumption item.[5] In constructing our measure of incidence, we define economic status using total household consumption. While income has also been used as a measure of household well-being, some studies have argued that consumption is a better measure of economic status because it captures expected income changes in transitory households, such as students who may undergo large increases in income after matriculation and senior citizens who are more likely to spend down accrued savings.[6]

We sort households into deciles and quintiles as determined by their consumption levels, and then provide distributional estimates through two sets of calculations. The first portion of the analysis estimates, for each item, the percentage of the total consumption attributable to each expenditure category, allowing for intergroup comparison. For instance, consider a scenario where the lowest quintile generates 14 percent of total consumption, while the highest quintile generates 25 percent. Suppose also that the lowest quintile generates 10 percent of total motor fuel consumption, while the highest quintile has 45 percent of total motor fuel consumption (with a consistently rising consumption pattern across quintiles in both categories). Then we would say that the excise tax on motor fuels is less progressive than a tax levied on all types of consumption.

The second portion of the distributional analysis uses consumption and price information to provide effective tax rate estimates across expenditure categories. These effective tax rates represent the amount paid in taxes for each product as a percentage of total reported income. Motor fuel effective tax rates use consumption data from the CEX, while effective tax rates for alcohol and tobacco products use quantity consumption data from the Vital Health and Statistics Report.

For the monetary consumption analysis, the CEX data directly assigns households to expenditure categories: deciles are used for this portion of the analysis. The Vital and Health Statistics Report contains information on household consumption spread across the following income categories: income at or below the poverty level, income between one and two times the poverty level, income between two and four times the poverty level, and income greater than four times the poverty level. However, we can use CEX data on income related to the poverty level for each household to assign values found in the Vital and Health Statistics Report across expenditure quintiles in both Louisiana and in the southern region.[7,8] For example, if the CEX data revealed that 25 percent of households had incomes below the poverty level and 18 percent of households had incomes between one and two times the poverty level, we would assign the lowest quintile with the CDC values reported for the below-poverty population, and assign the second lowest quintile with consumption values equal to one-fourth of the below-poverty population (as 5 of the 20 percent of the total households in this quintile belong to that group) and three-fourths of the numbers reported for the population with incomes between one and two times the population level (as 15 of the 20 percent of households in this quintile were in that category).

The level of detail offered by the Vital Health and Statistics Report requires the use of some assumptions in generating distributional analysis. For tobacco consumption, the report assigns individuals into three categories: nonsmokers, nondaily smokers, and daily smokers. It then computes the average number of cigarettes smoked per day for each group (and each expenditure category). We combine these numbers with the distributional sorting described earlier to generate consumption estimates for tobacco.

The information offered by the CDC report on alcohol consumption is less specific, sorting individuals into five categories: nondrinkers (no drinks in the past year), infrequent drinkers (between one and eleven drinks in the past year), light drinkers (three drinks or less per week), moderate drinkers (between three and seven drinks per week for women, and three and fourteen drinks for men), and heavy drinkers (more drinks than what is reported in the moderate category). Given this data, we assume that all individuals consume the average number of drinks available in each category (for heavy drinkers, we assume that the maximum number of drinks per week is twenty-five for men and eleven for women, making the bandwidth equal to the moderate drinker category). These numbers are then used to inform consumption estimates for alcohol consumption.

Note that for both portions of the distributional analysis we are not able to capture any behavioral effects that might stem from the imposition of increased excise tax rates. Taxes on services will increase the price of excise-related goods, which will in turn reduce the quantity demanded of services. Our analysis does not include such a behavioral response. If lower income households reduce their quantity demanded for services more than higher income households as a result of the sales tax expansion, then their consumption of services after the imposition of a tax will be lower than our estimates suggest, which would in turn make the taxation of services more progressive than suggested by our estimates.

Results. Table 9.4 summarizes the results of the standard incidence analysis across deciles across all measures of consumption in the CEX for the subsample of Louisiana households only. These results show reduced motor fuel consumption burden at the tails of the distribution when compared to both total consumption and disposable income. For the lowest consumption deciles, this reduced burden may stem from lower vehicle ownership levels. The lighter burden on higher-consuming households may be reflective of driving consumption failing to keep pace with rises in income at the upper portion of the distribution. Households in the middle deciles therefore receive an increased financial burden of motor fuel consumption as compared to total spending and income. (While distributional estimates of alcohol and tobacco consumption are included for completeness, the distributional ramifications of tax increases on these products are reserved for discussion in Tables 9.6 and 9.7.)

Table 9.5 summarizes the monetary consumption distributional findings for the southern region. Unlike with the results for only Louisiana, this subset of data produces an increased motor fuel burden for each of the lowest eight deciles when compared to total spending and income—including for

TABLE 9.4. Louisiana Consumption Burden (in Dollars) by Consumption Decile, Selected Items

					Decile					
	1 (Lowest)	2	3	4	5	6	7	8	9	10 (Highest)
Measure										
Total consumption	2.2%	3.4%	6.0%	7.6%	8.8%	9.0%	9.4%	11.4%	18.5%	23.7%
Total disposable income	1.9%	3.2%	4.9%	6.7%	8.5%	10.0%	12.2%	12.4%	17.0%	23.1%
All Excise Goods	1.7%	4.3%	4.1%	7.4%	8.5%	10.0%	12.1%	17.3%	15.9%	18.8%
Motor fuel	1.8%	3.2%	3.8%	7.2%	7.9%	11.0%	13.1%	17.6%	16.2%	18.1%
Alcohol	1.2%	7.0%	4.9%	3.6%	13.0%	7.4%	5.4%	10.3%	21.3%	25.9%
Tobacco	2.0%	10.2%	5.2%	13.5%	8.3%	4.3%	11.0%	21.2%	8.0%	16.3%

Note: Percentages represent the share of the overall consumption level attributable to the decile, based on a sample of 275 households.

TABLE 9.5. Southern Consumption Burden (in Dollars) by Consumption Decile, Selected Items

	1 (Lowest)	2	3	4	5	6	7	8	9	10 (Lowest)
					Decile					
Measure										
Total consumption	2.1%	3.6%	4.9%	6.3%	7.5%	9.0%	10.5%	12.2%	16.8%	27.1%
Total disposable income	2.2%	3.5%	4.7%	6.2%	7.3%	9.2%	10.6%	12.7%	17.1%	26.6%
All Excise Goods	3.1%	5.1%	6.9%	8.1%	9.4%	10.6%	12.9%	13.3%	14.5%	16.2%
Motor fuel	2.9%	4.7%	6.6%	7.9%	9.4%	10.7%	12.8%	13.8%	14.8%	16.2%
Alcohol	2.8%	3.7%	6.0%	8.2%	7.6%	9.7%	14.8%	14.0%	15.1%	18.1%
Tobacco	4.5%	7.6%	8.6%	8.7%	9.9%	10.4%	12.7%	10.3%	12.2%	15.0%

Note: Percentages represent the share of the overall consumption level attributable to the decile, based on a sample of 4,591 households.

the lowest categories of earners. As with the previous table, reductions in the relative burden can be seen in the upper two deciles. Taken together, these tables suggest that raising the excise taxes on motor fuels will result in additional spending that is less progressive than general spending and income for the middle- and upper-income households; more research is needed to determine the effect on lower-income families.

Figures 9.1 and 9.2 display the results of the Vital Health and Statistics report data on alcohol and tobacco consumption. Figure 9.1 shows that lower-income households are more likely to abstain from alcohol consumption or drink infrequently than the general population, while upper-income households are more likely to be light or moderate drinkers. Heavy drinking does not produce an obviously detectable pattern across consumption groups. Figure 9.2 shows that the income trend for tobacco use is roughly the opposite of that for alcohol. Here, individuals at the lower end of the consumption spectrum are significantly more likely to participate in daily smoking and slightly more likely to be nondaily smokers than individuals in higher-consuming households.

Table 9.6 compares the distribution of alcohol and tobacco consumption with that of monetary consumption and income, in order to provide a like-for-like comparison with the incidence effects of excise tax increases

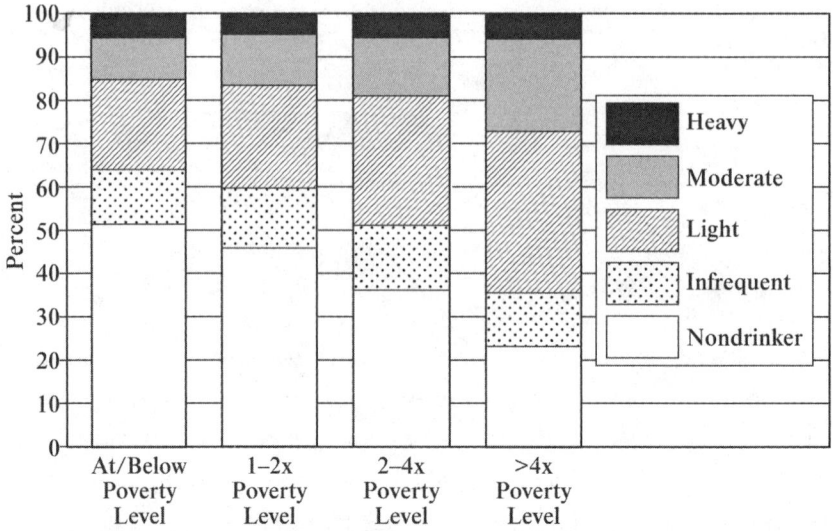

FIGURE 9.1. Drinking and Income Status for US Adults, 2008–2010

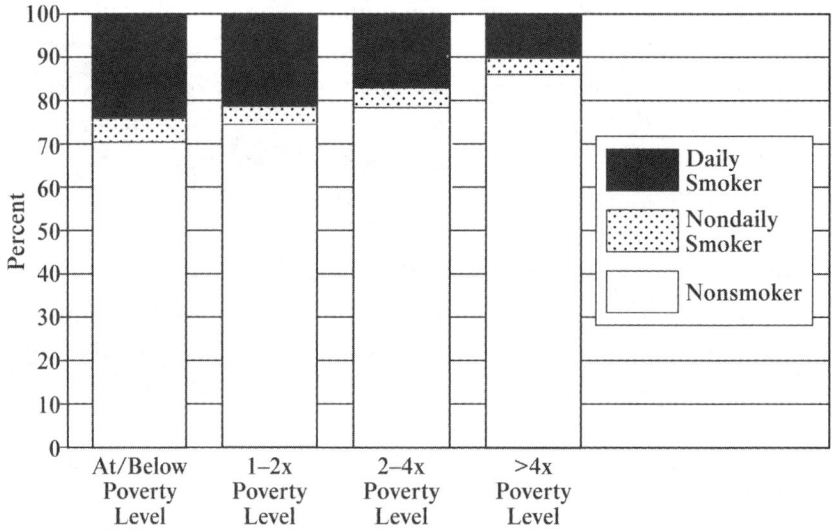

FIGURE 9.2. Smoking and Income Status for US Adults, 2008–2010

on alcohol and tobacco. The results show that the consumption burden of both products is much higher on the lowest consumption quintile than general measures—by roughly three times in the case of alcohol and five times for tobacco products. Conversely, the burden on the highest-consumption household quintile is significantly reduced compared to general spending and income measures. Alcohol consumption in the middle quintiles falls roughly in line with general consumption patterns from those households: with tobacco products, an increased burden is placed on the second-lowest quintile, with the consecutively higher quintiles exhibiting consumption behaviors similar to their general spending.

Table 9.7 displays the results of the same analysis extended to the entire southern region. The results are strikingly similar with what is presented in the previous table, with heavier excise tax burdens placed on the lower-

TABLE 9.6. Louisiana Alcohol and Tobacco Consumption Burden (in Quantity) by Consumption Quintile

	Quintile				
Measure	1 (Lowest)	2	3	4	5 (Highest)
Total (monetary) consumption	5.6%	13.6%	17.8%	20.8%	42.2%
Total disposable income	5.1%	11.6%	18.5%	24.6%	40.1%
Alcohol (quantity)	16.5%	16.8%	19.0%	20.8%	26.9%
Tobacco (quantity)	25.3%	24.6%	20.7%	18.3%	11.1%

Note: Percentages represent the share of the overall consumption level attributable to the quintile, based on a sample of 275 households.

TABLE 9.7. Southern Alcohol and Tobacco Consumption Burden (in Quantity) by Consumption Quintile

	Quintile				
Category	1 (Lowest)	2	3	4	5 (Highest)
Total (monetary) consumption	5.7%	11.2%	16.5%	22.7%	43.9%
Total disposable income	5.7%	10.9%	16.9%	23.3%	43.7%
Alcohol (quantity)	17.4%	16.8%	18.5%	20.7%	26.6%
Tobacco (quantity)	25.5%	24.3%	21.3%	17.7%	11.2%

Note: Percentages represent the share of the overall consumption level attributable to the quintile, based on a sample of 4,591 households.

consumption households and lower burdens placed on high-consumption families, again with greater magnitudes for consumption of tobacco products. These results indicate that excise tax increases on alcohol and tobacco would likely be more regressive than taxes on general consumption and income.

Table 9.8 uses the consumption information obtained from the first portion of the distributional analysis to estimate effective tax rates for levies on motor fuels, alcohol, and tobacco products using consumption data from residents in the state of Louisiana. The results in Table 9.8 produce an effective excise tax rate on motor fuels that is relatively consistent across measures of household consumption: each tax rate was between 0.22 percent and 0.27 percent for the deciles on the bottom, middle, and top of the distribution. Meanwhile, the effective tax rates for alcohol and tobacco products revealed a relatively regressive tax structure, as the bottom quintile face a tax rate three and ten times that faced by the top quintile for alcohol and tobacco respectively.

Table 9.9 extends the CEX subsample to include residents of all southern states. The results for motor fuel are largely consistent with the steady trend produced in the previous table, although in this subsample the bottom two deciles have slightly lower tax rate values (0.24 percent and 0.27 percent) than those faced by the remaining eight categories (which range from 0.30 percent to 0.34 percent). The tax rates for tobacco products is

TABLE 9.8. Louisiana Effective Tax Rate by Consumption Decile and Quintile, Selected Items

Product						Decile				
	1 (Lowest)	2	3	4	5	6	7	8	9	10 (Highest)
Motor fuel	0.26%	0.27%	0.20%	0.26%	0.26%	0.27%	0.34%	0.40%	0.25%	0.22%

			Quintile		
	1 (Lowest)	2	3	4	5 (Highest)
Alcohol	0.09%	0.05%	0.04%	0.03%	0.03%
Tobacco	1.67%	0.92%	0.49%	0.30%	0.17%

Note: Motor fuel estimates are based strictly on data obtained from the Consumer Expenditure Survey, alcohol and tobacco product estimates are based on distributional data from the Vital Health and Statistics Report, and consumption data are from the Consumer Expenditure Survey.

TABLE 9.9. Southern Effective Tax Rate by Consumption Decile and Quintile, Selected Items

Product	Decile									
	1 (Lowest)	2	3	4	5	6	7	8	9	10 (Highest)
Motor Fuel	0.24%	0.27%	0.32%	0.31%	0.34%	0.33%	0.33%	0.31%	0.30%	0.31%

	Quintile				
	1 (Lowest)	2	3	4	5 (Highest)
Alcohol	0.03%	0.02%	0.02%	0.02%	0.02%
Tobacco	1.31%	0.85%	0.62%	0.44%	0.25%

Note: Motor fuel estimates are based strictly on data obtained from the Consumer Expenditure Survey, alcohol and tobacco product estimates are based on distributional data from the Vital Health and Statistics Report, and consumption data are from the Consumer Expenditure Survey.

once again regressive in this sample, with the top consumption quintile having an effective tax rate more than five times lower than that faced by the bottom consumption quintile. Notably, the effective tax rate information for alcohol is different from that seen in the Louisiana-only information: consumption of alcohol from the southern region is around one-third of that produced by Louisiana residents, lowering the tax rates across all quintiles. This decrease was largest among the lower-consumption households, and produces a distributional pattern that is much more consistent than what was found in Table 9.8, with each quintile having an effective tax rate of 0.02 percent or 0.03 percent.

REVENUE EFFECTS

Methodology. Our revenue projections are based upon the collections information provided by the Louisiana Department of Revenue, and updated to 2015 using Louisiana GDP growth over this period. Revenue estimates were generated through a three-step process. First, each service was assigned a tax base that corresponded to the 2013 estimates from Louisiana Department of Revenue data. Second, we assumed that all taxes on motor fuels, alcohol, and tobacco products with rates below the national median would be raised to median values.[9] Third, as noted, we updated our estimates of services by GDP growth to represent consumption in 2015, given that the estimates from the Jindal proposal were produced in 2013. Accordingly, our estimates reflect a passage of sales tax expansion effective in the beginning of calendar year 2015.

As with the distributional work, the specific nature of the taxes on alcohol and tobacco required manipulations worthy of discussion. For the excise tax on alcohol, the total amount of current revenue collected was available but was not broken out by source (beer, wine, and liquor). Therefore, in order to calculate current consumption levels, we backed out national consumption rates of each category from their federal tax rates and collection levels, and applied the share of total alcohol consumption devoted to each category to Louisiana activity, so that total consumption matched current revenue collection levels.

Source detail on tobacco revenues was also unavailable for this analysis. However, unlike with alcohol, tobacco product consumption is dominated by a single source, that of cigarettes.[10] Moreover, the national ranks of Louisiana tax rates on cigarettes, cigars, and snuff and chewing tobacco are roughly equal to one another, with the state placing in the lowest quintile of states in each case. Therefore, in our calculations we assumed that tax increases on all tobacco products would be equivalent to the percent increase needed to move the tax rate on cigarettes to the national median rate.

Revenue projections are calculated under two scenarios. The first scenario mirrors what was done in the distributional analysis, and assumes that changes in excise tax rates produce no behavioral effects: these estimates may be viewed as an "upper bound" for actual revenue effects. In practice, the rise in the prices of these products is likely to decrease their consumption. Therefore, we took price elasticity of demand estimates from the existing literature that were relatively strong to provide a "lower bound" for the revenue effects of increasing excise tax rates to fall in line with national median values.[11]

Federal budget organizations include an "excise tax offset" when estimating a policy change in those types of taxes, as increases in excise tax collections are likely to reduce the amount of money collected by income and payroll taxes.[12] We choose not to include such an offset, as the relative size of income and payroll revenue sources at the state level is small compared to that of the federal government.

Results. Table 9.10 displays the results for increasing all excise tax rates to national average values. In total, raising the tax rates on motor fuels, alcohol, and tobacco products is forecast to increase 2015 revenues by $494 million if strong behavioral effects are assumed, and $540 million if no behavioral effects are incorporated. The majority of this rise comes from increased collections from tobacco taxes, which are forecast to bring in $357 million and $391 million in revenues under the two scenarios. Increasing the tax on gasoline and diesel fuel by four cents per gallon is responsible for between $116 million and $128 million in additional revenues, while tax increases on alcohol raise around $20 million. The difference in revenue projections across each scenario is largely attributable to changes in estimates for the tax on tobacco products: this is because the proposed change in the tax rate on that product is the largest in both nominal terms and as a percentage of the pretax price. The remaining difference is almost entirely due to changes in the gas tax estimate: although the relative tax change (and assumed behavioral effects) is relatively small for this revenue source, the

TABLE 9.10. Revenue Projections for Excise Tax Increases to National Median Values

Product	Current Tax Rate	Current Revenue	Suggested Tax Rate	No Behavioral Response		Strong Behavioral Response	
				New Revenue	Revenue Increase	New Revenue	Revenue Increase
Motor fuels	$0.20 per gallon	$583.0	$0.24 per gallon	$699.6	$116.6	$697.5	$127.6
Alcohol							
Liquor	$2.50 per proof gallon	$20.1	$3.75 per proof gallon	$30.1	$10.0	$29.9	$11.0
Wine	$0.11 per proof gallon	$1.5	$0.81 per proof gallon	$11.2	$9.7	$10.9	$10.6
Beer	$0.32 per proof gallon	$42.7	$0.32 per proof gallon	$42.7	$0.0	$42.7	$0.0
Total Alcohol		$64.3	—	$84.0	$19.7	$83.6	$21.6
Tobacco	$0.36 per pack	$128.7	$1.36 per pack	$486.1	$357.4	$446.8	$391.3
Total		$776.0	—	$1,269.7	$493.7	$1,227.8	$540.5

Note: All estimates are in millions of dollars. The Strong Behavioral Response category assumes price elasticities of demand of –0.25 for motor fuels, –0.679 for liquor, –0.70 for wine, –0.36 for beer, and –0.44 for tobacco products.

large levels of motor fuel consumption generate an $11 million difference across estimates.

Summary and Recommendations

At present, Louisiana excise taxes are lower, and in some cases significantly lower, than regional or national average excise taxes. *We recommend that in all cases the Louisiana excise taxes be aligned to national or regional averages.*

For *beer and alcoholic beverages,* Louisiana taxes alcoholic beverages on a volumetric basis at the wholesale level. The tax is organized into a low alcohol content beverage tax (beer and malts) and a high alcohol content beverage tax (liquor and wine). In fiscal year 2013, receipts from alcoholic beverages totaled approximately $57 million, a slight increase from the previous year. Beer and malts are taxed at a rate of $10.00 per 31-gallon barrel, or $0.32/gallon. This rate is relatively low compared to the rate in states in the southern region; nevertheless, it is slightly higher than the national average of $0.28/gallon. The average beer tax in Alabama, Georgia, Kentucky, Mississippi, North Carolina, South Carolina, and Tennessee averaged 83 cents per gallon or over 2.5 times the Louisiana rate. Texas has a beer tax of 20 cents per gallon. If we compare Louisiana to its neighboring states, the average beer tax is 32.3 cents per gallon or just about the Louisiana rate. At $34.9 million, beer receipts in Louisiana account for a majority of total alcoholic beverage revenue despite its leveling growth patterns.

Growth in alcohol revenue can be attributed to liquor and wine sales. Liquor and wine are taxed at a rate of $0.66/liter ($2.50/gallon) and $0.03/liter ($0.11/gallon), respectively. Louisiana's liquor excise rate falls well below the national average, while the wine excise is the lowest in the United States. In addition, the state imposes a graduated tax on wine of higher alcohol content. Just as a comparison, the average liquor tax is $8.78 per gallon for Alabama, Georgia, Kentucky, North Carolina, South Carolina, and Tennessee, an average rate that is 3.6 times the Louisiana tax rate. Using comparable rates in Texas, Arkansas, and Mississippi, the average liquor rate is $5.46 per gallon. Regardless of what average we use, the liquor rate in Louisiana is extremely low compared to the rate in other states.

Based on regional comparisons, these taxes can be raised in an overall attempt to update the tax structure and produce a certain amount of revenues for the state general fund. We may also want to index the taxes so that the tax rates will grow with inflation. The tax will still be a volume tax but the rate will change from year to year.

As noted earlier, in 2016 the tax on high alcoholic content was raised to $0.80 per liter from $0.66 per liter; the tax on sparkling wines was raised to $0.55 per liter from $0.42 per liter; and the tax on beer was increased to $12.50 per barrel from $10.00 per barrel (31 gallons).

The *tobacco* tax in Louisiana was 36 cents per pack. The average tobacco tax in Texas, Arkansas, and Mississippi is $1.08 per pack, while the average for Alabama, Georgia, Kentucky, North Carolina, South Carolina, and Tennessee is 53 cents per pack. According to the Tax Foundation, Louisiana is the forty-eighth state in the country in terms of the tobacco tax. Tobacco taxes can be increased with a minimal impact on revenue collections unless the rates are increased in order to deter smoking. Very high tax rates can create activity on the part of citizens to avoid the tax entirely by purchasing tobacco in other venues, so any increase in tobacco taxes must recognize that there are limits on any tax increase by the state. However, the evidence suggests that Louisiana could implement a substantial increase in the tobacco tax without encouraging persons to find alternative venues for purchasing tobacco. In 2015 and 2016 the state raised the tax on cigarettes from $0.36 per pack to $1.08 per pack, which is the average rate as charged in Arkansas, Texas, and Mississippi, the three states that border Louisiana. The $1.08 per pack is lower than the tax in Arkansas and Texas and higher than the tax in Mississippi. This increase was done in two stages; raising the rate by $0.50 per pack in 2015 and then by $0.22 per pack in 2016. Taxes on cigars, smoking tobacco, and smokeless tobacco were not changed.

The *gasoline* tax is a tax that is used to pay for the Department of Transportation and Development, highway maintenance, and other highway improvements in Louisiana. The gasoline tax is a tax related to the volume of gasoline purchased. The amount of gasoline required to drive on the state highways and roads depends on the gas mileage relating to the fleet of cars and trucks that are on the road. The method of paying for roads and highway maintenance has not changed over many years, but the relationship between driving, gasoline mileage, and miles driven has changed over time. In comparing Louisiana to other states, Louisiana imposes a relatively similar tax burden. The average gasoline tax for Alabama, Georgia, Kentucky, Mississippi, North Carolina, South Carolina, and Tennessee is 22 cents per gallon; the average gasoline tax for Texas, Arkansas, and Mississippi is 20.2

cents per gallon. In both cases the average gasoline tax in these two groups of states is very close to Louisiana's rate of 20 cents per gallon. However, nationwide the average tax rates are slightly higher, at 24 cents per gallon.

An increase in the gasoline tax from 20 cents per gallon to 24 cents per gallon would be compatible with good tax policy since the tax is similar to a user's fee. It would not drive many people from the market; it would provide additional revenues of $120 million; and it would be assigned to those persons using the streets. Given that the gasoline tax is dedicated to the transportation trust fund, it is appropriate to connect any tax changes in the gasoline tax to any suggestions for highway maintenance and additional infrastructure. In the 2017 regular legislative session it was proposed that the gasoline tax be raised by 17 cents per gallon, and then the suggestion was to increase the gasoline tax by only 10 cents per gallon. Both of these measures failed.

It would also be appropriate to initiate a study connecting the demand for highway maintenance with the appropriate method of funding such maintenance if the current tax sources cannot provide sufficient revenues. This would be the time to rethink the way in which we pay for the use of roads and highways in Louisiana, given that fuel efficiency is improving steadily and the gasoline tax does not account for inflationary trends.

Table 9.11. State Excise Taxes

State	Beer ($ per Gallon)	Distilled Spirits ($ per Gallon)	Wine ($ per Gallon)	Cigarettes ($ per Gallon)	Gasoline Tax (Cents per Gallon	Diesel (Cents per Gallon)
Alabama	$0.53	*	$1.70	67.5	18.0	19.0
Alaska	1.07	$12.80	2.50	200	8.95	9.0
Arizona	0.16	3.00	0.84	200	19.0	27.0
Arkansas	0.23	2.50	0.75	115	21.8	22.8
California	0.20	3.30	0.20	87	32.8	33.0
Colorado	0.08	2.28	0.28	84	22.0	20.5
Connecticut	0.24	5.40	0.72	390	25.0	41.7
Delaware	0.16	3.75	0.97	160	23.0	22.0
Florida	0.48	6.50	2.25	133.9	30.925	31.8
Georgia	0.32	3.79	1.51	37	26.3	29.4
Hawaii	0.93	5.98	1.38	320	16.0	16.0
Idaho	0.15	*	0.45	57	33.0	33.0

Illinois	0.231	8.55	1.39	198	20.1	22.6
Indiana	0.115	2.68	0.47	99.5	18.0	16.0
Iowa	0.19	*	1.75	136	30.7	32.5
Kansas	0.18	2.50	0.30	129	25.03	27.0
Kentucky	0.08	1.92	0.50	60	26.0	23.0
Louisiana	0.40	3.03	0.76	108	20.125	20.1
Maine	0.35	*	0.60	200	30.0	31.2
Maryland	0.09	1.50	0.40	200	33.5	34.3
Massachusetts	0.11	4.05	0.55	351	24.0	24.0
Michigan	0.20	*	0.51	200	26.3	26.3
Minnesota	0.15	5.03	0.30	304	28.6	28.6
Mississippi	0.4268	*	0.35	68	18.4	18.4
Missouri	0.06	2.00	0.42	17	17.3	17.3
Montana	0.14	*	1.02	170	27.0	27.8
Nebraska	0.31	3.75	0.95	64	28.2	27.6
Nevada	0.16	3.60	0.70	180	24.805	27.8
New Hampshire	0.30	*	0.30	178	23.825	23.8
New Jersey	0.12	5.50	0.875	270	37.10	33.4
New Mexico	0.41	6.06	1.70	166	18.875	22.9
New York	0.14	6.44	0.30	435	24.2	22.5
North Carolina	0.6171	*	1.00	45	34.55	34.6
North Dakota	0.16	2.50	0.50	44	23.0	23.0
Ohio	0.18	*	0.32	160	28.0	28.0
Oklahoma	0.40	5.56	0.72	103	17.0	14.0
Oregon	0.08	*	0.67	132	30.0	30.0
Pennsylvania	0.08	*	*	260	58.2	74.7
Rhode Island	0.11	5.40	1.40	375	34.0	34.0
South Carolina	0.77	2.72	0.90	57	16.75	16.8
South Dakota	0.27	3.93	0.93	153	30.0	30.0
Tennessee	1.29	4.40	1.21	62	21.4	18.4
Texas	0.20	2.40	0.204	141	20.0	20.0
Utah	0.41	*	*	170	29.4	29.4
Vermont	0.265	*	*	308	30.46	32.0
Virginia	0.26	*	0.55	30	16.2	20.2
Washington	0.26	14.27	1.51	302.5	49.4	49.4
West Virginia	0.18	*	0.87	120	32.2	32.2
Wisconsin	0.06	3.25	1.00	252	32.9	32.9
Wyoming	0.02	*	0.25	60	24.0	24.0

Note: "*" denotes that the state does not impose this tax.

Notes

1. There are two main sources of price differentiation in motor fuels that this analysis ignores. The first is geographic differentiation, or varying price levels in different parts of the state. Past work by Sarah E. West (2004) found this deviation to be relatively small, on the order of 2 percent of the total price; see "Distributional Effects of Alternative Vehicle Pollution Control Policies," *Journal of Public Economics,* 88 (3–4), 735–57. The other form of deviation is in the type of fuel itself (i.e., "unleaded" vs. "premium"). To our knowledge, no studies exist that quantify such differentiation.

2. Energy Information Administration. (2014). *Petroleum Price History, U.S. All Grades.* Washington, DC: Energy Information Administration.

3. Kulwin, N. (2014). What a Pack of Cigarettes Costs, State by State. *The Awl,* http://www.theawl.com/2014/08/how-much-a-pack-of-cigarettes-costs-state-by-state on 10 April 2015.

4. Young, D. J. (2010). Alcohol Taxes, Beverage Prices, Drinking and Traffic Fatalities in Montana. University of Montana Working Paper. Bozeman, MT.

5. Alm, J., E. Sennoga, and M. Skidmore. (2009). Perfect Competition, Urbanization, and Tax Incidence in the Retail Gasoline Market. *Economic Inquiry,* 47 (1), 118–34.

6. Poterba, J. M. (1991). Is the Gasoline Tax Regressive? In *Tax Policy and the Economy, Volume 5,* J. M. Poterba (Ed.). Cambridge, MA: The MIT Press and National Bureau of Economic Research, 145–64; Chernick, H., and A. Reschovsky. (1997). Who Pays the Gasoline Tax? *National Tax Journal,* 50 (2), 233–59; Metcalf, G. E. (1998). A Distributional Analysis of an Environmental Tax Shift. NBER Working Paper 6546. Boston, MA: National Bureau of Economic Research.

7. The poverty level adopted in all analysis refers to the definitions used by the US Census Bureau in 2013. The poverty threshold for each household varies with the number of adults and children present. Each data source is consistent in changing the threshold to match observations.

8. Decile measures were considered inappropriate given the level of information available.

9. The excise tax on beer is currently above the national median, and thus is projected to remain unchanged.

10. Using federal collection and tax information, cigarettes accounted for 93 percent of tobacco consumption in 2013.

11. Price elasticities of demand were set as follows: –0.25 for motor fuel, in response to long-run analysis from Hughes, Knittel, and Sperling (2008) and Lin and Prince (2013); –0.36 for wine, –0.679 for spirits, and –0.7 for beer, as cited in meta-analysis by Gallet (2007); and 0.44 for tobacco products, using meta-analysis from Gallet and List (2003). See Jonathan E. Hughes, Christopher R. Knittel, and Daniel Sperling (2008), "Evidence of a Shift in the Short-run Price Elasticity of Gasoline Demand," *The Energy Journal* 29 (1), 113–34; C.-Y. Cynthia Lin and Lea Prince (2013), "Gasoline Price Volatility and the Elasticity of Demand for Gasoline," *Energy Economics* 38 (2), 111–17; Craig A. Gallet (2007), "The Demand for Alcohol: A Meta-analysis of Elasticities," *Australian Journal of Agricultural*

and Resource Economics 51 (2), 121–35; and Craig A. Gallet and John A. List (2003), "Cigarette Demand: A Meta-analysis of Elasticities," *Health Economics* 12 (1), 821–35.

12. Federal estimators at the Joint Committee on Taxation and Congressional Budget Office have historically used an offset value of 25 percent.

10

PROPERTY TAXES IN LOUISIANA

Steven M. Sheffrin and Daniel Teles

Introduction

Nationally, the property tax is an important revenue source for local governments. As we discussed in earlier chapters, Louisiana relies less on the property tax for local support than other states and does not impose any state-wide property tax unless one wants to consider the corporate franchise tax a property tax. While nominal property tax rates are similar to those in other states, the base of the property tax in Louisiana is reduced through a series of exemptions and exclusions. This chapter explores the consequences of these decisions. The first section of this chapter describes the mechanics of property taxes in Louisiana. The next section discusses the level of residential property taxes in the state and does so, in large part, by comparing property taxes in Louisiana to those in other states. The third section describes the way in which Louisiana has distributed the burden of paying the property tax. This section also explores differential tax treatment between residential and commercial property, between rental and owner-occupied property, and between different industries. The fourth section discusses the property tax as a source of revenue, describes where revenue is spent, and discusses the impact of policy on revenue levels. We conclude with some overall recommendations on the property tax in Louisiana.

The Mechanics of Property Taxes in Louisiana

Property taxes are governed by a web of interrelated state and local laws and regulations. In Louisiana and in most states, a framework for property taxation is determined at the state level, while rates are determined and the taxes are collected at a local level. This means that, in general, the tax base is determined by the state and tax rates are determined locally.

How is the tax base determined? The Louisiana Constitution is fairly specific on this subject. First, the tax base is defined by the assessment value rather than the true market or use value of a property. Residential property is assessed at 10 percent of its market value. Commercial and agricultural land is also assessed at 10 percent. All other commercial properties (buildings, equipment, etc.) are assessed at 15 percent, and "public service properties" (properties owned by utility companies) are assessed at 25 percent (Louisiana Constitution art. 7 section 18).[1] Second, the state defines a homestead exemption that reduces the assessed value of owner-occupied housing by $7,500 (Louisiana Constitution art. 7 section 20). Since residential property is assessed at 10 percent, this has the effect of excluding the first $75,000 of value of homesteads from taxation. The exemption, as defined constitutionally, "shall not extend to municipal taxes. However, the exemptions shall apply (a) in Orleans Parish, to state, general city, school, levee, and levee district taxes and (b) to any municipal taxes levied for school purposes." Third, the constitution specifically exempts a variety of property types from taxation. No property taxes are levied against public property and property owned by tax-exempt, nonprofit organizations.[2] Further exemptions apply to medical equipment leased by nonprofits and the property of unions, fraternal groups, trade organizations, and professional associations.[3] Additionally, personal property; agricultural products, machinery, and equipment; animals; boats that either use gasoline or are used for fishing; motor vehicles subject to the motor vehicle tax; and all art and property used for "cultural, Mardi Gras carnival, or civic activities and not operated for profit" are exempt from the property tax base (Louisiana Constitution art. 7 section 21). Fourth, the state has the power to offer additional property tax exemptions, the most notable of which is the Industrial Tax Exemption, which we discuss in detail below.

Tax rates are determined locally. In Louisiana, tax rates are represented as "mills," where 1 mill represents a tax bill of $1 for every $1,000 in assessed value. Thus, a rate of 150 mills would be a 15 percent rate on the taxable property or the assessed value of the property. "Millage rates" vary both between and within parishes, as parishes, cities, school districts, and special districts (such as levee districts) select their own millage rates. Moreover, parishes and municipalities may choose to have specific millages earmarked for specific funds. In fact, there is significant variation in those public services receiving funding from a direct millage and those funded by parish or city general funds. In Orleans Parish, for example, there are sixteen different funds that receive a portion of the property tax revenue. Each of these funds levees its own millage rate, with the largest generally being the local school district.

With a few exceptions, properties are appraised by the office of the assessor in each parish and taxes are collected by a separate office. The state constitution mandates that each parish elect an assessor to serve a four-year term (Louisiana Constitution art. 7 section 24). At the state level, the Louisiana tax commission is tasked with ensuring fair, accurate, and uniform ad valorem taxation throughout the state. This entails providing taxpayers with a centralized place to obtain property tax information, including access to legislation, and the publishing of annual reports. Additionally the commission monitors the parish assessors to ensure that assessments are fair and equitable across the state. Taxpayers may appeal their assessments to the commission, and the commission publishes statutes and regulations regarding the assessment and appeals processes. Other responsibilities of the commission include assessing banks and insurance property, assessing public service properties (utilities), and providing assessors with guidelines to enable their compliance with state law.

Taxing Residential Property: How do Louisiana's Property Tax Rates Compare?[4]

Compared with their counterparts in other states, voters in Louisiana have chosen property taxes that are, at least for homeowners, both lower and more progressive.[5] The primary mechanism for implementing both of these choices is a large homestead exemption. Tax rates on nonexempt, residential properties are not especially low at all. Statutory tax rates on the assessed value range from 50.2 mills (or 5.02 percent) in East Feliciana Parish to 172.6 mills (or 17.26 percent) in Grant Parish (Louisiana Tax Commission, 2013a). From this vantage point, taxes in Louisiana seem in line with the national average of 1.24 percent, with this national average relating to fair market value as opposed to assessed value. What homeowners actually pay after accounting for the homestead exemption, however, tells a different story.

The American Community survey asks homeowners the value of their home and the amount that they pay in property taxes. From these self-reported statistics, and assuming they are a reasonably accurate reflection of actual payments, it is possible to calculate an average effective tax rate on owner-occupied housing—the rate homeowners actually pay—for each state. These self-reported rates include the reduction in tax liability from the homestead exemption. Table 10.1 displays the average effective residential property tax in Louisiana, nearby states, and the national average, with the tax being related to the fair market value of the property. With the exception of Texas, southern states tend to have lower property taxes than do states in the Northeast or on the West Coast.[6] Yet Louisiana's average effective tax rate (on the fair market value of owner-occupied residential property) of 0.51 percent is lower than any of its neighbors' and less than half of the national average. Only one parish, East Feliciana, has a statutory tax rate below 0.51 percent of fair market value.

Since property taxes are determined locally, there is significant variation in the level of property taxes within states. The variation within Louisiana is compared to that within Arkansas, Mississippi, Florida, and Texas in Table 10.2. The table shows the average property tax rates in the parishes or counties with the lowest, median, and highest property tax rates in each state. Variation is greatest in Louisiana and Mississippi, where the highest tax rate is more than three times the lowest tax rate. Of these states, Arkansas has the least in-state property tax rate variation.

One reason for geographic variation in property tax rates, both within and between states, is the tendency of large cities to have higher tax rates

TABLE 10.1. Average Self-Reported Effective Tax Rates by State

State	Effective Tax Rate
Louisiana	*0.510%*
Alabama	0.525%
Arkansas	0.745%
Mississippi	0.865%
Oklahoma	0.926%
Tennessee	0.936%
Georgia	0.946%
Florida	1.093%
Texas	1.875%
US Average	1.240%

Note: Effective Tax Rates are calculated from the American Community Survey and reflect the years 2008–2012. The Effective Tax Rate is calculated as the property tax paid divided by the property value. Both the tax paid and the property value are self-reported.

Sources: American Community Survey and authors' own calculations.

TABLE 10.2. Statutory Residential Property Tax Rates in Southern States Based on Fair Market Value

| State | Statutory Tax Rate on Residential Property | | |
	Lowest County	Median County	Highest County
Louisiana	0.50%	1.03%	1.73%
Arkansas	0.76%	0.93%	1.17%
Mississippi	0.40%	1.09%	1.59%
Florida	1.02%	1.74%	2.38%
Texas	1.19%	2.03%	2.91%

Note: Columns represent the total statutory tax rates on residential property in the counties or parishes with the lowest, median, or highest statutory tax rate, except in Texas, where rates are total rates in the incorporated city or town with the lowest, median, and highest combined county and municipal property tax rates. Average, countywide tax rates for Alabama, Oklahoma, Georgia, and Tennessee were unavailable. Sources are available from the authors.

than rural counties do. Table 10.3 displays the average statutory property tax rates in the large urban areas of eight southern states. In Louisiana, the average (population-weighted) property tax rate in New Orleans, Baton Rouge, and Shreveport is 1.36 percent. The property tax rates in Orleans, East Baton Rouge, and Caddo Parishes are all higher than the median rate shown in Table 10.2. Both 10.2 and 10.3 show that statutory tax rates in Louisiana are similar to those in neighboring Mississippi and Arkansas, and lower than in Texas and Florida.

The homestead exemption changes the property tax level significantly. Many states offer some form of homestead exemption, reducing the tax burden significantly on smaller, owner-occupied homes. Generally, the exemption allows individuals to declare a single property a homestead, provided that it is their primary residence. Homestead properties then receive an exemption from some classes of property tax, up to a particular property value. Many states, including Louisiana, offer larger homestead exemptions to qualifying veterans and senior citizens. Because the homestead exemption is available for only one property and only for a portion of the property's value, the homestead exemption has the additional feature of making ad valorem property taxes more progressive.

Louisiana has a far more generous homestead exemption than any of its neighboring states. As noted, the Louisiana homestead exemption extends to the first $7,500 in assessed value, which is equivalent to the first $75,000

TABLE 10.3. Average Statutory Tax Rate in Urban Areas (Cities over 180,000) Compared to Fair Market Value

State	Average Tax Rate
Alabama	0.57%
Oklahoma	1.33%
Louisiana	1.36%
Arkansas	1.40%
Tennessee	1.59%
Georgia	1.59%
Florida	2.02%
Texas	2.05%

Note: This table displays a population-weighted average of the statutory tax rates in the largest cities in each state. Cities over 180,000 in population were included. Population data are from the US Census Bureau. The Orlando rate represents the median tax district in Orange County. The Atlanta rate is based on the Fulton County portion of the city. The Columbus rate encompasses urban service district 1 and assumes it is not part of a business improvement district. The Oklahoma City rate includes the Oklahoma City School District and Metro Tech Community College District. The Tulsa rate is for properties within city limits, in the Tulsa School District, and with less than five acres. Sources are available from the authors.

of market value (Louisiana Constitution art. 7 section 20). This exemption is constitutionally established, and it has not been increased since 1982. Even with this caveat, in 2015 only Mississippi allows as large a deduction, but there the total savings are capped at $300. In most states, the homestead exemption applies to some, but not all, portions of the property tax. Here, too, Louisiana is fairly generous. The constitution exemption applies to all taxes levied by a parish, to all school taxes, and in Orleans Parish, to general municipal and levee taxes (Louisiana Constitution art. 7 section 20). The effect is that one in five properties, and about 40 percent of homeowners in Louisiana, are fully exempt from parish and school taxes.

Property Tax Burden

Among homeowners, the property tax in Louisiana is quite progressive. Using the American Community Survey figures displayed in Table 10.1 as a starting point, we estimated the average statutory rate on residential property in Louisiana and eight nearby states. We began by assigning the average effective tax rate from Table 10.1 to the median valued property. We then imputed a statutory rate that would be consistent with the median household paying the average effective rate. Based on these imputed statutory rates, we calculated the effective rates on homesteads for the 5th, 25th, 75th, and 95th percentile property values, which are displayed in Table 10.4. In Louisiana, an imputed statutory rate of 120.6 mils produces the effective rates displayed in the table. The calculations for Table 10.4 assume all properties to be homesteads.

No other nearby state is nearly as progressive—at least among owner-occupied residences—as Louisiana. At the high end (the rightmost column of Table 10.4), effective tax rates in Louisiana are very similar to rates in Mississippi, Tennessee, Arkansas, and Georgia. At the low end, Mississippi, Florida, Arkansas, and Alabama have similarly low tax rates. Where Louisiana is most different is in the middle of the property tax distribution.

Table 10.4 shows that the effective tax rate on the most expensive homes in Louisiana is roughly twice the rate on a home of median value. It should be noted, however, that the level of the homestead exemption in Louisiana is pegged to neither inflation nor median property values. As property rates rise, other states may raise the level of their exemptions. The effect of the generous homestead exemption on the tax base is discussed in the next section.

Using the same methodology as in Table 10.4, we estimated that the effective tax rate on residential rental property in Louisiana is 1.21 percent. The Louisiana Tax Commission does not report the share of property taxes that come from residential rental properties, but we derived an upper-bound estimate using data from the Tax Commission as a starting point. We assumed that the distribution of land value between homesteads and residential rentals is the same as the distribution between households that own and households that rent—65.7 percent own and 34.3 percent rent. Given that homeowners are, on average, wealthier than renters, this assumption is likely to overestimate the total amount of residential rental real estate. The total value of all homestead land in Louisiana was $17.3 billion in 2012; so an upper bound estimate for residential rentals would be $9.0 billion. The total value of all (homestead or otherwise) residential structures was $151.9 billion—giving an upper bound estimate of rental structures as $52.1 billion. Under this upper-bound estimate, residential rental property has a total value of $61.1 billion and an assessed value of $6.1 billion, and pays 16 percent of all property taxes. In comparison, homesteads value $117.1 billion,

TABLE 10.4. Distribution of Effective Residential Tax Rates on Homesteads by Property Value

State		5th	25th	Median	75th	95th
				Percentile		
Alabama	Value	$15,000	$65,000	$120,000	$195,000	$410,000
	Estimated Tax Rate	0.00%	0.43%	0.53%	0.57%	0.61%
Arkansas	Value	$15,000	$60,000	$100,000	$165,000	$350,000
	Estimated Tax Rate	0.00%	0.51%	0.74%	0.88%	0.99%
Florida	Value	$35,000	$129,000	$200,000	$300,000	$700,000
	Estimated Tax Rate	0.10%	0.91%	1.09%	1.20%	1.33%
Georgia	Value	$25,000	$100,000	$160,000	$250,000	$550,000
	Estimated Tax Rate	0.78%	0.93%	0.95%	0.96%	0.97%
Louisiana	*Value*	*$15,000*	*$75,000*	*$130,000*	*$200,000*	*$380,000*
	Estimated Tax Rate	*0.00%*	*0.00%*	*0.51%*	*0.75%*	*0.97%*
Mississippi	Value	$12,000	$50,000	$97,000	$160,000	$325,000
	Estimated Tax Rate	0.00%	0.57%	0.87%	0.99%	1.08%
Oklahoma	Value	$17,000	$63,000	$100,000	$160,000	$325,000
	Estimated Tax Rate	0.47%	0.87%	0.93%	0.96%	0.99%
Tennessee	Value	$22,000	$80,000	$130,000	$200,000	$450,000
	Estimated Tax Rate	0.94%	0.94%	0.94%	0.94%	0.94%
Texas	Value	$24,000	$75,000	$125,000	$192,000	$410,000
	Estimated Tax Rate	1.15%	1.69%	1.79%	1.84%	1.89%

Note: Property values are reported as the 5th percentile, 25th percentile, median, 75th percentile, and 95th percentile property values according to the American Community Survey between 2008 and 2012. For each state, a constant statutory rate was imputed such that the median household would pay the effective tax rate displayed in Table 9.1. These imputed statutory rates were 64.3 mills for Alabama, 54.7 mills for Arkansas, 16.7 mills for Florida, 24.4 mills for Georgia, 120.6 mills for Louisiana, 117.4 mills for Mississippi, 92.6 mills for Oklahoma, 3.7 mills for Tennessee, and 2.11% for Texas. For state-by-state property tax law information, see Appendix A. Sources: American Community Survey and authors' calculations.

have an assessed value of $11.7 billion, and after homestead exemptions pay only 13 percent of property taxes.

While this estimate of the tax burden on residential rental property is likely an upper bound, the mechanics of the homestead exemption mandate that rental property carries a heavier tax burden than owner-occupied housing. The next logical question is who ends up paying this higher tax: landlords or renters? Unfortunately, there is no clear answer, as it depends on the actual incidence of the tax. If we assume that owners pass the full cost of property taxes on to their tenants, then the property tax system in Louisiana looks a lot less progressive. If, on the other hand, property taxes are taxes on capital, then the incidence falls on owners of capital. From this viewpoint, taxes in Louisiana still look progressive.

The homestead exemption is not the only way in which Louisiana has shifted the tax burden away from homeowners. It also assesses commercial and industrial property at higher rates. This is not uncommon; Alabama, Mississippi, and Tennessee also tax commercial property at higher rates.[7] In all of these states, the primary mechanism for a higher tax on commercial property is a higher assessment ratio. Table 9.5 displays the statutory assessment ratios in Louisiana and five nearby states. Alabama assesses commercial properties at double the rate of residential properties, while Georgia and Arkansas assess all property at the same rate. We estimate effective tax rates for residential (non-homestead) and commercial property using these ratios and the same statutory tax rates we calculated in Table 10.4.

These estimates are displayed in the fourth and fifth columns of Table 10.5. It appears that businesses in Louisiana pay, on average, higher property tax rates than those in Alabama, Arkansas, Georgia, Mississippi, or Tennessee. A 2012 study from the Minnesota Center for Fiscal Excellence examines property taxes in the largest city and one rural city in each state. Their study suggests that New Orleans taxes "Commercial" properties at about average rates and "Industrial" properties at below average rates.[8] For businesses, Louisiana has property tax rates that are average nationally, but high for the region. One exception is for manufacturing, which we discuss below.

Table 10.6 displays the ratio of business tax rates to homestead tax rates. The second column displays the statutory ratio: the assessment ratio on business property divided by the assessment ratio on residential property.

TABLE 10.5. How Commercial and Residential Rates Differ

State	Residential Assessment Ratio	Commercial Assessment Ratio*	Estimated Statutory Residential Tax Rate***	Estimated Commercial Tax
Alabama	10%	20%	0.64%	1.29%
Arkansas	20%	20%	1.09%	1.09%
Georgia	40%	40%	0.98%	0.98%
Louisiana	*10%*	*15%*	*1.21%*	*1.81%*
Mississippi	10%	15%	1.17%	1.76%
Tennessee	25%	40%	0.94%	1.50%

Note: Tax assessments in Oklahoma, Florida, and Texas are determined at the county level.
*In Louisiana, commercial land is assessed at 10%, but improvements to the property and the value of machinery and equipment are assessed at 15%.
**The residential tax rate shown in this table is the average statutory rate implied by the ACS survey. It was calculated by the authors so that the owner of a residential property of median value paid the average effective tax rate shown in Table 9.1. These imputed statutory rates were 64.3 mills for Alabama, 54.7 mills for Arkansas, 16.7 mills for Florida, 24.4 mills for Georgia, 120.6 mills for Louisiana, 117.4 mills for Mississippi, and 3.7 mills for Tennessee.
***The estimated commercial tax rate is calculated as the estimated statutory residential tax rate multiplied by the commercial assessment ratio divided by the residential assessment ratio.

With a ratio of 1.5, Louisiana falls roughly in the middle. Looking only at assessment ratios, however, ignores Louisiana's large homestead exemption. Once the homestead exemption is considered, the difference between commercial and residential rates is larger. The estimates of statewide average rates are calculated by dividing the estimated commercial rate in Table 10.5 by the average effective rate from Table 10.1. We estimate that businesses in Louisiana face tax rates more than three and a half times higher than what a neighboring owner-occupied property would pay.

The right side of Table 10.6 displays ratios calculated in the Lincoln Institute for Land Policy and Minnesota Center for Fiscal Excellence's *50 State Property Tax Comparison Study*.[9] Their calculations are for representative urban and rural cities in each state. The ratios displayed in the table were calculated as the effective tax rate on commercial property divided by the effective tax rate on homestead property. In Louisiana, the effective tax rate on a typical rural homestead property, one with a value of $70,000, is zero; therefore, the ratio cannot be calculated. The ratio in New Orleans, 2.61,

TABLE 10.6. Ratio of Commercial to Homestead Tax Rates

	Authors' Calculations			Lincoln Institute for Land Policy and Minnesota Center for Fiscal Excellence's 50 State Property Tax Comparison Study		
	Statutory Assessment Level	Statewide Average	Urban City	Urban Ratio	Rural City	Rural Ratio
Alabama	2.00	2.45	Birmingham	2.10	Monroeville	2.39
Arkansas	1.00	1.47	Little Rock	1.26	Pocahontas	3.94
Georgia	1.00	1.03	Atlanta	2.51	Fitzgerald	1.19
Louisiana	1.50	3.55	New Orleans	2.61	Natchitoches	n/a
Mississippi	1.50	2.04	Jackson	1.77	Aberdeen	2.01
Tennessee	1.60	1.60	Memphis	1.52	Savannah	1.54

Note: The columns under "Authors' Calculations" display the crude ratio of statutory assessment rates calculated as the ratio of the estimated commercial tax rate from Table 9.5 to the average effective residential tax rate shown in Tables 9.1 and 9.4. In Louisiana, commercial land is assessed at 10%, but improvements to the property and the value of machinery and equipment are assessed at 15%; the 15% figure is used here. The right side of the table contains information from Lincoln Institute for Land Policy and Minnesota Center for Fiscal Excellence's 50 State Property Tax Comparison Study. The urban ratio is the effective rate on a commercial property divided by the effective rate on a homestead of median value. The rural ratio is the effective rate on a commercial property divided by the effective rate on a homestead valued at $70,000. Tax assessments in Oklahoma, Florida, and Texas are determined at the county level, and statewide averages could not be calculated. The ratios of commercial to homestead effective tax rates for Houston, Oklahoma City, and Jacksonville are 1.27, 1.11, and 1.40, respectively. The ratios for Fort Stockton, Texas; Mangum, Oklahoma; and Moore Haven, Florida are 1.46, 1.18, and 2.50, respectively.

ranks Louisiana forty-second nationally—although it is far closer to the states ranked first (who treat business and residential property equally) than it is to the state ranked fiftieth (New York, with a ratio of 6.01).[10]

Based on data from the Louisiana Tax Commission, the total market value of the property tax base is $353 billion, of which 50.5 percent is industrial or commercial, 43.5 percent is (potential) homesteads, and 6.0 percent is public service properties. After the assessment ratios are applied (but before exemptions), the total assessed value of all property in Louisiana is $50.5 billion, of which 53.6 percent is industrial or commercial properties, 34.5 percent is (potential) homesteads, and 11.9 percent is public service properties. The homestead exemption reduces the burden on owner-occupied housing even further. Property that qualifies for the homestead exemption accounts for only 23.2 percent of total revenue, while industrial and commercial properties combine to pay 63.6 percent of taxes. Public service properties pay 13.2 percent.

These figures, however, do not factor in the Industrial Tax Exemption Program (ITEP). Operated by Louisiana Economic Development (LED) and the Board of Commerce and Industry, ITEP offers property tax abatement on new manufacturing investment for up to ten years. The exemption covers manufacturing establishments and additions, including taxable capital equipment but not the value of the land or the inventory contained within the establishment. Additions and establishments are classified as manufacturing if the site is engaged in "the business of working raw materials into wares suitable for use or which give new shapes, qualities, or combinations to matter which already has gone through some artificial process" (Louisiana Administrative Code, Title 13, Part I, Chapter 5, Section 507, Article A). At least 51 percent of the site must qualify under this description to qualify for the exemption.

Between 2004 and 2013, the Board of Commerce and Industry approved $67.4 billion of new investments for the industrial tax exemption.[11] The ten-year tax savings for those projects is unclear for two reasons. First, some property may depreciate or be sold before the ten-year period is over. Second, local assessors may reappraise the property during that time. As an upper bound, if all investment stayed on the tax rolls at the amount approved, the total savings in 2013 would have been $1.15 billion.[12] In 2013, the total tax bill for property not classified as either homesteads or public service companies was $2.58 billion.[13] This suggests that Industrial Tax Exemptions could reduce the total tax bill for businesses by as much as 30.9 percent. To get a lower bound estimate, assume that the combination of depreciation, sales, and business closures causes value of preexisting property qualifying as tax exempt to decline by 10 percent of the initial value each year. Thus the exemption for an investment falls to zero by the time the exemption expires. In this case, ITEP results in a $704 million, or 21 percent, tax reduction for qualifying businesses. This large savings is concentrated in the manufacturing sector, which makes up only the 3.2 percent of businesses in Louisiana (U.S. Census Bureau, 2012). For some manufacturers, the effective tax rate is nearly zero.[14]

The governor of Louisiana made a significant change in the ITEP program by issuing an executive order in 2016. Working through the Board of Commerce and Industry, he made the following changes: (1) local governments (parish governing boards, municipal governing boards, school boards, and law enforcement) will have to sign off on the level of local tax exemption and (2) all ITEP contracts must be accompanied by a Cooperative Endeavor Agreement that outlines a job creation or job retention component.[15]

Who pays the property tax in Louisiana? Businesses pay the greatest amount. Based on assessments reported by the Louisiana Tax Commission, businesses pay more than 75 percent of all property taxes. However, the burden is not shared proportionally across all types of businesses. While manufacturing firms qualify for large tax cuts under ITEP, public utility companies are taxed at the highest rates, but these property taxes may be passed on to consumers. They make up only 6 percent of all property and account for 13 percent of all tax revenue. Relative to their share of property value, residential properties—in particular, homestead properties, bear less of a burden. Property subject to homestead exemptions accounts for more than 40 percent of property value in Louisiana.[16] With a more favorable assessment ratio and the homestead exemption, residential properties pay less than 30 percent of taxes. Owner-occupied homesteads pay between 13 percent and 23 percent. Property tax policy in Louisiana clearly shifts the tax burden away from homeowners and manufacturers and onto the rest of the commercial and industrial sector.

Property Tax Revenue

Property taxes raise more than $4 billion for parishes, school districts, municipalities, and other special districts in Louisiana. They generate more government revenue than the state sales or income taxes do and are a primary source of local government and school district funding. Nationally, property taxes generate more than 20 percent of local revenue and more than 70 percent of local tax revenue. In Louisiana, local sales taxes are also used as a significant source of own-source revenue. However, parishes, municipalities, school districts, and special districts still rely heavily on property taxes to meet funding needs.

Parishes and municipalities differ in their use of property and sales taxes to fund different needs. Separate millages raise revenue for general funds for parishes, municipalities, and school districts, and to fund specific agencies and programs that vary by parish. Figure 10.1 displays the amount of revenue collected by different taxing authorities. Schools receive the largest share of property taxes statewide, raising $1.54 billion, or 38 percent, of total property tax revenue. Parishes levy the second largest share, $1.38 billion, or 34 percent of total revenue. Funds levied by the parishes may pay into parish general funds; fund specific agencies such as the Public Health Unit or the Office of the Assessor; pay off bonds; or pay for specific programs such as Mosquito Control or building maintenance. No other taxing authority levies property taxes in any parish, but dedicated millages for road, levee, and drainage districts are common. Of the sixty-four parishes, twenty-three have dedicated millages to fund roads, twenty-seven have millages for levee districts, and thirty-three have millages for drainage districts. More than $833 million is raised by miscellaneous districts and taxes. Common among these are special fire protection districts, hospital districts, forestry districts, and recreation districts.

Even with all these varied taxing authorities, Louisiana's residential property taxes are lower than those in most other states. How does the $4 billion in revenue compare? On a per capita basis, Louisiana brings in well

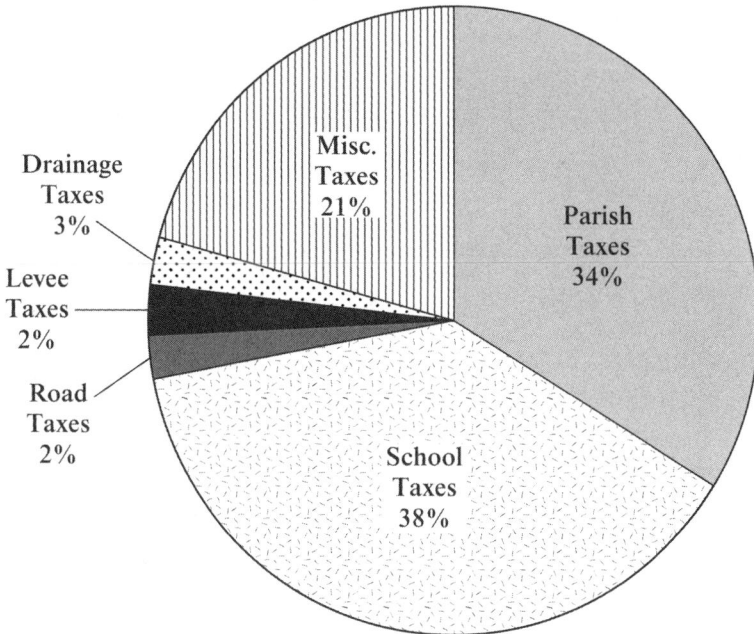

FIGURE 10.1. Property Tax Collections by Percentage of Revenue Collected, 2013

below the national average. However, per capita property tax revenue varies greatly by state. In general, per capita revenue is lower among southern states and highest in the Northeast. Table 10.7 displays per capita property tax collections for Louisiana and nearby states in 2010—the latest year for which a national, cross-state study was available. While well below the national average, the revenue brought in from property taxes in Louisiana is similar to the levels raised in the nearby states of Mississippi, Arkansas, and Tennessee. Texas and Florida raise more than double the property tax revenue as Louisiana, but other taxes in Texas and Florida are much lower. The per capita tax rate in Louisiana rose 17 percent between 2010 and 2013 and now stands at $876 per person (current year dollars).

A similar story is told when revenue is examined as a percentage of either personal income or state GDP. Table 10.8 displays property tax revenue as a percentage of personal income and state GDP. Louisiana property taxes generated revenue equivalent to 2 percent of total personal income, or 1.5 percent of state GDP, in 2010. Again, these figures are well below US averages and generally similar to those in Alabama, Arkansas, Oklahoma, and Tennessee. These numbers have been relatively stable over the last few years. GDP per capita in Louisiana rose by 9.6 percent between 2010 and 2013 in current year dollars (Bureau of Business and Economic Research, 2013b; Federal Reserve Bank of St. Louis, 2014), and property taxes have risen from 1.5 percent to 1.6 percent of state GDP. Whether examined from a per cap-

TABLE 10.7. Per Capita Property Tax Revenue (2010)

State	Collections Per Capita	State Rank
Alabama	$539	50
Arkansas	$598	49
Oklahoma	$642	47
Louisiana	$748	43
Tennessee	$795	42
Mississippi	$853	39
Missouri	$960	37
Georgia	$1,096	33
Florida	$1,507	15
Texas	$1,562	14
US Average	$1,434	–

Sources: US Census Bureau; Tax Foundation (2013)

TABLE 10.8. Property Tax Revenue as a Percent of Income (2010)

State	As a Percent of Personal Income	As a Percent of GDP
Alabama	1.60%	1.49%
Arkansas	1.85%	1.69%
Oklahoma	1.81%	1.63%
Louisiana	2.02%	1.50%
Tennessee	2.26%	1.99%
Mississippi	2.77%	2.65%
Missouri	2.64%	2.36%
Georgia	3.17%	2.65%
Florida	3.93%	3.90%
Texas	4.09%	3.21%
US Average	3.60%	3.08%

Sources: US Census Bureau; Tax Foundation; Bureau of Business and Economic Research, UNM

ita basis, or as a percentage of income, property tax revenue in Louisiana is in line with most neighboring states (with the exception of Texas) but far below the national average.

Various exemptions further reduce the tax base. One of the largest exemptions is the homestead exemption. In total, 1,164,392 properties and half of all taxpayers received the homestead exemption in 2013. Table 10.9 shows the breakdown of number of homesteads and number of properties that are fully exempted from parish and school property taxes. How much of the tax base is eroded by the property tax exemption?

We find that the homestead exemption reduced the property tax base by more than 15 percent. This number, however, varies greatly by parish. Parishes with higher proportions of residential property tend to be more affected by the homestead exemption. Grant Parish loses the largest share of its tax base, just over 40 percent; more than 64 percent of the property value in the parish is residential.[17] Four parishes—Bienville, Cameron, Plaquemines, and Red River—lose less than 5 percent of their tax base to the homestead exemption. In all four, business and commercial property make up more than 60 percent of the tax base, and public service companies (utilities) make up more than 10 percent. The exceptions to this trend are the parishes around New Orleans, Baton Rouge, and Shreveport, which likely have more high-density housing and higher property values.

Higher property values also affect the impact of the homestead exemp-

Table 10.9. Number of Homestead Exemptions (2013)

Parish	Total # of Taxpayers	Total # of Homesteads	Percent of Properties That Are Homesteads	# of 100% Exempt Homesteads	Percent of Properties That Are 100% Exempt
Acadia	32,529	16,921	52%	9,676	30%
Allen	8,801	7,275	83%	6,071	69%
Ascension	43,457	32,713	75%	10,337	24%
Assumption	12,744	6,299	49%	3,170	25%
Avoyelles	26,955	12,847	48%	8,290	31%
Beauregard	16,868	10,362	61%	6,792	40%
Bienville	13,204	4,497	34%	3,828	29%
Bossier	60,511	28,693	47%	8,039	13%
Caddo	155,244	56,629	36%	24,342	16%
Calcasieu	91,856	49,020	53%	23,782	26%
Caldwell	8,567	3,854	45%	3,186	37%
Cameron	13,155	2,851	22%	1,917	15%
Catahoula	8,983	3,928	44%	3,070	34%
Claiborne	14,221	4,673	33%	3,391	24%
Concordia	9,550	6,591	69%	4,686	49%
Desoto	17,864	9,277	52%	7,096	40%
East Baton Rouge	213,012	101,105	47%	24,014	11%
East Carrol	5,223	1,552	30%	1,171	22%
East Feliciana	12,125	6,260	52%	3,050	25%
Evangeline	15,400	9,728	63%	6,686	43%
Franklin	8,934	6,931	78%	5,282	59%
Grant	7,612	7,023	92%	4,963	65%
Iberia	30,565	21,462	70%	11,959	39%
Iberville	11,777	8,206	70%	4,514	38%
Jackson	9,905	4,523	46%	2,956	30%
Jefferson	160,192	103,288	64%	16,036	10%
Jefferson Davis	20,236	8,572	42%	4,961	25%
Lafayette	112,412	54,496	48%	13,462	12%
Lafourche	37,070	28,710	77%	13,760	37%
Lasalle	10,669	4,581	43%	3,137	29%
Lincoln	29,326	9,720	33%	9,625	33%
Livingston	53,523	35,670	67%	13,098	24%
Madison	6,592	2,443	37%	2,043	31%
Morehouse	20,867	7,954	38%	4,977	24%
Natchitoches	20,451	9,938	49%	5,347	26%

Parish	Total # of Taxpayers	Total # of Homesteads	Percent of Properties That Are Homesteads	# of 100% Exempt Homesteads	Percent of Properties That Are 100% Exempt
Orleans	148,251	62,267	42%	9,500	6%
Ouachita	72,139	36,117	50%	9,710	13%
Plaquemines	45,024	5,432	12%	2,456	5%
Pt. Coupee	14,620	7,337	50%	3,803	26%
Rapides	69,886	36,382	52%	20,998	30%
Red River	4,900	2,605	53%	2,105	43%
Richland	10,973	6,540	60%	4,679	43%
Sabine	18,369	7,844	43%	5,785	31%
St. Bernard	20,749	8,865	43%	3,728	18%
St. Charles	24,981	14,157	57%	3,354	13%
St. Helena	7,312	3,668	50%	3,066	42%
St. James	11,652	6,602	57%	3,275	28%
St. John	18,582	12,867	69%	4,610	25%
St. Landry	42,249	23,038	55%	12,870	30%
St. Martin	30,975	15,639	50%	8,553	28%
St. Mary	42,669	16,781	39%	10,693	25%
St. Tammany	128,897	70,315	55%	7,384	6%
Tangipahoa	64,398	31,028	48%	13,012	20%
Tensas	4,594	1,555	34%	1,264	28%
Terrebonne	53,778	28,156	52%	10,365	19%
Union	20,091	6,831	34%	4,029	20%
Vermilion	39,525	16,706	42%	8,725	22%
Vernon	15,633	12,155	78%	9,204	59%
Washington	19,611	13,513	69%	9,066	46%
Webster	23,898	12,607	53%	9,029	38%
West Baton Rouge	10,262	6,130	60%	1,743	17%
West Carroll	7,022	3,603	51%	2,784	40%
West Feliciana	5,401	2,638	49%	713	13%
Winn	12,318	4,422	36%	3,523	29%
Total	*2,309,159*	*1,164,392*	*50%*	*468,740*	*20%*

Source: Louisiana Tax Commission, 2013

tion, but not as much as proportions of business and residential property. The effect of property values is largest in Orleans, St. Tammany, Jefferson, East Baton Rouge, and St. Charles. In these parishes fewer than one in four homesteads is fully exempt. Yet St. Tammany, which is more than 60 percent residential, still loses more than 20 percent of its tax base to the homestead exemption. On the other extreme, more than 80 percent of the homesteads in Allen, Bienville, Caldwell, Lincoln, Madison, Red River, and Tensas are fully exempt. In Lincoln, 99 percent of homestead properties are valued at less than $75,000. Yet Bienville and Red River lose less than 5 percent of their tax base, and Lincoln still retains more than 86 percent of its tax base.

Because the homestead exemption is not tied to inflation, its effect has steadily declined. In 1990, 83 percent of properties in Louisiana qualified as 100 percent exempt under the homestead exemption—that is, they paid no parish or school property taxes. This reduced the tax base and total revenue from property taxes by 28 percent. As of 2000, 69 percent of properties qualified as 100 percent exempt, and the exemption reduced the tax rolls by about one-fourth.[18] The number of 100 percent exempt properties fell more sharply in the 2000s. By 2010 only 43 percent of properties were 100 percent exempt, and the reduction of the exemption's effect on the tax base had declined to a 17 percent reduction. In 2013, 40 percent of properties qualified as 100 percent exempt through the homestead exemption, and the exemption reduced the tax base by only 16 percent. The further property prices rise, the smaller the effect of the homestead exemption on revenues will be.

There is no official figure of the amount by which the Industrial Tax Exemption Program shrinks the property tax base. With $67.4 billion of investment approved under the ITEP between 2004 and 2013, we know the figure is quite large. Based on the values of the projects and the estimated tax savings provided by Louisiana Economic Development, we estimated—using the method described above—that ITEP reduces the property tax base by between 11.2 percent and 18.5 percent—making it potentially larger than the homestead exemption.[19]

Unlike the homestead exemption, ITEP exemptions are for the full value of the new property (exclusive of land) or infrastructure improvement. As such, the size of the exemptions keeps up with inflation. Moreover, the value of the investments approved by ITEP has increased by more than 380 percent since 2000. Figure 10.2 displays the amount of manufacturing invest-

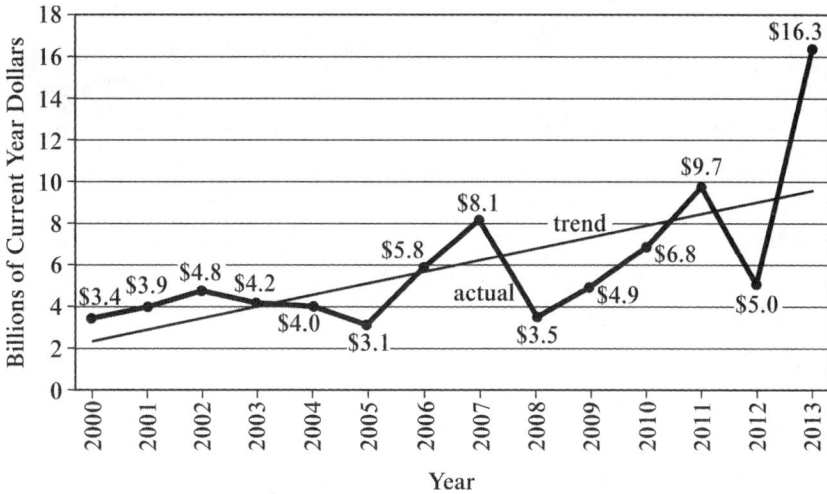

FIGURE 10.2. Manufacturing Investment Approved to be Property Tax–Exempt

ment approved under ITEP each year between 2000 and 2013. The ITEP has increased the value of exemptions given by an average rate of 13 percent. Even if the $16.3 billion approved last year is an outlier, the trend line shows average growth of almost $1 billion per year.

The total effect of the ITEP on revenue is unclear for two reasons. First, we do not know how much of the new manufacturing investment would have happened were the ITEP not in place. The cost of the program is only in the revenue lost from manufacturing property that would have existed even without the exemption. Since the program is statewide, there is no strong counterfactual against which we can compare. Second, there may be significant spillover effects on the value of other properties. The construction of a new plant could reduce the value of residential property nearby, further eroding the tax base. On the other hand, a new plant could bring new jobs to an area, create opportunities for other businesses, and raise the value of property nearby. It is important to note that while any effect on revenue occurs locally, the ITEP is administered at the state level.

Other Property Tax Issues

There are two other issues that are frequently discussed with respect to the property tax. They are the possibility of a statewide property tax and the consequences of removing inventories from the local ad valorem tax. While property tax exemptions for new manufacturing property and homestead are regulated by state law, Louisiana does not currently levy any statewide property taxes. Constitutionally, the state has limited power to levy property taxes. The Louisiana Constitution allows the state to levy an ad valorem tax on the assessed value of all property at a rate not to exceed five and three-quarter mills (Louisiana Const. art. VII, section 19). Taking into account that residential property is assessed at 10 percent of market value in Louisiana, a tax of 5.75 mills implies an additional residential property tax of 0.0575 percent.

While most states do not levy a statewide property tax, Alabama imposes a statewide tax of 6.5 mills (which translates into 0.065 percent on residential property with its 10 percent assessment ratio), and Georgia imposes a nominal statewide tax of 0.15 mills (which translates into 0.006 percent on residential property with its 40 percent assessment ratio). These taxes brought in $339 million and $51 million, or 4 percent and 0.3 percent of the state budgets, in fiscal year 2013 (Alabama Department of Revenue, 2013; The Governor's Office of Planning and Budget, 2013).

In Louisiana, the potential revenue stream of a 5.75 mill state property tax would represent a property tax increase of 5.3 percent. At 2013 assessment levels, the tax would bring in over $200 million to the state. While significant, it would represent only about 2.5 percent of total state revenue. It would also then require the state and parishes to "equalize" property assessments in order to avoid shifting the distribution of the tax burden from one parish to another. This would entail substantial administrative costs and complexity for relatively little gain.

Inventory held by manufacturers, retailers, and distributors is taxed as personal property at the local level. However, as we described in earlier chapters, businesses are allowed a credit against these ad valorem tax payments, and until 2015, they were fully refundable. Thus, the state offsets the taxes on inventories faced by business. In recent years, these credits have been in the neighborhood of $450 million, or approximately 11 percent of the property tax base. Thus, simply prohibiting local governments from taxing inventories would lead to a substantial revenue loss.

Some have suggested that phasing down the industrial tax exemption could be coupled with repealing the property tax on inventories. On an aggregate level, this might seem possible, as we estimated over $700 million as a lower bound from fully phasing out the industrial tax exemption, while the cost of the inventory tax credit is only about $450 million. Careful examination on a parish-by-parish base suggests that a simple swap is not likely to work. The biggest losers from such a change would be the largest parishes in terms of population. Jefferson Parish, for example, has a large number of large retail outlets but relatively few new projects that qualify for the industrial tax exemption. Parishes that have received much of the new investment in the state in recent years—for example, Cameron Parish—on paper would be the big winners. None of these calculations take into account what investment levels would have been without the credit.

Thus, while scaling down the industrial tax exemption may be a worthwhile reform objective in terms of increasing local revenues and equalizing effective tax rates across classes of properties, even a complete phaseout would not provide a solution to the inventory tax credit issue at the state level. In practice, any change to the industrial tax exemption would need to be phased in. Finally, we do need to consider the extent to which the tax exemption does increase investment levels.

Concluding Thoughts and Recommendations

Key property tax policies in Louisiana are embedded in the state constitution. The constitutionally provided homestead exemption, and the state's constitutional authority to provide industrial tax exemptions, leave local governments with little ability to tailor the property tax to suit their needs. Instead, local governments offer very different millage rates and different levels of property taxes. For homeowners, property taxes in Louisiana appear moderately low and very progressive. This is due to a generous homestead exemption which, in turn, leads to an increased burden on residential rental and commercial properties. Industrial properties can avoid large portions of the property tax if they invest in new manufacturing property that qualifies for the industrial tax exemption. Louisiana tax policy incentivizes homeownership and manufacturing, and forces residential rental and other commercial properties to pick up the remainder of the tax burden. What reforms should be made for the property tax?

First, we should recognize that, despite political pressure, the current level for the homeowners' exemption has not changed since 1982. Since the homestead exemption has not been changed for thirty-six years, its effects on the tax base have eroded over time as property values increased. In 1990, the homestead exemption reduced the taxable base by approximately 28 percent; in 2013, the taxable base was reduced by only 16 percent. One recommendation would be to maintain the $7,500 homestead exemption, but not let it increase above the current $7,500.

This is not the case for the industrial tax exemption. The exemption in Louisiana offers full property tax abatement on new manufacturing investment for up to ten years (an initial five years with a five-year renewal), including taxable equipment but excluding land and inventories. While other states have similar exemptions, most states are not as generous, limiting their exemption period to five years. In addition, in other states, local governments must first request the exemption, while in Louisiana the exemptions are determined at the state level, and the local parishes have no say in the process. Our estimates suggest that the reduction of the property tax base from the industrial tax exemption program is greater than the homestead exemption in terms of reducing the tax base, although the differences vary sharply across parishes.

Unlike the homestead exemption (which is naturally reduced by increases in property values over time as long as the exemption is not increased), there are no mechanisms to decrease the industrial property tax exemption. One simple proposal would be to limit the amount of the exemption to 80 percent and to limit it to one seven-year period. This is still a generous incentive for manufacturing, but would put a partial brake on the expansion of this exemption. Local parishes would then regularly assess and tax the other 20 percent. A more aggressive proposal would be to completely phase out the industrial tax exemption, though we have to be aware of the fact that thirty-nine other states have versions of the industrial tax exemption. Our revenue estimates suggest that this eventually would raise more than enough total revenue to equal the loss of exempting inventories from the ad valorem tax, but the revenues do not match up well on a parish-by-parish basis. Regardless of the specific plan adopted, an important additional change would be to require approval by the local parish before approving any exemptions.

Notes

1. The tax base for a business would then be calculated as 10% × Land Value + 15% × (Building Value + Equipment Value).

2. Notably, this exempts churches and universities from the property tax base.

3. In general, Louisiana has significantly broader exemptions for nonprofits than other states. For a discussion, see Janelle Sharer, "Subsidizing Rental Properties, Country Clubs, and Blight: The Unintended Consequences of Louisiana's Overbroad Property Tax Exemption," 2015, available from the authors.

4. Details and sources for all our calculations are contained in the working paper version of this chapter, which is available from the authors.

5. The differential treatment between rental and owner-occupied housing is discussed in the next section.

6. The Tax Foundation (2011, June 02), *Median Property Taxes Paid by County, 2005–09*. Retrieved June 16, 2014, from http://taxfoundation.org/article/median-property-taxes-paid-county-2005–09.

7. In Louisiana, commercial and agricultural lands are taxed at the same rate as residential property, but all improvements and equipment are taxed at a higher rate.

8. Lincoln Institute for Land Policy and Minnesota Center for Fiscal Excellence (2013), *50 State Property Tax Comparison Study*.

9. Lincoln Institute for Land Policy and Minnesota Center for Fiscal Excellence (2013), *50 State Property Tax Comparison Study*.

10. J. Henchman (November 21, 2012), *State and Local Property Taxes Target Commercial and Industrial Property*. Retrieved from The Tax Foundation, http://taxfoundation.org/sites/taxfoundation.org/files/docs/ff342.pdf.

11. Figures are based on calculations from data exported from a Fast Lane applicant search at https://fastlane.louisianaeconomicdevelopment.com/ApplicationSearch.aspx. Dollar amounts available through Louisiana Economic Development are either estimated or self-reported; actual property values are determined by local assessors.

12. This figure was calculated by multiplying the exemptions from 2004–2013 in each parish by the average millage rate in the parish.

13. This figure was calculated by multiplying assessed value of all property types not classified as eligible for homestead exemption or public service properties in each parish—as listed in the Louisiana Tax Commission's Annual Report—and multiplying it by the average millage in the parish.

14. We looked up individual assessments of ten properties listed as having received the Industrial Tax Exemption. The lowest effective tax rate that I found was 0.05% for a recycling plant in New Orleans.

15. "LED Announces Changes in Industrial Tax Exemption Program," June 24, 2016.

16. Factoring in rental properties, I estimate that owner-occupied housing accounts for 33 percent of all property value in Louisiana.

17. This missing tax base may help explain why Grant Parish has the highest millage rates in the state.

18. These comparisons derive from data from various reports of the Louisiana Tax Commission.

19. To calculate the high estimate, we took the total value of projects approved under ITEP from 2004–2013 and multiplied them by the 0.15 assessment ratio for commercial and industrial improvements to obtain an estimate of $10.1 billion in assessments lost from the tax base. To calculate the low estimate, I assumed that the projects lost 10 percent of initial value each year, thus having no value after ten years. We then multiplied these depreciated values by the 0.15 assessment ratio to get an estimate of $5.6 billion in assessments lost from the tax base.

11

THE ROLE OF TAX EXEMPTIONS, DEDUCTIONS, AND CREDITS

James Alm and Bibek Adhikari

Introduction

It is well known that Louisiana's major tax bases have been narrowed significantly by giving extensive and generous tax exemptions and tax credits. The property tax base has been narrowed by the homestead exemption and the industrial tax exemption. The corporate income tax base has been reduced by fifty-two tax credits and numerous additional tax incentives offered through the Louisiana Economic Development (LED). The sales tax has nearly two hundred tax-exempt personal property transactions, there are exemptions for sales tax holidays, and, by constitutional provision, there are exemptions for food consumption at home, residential utilities, gasoline and special fuels, and prescription drugs. The personal income tax base is narrowed by a deduction for federal tax liability, by retirement exclusions, by credits for rehabilitation of historic structures, by excess itemized deductions, and by other provisions.

In total, there are 462 separate tax exemptions, which the Louisiana Department of Revenue (LDR) estimates led to a total loss of $7.1 billion in revenues in 2013–2014 (*Tax Exemption Budget 2013–2014*). These revenue losses have continued to grow in recent years. These many tax preferences have been placed in the tax code for specific and different reasons, such as defining income or consumption more accurately, enhancing fairness, stimulating economic development, or even rewarding political constituents. However, they also come at obvious costs: the narrowed bases require higher tax rates on the bases that remain to generate revenues, they create distortions both within Louisiana and across state borders, they lead to unequal treatment of similarly situated individuals and businesses, and they increase the burden on the tax administration.

The tax preferences can be broadly classified into two groups: statutorily imposed exemptions and constitutionally imposed exemptions. Statutorily

imposed exemptions emerge from the usual legislative process. Constitutionally imposed exemptions include exemptions that are prohibited from
taxation by the state constitution, federal laws, or existing reciprocal agreements between states.

This chapter examines the practice and results of tax preferences in Louisiana, focusing especially on tax exemptions in the general sales tax and the
vehicle sales tax (referred to for simplicity as the "sales tax"), as well as tax
exemptions in the personal income tax (PIT); we also discuss some of the
larger tax credits designed for economic development, although this discussion is brief. We present information on historic trends of the amount
of revenue loss due to all tax exemptions in Louisiana, and also for the sales
tax and the PIT, over the period 1997 to 2013. We also suggest specific policies to rationalize the many exemptions and to ensure they meet the state's
policy goals.

Data and Methodology

Our primary source of data is the *Tax Exemption Budget* (TEB) published
by the Louisiana Department of Revenue (LDR) in various issues from fiscal years 1999 to 2014. The LDR is required by Section 1517 of Title 47 of the
Louisiana Revised Statues to prepare an annual tax exemption budget report. The TEB provides general information on each tax exemption: legal
citations, brief descriptions of purpose of each exemption, legislative origins, effective dates, beneficiaries, administration, and estimated fiscal effects for the preceding two years, the current year, and two ensuing fiscal
years. When possible, the estimated amounts of exemptions in the TEB are
calculated from the actual tax returns; however, in many cases the necessary information is not reported in the tax returns, so alternative sources
are used (e.g., information from specific taxpayers and estimates from the
Louisiana Legislative Fiscal Office). See Table 11.4 at the very end of the
chapter for a detailed listing of all Louisiana tax exemptions and their associated revenue loss, broken down by type, for a recent representative year.

The LDR began publishing the TEB annually in fiscal year 1983, and it
has been available in electronic form since fiscal year 1999. We collect the
data on current fiscal effects of tax exemptions for all major categories of
tax types such as the general sales tax, the PIT, the corporate income tax,
the corporate franchise tax, the gift tax, the inheritance tax, the liquors–al-

coholic beverages tax, the petroleum products tax, the severance tax, the tobacco tax, and tax exemption and incentive contracts.

Our focus is on the PIT and the sales tax, although we also briefly discuss economic development tax preferences. For the PIT and the sales tax, we collect data on all reported exemptions. In some instances, revised estimates for exemptions are published in the TEB to reflect revenue losses obtained from more reliable sources. In all cases, we use the most recent and up-to-date data available. This gives us annual data on exemptions from fiscal years 1997 to 2013.

We also collect quarterly data on revenues for the PIT, the general sales tax, and total tax revenues from the Rockefeller Institute of Government, for which the original source of data is the US Census Bureau *Quarterly Summary of State and Local Government Tax Revenue*. The fiscal calendar in Louisiana spans July to June, so we sum quarterly data to create an annual series based on the fiscal year. For example, we sum data for the third and fourth quarter of 2004 and the first and second quarter of 2005 to get the series for the fiscal year ending in 2005, which for simplicity we call "fiscal year 2005."

We calculate several measures for the tax exemptions. We sum the "actual tax collections" plus the "revenue losses" from each of the exemptions, and we call this "total potential collections." Dividing the revenue loss by the total potential collections gives the percentage of tax loss due to exemptions, which can be interpreted as the percentage of revenue collection forgone due to the exemptions. We also measure the relative size of individual exemptions by dividing the individual exemptions by the total exemptions (or the share of revenue loss due to individual exemptions). These are gross measures of losses as they do not account for any behavioral changes induced by exemptions; these measures also assume that all other elements of the tax system remain unchanged, so that any potential cross effects across exemptions are not considered. Note that total exemptions include exemptions that are prohibited from taxation by the state constitution, federal laws, or existing reciprocal agreements, so that obtaining a zero revenue loss would be impossible in the current institutional environment.

In the next section we present our estimates for the overall tax system. We then examine the sales tax and the personal income tax separately and in detail, followed by a brief discussion of economic development tax preferences. We conclude with a summary and recommendations.

Tax Exemptions in the Overall Tax System

Figure 11.1 graphs total revenue from taxes, total revenue losses from tax exemptions, and the percentage of revenue losses due to tax exemptions. Both the revenues and the losses are increasing over the years. For example, in fiscal year 1997 total revenue was $5.5 billion and total loss was $5.3 billion; in fiscal year 2013 revenue increased to $9.2 billion and total loss increased to $7.1 billion; projected revenue losses for fiscal year 2015 are $7.9 billion. The percentage of loss due to various exemptions ranges from 35.5 percent in fiscal year 2002 to 50.0 percent in fiscal year 1999, with an average percentage loss of 43.5 percent. This result implies that, if all exemptions were removed, total revenue could be increased by 43.5 percent on average. See Table 11.1 for the estimated revenue losses for the major taxes.

How much of the revenue and losses are due to the sales tax and the PIT? Figure 11.2 graphs sales tax revenues as a percentage of total revenues and the loss of revenues from sales tax exemptions as a percentage of loss of revenues from total exemptions. The sales tax is the major source of Louisiana's revenue system, accounting for roughly one-third of total revenues across the years, and its importance has remained roughly the same in the last sixteen years. However, the share of sales tax revenue loss relative to total revenue loss has increased steadily, with a sharp spike during the post-Katrina years. By 2006 the proportional loss from sales tax exemptions was greater

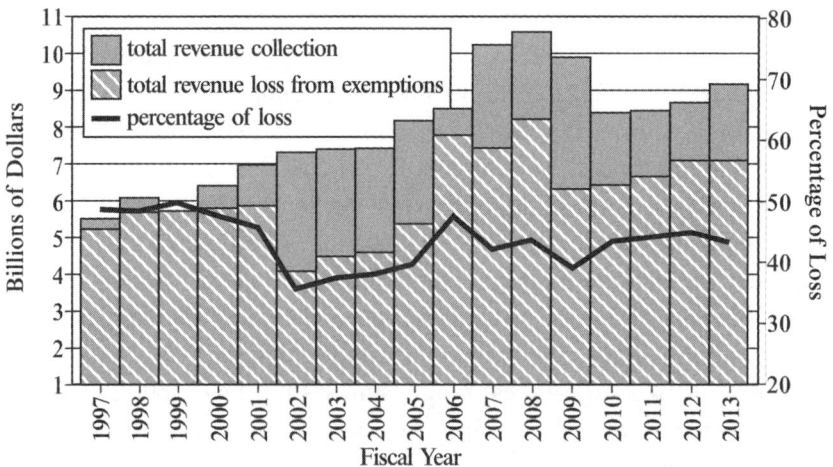

FIGURE 11.1. Total Revenue Collections and Total Revenue Losses from Exemptions

TABLE 11.1: Revenue Loss from Tax Exemptions

Type	Revenue Loss, FY 2013 ($)	Projected Revenue Loss, FY 2015 ($)
Sales tax	$2,663,450,562	$3,148,155,000
Personal income tax	1,961,388,192	2,103,603,000
Tax incentives and exemption contracts	319,403,814	456,325,000
Corporate franchise tax	19,812,262	19,710,000
Corporation income tax	1,502,155,325	1,722,720,000
Gift tax	—	—
Inheritance tax	—	—
Liquors: alcoholic beverage taxes	2,776,055	2,721,000
Natural resources: severance tax	462,887,099	328,195,677
Petroleum products tax	73,337,375	91,225,000
Tobacco tax	75,997,300	84,440,000
Public utilities and carriers tax	3,196,000	3,000,000
Hazardous waste disposal tax	13,700	20,000
Total revenue loss	$7,084,434,484	$7,932,588,377

Note: "—" denotes a negligible amount of revenue loss.
Source: *Tax Exemption Budget, 2013–2014 and 2014-2015*, Louisiana Department of Revenue (Baton Rouge, LA)

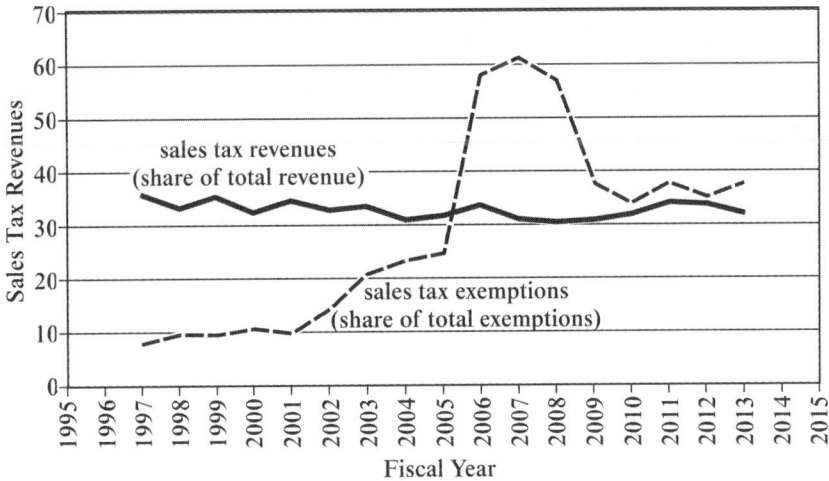

FIGURE 11.2. Sales Tax Revenues as Share of Total Revenues and as Share of Tax Exemptions

than the proportion of revenue collected from sales tax. In the next section we discuss in detail the changes in various sales tax exemptions over the years.

Figure 11.3 graphs PIT revenue as a percentage of total revenue and the loss of revenues from PIT exemptions as a percentage of loss of revenues from total exemptions. The PIT is the second biggest source of Louisiana's revenue system, accounting for 23.1 to 30.8 percent of total revenue across the years, and its importance has increased in the last sixteen years.

The share of revenue loss from the PIT has also increased over the years, although the share was generally decreasing during 2003–2006, largely due to the Stelly plan. The percent of loss was 23.1 percent in 1997, and increased to 29.7 percent in 2013. In the next sections we discuss the changes in various tax exemptions that have caused the pattern of revenue loss over the years.

Sales Tax Exemptions: Structure and Trends

Louisiana is one of the forty-five states that levy a sales tax, adopting a sales tax in 1936 by charging a 2 percent tax on luxury sales. In 1938, the luxury sales tax was replaced with a more general sales tax at a rate of 1 percent. The first permanent sales tax was enacted in 1944 at a rate of 1 percent, which

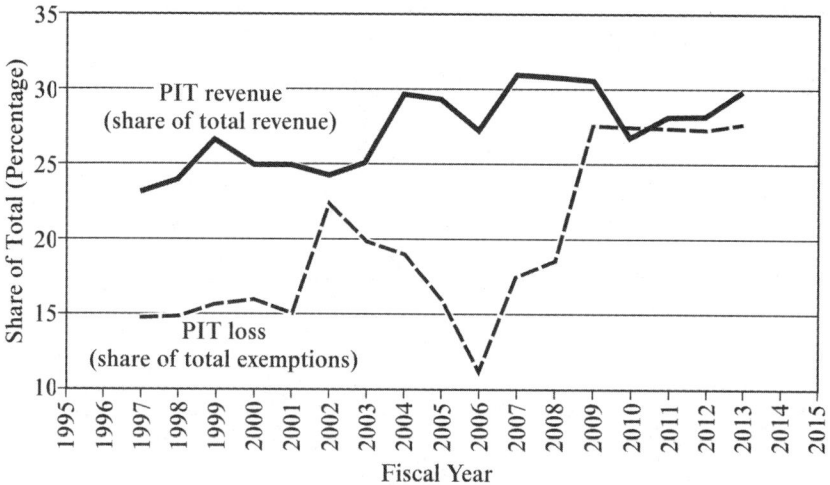

FIGURE 11.3. Personal Income Tax Revenues as Share of Total Revenues and as Share of Tax Exemptions

was increased to 2 percent in 1948, 3 percent in 1970, and 4 percent in 1984. The state tax rate remained at 4 percent until it was increased to 5 percent in a special session of the legislature in 2016 to deal with a major shortfall in revenues.

The base of the sales tax has changed numerous times over the years. The tax base consists of retail sales of tangible personal property, rental or lease of movable property, and sales of selected services. Consumers pay the sales tax on the price of goods and select services at the point of sale, and the sales tax is collected by the qualified seller and remitted to the LDR. Businesses with a physical presence, or "nexus" (e.g., offices, branches, warehouses, employees in the state), are responsible for the collection and the remittance of the state and local sales tax. The tax base also includes a use tax on the cost of tangible personal property imported into Louisiana or purchased within the state without the proper payment of sales tax.

Exemptions have existed since the beginning, with the number of exemptions increasing significantly in recent years. The number of sales tax exemptions increased from 143 in 1999 to 192 in 2013, a 34.3 percent increase. As many as fifteen new exemptions have been enacted in a single year. See Table 11.2.

Another complication to the sales tax structure is the suspension of the exemptions. Most of the sales tax exemptions were suspended beginning in 1986. As a result of the suspension, traditionally exempt items, including food and utilities, were taxed at the 1 percent suspended rate. The suspended rate was increased to 3 percent on 1 August 1989 and remained so for the most part until 30 June 2000, except that the suspension rate was 2 percent from 1 January 1990 to 9 July 1990 and 4 percent from 1 July 1993 to 30 September 1996. The suspension rate was increased to 4 percent from 1 July 2000 to 30 June 2009. From 1 July 2009, the suspended rate decreased to 1 percent again.

Local governments in Louisiana can also levy and collect the sales tax. The local sales tax rate for all local governments cannot exceed 3 percent unless approved by the state legislature and approved by electors voting in a special election.

Figure 11.4 graphs revenue collected from the sales tax and the revenue loss due to sales tax exemptions. The revenue was $2.0 billion and the exemptions were $0.4 billion in 1997; by 2013 the revenue increased to $2.9 billion and the exemptions also increased to $2.7 billion, or by $2.3 billion.

TABLE 11.2: Number of Exemptions in the PIT and the Sales Tax, 1999–2013

Fiscal Year	PIT	Sales Tax	Change in Number of PIT Exemptions from Prior Year	Change in Number of Sales Tax Exemptions from Prior Year
1999	35	143	—	
2000	39	145	4	2
2001	40	146	1	1
2002	50	156	10	10
2003	50	156	0	0
2004	50	163	0	7
2005	46	162	−4	−1
2006	47	162	1	0
2007	61	177	14	15
2008	73	177	12	0
2009	76	188	3	11
2010	76	188	0	0
2011	78	191	2	3
2012	78	191	0	0
2013	79	192	1	1

Source: *Tax Exemption Budget*, various years, Louisiana Department of Revenue (Baton Rouge, LA)

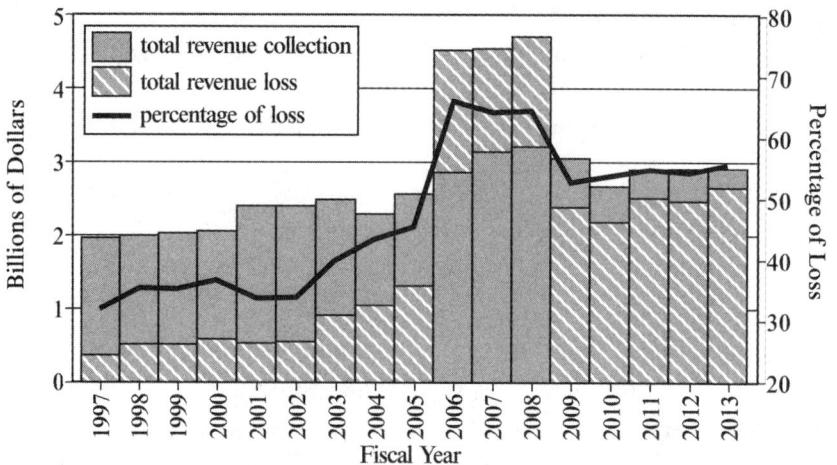

FIGURE 11.4. Sales Tax Revenues and Sales Tax Revenue Losses Due to Exemptions

For fiscal years 2006, 2007, and 2008, exemptions were greater than the actual revenue collected, so that for every dollar raised in revenue, more than one dollar was forgone in exemptions. Figure 11.4 also shows the percentage of loss due to sales tax exemptions. There is an increasing trend in the percentage of loss, starting from close to 20 percent in 1997 and ending at 50 percent in 2013. The highest amount of loss is close to 60 percent during fiscal years 2006, 2007, and 2008. The increasing trend in exemptions does not necessarily mean that it is an undesirable development. The spike in tax exemptions during 2006–2008 was created by tax expenditures enacted to offset the damages caused by Hurricanes Katrina and Rita. The trend in exemptions has reverted back to the pre-Katrina level since 2009.

Figure 11.5 breaks down total sales tax exemptions into constitutionally protected exemptions and statutorily protected exemptions. Out of 192 sales tax exemptions, only 10 are constitutionally imposed. Both categories follow similar trends, with statutorily protected exemptions being slightly larger in number than constitutionally protected exemptions until 2005. Statutorily protected exemptions jumped in 2006 and stayed at that level through 2008 before falling back to the previous trend in 2009.

The jump in 2006–2008 was created by various exemptions that were in place due to Hurricanes Katrina and Rita. These include the following: the purchase or rental of machinery and equipment to replace equipment

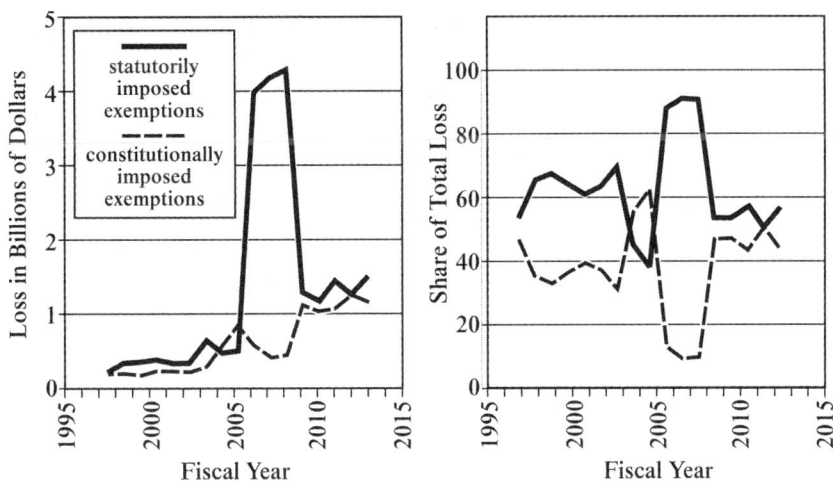

FIGURE 11.5. Sales Tax Revenue Losses Due to Constitutionally Imposed versus Statutorily Imposed Exemptions

damaged or destroyed by Hurricanes Katrina or Rita; a 2005 sales tax holiday for business purchases, an exemption available for those businesses that were located in Hurricanes Katrina or Rita Federal Emergency Management Agency Individual Assistance Areas that acquire property to replace property that was damaged, destroyed, or lost as a result of conditions created by the hurricanes; hurricane preparedness Louisiana sales tax holiday; and sales of construction materials to Habitat for Humanity.

Major Sales Tax Exemptions

In this subsection we describe twelve of the largest sales tax exemptions, ordered according to their average rank across all active years from 1997 to 2013. See Figures 11.6 to 11.8 for more detail on these exemptions.

Sales of Gasoline, Gasohol, and Diesel. Some form of exemption on the sale of gasoline has been in place since 1948, and some form of exemption on the sale of gasohol has been in place since 1979. In 1990, a constitutional amendment was passed that prohibited the taxation of fuel that is subject to the road use excise tax. Unlike most other exemptions, this exemption applies at both the state and local levels. (Note that only state revenue loss due to the exemption is reported in TEB reports.) This exemption excludes most fuel sales, as most gasoline, gasohol, and diesel will be subject to the road

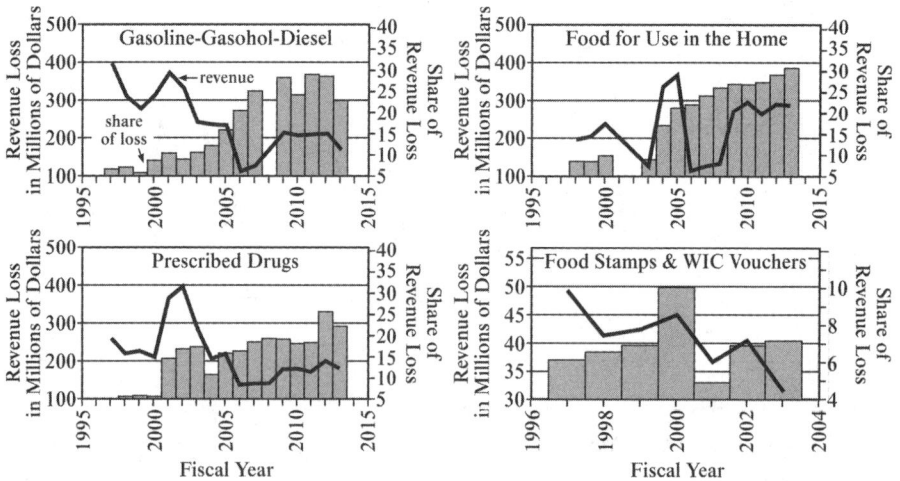

FIGURE 11.6. Revenue Losses from Specific Sales Tax Exemptions

use tax. Gasoline not subject to the road use excise tax is exempt from taxation of sales tax under R.S. 47:301(D)(1)(a). Gasohol not subject to the road use excise tax is exempt from taxation under R.S.47:305.28 for gasohol produced, fermented, and distilled in Louisiana. The purpose of this prohibition is to give a tax break to consumers. This exemption is one of the largest of the sales tax exemptions, ranking as one of the largest three exemptions

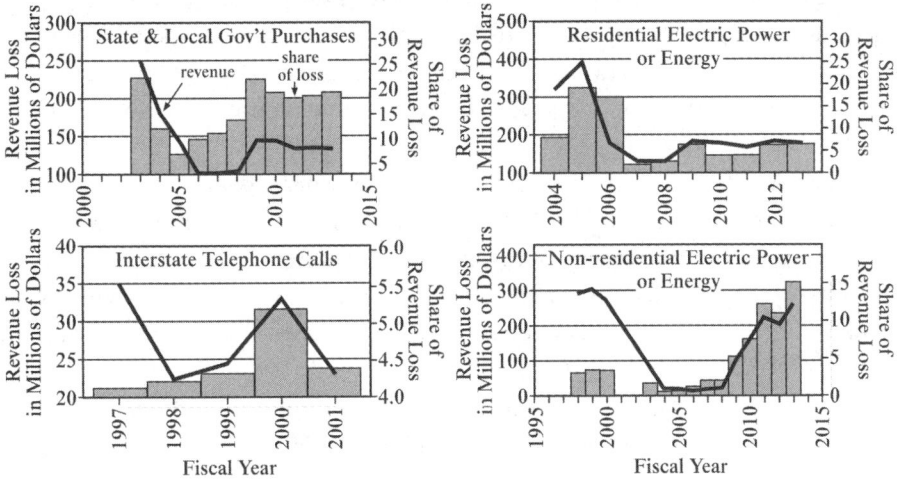

FIGURE 11.7. Revenue Losses from Various Sales Tax Exemptions

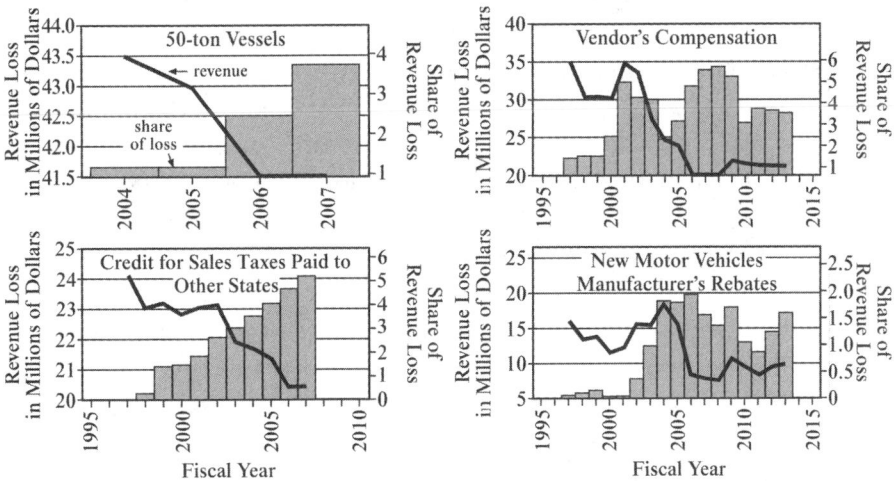

FIGURE 11.8. Revenue Losses from Various Sales Tax Exemptions

each year from 1997–2013 and accounting for 11.3 percent (or $301 million) of total sales tax losses in 2013. In 1997, it accounted for 31.5 percent (or $119 million) of total sales tax exemptions. Its share of total tax expenditures has been on a decreasing trend since 1997.

Sales of Food for Preparation and Consumption in the Home. This exemption was enacted in 1973, and allows tax-free sales of food for preparation and consumption in the home but does not include sales of single-serving portions or prepared food sold to the general public. Meals furnished to staff and students of educational institutions, the staff and patients of hospitals and mental institutions, and boarders in rooming houses are also exempt if the facility does not serve food to the general public. The purpose of this exemption is to provide financial relief to the general public on food purchases and to the staff and patients/boarders of certain institutions. Sales of prepared foods by grocery stores, department stores, variety stores, drugstores, delicatessens, convenience stores, meat markets, seafood markets, and similar businesses do not qualify for the exclusion, and are instead subject to the state sales tax.

After the suspension of exemptions in 1986, the sales of food for preparation and consumption in the home were taxed at the suspended rate, which varied from 1 percent to 4 percent (implying no effective exemption at all in 2001 and 2002). A constitutional amendment was passed on 5 November 2002 that prohibited the taxation of food sold for preparation and consumption in the home. Effective 1 January 2003, food items were taxed at 2 percent until 1 July 2003, when they were fully excluded from the state sales tax.

This is one of the largest sales tax exemptions, accounting for 14.5 percent ($388 million) of total sales tax losses in 2013. In 2005, it accounted for 18.5 percent ($245 million) of total sales tax exemptions. There is a general upward trend in the amount of exemptions given each year.

Drugs Prescribed by Physicians or Dentists. This exemption allows drugs prescribed by a physician or dentist and drugs that are dispensed to patients by hospitals under orders of the physician to be purchased free from sales tax. The purpose of this prohibition is to provide financial assistance to consumers.

This statute originally exempted only drugs prescribed by a physician. In

1974, the exemption was expanded to include drugs prescribed by a dentist. In 1985, Act 901 defined drugs under R.S. 47:301(20) to include all pharmaceuticals and medical devices. The inclusion of medical devices added a new exempt classification and greatly increased the fiscal effect of this exemption. On 5 November 2002, voters approved a constitutional amendment effective 1 January 2003 that prohibits the taxation of prescription drugs.

This is one of the major sales tax exemptions. It is also one of the few exemptions that was not suspended when many other exemptions were suspended beginning in 1986. It accounted for 10 percent ($150 million) of total sales tax exemptions in 2013. At its peak in 2002, it accounted for 40 percent ($350 million) of total sales tax exemptions.

Purchases Made with Food Stamps and WIC Vouchers. This exemption originated in 1986, and allows tax-free purchases of eligible food items if purchased with either USDA food stamps or Women, Infants, and Children (WIC) vouchers. The federal government issues food stamps and WIC vouchers to qualified participants to purchase eligible food items. States are not allowed to tax these purchases as a requirement for receiving federal funding for the food stamp and WIC programs. Repeal of this exemption would cost the state federal food stamp funding. A constitutional amendment was passed on 5 November 2002 that fully exempted sales of food for preparation and consumption in the home effective 1 July 2003. Food items eligible to be purchased with food stamps or WIC vouchers would be exempted under the food exclusion.

This exemption accounted for 4.4 percent ($40.3 million) of total sales tax losses in 2003, when it was superseded by the general exemptions of grocery items. In 1997, when it was at its highest, it accounted for 9.8 percent ($37 million) of total sales tax exemptions.

Purchases by State and Local Governments. This exemption allows all boards, agencies, or commissions of the State of Louisiana or any local authority within Louisiana to purchase or rent/lease tangible personal property, or receive services without being subject to general sales tax by excluding Louisiana state and local governments from the definition of person. It originated in 1991, and was effective from 1 September 1991. However, the revenue lost due to the exemption was not reported until fiscal year

2002. This exemption accounted for 8 percent ($210 million) of total sales tax losses in 2013. In 2003, it accounted for 25 percent ($250 million) of total sales tax exemptions, but then decreased from 2003 to 2005 and then started increasing again. The exemption as a share of total has remained almost flat in the last five years.

Sales of Electric Power or Energy—Residential. The Louisiana Constitution prohibits the taxation of natural gas, electricity, and water sold directly to the consumer for residential use. This constitutional amendment was passed on 5 November 2002. Effective 1 January 2003, these items were taxed at 2 percent until 1 July 2003, when they were fully excluded from the state sales tax. The purpose of the exclusion is to benefit the residential consumers of electrical utility services. This exemption accounted for 6.6 percent ($177 million) of total sales tax losses in 2013, down from its peak in 2005 when it accounted for 25 percent ($330 million) of total sales tax exemptions.

Sales of Electric Power or Energy—Nonresidential. This exemption allows the tax-free sale of electric power or energy and any materials or energy sources used to fuel the generation of electric power for resale or used by an industrial manufacturing plant for self-consumption or cogeneration. As the sale of electricity for residential use is constitutionally protected, this exemption benefits the nonresidential users of electrical utility services. It first originated in 1948. Then in 1980, Act 159 expanded the exemption to include any material or fuel used to generate electric power, and Act 183 in 1984 limited the exemption to material or fuel used to generate electric power to be resold or electric power in industrial manufacturing plants used for consumption or cogeneration. This exemption accounted for 12.2 percent ($326 million) of total sales tax loss in 2013.

Telecommunication Services through Interstate Telephone Calls. This exclusion was enacted in 1990, and allowed interstate telephone calls to be excluded from the definition of telephone services and therefore not subject to 3 percent communication tax. The purpose of this exclusion was to prohibit the taxation of out-of-state telephone calls. This exclusion was repealed by Act 2000, No. 22, effective 1 April 2001, which levied the new tax on amounts paid for interstate telecommunication services that either originate or terminate in the state and are charged to a service address in the state regardless of where the amounts are billed or paid. Before its repeal, it accounted for 5.6 percent ($21 million) of total sales tax losses.

Sales of Fifty-Ton Vessels and New Component Parts and Sales of Certain Materials and Services to Vessels Operating in Interstate Commerce. This exemption was enacted in 1959, and it allows for the exempt purchase of materials, equipment, and machinery that become component parts of ships, vessels, and barges with a fifty-ton and over load displacement and the sale of qualifying ships, vessels, and barges. Drilling ships and barges are also exempt. The purpose of this exemption is to make Louisiana boat builders and boat-service businesses competitive with similar companies in other states. Since the courts have declared that tax laws cannot discriminate against interstate commerce, the LDR has been unable to enforce the restrictive "built-in–Louisiana" language contained in the statute. Consequently, out-of-state builders have also benefited from this exemption.

The revenue loss for this exemption is hard to estimate, and there were no estimates until 2004. In 2004, the exemption was estimated to generate 4 percent ($41.6 million) of total sales tax loss. Starting from 2008, its revenue loss has been reported under "miscellaneous loss." In all of the four years with data, this exemption has been among the ten highest sales tax exemptions.

Vendor's Compensation. This credit is intended to compensate the dealer in accounting for and remitting the sales tax. Each dealer is allowed to deduct a certain percentage from the tax due, provided the reports are submitted and paid to the LDR on a timely basis. The amount of the vendor's compensation is computed on the sales tax collections before the credit is taken for taxes paid on goods for resale. This provision as originally enacted in 1948 allowed a credit of 1.5 percent. Act 916 of 1986 reduced the credit to 1.1 percent. Effective 1 July 2013, the vendor's compensation rate was reduced to 0.935 percent. This exemption accounted for 1.1 percent ($28 million) of total sales tax losses in 2013.

Credit for Sales Taxes Paid to Other States on Property Imported into Louisiana. This credit originated in 1964. It allows a person or company to reduce any use tax due by the equivalent sales/use tax lawfully paid to another qualified state. In order to qualify, the other state must allow a similar credit for Louisiana taxes, and the tax charged must be similar in nature. The state of Louisiana has entered into agreements with other states to allow similar credits for Louisiana residents. The purpose of this provision is to recipro-cate for the credit allowed by other states.

The estimated revenue loss from this exemption has declined steadily over time. During the 1990s and the early 2000s, it was one of the major sales tax exemptions, accounting for 5.2 percent ($19.8 million) of total sales tax expenditures at its peak. Now its share of total sales tax exemptions was only 0.5 percent ($24.2 million) in 2013. The estimated loss of revenue from this exemption has been reported as "other exemptions" since 2008.

Manufacturers Rebates on New Motor Vehicles. This exclusion was enacted in 1991, and it allows the taxable amount of a new vehicle to be reduced by the amount of a manufacturer's rebate allocated directly to the consumer. The purpose of this exclusion is to relieve the new-car buyer of the tax on the rebate, which represent reductions in the sales price. It generated 0.6 percent ($17 million) of total sales tax losses in 2013, down considerably from its peak in 2004.

SUMMARY OF MAJOR SALES TAX EXEMPTIONS

Calculating the sales-tax base is more complicated than for most of the other taxes. Furthermore, the complexity is increasing with time. One pos-itive trend with sales tax exemptions is the elimination of business-to-busi-ness transactions from the tax base through various exemptions. Effective 1 January 2009, advance sales tax was repealed, so that all sales for resale be-came excluded from sales tax and only the final sale to the consumer is now subject to the state sales tax. As of July 2013, Louisiana exempts many busi-ness-to-business transactions, including: insecticides and pesticides, fertil-izer, seed and feed, manufacturing machinery, manufacturing utilities/fuel, transportation services, professional and personal services, custom soft-ware, modified canned software, raw material, and water and air pollution control equipment. Even so, several business-to-business transactions are still taxed: seedlings, plants and shoots, general cleaning services, repair services, downloaded software (partially taxable), leasing motor vehicles, leases/rentals of tangible personal property, leasing rooms and lodgings, and office equipment. One possible solution is to broadly exempt business inputs across the board or even to apply a low flat rate of tax on all inputs.

Note that these business-to-business exemptions generate revenue losses. Even so, they improve the efficiency of the sales tax.

Exemptions in the Personal Income Tax: Structure and Trends

Louisiana is one of the forty-three states that levy a PIT. Louisiana adopted its PIT in 1934, two years before the introduction of the sales tax. Unlike the sales tax, the Louisiana Constitution does not allow local governments (e.g., municipality or parish) to levy the income tax. The PIT rate structure consists of three separate brackets (2, 4, and 6 percent), and these have not been changed since 1934. The tax brackets have also been quite stable, with only two changes since 1934. The first one was in 2002, commonly referred to as the Stelly plan, which attempted to shift the burden of revenue collection from the sales tax to the PIT. The second bracket change, which was effective in 2009, basically reverts back to the tax brackets before the Stelly plan. This general stability has been achieved in part due to a constitutional amendment of 1974, which provided for strict restrictions that prohibit most changes to the tax rates and income brackets. Table 11.3 provides the tax rates and brackets from 1934 to the present.

The tax is assessed on a resident individual's income derived from all sources and a nonresident individual's income derived from Louisiana sources. Louisiana taxable income is defined as federal adjusted gross in-

TABLE 11.3: Personal Income Tax—Rates and Brackets, 1934–2016

Years Effective	Single, Head of Household, Married Filing Separately	Married Couple Filing Joint Return or Qualifying Widow
1934–2002	2% on the first $10,000; 4% on the next $40,000; 6% on the taxable income above $50,000	2% on the first $20,000; 4% on the next $80,000; 6% on the taxable income above $100,000
2003–2008	2% on the first $12,500; 4% on the next $12,500; 6% on the taxable income above $25,000	2% on the first $25,000; 4% on the next $25,000; 6% on the taxable income above $50,000
2009–Present	2% on the first $12,500; 4% on the next $37,500; 6% on the taxable income above $50,000	2% on the first $25,000; 4% on the next $75,000; 6% on the taxable income above $100,000

come less the following: the personal exemption and standard deduction, the federal tax liability, and excess itemized deductions. Excess itemized deductions were partially eliminated starting in 2000 and completely by 2003, but they were reinstated effective 2008. Exemptions have existed since the beginning of the PIT in 1934, and their number has increased significantly recently, doubling from thirty-five in 1999 to seventy-nine in 2013.

Figure 11.9 graphs revenue collected from the PIT and revenue loss from PIT exemptions. Revenues were $1.28 billion in 1997, and slowly trended upwards until 2005 when they reached $2.4 billion. Revenues then decreased slightly to $2.3 billion in 2006 and then jumped to $3.2 billion in 2007. In 2010, the revenue trend shifted back to its pre-Katrina level. Exemptions remained relatively flat until 2006, at which point they started increasing slowly, reaching $2 billion in 2013. The percentage of revenue loss from PIT exemptions was 37.8 percent in 1997, and followed a modest downward trend until 2005, when it reached 26.5 percent; it has increased steadily since then, ending with 41.2 percent in 2013.

Figure 11.10 divides the income tax exemptions into those that were constitutionally imposed and those that were statutorily imposed. Out of seventy-nine income tax exemptions active in 2013, only three are constitutionally imposed: the federal income tax deduction, interest on US debt obligations, and Native American income. In 1997 constitutionally imposed exemptions were $363.2 million (46.8 percent of total exemptions), and statutorily im-

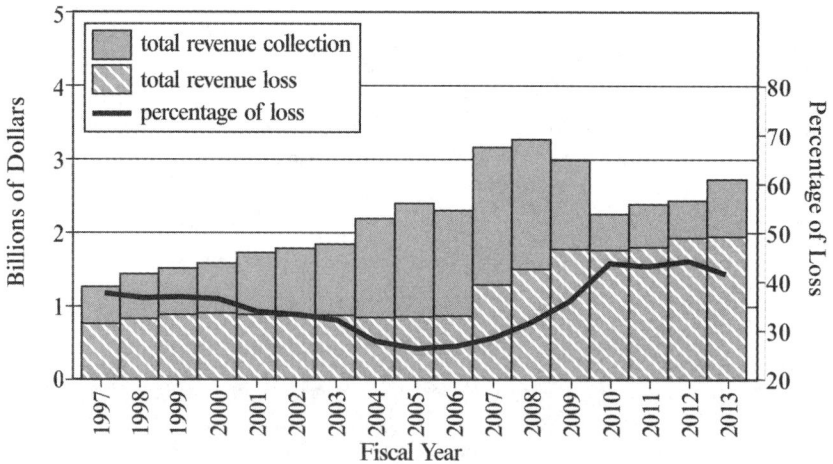

FIGURE 11.9. PIT Revenues and PIT Revenue Losses Due to Exemptions

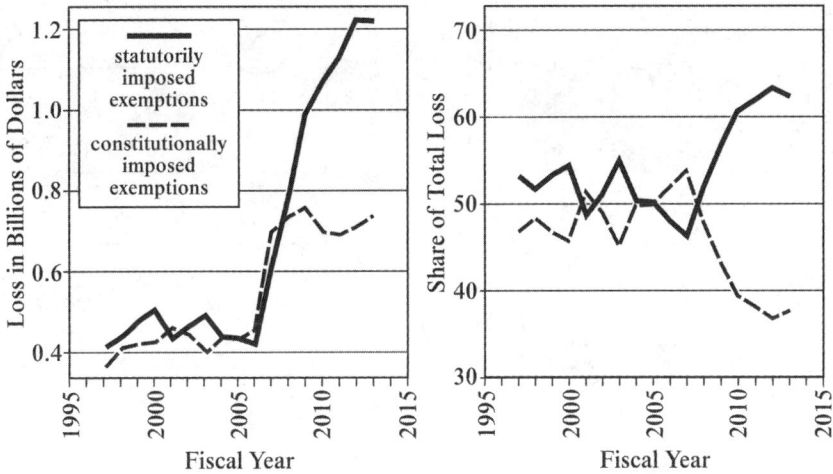

FIGURE 11.10. PIT Revenue Losses: Constitutionally Imposed and Statutorily Imposed

posed exemptions were $412 million (53.2 percent of total exemptions). In 2006, both categories of exemptions increased, but the statutorily imposed exemptions increased substantially, accounting for as much as 62.4 percent of the share of total exemptions, due largely to the introduction of hurricane recovery tax exemptions such as the credit for the Louisiana citizens' property insurance corporation assessments and the deduction for Hurricane Recovery Entity Benefits.

MAJOR PIT EXEMPTIONS

In this subsection we describe twelve of the largest PIT tax exemptions, ordered according to their average rank across all active years from 1997 to 2013. See Figures 11.11 to 11.16.

Federal Income Tax Deduction. The federal income tax deduction was enacted in 1974, and is protected by the Constitution. A deduction is allowed for federal income tax on income for which the Louisiana income tax is paid. The purpose of this deduction is to shelter from taxation the portion of a taxpayer's income that represents federal income taxes paid.

This is the largest of the PIT exemptions for every year between 1997 and 2013. Its share of revenue loss ranges from 36.5 percent ($709.7 million) in 2012 to 53.2 percent ($696.7 million) in 2007. Its share has slightly decreased

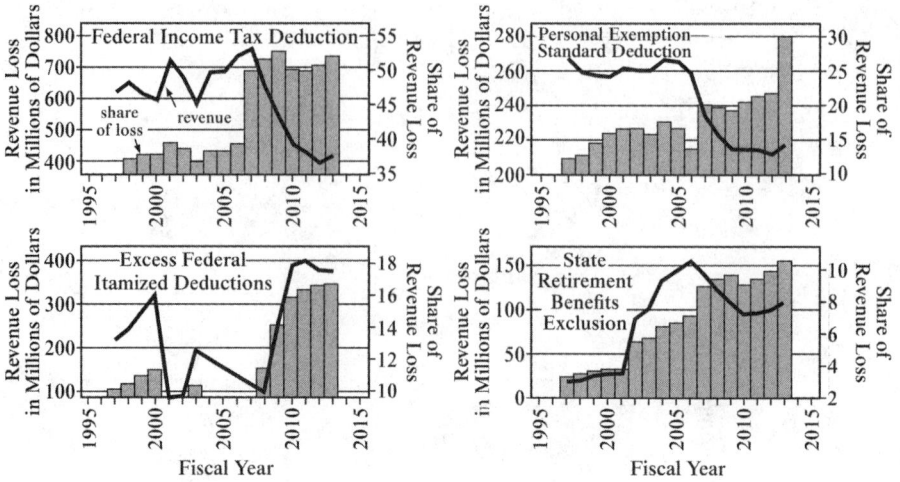

FIGURE 11.11. Revenue Losses from Various PIT Exemptions

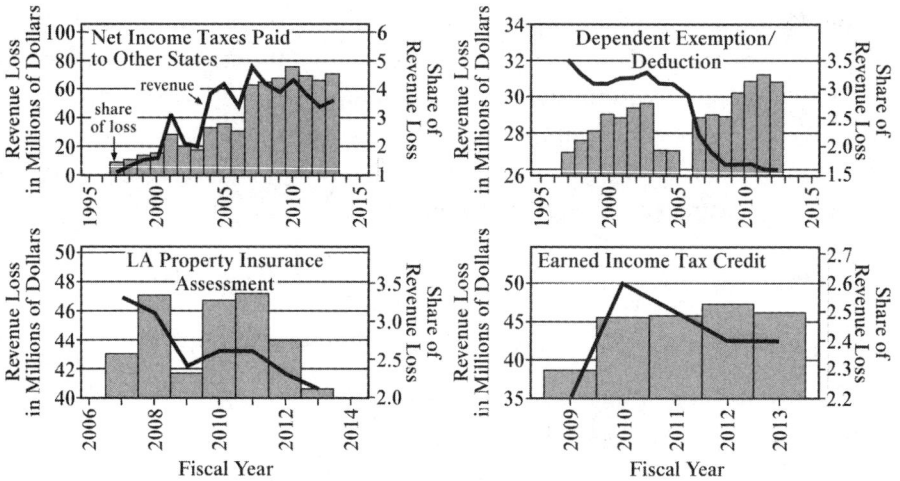

FIGURE 11.12. Revenue Losses from Various PIT Exemptions

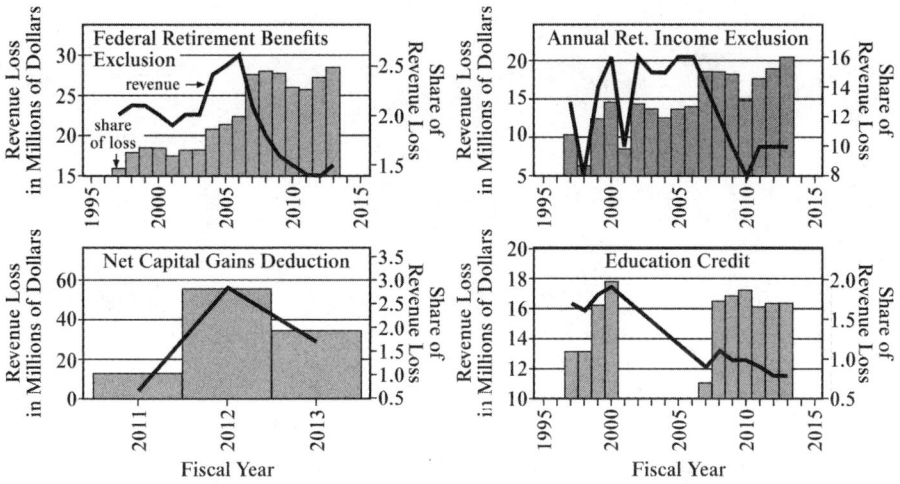

FIGURE 11.13. Revenue Losses from Various PIT Exemptions

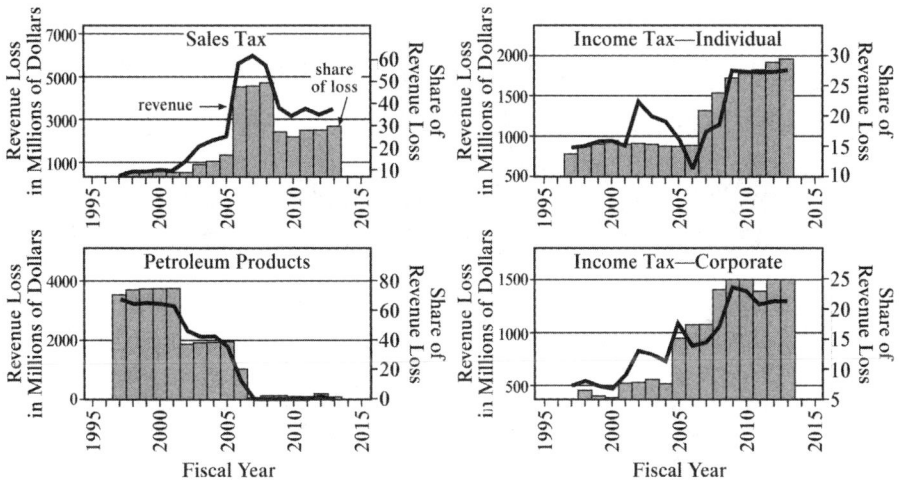

FIGURE 11.14. Revenue Losses from Sales Tax, PIT, Taxes on Petroleum Products, and Corporate Income Tax

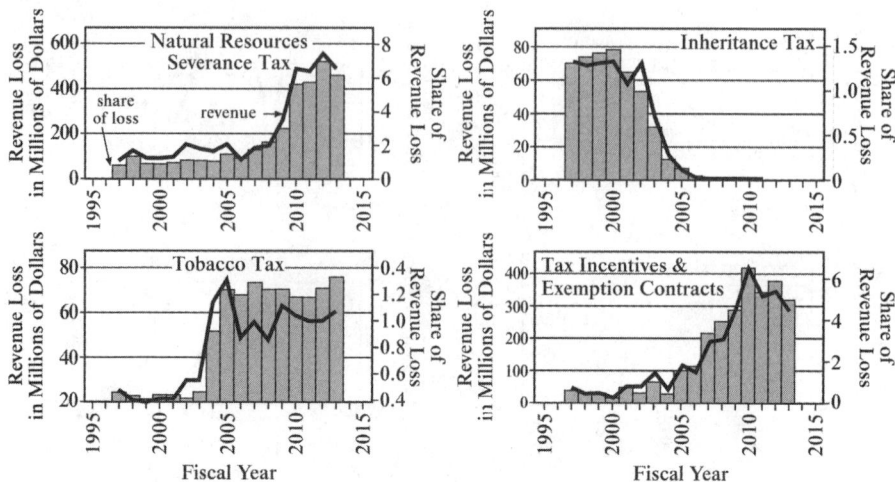

FIGURE 11.15. Revenue Losses from Natural Resources Severance Tax, Tobacco Tax, Inheritance Tax, and Other Contractual Exemptions

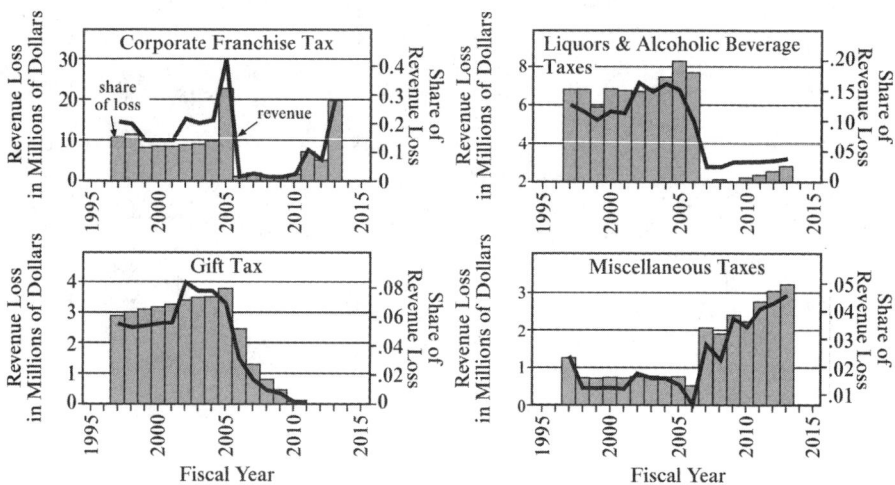

FIGURE 11.16. Revenue Losses from Corporate Franchise Tax, Gift Tax, Liquors and Alcoholic Beverages Tax, and Miscellaneous Taxes

in the recent years. Only five other states (Alabama, Iowa, Missouri, Montana, and Oregon) allow this deduction.

Personal Exemption/Standard Deduction. Taxpayers are allowed a standard deduction from taxable income. The combined personal exemption/standard deduction is $4,500 for taxpayers filing single or separate returns and $9,000 for taxpayers filing joint returns or as head of household; in all cases the amount is deducted from the lowest tax bracket. This deduction was introduced in 1934 with the enactment of the PIT, and it is intended to shelter a portion of a taxpayer's income from state income tax. It is one of the major PIT exemptions, accounting for 14.2 percent ($279.3 million) of total income tax losses in 2013. Its share has slightly decreased in recent years.

Excess Federal Itemized Deductions. This provision was enacted in 1980, and it allows taxpayers who itemize their federal deductions to deduct 100 percent of the portion of federal itemized deductions that are in excess of the federal standard deduction. The deduction for excess federal itemized deductions was repealed for tax years 2003 through 2006, and was reinstated in 2007 but was phased in over three years. In 2007, a deduction for 57.5 percent of "excess itemized deductions" was allowed; in 2008, the allowable percentage was 65 percent, and full deduction of the excess itemized deduction was allowed for tax years 2009 and forward. The purpose of this deduction is to shelter a portion of a taxpayer's income from state income tax. Only Alabama and Iowa allow a deduction for the full amount of federal income taxes paid. Most of the states with a similar provision place a cap on the deduction. This is one of the largest three PIT exemptions. It accounted for 17.5 percent ($344.1 million) of total PIT tax losses in 2013.

State Employees, Teachers, and Other Retirement Benefits Exclusion. This provision was enacted in 1946, and has been modified several times to include different retirement systems. It allows individuals receiving benefits from certain state, statewide, and local government retirement systems to fully exclude those benefits from their Louisiana taxable income. The purpose of this exclusion is to shelter certain retirement benefits from the income tax. The benefits from forty-nine public retirement systems across the state are excluded. This exemption accounted for 8 percent ($156 million) of total PIT tax losses in 2013, down slightly from its peak in 2006.

Net Income Taxes Paid to Other States. A credit is allowed for taxes paid to other states. Enacted in 1946, the purpose of this credit is to allow taxpayers to deduct the income tax paid to other states on income also taxed by Louisiana, so as not to subject the taxpayer to double taxation. It generated 3.6 percent ($71.4 million) of total PIT losses in 2013. There is a general upward trend in the amount of exemptions given each year. This tax deduction was redefined in 2016 to relate the loss in revenues to the taxes as assessed in Louisiana as opposed to the other state in which the taxes were being assessed.

Dependent Exemption/Deduction. Enacted in 1935, this provision allows a $1,000 deduction (increased from $400 effective 1980) from the lowest tax bracket for each dependent. The purpose of this deduction is to reduce the tax burden for taxpayers with dependents. It generated 1.6 percent ($30.1 million) of total PIT losses in 2013, with a slight downward trend in recent years.

Credit for the LA Citizens Property Insurance Corporation Assessments. Enacted in 2006 after Hurricanes Katrina and Rita, this refundable credit allows a credit in the amount of surcharges, market equalization charges, or assessments paid as a result of the assessments levied by the Louisiana Citizens Property Insurance Corporation due to Hurricanes Katrina and Rita. This credit is available to taxpayers who paid the assessments as a part of their property insurance premium. For assessments paid on or after 1 January 2007, a corporation can claim the credit after payment is made on a form provided by the secretary instead of on their Louisiana corporation income tax return. It accounted for 2.1 percent ($40.5 million) of total PIT losses in 2013.

Earned Income Tax Credit. This provision was enacted in 2008, and it provides a credit for residents of the state who are eligible for the federal earned income tax credit. The credit is equal to 3.5 percent of the federal earned income tax credit taken on a resident's federal income. It generated 2.4 percent ($46.2 million) of total PIT losses in 2013.

Federal Retirement Benefits Exclusion. Since its enactment in 1989, this provision has allowed federal retirement benefits received by federal retirees, both military and nonmilitary, to be excluded from Louisiana taxable income. The purpose of this exclusion is to shelter federal retirement benefits from the income tax. It accounted for 1.5 percent ($28.5 million) of total PIT losses in 2013.

Annual Retirement Income Exclusion. Persons 65 years or older may exclude up to $6,000 of annual retirement income from their taxable income. The purpose of this exclusion, which was enacted in 1981, is to reduce the tax burden for persons 65 years or older. It is one of the larger tax exemptions, accounting for about 1 percent ($20.3 million) of total PIT losses in 2013.

Deduction for Net Capital Gains. This provision, enacted in 2009, allows a deduction for net capital gains, limited to gains recognized and treated for federal income tax purposes as arising from the sale or exchange of an equity interest in or substantially all of the assets of a nonpublicly traded corporation, partnership, limited liability company, or other business organization commercially domiciled in this state. It accounted for 0.7 percent ($12.6 million) of total sales tax loss in 2013, 2.8 percent ($55 million) in 2012, and 1.7 percent ($34.2 million) in 2013.

Education Credit. A credit of $25 is allowed for each qualified dependent child who was in school in kindergarten through grade 12 at least part of the year. This credit was enacted in 1980, and was suspended beginning with the tax year 1986 through tax year 1995 and again beginning with tax year 2000 through 2005. The purpose of this credit is to assist taxpayers with education expenses. It accounted for 0.8 percent ($16.4 million) of total PIT losses in 2013, down considerably from its peak in 2000.

SUMMARY OF EXEMPTIONS IN THE PERSONAL INCOME TAX

Although the state's top PIT marginal rate is 6 percent, Louisiana taxpayers actually pay closer to an average effective rate of 2.3 percent. This is due in large part to the federal income tax deduction and various other exemptions that have the effect of lowering the tax burden for families, small businesses, and retirees. Given that only five other states allow the federal income tax deduction and only two other states allow full deduction of excess itemized deductions, there is some room for increasing the base of the income tax. Note that two of the states in the Southeast region (Texas and Florida) do not impose a personal income tax.

Some Other Major Tax Preferences:
Economic Development Tax Preferences

Many of Louisiana's tax preferences represent tax incentives offered through Louisiana Economic Development (LED) in an attempt to stimulate economic development. These tax incentives are of several major types: investment tax credits and deductions; accelerated depreciation; tax holidays; investment grants; and miscellaneous incentives such as reduced corporate income tax rates, reduced tax rates on some activities, exempt purchases, and the like. Like other states, Louisiana uses most of these tax incentives in some form or another through the Louisiana Economic Development, tax incentives that are intended to encourage businesses to expand their operations in Louisiana or to move their operations to the state.

The *Tax Exemption Budget 2013–2014* lists twenty-eight separate tax incentives and exemption contracts, including (among other programs):

- Angel Investor Tax Credit: 35 percent tax credit of amount invested
- Competitive Projects Payroll Incentive Program: up to 15 percent of payroll for ten years
- Quality Jobs Program: 6 percent rebate of payroll for ten years + 4 percent sales tax rebate OR 1.5 percent tax credit on investment spending
- Enterprise Zone Program: $2,500/job tax credit + 4 percent sales tax rebate OR 1.5 percent tax credit on investment spending
- Research and Development Tax Credit: tax credit up to 40 percent of expenditures
- Technology Commercialization Credit and Jobs Program
- Restoration Tax Abatement: five-year 100 percent property tax abatement
- Industrial Tax Exemption: ten-year 100 percent property tax abatement
- Motion Picture Investor Tax Credit: 30 percent tax credit on in-state spending + 5 percent on resident payroll

- Sound Recording Investor Tax Credit: 25 percent tax credit on spending
- Digital Interactive Media and Software Development Incentive: tax credit of 25 percent of in-state spending + 35 percent credit on in-state payroll
- Musical and Theatrical Production Tax Incentive: 25 percent to 35 percent tax credits on production and infrastructure spending + additional credits for payroll and transportation spending
- Retention and Modernization: tax credit of 5 percent of expenditures
- Tax Equalization Program: ten-year contracts to equalize LA taxes with those of alternative locations
- Manufacturing Establishments: fifteen-year contracts for exemption from essentially any and all state taxation

There are also several programs that target small businesses (Economic Gardening Initiative, Hudson Initiative, Small Business Loan and Guaranty Program, Small and Emerging Business Development Program, Veteran Initiative—a detailed listing of these programs can be found at http://www.opportunitylouisiana.com/index/incentives.) The total estimated revenue loss in 2013–2014 from all tax incentives and exemption contracts was $319.4 million, and these revenue losses have averaged roughly $350 million over the last three years. The largest programs in 2013–2014 were the Motion Picture Investor Tax Credit ($148.2 million in estimated revenue losses), Louisiana Quality Jobs Program ($51.3 million), and Enterprise Zone Program ($50.9 million). These three programs are discussed separately.

MOTION PICTURE INVESTOR TAX CREDIT

Louisiana's motion picture investor tax credit (commonly called the "film credit") provides a 30 percent transferable tax credit on total in-state expenditures, including resident and nonresident labor, with no cap, subject to a $300,000 minimum expenditure. The credits can offset personal or corporate tax liability, sold or transferred to third parties, or sold back to the state for 85 percent of face value. For productions using in-state labor, there is an additional 5 percent payroll tax credit. In the last year, Louisiana awarded approximately $250 million in credits.

There have been a number of formal and informal analyses of the motion picture investment credit, including those commissioned by the Louisiana Economic Development Agency. This research suggests the following four points:

1. The credit has been successful in attracting production of films to Louisiana and generating local economic activity. Louisiana has become a leader in film production. While the benefits of this job creation have accrued to many areas of the states, it is highly concentrated in a few areas, such as New Orleans.

2. The credit has cost the state considerable revenue, even after allowing for offsets due to the generation of new economic activity. The most recent study from the Louisiana Economic Development Agency pegged the budgetary cost for 2012 at approximately $170 million, while allowing for roughly a 33 percent offset from increased activity. Note that these types of offsets are not typically measured for regular state spending programs, such as those on infrastructure, education, or health. Moreover, there are no effective limits on the budgetary costs to the state—it is totally dependent on the utilization of the credit.

3. There is no natural ending point to the subsidization of the film industry. While there has been some infrastructure development, most observers believe that the level of film production we have witnessed in Louisiana is contingent upon the program continuing. These same observers expect that North Carolina, which recently sharply restricted its program, will experience a much lower level of production activity. The film credit cannot be justified as an "infant industry" that will no longer need subsidies in the future.

4. Although the program is structured as providing tax credits, it really has nothing to do with taxes and is effectively a subsidy program to the industry. Film production is not deterred from locating in Louisiana because of high personal or corporate tax rates. Tax credits are simply a vehicle to transfer benefits. Fully transferable tax credits are effectively equivalent to a subsidy program. The only difference is that there may be some transactions costs in selling the credits to third parties or receiving a reduced amount by returning them to the state.

These points can be summarized simply. *The film tax credit should be viewed as an ongoing spending program that provides some benefits to the state.* As such, it should be treated by the legislature on par with other spending programs. Viewing the film program as a spending program means explicitly weighing its benefits and costs against other worthwhile state programs. How does spending an additional dollar attracting production of films to Louisiana compare to spending an additional dollar on infrastructure or education? It also means applying the same type of analysis to the film tax credit as to other programs. When the legislature considers a major infrastructure program, it does not reduce its budgetary cost by "offsets" from the additional job creation or sales that the program would generate. This is not to say that increased infrastructure spending does not produce more jobs and eventually more revenue for the state. However, it is not appropriate to use one measuring rod for traditional spending programs and another, more favorable one, for spending programs in the guise of tax incentives.

QUALITY JOBS (QJ) PROGRAM

Louisiana's Quality Jobs (QJ) program provides a cash rebate to companies that create well-paid jobs and promote economic development. The benefits include up to a 6 percent cash rebate of annual gross payroll for new, direct jobs for up to ten years; the benefits also provide either a 4 percent sales and use tax rebate on capital expenditures or a 1.5 percent investment tax credit for qualified expenses. The intent of the QJ program is to give an incentive to firms to locate or to expand their operations in the state. (Details of the Louisiana QJ program can be found at http://www.opportunitylouisiana.com/page/quality-jobs.)

The Louisiana Department of Revenue annual *Tax Exemption Budget 2013–2014* estimates that the QJ program led to a loss of $51.3 million in 2013–2014, of which $5.0 million was due to the sales tax rebate, $35.2 million was due to the jobs credit, and $11.1 million was due to the investment tax credit. The estimated annual revenue loss has averaged $43.9 million over the last three years, an average that is somewhat lower than in previous years. Many firms that receive QJ benefits also are eligible for benefits from Louisiana's Enterprise Zone (EZ) program.

Job incentive programs in other states have been frequently studied.

Despite some differences in the specific conclusions of these studies, several general conclusions about the programs emerge from all of these studies:

1. Job incentive programs have often been at best only modestly successful in encouraging new job creation.
2. There is seldom firm evidence that the job incentive programs have encouraged economic development that would not have occurred anyway, in the absence of the programs.
3. The main beneficiaries of the job incentive programs have not been "mobile" workers but instead have been "immobile" factors of production, especially owners of land and commercial real estate.
4. The job incentive programs have cost the government considerable tax revenue, even after allowing for offsets due to the possible generation of new economic activity.

These points can be summarized simply. *Job incentive programs have been largely ineffective in encouraging new job creation, despite their considerable revenue cost.*

ENTERPRISE ZONES (EZ) PROGRAM

Louisiana's Enterprise Zone (EZ) program is a jobs incentive program that provides income and franchise tax credits to a new or existing business located in Louisiana, creating permanent net new full-time jobs, and hiring at least 50 percent of those net new jobs from targeted groups. The benefits include a one-time $2,500 job tax credit for each net new job created; the benefits also provide either a 4 percent rebate of sales and use taxes paid on qualifying materials, machinery, furniture, and/or equipment purchased, or a 1.5 percent refundable investment tax credit on the total capital investment, excluding tax-exempted items. The intent of the EZ program is to encourage economic development in areas with high unemployment and/or low income, especially in areas with high concentrations of individuals on public assistance. (Details of the Louisiana EZ program can be found at http://www.opportunitylouisiana.com/page/enterprise-zone.)

The Louisiana Department of Revenue's annual *Tax Exemption Budget 2013–2014* estimates that the EZ program led to a loss of $50.9 million in 2013–2014, of which $8.0 million was due to the sales tax rebate, $11.6 million was due to the jobs credit, and $31.3 million was due to the investment tax credit. The estimated annual revenue loss has averaged $61.0 million over the last three years.

The Louisiana program has been extensively studied by the Louisiana Economic Development (LED). In its *Enterprise Zone 2009 Annual Report* (2010), the LED concluded that:

A wide range of businesses across the state utilize the EZ program, but on average most of the activity involves larger businesses (e.g., national retail chains, manufacturers, hospitals, hotels, industrial/offshore construction and services, distribution, commodity storage and transportation) in relatively affluent, urban/suburban areas of the state that are not designated Enterprise Zones. Over the past four years, more than 95 percent of the value of incentives made available through the EZ program has been provided to large businesses (more than 500 employees). Despite being one of the state's most active incentive programs, less than one percent of Louisiana employers have historically accessed the program. Furthermore, Louisiana's EZ program appears to have fewer mechanisms in place to encourage net new permanent job growth for the state than similar programs in neighboring states. For example, four nearby southern states target their programs towards industry sectors that drive new economic growth and net new permanent jobs, and generally avoid providing incentives to certain industries that typically follow local demand and/or suffer from substitution effects (e.g., retail, restaurants and other sectors serving primarily local demand).

These conclusions are similar to those of other studies in other states. Despite some differences in the specific conclusions of these studies, several general conclusions about the programs emerge from all of these studies:

1. Enterprise zone programs have often been at best only modestly successful in encouraging new economic development, especially the creation of new jobs. Any economic development that has been generated has seldom been concentrated in geographic areas most in need of economic development.
2. There is seldom firm evidence that the enterprise zone programs have encouraged economic development that would not have occurred anyway, in the absence of the programs.

3. The main beneficiaries of the enterprise zone programs have not been "mobile" (especially low-income) workers but instead have been "immobile" factors of production, especially owners of land and commercial real estate.
4. The incentive programs have cost the government considerable tax revenue, even after allowing for offsets due to the possible generation of new economic activity.

These points can be summarized simply. *Enterprise zone programs have been largely ineffective in encouraging targeted economic development, despite their considerable revenue cost.*

SUMMARY OF OTHER MAJOR TAX PREFERENCES

A common rationale for these (and other similar if smaller) incentives is that, without these incentives, Louisiana firms cannot compete in the national and the world economy. Also, incentives allow the state government to adopt a system of differential capital income taxation, applying relatively low rates on highly mobile capital while maintaining comparatively high statutory tax rates for relatively immobile capital. This pattern of taxation can be consistent both with economic efficiency and with economic growth.

A counterargument is that incentives (and the resulting preferential tax treatments) involve the state government in industrial policies, picking winners and losers. Also, these incentives have created a misallocation of investment that has led in turn to a loss in competitiveness and have also led to unequal treatment of similarly situated businesses. They also complicate considerably the tasks of the tax administration that must administer the incentives. Further, there is the likelihood that the introduction of an incentive by one state leads to strategic responses by other, rival states, so that the incentives have little impact on investment because other states have similar incentives and simply act to transfer revenues to large enterprises. Of most note, there is little question that exemptions are a significant fiscal drain on the budget, a cost that can be reflected in higher taxes on other tax bases or in public investments that have been forgone.

Overall, a plausible economic argument can be made for at least some incentives. The possible *benefits* to a state that offers incentives may include increases in investment, gains from industrialization, the creation of jobs for persons who otherwise would be unemployed or employed at lower wages, the transfer of technology and training, and increases in revenues from taxes to which the incentives do not apply or from taxes payable after the initial reduction has ended. As for the *costs,* these include the loss of revenue, distortions in investment behavior leading to investments that are socially unproductive, administrative complications, political discord generated by favors to out-of-state businesses, and discrimination against smaller firms that lack the resources and/or the influence to apply for the incentives.

Even so, in the few instances in which the actual evaluation of benefits and costs has been done, the benefits have generally been found to be positive but small, and significantly smaller than their costs. The reasons for this were several. There is evidence that few if any incentives have the desired effects. Their main effect is a massive loss in tax revenues. Further, although investment may be attracted, it is not always on balance beneficial to the state economy. The administrative problems associated with the tax incentives are also enormous, especially for tax holidays. The presence of tax incentives for some groups of taxpayers requires higher tax rates on other nonfavored taxpayers, and these taxpayers often lobby for their own special treatment. Finally, smaller firms do not generally receive tax incentives, and these firms are often an important source of job growth in the state. On balance, these costs are often deemed to be far in excess of the potential benefits. In particular, there is seldom much evidence that the incentives are more important to potential investors than such factors as political transparency, potential market size, economic growth, quality labor, local amenities, or solid infrastructure.

Indeed, there is now some evidence that the best way to encourage investment is simply to lower the overall tax rate in the corporate income tax, not to offer targeted incentives. There is also increasing evidence that the main effect of incentives is on the transfer of income across jurisdictions, rather than on the location of real activity across jurisdictions. In short, the main messages of this research are that incentives can stimulate investment, but that a state's overall economic characteristics are much more important than any incentives package both for the success or the failure of industries and as potential "drivers" of investment decisions by long-term investors. Moreover, even if/when incentives stimulate some additional investment, they are not generally cost-effective.

Again, this is not to deny that incentives can affect the movement of "capital," broadly defined. It is to question whether any such movement represents a transfer of "real" economic activity as opposed to simply a transfer of "paper" transactions that reduce a firm's tax liabilities without generating any real economic activity. It is also to question whether the benefit-cost ratio of any such incentive is greater than one. Overall, then, in the few instances in which detailed analyses have been performed, the benefits of tax exemptions are less than their costs.

Overall, then, the general conclusions on the impacts of these incentive programs can be summarized simply. *The incentive programs should be viewed as an ongoing spending program that encourages development initiatives that would likely have occurred in their absence and whose economic costs exceed their economic benefits.* Recommendations that reflect these general conclusions are presented in the conclusions.

Summary and Recommendations

It is obvious that there is widespread use in Louisiana of tax exemptions. Various tax credits intended to encourage economic development expand even more the presence in Louisiana of these fiscal, financial, and other tax incentives.

The presence of these provisions raises a variety of different considerations, mainly related to their different justifications. In some cases, these exemptions are present because of constitutional provisions, which make changes to them difficult if not impossible. In other cases, these exemptions are present because of attempts to make taxable income (or consumption) more aligned with standard economic definitions. Included here are PIT provisions such as the personal exemption, the standard deduction, the dependent exemption, or taxes paid to other states; similarly, sales tax provisions that, say, remove business-to-business transactions from the tax base have a sound economic rationale. In still other cases, these exemptions are present largely because of fairness concerns (e.g., the EITC, sales of food for preparation or consumption in the home, drugs prescribed by physicians). In these cases, it is possible to make reasoned arguments for the retention of these exemptions in at least some form, even if the magnitude of the exemptions remains arguable. Exemptions that are intended to attract or to retain business activities are more problematic. Most evidence suggests that these development incentives do not generate benefits anywhere close to their costs.

All of this suggests some *specific* lessons related to the use of exemptions and incentives:

- *Use exemptions mainly to help lower income households.*
- *Use exemptions mainly to better define income or consumption.*
- *Resist the use of incentives for investment.* Incentives generally have little impact on investment, and seem mainly to reduce tax revenues and to induce other states to offer similar incentives. Even where they do attract investment, the investment is not often socially productive.
- *Resist the temptation to promote industrial or social policies through the tax system.* Such attempts are likely to result in a proliferation of incentives to enterprises and in the preferential treatment of particular groups of taxpayers, which will lead to other groups requesting them. Also, it is difficult to get rid of incentives once they are in place.
- *Establish tax policies that keep tax rates low and in line with those of neighboring states.*

However, if exemptions and other incentives are desired as part of an attempt to encourage investment and attract out-of-state business, then appropriate policy suggests some *general* guidelines:

- *Include in any legislation that introduces an exemption or an incentive a specific justification for the special provision;* that is, what are the specific, achievable objectives of the provision?
- *Define clearly in the legislation the types of activities that will receive exemptions and then grant these incentives automatically,* minimizing discretion and negotiation.
- *Do not favor out-of-state over in-state investors.* This is unfair to Louisiana entrepreneurs, it encourages questionable joint ventures, and it discourages the development of a state entrepreneurial class.
- *Set sunset provisions for all exemptions,* so that their retention requires hearings and votes by lawmakers.
- *Rationalize all exemptions.* Here "rationalize" means the adoption of schemes in which the scheme does not alter the relative ranking of eligible activities, even though it makes all eligible projects more

profitable. A rational scheme does not lead an individual to choose project A over project B when, in the absence of the scheme, project B is more profitable than project A.

- *Limit the magnitude of the tax incentive, either by designing the incentive program as an explicit expenditure program or by capping the magnitude of the tax credit or exemption and limiting its transferability.*
- *Evaluate any program regularly with rigorous and impartial analysis to determine whether it has achieved its stated justification, and at what cost.*
- *For the time being, there should be a moratorium on any new incentive program, until existing programs can be fully examined.*

More specific recommendations for the PIT, sales tax, and economic development tax preferences are discussed in the final chapter.

TABLE 11.4. All Tax Exemptions (Tax Exemption Budget, 2013–2014, Louisiana Department of Revenue)

Personal Income Tax Exemptions	Last Fiscal Year	Revenue Loss (Current $)
Accessible and barrier-free constructed home	2013	28,211
Ad valorem tax credit for offshore vessels	2013	12,982,073
Ad valorem tax on natural gas	2013	370,008
Ad valorem tax paid by certain telephone companies	2013	0
Alternative-fuel usage	2006	18,000
Amounts paid by certain military service members for obtaining Louisiana hunting and fishing licenses	2013	123,362
Annual retirement income exclusion	2013	20,295,707
Apprenticeship tax credit	2013	387,739
Bone-marrow donor expenses	2008	4,472
Cash donations to dedicated research investment fund	2012	0
Certain disabilities	2013	2,810,513
Contribution of tangible property of a sophisticated nature to educational institutions	2013	819,714
Conversion of vehicles to alternative fuel	2013	643,466
Credit for certain child care expenses	2013	18,299,092
Credit for debt issuance costs	2013	28,567

Credit for purchases from prison industry enhancement contractors	2006	0
Credit for rehabilitation of historic structures	2013	27,357,792
Deduction for construction code retrofitting	2010	12,232
Deduction for fees and other educational expenses for a quality public education	2013	2,311,533
Deduction for hurricane recovery entity benefits	2013	66,671
Deduction for I.R.C. Section 280C expense	2013	1,031,309
Deduction for net capital gains	2013	34,240,997
Deduction for recreation volunteer	2013	19,055
Deduction for START savings program contribution	2013	1,816,416
Deduction for teachers	2010	17,435
Deduction for volunteer firefighters	2013	57,771
Dependent exemption/deduction	2013	30,796,945
Disability income exclusion	2013	6,429,627
Donations of materials, equipment, or instructors made to certain training providers	2013	192,815
Donations of property to certain offices and agencies	2013	0
Donations to assist qualified playgrounds	2013	38,158
Earned income tax credit	2013	46,170,871
Education credit	2013	16,370,759
Educational expense incurred for a degree related to law enforcement	2013	105,668
Educational expenses for home-schooled children deduction	2013	185,616
Elementary and secondary school tuition deduction	2013	20,659,171
Employment of certain first time drug offenders	2012	14,945
Employment of certain first-time nonviolent offenders	2013	44,781
Employment of the previously unemployed	2013	83,185
Employment related expenses for maintaining households for certain disabled dependents	2013	293,760
Excess federal itemized deductions	2013	344,150,831
Family responsibility	2013	49,874
Federal income tax deduction	2013	735,538,062
Federal retirement benefits exclusion	2013	28,516,374
Gasoline and special fuels taxes for commercial fishermen	2013	23,374

TABLE 11.4. (*continued*)

Personal Income Tax Exemptions	Last Fiscal Year	Revenue Loss (Current $)
Income reported to shareholders of banks organized as S corporations	2006	884,000
Interest on US obligations	2013	2,062,109
Inventory tax/ad valorem tax	2013	11,457,440
Louisiana property insurance assessment	2013	40,537,244
Living organ donation credit	2013	11,736
Louisiana basic skills training	2013	18,402
Louisiana community development financial institutions act	2013	0
Low-income housing	2013	0
Military pay exclusion	2013	5,404,525
Milk producers	2013	1,515,000
Native American income	2013	210,681
Net income taxes paid to other states	2013	71,427,762
Personal exemption—standard deduction	2013	279,333,129
Property insurance	2013	114,158
Property taxes paid by telephone companies	2006	0
Purchase of a qualified recycling equipment	2013	78,946
Purchase of bulletproof vest	2013	15,253
Purchases from prison industry enhancement contractors	2013	0
Rehabilitation of an owner occupied residential or mixed-use property	2013	303,818
School readiness business supported child care credit	2013	164,045
School readiness child care credit	2013	2,872,501
School readiness child care directors and staff	2013	7,093,663
School readiness child care provider	2013	2,412,408
School readiness fees and grants to resource and referral agencies	2013	296,384
Small town doctor/dentist	2013	1,098,387
Special allowable credits	2013	944,615
State retirement benefits exclusion	2013	156,071,376
Student tuition assistance	2006	568,000
Sugarcane transport credit	2013	496,500

Vehicle alternative fuel usage	2012	166,991
Wind and solar energy system	2013	24,108,243

Note: "Last Fiscal Year" indicates the last fiscal year for which the exemption is reported in the *Tax Expenditure Report*. "Revenue Loss" indicates the estimated nominal revenue loss for that year.

Sales Tax Exemptions	Last Fiscal Year	Revenue Loss (Current $)
Adaptive driving equipment and motor vehicle modification	2000	50,000
Additional tax levy on contracts entered into prior to and within days of tax levy	2013	0
Admissions to athletic or entertainment events by educational institutions and membership dues of certain nonprofit, civic organizations	2007	2,274,000
Admissions to museums	2007	1,252,000
Advertising services	2013	0
All sales tax holidays	2013	3,320,341
Apheresis kits and leuko reduction filters	2007	182,000
Cable television installation and repair services	2013	0
Cash-basis reporting procedure for rental and lease transactions	2013	0
Cash-basis sales tax reporting and remitting for health/ fitness club membership contracts	2013	0
Catalogs distributed in Louisiana	2000	42,000
Certain aircraft assembled in Louisiana with a capacity of 2 people or more	2003	0
Certain contract carrier buses used 80% in interstate commerce	2010	853,867
Certain digital television and digital radio conversion equipment	2007	841,000
Certain educational materials and equipment used for classroom instruction	2007	602,000
Certain geophysical survey information and data analyses	2013	0
Certain interchangeable components; optional method to determine	2007	614,000
Certain seafood-processing facilities	2007	238,000
Certain transactions involving the construction or overhaul of US Navy vessels	2007	602,750
Certain trucks and trailers used 80% in interstate commerce	2013	13,350,252
Coin bullion with a value of $1,000 or more	2007	216,000

TABLE 11.4. (*continued*)

Sales Tax Exemptions	Last Fiscal Year	Revenue Loss (Current $)
Construction materials and operating supplies for certain nonprofit retirement centers	2000	150,200
Cost price of refinery gas	2006	0
Credit for costs to reprogram cash registers	2013	16,111
Credit for sales taxes paid to other states	2007	24,170,000
Defined call centers	2006	8,274,616
Donation of toys	2007	40,000
Drugs prescribed by physicians or dentists	2013	288,472,992
Electricity for chlor-alkali manufacturing process	2007	6,475,000
Exemptions subject to 1% suspended rate	2013	11,187,076
Extended time to register mobile homes	2013	0
Farm products produced and used by the farmers	2007	81,000
Fees paid by radio and television broadcasters for rights to broadcast film, video, and tapes	2000	125,000
First $50,000 of new farm equipment used in poultry production	2004	150,000
First $50,000 of the sales price of certain rubber-tired farm equipment and attachments	2009	7,522,897
Food stamps and WIC vouchers purchases	2003	40,371,200
Helicopters leased for use in extraction, production, or exploration for oil, gas, or other minerals	1997	71,000
Interstate telecommunication services purchased by defined call centers	2007	9,023,276
Interstate telephone calls	2001	23,700,000
Lease or rental of certain vessels in mineral production	2000	13,000
Louisiana tax free shopping program	2013	871,581
Manufacturers rebates on new motor vehicles	2013	17,041,643
Manufacturers rebates paid directly to a dealer	2007	2,541,500
Materials used directly in the collection of blood	2007	624,000
Materials used in the construction, restoration, or renovation of housing in designated areas	2013	0
Materials used in the production or harvesting of catfish	2000	290,000
Materials used in the production or harvesting of crawfish	2000	390,000
Natural gas held, used, or consumed in providing natural gas storage services or operating natural gas storage facilities	2013	0

New vehicles furnished by a dealer for driver-education programs	2000	27,000
Nonresidential sales of electric power or energy	2013	325,678,464
Other exemptions	2013	769,017,447
Outside gate admissions and parking fees at fairs, festivals, and expositions sponsored by nonprofit organizations	2000	33,000
Piggy-back trailers or containers and rolling stock	2000	1,001,000
Pollution control devices and systems	2007	0
Purchase or rental of machinery and equipment to replace equipment damaged or destroyed by Hurricane Katrina or Hurricane Rita	2007	4,000,000
Purchases and leases by free hospitals	2007	49,000
Purchases and leases of durable medical equipment paid by or under provisions of Medicare	2013	2,282,028
Purchases and sales by Ducks Unlimited and Bass Life	2000	23,000
Purchases by a motion picture production company	2004	1,530,000
Purchases by a private postsecondary academic degree-granting institution	2007	56,000
Purchases by a public trust	2013	0
Purchases by motor vehicle manufacturers	2007	18,254
Purchases by nonprofit electric cooperatives	2000	1,502,000
Purchases by nonprofit entities that sell donated goods	2007	350,000
Purchases by regionally accredited independent educational institutions	2007	205,000
Purchases by state and local governments	2013	210,532,149
Purchases by the Society Of The Little Sisters Of The Poor	2006	25,000
Purchases of certain Bibles, song books, or literature by certain churches or synagogues for religious instructional classes	2006	624,500
Purchases of certain custom computer software	2008	801,630
Purchases of certain fuels for private residential consumption	2000	300,300
Purchases of consumables by paper and wood manufacturers and loggers	2013	1,578,426
Purchases of electric power and natural gas by paper or wood products manufacturing facilities	2009	7,481,867
Purchases of equipment by bona fide volunteer and public fire departments	2007	181,000
Purchases of manufacturing machinery and equipment	2013	60,436,437

TABLE 11.4. (*continued*)

Sales Tax Exemptions	Last Fiscal Year	Revenue Loss (Current $)
Purchases of new research equipment by a biotechnology company	2006	1,350,000
Purchases of school buses by independent operators	2007	395,000
Purchases of supplies, fuels, and repair services for boats used by commercial fishermen	2007	2,967,000
Purchases of tangible personal property for lease or rental	2013	11,536,271
Purchases of vehicles modified for use by an orthopedically disabled person	2013	59,304
Racehorses claimed at races in Louisiana	2000	200,000
Rail rolling stock sold or leased in Louisiana	2007	510,000
Raw materials used in the printing process	2000	521,000
Receipts from coin-operated washing and drying machines in commercial laundromats	2009	0
Refunds of sales tax to motion-picture production companies	2002	16,639
Rental or purchase of airplanes or airplane equipment and parts by Louisiana-domiciled commuter airlines	1999	420,000
Rentals or leases of certain oil-field property to be re-leased or re-rented	2007	966,500
Repair services performed in Louisiana when the repaired property is exported	2010	10,042,110
Residential sales of electric power or energy	2013	176,801,540
Room rentals at certain homeless shelters	2010	0
Sales by state-owned domed stadiums	2007	124,000
Sales of 50-ton vessels	2007	43,327,000
Sales of certain fuels used for farm purposes	2007	11,261,000
Sales of farm products direct from the farm	2007	330,000
Sales of fertilizers and containers to farmers	2009	0
Sales of food for use in the home	2013	387,523,862
Sales of food items by youth organizations	2007	169,000
Sales of gasoline, gasohol, and diesel	2013	301,026,374
Sales of motor vehicles to be leased or rented by qualified lessors	2013	47,216,045
Sales of newspapers	2000	871,000
Sales of newspapers by religious organizations	2007	38,000

Sales of pesticides for agricultural purposes	2007	1,813,000
Sales of raw agricultural products	2009	0
Sales of seeds for planting crops	2009	0
Sales of tangible personal property at or admissions to events sponsored by nonprofit groups	2007	2,856,000
Sales of telephone directories by advertising companies	2007	42,000
Sales of water	2010	4,806,687
Sales or purchases by blind persons operating small businesses	2007	201,000
Sales or purchases by certain sheltered workshops	2007	76,000
Sales price of refinery gas and other by products	2004	0
Sales tax collected by a qualified charitable institutions	2013	0
Sales tax remitted on bad debts from credit sales	2013	615,312
Sales through coin-operated vending machines	2007	3,350,000
Sales to nonprofit literacy organizations	2007	53,000
Specialty Mardi Gras items purchased by certain organizations	2000	27,000
State sales tax paid on property destroyed in a natural disaster	2012	34,104
Trucks, automobiles, and new aircraft removed from inventory for use as demonstrators	2000	220,000
Used manufactured homes and percent of cost of new manufactured homes	2013	6,800,602
Utilities used by steelworks and blast furnaces	1999	0
Vehicle rentals for re-rent to warranty customers	2007	114,500
Vendor's compensation	2013	28,086,286
Work products of certain professionals	2013	0
"Sales or cost price" of refinery gas	2013	0

Note: "Last Fiscal Year" indicates the last fiscal year for which the exemption is reported in the *Tax Expenditure Report*. "Revenue Loss" indicates the estimated nominal revenue loss for that year.

Tax Incentives and Exemption Contracts	Last Fiscal Year	Revenue Loss (Current $)
Angel Investor Tax Credit Program	2013	1,822,774
Atchafalaya Trace Heritage Area Development Zone Tax Exemption	2013	6,219
Brownfields Investor Tax Credit	2013	529,924
Cane River Heritage Tax Credit	2013	0

TABLE 11.4. (*continued*)

Tax Incentives and Exemption Contracts	Last Fiscal Year	Revenue Loss (Current $)
Digital Interactive Media and Software Tax Credit	2013	3,798,054
Enterprise Zone Tax Credit	2013	50,876,337
Exemptions for manufacturing establishments	2013	2,101,395
Green Jobs Industries Credit	2013	0
Industrial Tax Equalization Program	2013	6,067,950
Louisiana Biomedical Research and Development Park Program	2011	0
Louisiana Capital Companies Tax Credit Program	2013	24,686
Louisiana Community Economic Development	2013	0
Louisiana Motion Picture Incentive Program	2013	3,173,488
Louisiana Quality Jobs Program	2013	51,318,246
Mentor-protégé Tax Credit	2013	22,024
Motion picture Investor Tax Credit	2013	148,203,276
Musical and Theatrical Productions Tax Credit	2013	4,948,816
New Markets Tax Credit	2013	21,969,519
Ports of Louisiana Tax Credit	2013	0
Research and Development Tax Credit	2013	24,232,875
Retention and Modernization Credit	2013	857
Sound Recording Investor Tax Credit	2013	177,421
Technology Commercialization Credit and Jobs Program	2013	104,735
University Research and Development Parks Program	2013	1,994
Urban Revitalization Tax Incentive Program	2013	23,224

Note: "Last Fiscal Year" indicates the last fiscal year for which the exemption is reported in the *Tax Expenditure* Report. "Revenue Loss" indicates the estimated nominal revenue loss for that year.

Corporation Franchise Tax Exemptions	Last Fiscal Year	Revenue Loss (Current $)
Debt issuance costs	2013	0
Donations of materials, equipment, or instructors made to certain training providers	2013	0
Donations to assist qualified playgrounds	2013	0
Donations to public elementary or secondary schools	2013	0
Employment of the previously unemployed	2013	0

	Last Fiscal Year	Revenue Loss (Current $)
Insurance holding corporations	2004	123,000
Louisiana basic skills training	2013	0
Louisiana Capital Investment Tax Credit	2008	0
Louisiana Community Development Financial Institutions Act	2008	0
Low-income housing	2008	0
Members of controlled groups that include a telephone corporation	2007	1,336,000
Phase-out of borrowed capital in franchise tax base	2007	45,100,000
Public water utility companies	2007	111,000
Public-utility holding corporations	2007	8,467,000
Purchase of a qualified recycling equipment	2013	1,785,140
Regulated utility companies	2013	0
Rehabilitation of historic structures	2008	519,344
Vehicle, boat and equipment dealers	2003	0

Note: "Last Fiscal Year" indicates the last fiscal year for which the exemption is reported in the *Tax Expenditure Report.* "Revenue Loss" indicates the estimated nominal revenue loss for that year.

Corporation Income Tax Exemptions	Last Fiscal Year	Revenue Loss (Current $)
Ad valorem tax on natural gas	2013	3,652,547
Ad valorem tax on offshore vessels	2013	28,475,503
Ad valorem tax paid by certain telephone companies	2013	24,097,188
Alternative fuel usage	2006	0
Apprenticeship Tax Credit	2013	159,174
Bone marrow donor expense	2013	0
Cash donations to the Dedicated Research Investment Fund	2013	0
Certain refunds issued by utilities	2013	26,998
Contribution of tangible property of a sophisticated and technological nature to educational institutions	2013	1,714
Conversion of vehicles to alternative fuel	2013	2,820,589
Corporation jobs	2006	104,000
Credit for debt issuance costs	2013	0
Credit for purchases from prison industry enhancement	2006	0
Credit for rehabilitation of historic structures	2006	86,000
Credit for corporation jobs	2005	380,000

TABLE 11.4. (*continued*)

Corporation Income Tax Exemptions	Last Fiscal Year	Revenue Loss (Current $)
Deduction for hurricane recovery entity benefits	2008	0
Donations of materials, equipment, or instructors made to certain training providers	2013	0
Donations of property to certain offices and agencies	2013	0
Donations to assist qualified playgrounds	2013	0
Donations to public elementary or secondary schools	2011	0
Employee and dependent health insurance coverage credit	2013	0
Employment of certain first time drug offenders	2006	0
Employment of certain first-time nonviolent offenders	2013	0
Employment of the previously unemployed	2013	0
Federal income tax deduction	2013	174,461,066
Governmental subsidies for operating public transportation systems	2013	0
Hiring eligible re-entrants	2013	0
Income from carriage on high seas	2011	0
Insurance company premium tax	2013	23,602,003
Inventory tax	2006	227,374,680
Inventory tax/ad valorem tax credit	2013	407,849,402
LA Citizens Property Insurance Corporation Assessments Credit	2013	5,336,399
Louisiana basic skills training	2013	0
Louisiana capital companies	2005	8,300,000
Louisiana Community Development Financial Institutions Act Credit	2013	0
Low-income housing	2013	0
Milk producers	2013	295,000
Neighborhood assistance	2013	12,525
Net Louisiana operating loss	2013	318,106,502
New jobs	2013	295,681
Percentage depletion	2010	18,000,000
Purchase of a qualified recycling equipment	2013	3,895,969
Purchases from prison industry enhancement contractors	2013	0

	Last Fiscal Year	Revenue Loss (Current $)
Rehabilitation of historic structures	2013	7,837,164
School Readiness Business-supported Child Care Credit	2013	257,595
School Readiness Child Care Provider Credit	2013	3,094,412
School Readiness Fees and Grants to Resource and Referral Agencies Credit	2013	172,400
Subchapter S corporation	2013	477,482,318
Sugarcane Transport Credit	2013	5,237,193
Vehicle alternative fuel usage	2013	0
Wind and solar energy system	2013	14,895,799

Note: "Last Fiscal Year" indicates the last fiscal year for which the exemption is reported in the *Tax Expenditure Report*. "Revenue Loss" indicates the estimated nominal revenue loss for that year.

Gift Tax Exemptions	Last Fiscal Year	Revenue Loss (Current $)
Annual exclusion per donee	2011	16,000
Gifts made to charitable, religious, or educational institutions located in Louisiana	2013	0
Gifts made to US, State of Louisiana, or any other political subdivision or civic organization	2013	0
Gifts to spouse	2013	0
Specific lifetime-donor exemption: $30,000	2013	0

Note: "Last Fiscal Year" indicates the last fiscal year for which the exemption is reported in the *Tax Expenditure Report*. "Revenue Loss" indicates the estimated nominal revenue loss for that year.

Inheritance Tax Exemptions	Last Fiscal Year	Revenue Loss (Current $)
Bequests to charitable, religious, or educational institutions in Louisiana	2011	11,000
Bequests to out-of-state charitable, religious, or educational institutions	2008	4,000
Bequests to state, incorporated municipalities, or political subdivisions for exclusive public use	2009	10,000
Collateral relations; $1,000 exemption	2010	11,000
Direct descendants by blood or affinity	2011	40,000
Proceeds of life insurance payable to named beneficiaries	2011	18,000

TABLE 11.4. (*continued*)

Inheritance Tax Exemptions	Last Fiscal Year	Revenue Loss (Current $)
Strangers or nonrelated persons: $500 exemption	2008	6,000
Surviving spouse	2011	11,000

Note: "Last Fiscal Year" indicates the last fiscal year for which the exemption is reported in the *Tax Expenditure Report*. "Revenue Loss" indicates the estimated nominal revenue loss for that year.

Liquors—Alcoholic Beverage Taxes Exemptions	Last Fiscal Year	Revenue Loss (Current $)
Discount of 2% on beer	2013	731,700
Discount of 3.33% on liquor and wine	2013	761,850
Interstate shipments of alcoholic beverages	2013	125,450
Interstate shipments of beer	2013	912,250
Products returned to manufacturer or destroyed by a dealer	2013	70,480
Sales of beer to federal government and its agencies	2013	152,800
Sales of beer to ships engaged in interstate or foreign commerce	2005	30,000
Sales of liquor and wine to the federal government and its agencies	2013	21,525

Note: "Last Fiscal Year" indicates the last fiscal year for which the exemption is reported in the *Tax Expenditure Report*. "Revenue Loss" indicates the estimated nominal revenue loss for that year.

Miscellaneous Tax Exemptions	Last Fiscal Year	Revenue Loss (Current $)
Commercial mobile service exclusion	2006	75,000
Hazardous waste disposal tax—deduction for compliance	2013	13,700
Public utilities and carriers taxes—power cost exclusion	2006	150,000
Telecommunication tax—deduction of 2%	2013	16,800
Transportation and communications tax—seven-mile-zone exclusion	2013	3,196,000

Note: "Last Fiscal Year" indicates the last fiscal year for which the exemption is reported in the *Tax Expenditure Report*. "Revenue Loss" indicates the estimated nominal revenue loss for that year.

Natural Resources—Severance Tax Exemptions	Last Fiscal Year	Revenue Loss (Current $)
Consumed in field operations	2013	6,527,678
Consumed in the production of natural resources in State of Louisiana	2009	7,000
Contract gas at less than 52¢ per Mcf	2002	0
Flared or vented	2013	526,283
Horizontal mining and drilling projects	2013	0
Incapable gas-well gas	2013	23,617,328
Incapable oil	2013	13,930,093
Incapable oil-well gas	2013	965,106
Injection	2013	331,326
Natural gas suspensions—deep wells	2013	7,411,805
Natural gas suspensions—horizontal wells	2013	227,564,460
Natural gas suspensions—inactive wells	2013	2,285,192
Natural gas suspensions—new discovery wells	2004	1,000,000
Oil suspensions—deep wells	2013	20,076,267
Oil suspensions—horizontal wells	2013	7,667,963
Oil suspensions—inactive wells	2013	62,989,223
Oil suspensions—new discovery wells	2004	1,100,000
Oil suspensions—tertiary recovery	2013	40,789,524
Owned and severed by political subdivisions	2013	0
Produced outside the State of Louisiana	2013	5,162
Produced water injection incentive	2013	298,144
Salvage oil	2011	86,000
Stripper oil	2013	47,016,971
Stripper oil value less than 20$ per barrel	2013	0
Stripper oil wells	2001	1,500,000
Subdivisions	2001	0
Trucking, barging, and pipeline fees	2013	521,201
Used in the manufacture of carbon black	2013	363,373

Note: "Last Fiscal Year" indicates the last fiscal year for which the exemption is reported in the *Tax Expenditure Report*. "Revenue Loss" indicates the estimated nominal revenue loss for that year.

TABLE 11.4. (*continued*)

Petroleum Products Tax Exemptions	Last Fiscal Year	Revenue Loss (Current $)
Aviation gasoline	2013	117,400
Casinghead gasoline	2013	0
Diesel fuels tax refunds—school-bus drivers	2013	263,500
Diesel fuels used in licensed vehicles by commercial fishermen	2013	0
Diesel fuels used in or distributed to seagoing vessels	2013	812,500
Discount for timely filing and payment by licensed distributors and importers	2005	700,000
Discount for timely filing and payment by suppliers	2013	2,299,900
Discount of 3%	2006	4,000,000
Discount of 3% for a gasoline dealer	2006	700,000
Discount of 3% for a gasoline jobber	2006	700,000
Exports of gasoline or diesel fuels	2013	587,500
Gasoline and diesel fuel tax refunds—farmers, fishermen, and aircraft	2005	115,000
Gasoline and diesel fuel tax refunds—school-bus drivers	2005	140,000
Gasoline and undyed diesel brought into Louisiana in fuel supply tanks of interstate motor fuel users	2013	19,100
Gasoline discount for timely filing and payment by suppliers	2013	7,755,900
Gasoline for premixed two-cycle engine fuel	2012	0
Gasoline sales to federal government and its agencies	2013	133,500
Gasoline tax refunds—farmers, fishermen, and aircraft	2013	21,500
Gasoline tax refunds—school-bus drivers	2013	15,325
Interstate gasoline and diesel shipments/exports	2013	61,311,250
Interstate gasoline shipments/exports	2007	1,000,000,000
Special fuels tax refunds—school-bus drivers	2005	360,000
Undyed diesel fuel used by commercial fishermen	2013	0

Note: "Last Fiscal Year" indicates the last fiscal year for which the exemption is reported in the *Tax Expenditure Report*. "Revenue Loss" indicates the estimated nominal revenue loss for that year.

Tobacco Tax Exemptions	Last Fiscal Year	Revenue Loss (Current $)
Discount of 6% for timely filing reports	2013	1,353,500
Discount of 6% for tobacco stamps	2013	6,380,300
Interstate shipments of cigarettes	2013	56,250,300
Interstate shipments of tobacco products	2008	56,106,000
Return of taxable cigarettes to the manufacturer	2013	151,200
Return of taxable product to the manufacturer	2008	101,250
Sales to federal government and its agencies	2008	32,000

Note: "Last Fiscal Year" indicates the last fiscal year for which the exemption is reported in the *Tax Expenditure Report*. "Revenue Loss" indicates the estimated nominal revenue loss for that year.

12

PAYING FOR STATE GOVERNMENT WITH GAMING TAXES

James A. Richardson and Nathan Babb

Introduction

Over the past few decades, many states have turned to lotteries and other forms of gaming to raise money for public activities. An appealing aspect of the gaming industry as it relates to a taxable base is that its tax revenue is generated voluntarily by the consumer; engaging in gaming activities is a choice. States have several authorized forms of taxable gaming. A list of states with various forms of gaming is given in Table 12.1 at the end of this chapter. Gaming activities include: state lotteries, land-based casinos or riverboats, gaming at racetracks, video poker machines, and tribal casinos. Two states, Louisiana and West Virginia, have each form of these gaming activities. And, we might add Louisiana is presently considering expanding its gaming base by allowing certain gaming establishments to engage in sports betting, a decision that will also be dependent on rulings of the U.S. Supreme Court as well as action of the Louisiana Legislature. Forty-four states have lotteries, with the only states not having a lottery being Alaska, Alabama, Hawaii, Mississippi, Nevada, and Utah. Seventeen states have casinos, either land-based and/or riverboats. Nevada has, by far, the largest number with 235 casinos, and South Dakota follows with 35 and then Mississippi with 30. Fourteen states have gaming activities at racing tracks, and seven states allow the establishment of video poker machines in restaurants, bars, hotels, truck stops, and other such places.

States have turned to gaming activities to meet state financial obligations. Gaming has to be examined in terms of its tax base and the persons who make up this tax base; its growth dynamics; and its role in the development of the overall economy. As an example, the lottery is primarily a local tax being paid by local residents. In a few cases, residents from another state will cross state borders to engage in gaming activities, such as the lottery.

Louisiana marginally benefits from Mississippi residents coming to Louisiana to engage in the state lottery, as Mississippi does not currently operate a state lottery. Findings have been fairly consistent that the purchase of lottery tickets is funded by a reduction in spending on some other consumer products or services.[1]

Gaming Taxes Revenues

As a state revenue source, direct taxation of gaming activities achieved a slice of just over 8 percent of total state tax receipts in fiscal year 2015. This slice is composed of five forms of gaming: the lottery, video draw poker, riverboat gaming, the New Orleans land-based casino, and slot machines at live racing facilities.[2] Three of these gaming activities are very typically paid by local residents, with those being the lottery, video poker, and slot machines at live racing facilities. Riverboat gaming and the land-based casino in New Orleans may be aimed at persons from outside the state. Expanding the consumer base by attracting out-of-state players is key to the riverboat markets of Lake Charles and Shreveport, whose proximity to Texas makes these markets especially attractive. Gaming activity, regardless of the origins of the players, generated $846.0 million in fiscal year 2014 and $887 million in fiscal year 2015. Of that total, about 5 percent funded enforcement and treatment expenses in the state budget, and 5 percent was distributed to local governments, while 90 percent funded other areas of the budget: 46 percent through the state general fund and 44 percent through special dedications that primarily supported what would otherwise be general fund expenditures. Thus, while not a large share of state tax receipts, gaming revenue is largely a consistent source supporting general operations of the state budget, as illustrated in Figure 12.1. Since 1994–95 gaming activities have provided over 7 percent of the state's taxes, licenses, and fees, and provided just over 9 percent of total state taxes, licenses, and fees in fiscal year 2010.

Annual gaming revenue for the state of Louisiana is depicted in Figure 12.2. Gaming revenues to the state started in fiscal year 1991 with the introduction of the lottery. In the years following, revenues quickly accelerated with the addition of other forms of gaming, reaching an early peak of roughly $600 million in fiscal year 1996. After a minor decrease, revenues began a steady year-over-year increase, peaking at nearly $900 million in fiscal year 2007 prior to the Great Recession. For the majority of the time

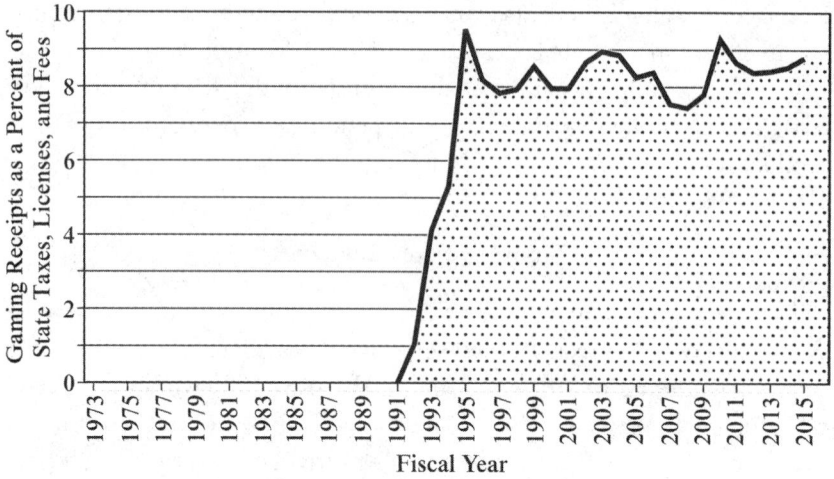

FIGURE 12.1. Gaming Receipts as Percentage of State Taxes, Licenses, and Fees

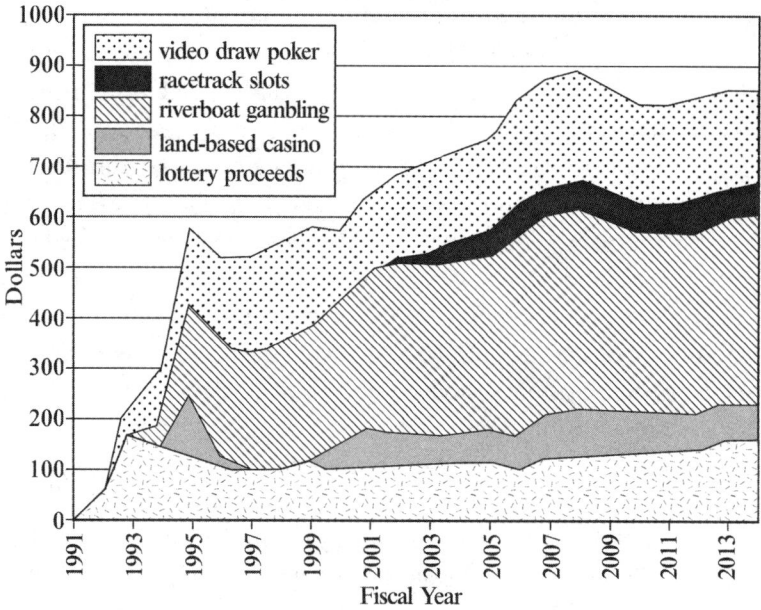

FIGURE 12.2. Gaming Revenues by Source

period selected, riverboat gaming accounted for the largest proportion of state revenue. The lottery has been a fairly consistent source of revenue, at around $150 million. Various forms of gaming have similar growth patterns. Take the time period of fiscal year 1993 through fiscal year 1996: all forms of gaming experience a sharp increase and then a sharp decrease of nearly equal magnitude. Similarly, other years see similar trends, whether increases or decreases. Gaming revenue is fairly consistent and predictable from the trends in the economy, as expenditures on gaming can be seen as outlets for disposable income. As the overall economy improves, so do gaming revenues.

Types of Gaming: An Overview

THE LOTTERY

Louisiana's history with lotteries dates farther back than that of almost any other state in the nation. In 1868, the Louisiana Lottery Company was granted a twenty-five-year charter to operate within the state and help generate revenues that would be used to finance the reconstruction periods following the Civil War. Corruption and bribery were rampant, though the company was able to continue doing business. While other state lotteries in the country were being repealed and prohibited in the late 1870s, the Louisiana Lottery Company was still in operation. In 1895 the company was disbanded, and legal forms of lottery gambling ceased to persist in the state.[3]

The recent era of lottery gaming in Louisiana was started in September of 1991[4] with the Louisiana Lottery Corporation running the operation as a regional monopoly. The state wanted to generate more revenue without increasing taxes and amended the constitution in the 1990 session. On October 6, 1990, Louisiana voters approved the measure by a two-to-one margin. Revenue to the state of Louisiana in the 1990s peaked in the first full year of 1992. Louisiana enjoyed a time period of no competition, but it was short-lived, as Texas voters approved the initiative by a two-to-one margin in 1992. Texas implemented its lottery in mid-1992. From 1992 to the present, Louisiana's revenues from the lottery have been steadily climbing to another peak of roughly $180 million in fiscal year 2017, after the drop in lottery revenues from its 1992 peak following the introduction of the Texas lottery. By 2013 lottery sales had achieved close to the 1992 peak year as the corporation marketed new instant-game mixes and price points, and joined the two multistate games of Powerball and mega-Millions, exploiting the large jackpot-driven sales nature of those games. By fiscal year 2017 the Louisiana lottery provided almost $180 million to the state treasury.

Lotteries, however, are primarily created to appeal to local markets. Individuals voluntarily decide to purchase lottery tickets, though one of the major responsibilities of the Lottery Corporation or organization is to advertise the winnings from any such game in a manner that promotes continued demand. Lotteries also provide different games with various odds of winning. The jackpots associated with the major prize money have extremely low odds of winning—estimated to be about 1 out of 175,000,000. Other lottery games will have better odds of winning, though the prizes will be lower in value. A larger risk premium, or seen another way, the probability of winning, is inversely associated with the amount of winnings at stake.

The lottery transfers 35 percent of its total sales and earnings to the state, plus any additional amount decided by its board.[5] In 2014 sales exceeded $450 million and transfers to the state budget were $170.6 million, making it the third-largest gaming sector contributor to the state budget revenue mix.

Lotteries are not growth-oriented; you cannot change the price of lottery tickets easily. When prices are fixed, say at the $1 or $2 mark, growth in tax receipts from the lottery then comes from an expansion in the consumer base. Thus, the major responsibility of the Louisiana Lottery Corporation is to market the lottery tickets to Louisiana citizens and people who might be visiting the state. Capturing out-of-state consumers is a convenient way to expand the consumer base, while also playing off the regional monopoly aspect of the Louisiana Lottery.

VIDEO GAMING DEVICES

Video draw poker devices followed the lottery in mid-1992,[6] ramping up to over 16,000 devices in nearly 4,000 bars, restaurants, truck stops, horse racing/betting venues, and hotels statewide by late 1995. A statewide referendum eliminated these devices in half the parishes in the state as of July 1999, cutting the device count to about 11,000 and the location count to 2,600. The number of devices climbed to nearly 15,000 by March of 2010, but has been declining since then, and there are around 14,500 as of July 2015. The locations having video poker machines increased to almost 2,900 by mid-2002, but have generally fallen since then to about 1,900 locations by July 2015.[7] Total gaming activity, as reflected in total device net revenue, dropped sharply with the referendum, generally rose in the period after, and has largely stabilized since mid-2009, as the lower device counts were effectively shifted to a growing number of truck stop locations, which are allowed more devices than the more numerous but declining bar and restaurant locations. In addition, truck stop devices have always earned more per device than devices in any of the other locations, supporting gaming activity total even as total locations and devices have fallen. Map 12.1 provides an illustration of the density of video gaming devices (VGDs) in the state.

Louisiana taxes this gaming activity with three tiers of rates dependent upon the venue location of the device: 22.5 percent at horse racing/betting venues; 26 percent at bars, restaurants, and hotels; and 32.5 percent at truck stops. The statewide effective tax rate is slightly over 30 percent, reflecting the heavy activity in the truck stop location. In fiscal year 2015 video draw

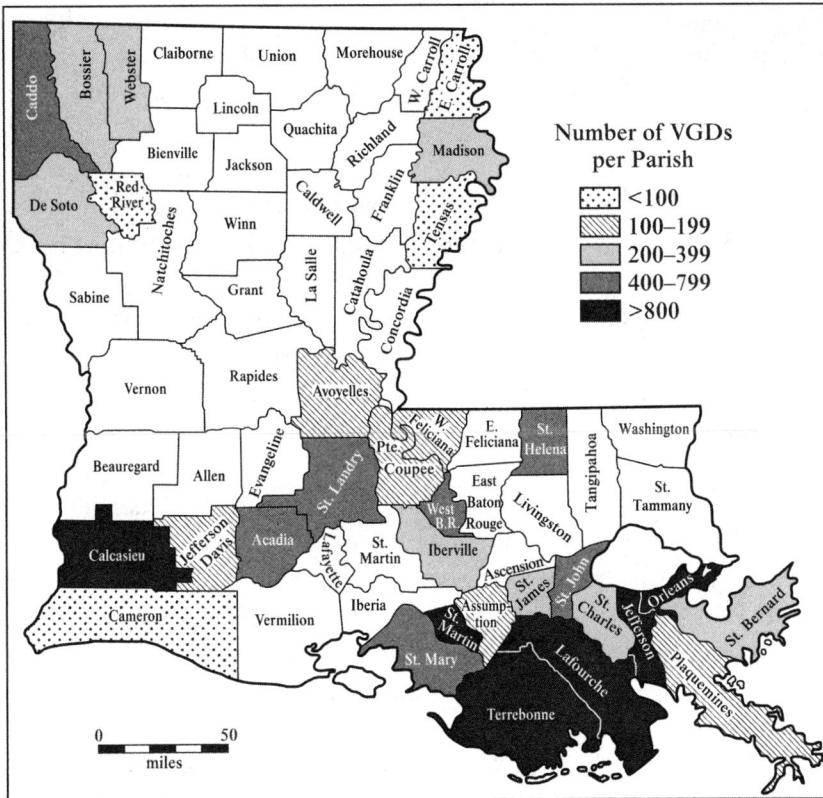

MAP 12.1. Video Gaming Devices (VGDs) in Louisiana

poker receipts to the state budget from gaming activity and various other fees paid by operators were $190.8 million; they were the second-largest gaming sector contributor to the state budget revenue mix.

Louisiana might profit marginally from out-of-state residents driving across the border to engage in this form of gaming. Neither Mississippi, Texas, nor Arkansas permit this type of gaming, thus giving the state a regional "monopoly" on this form of gaming revenue. The parishes of East Carroll, Madison, and Tensas all border Mississippi, and are competing against several riverboat casinos operating in Mississippi. Likewise, St. Helena and West Feliciana might benefit from out-of-state sales. The parishes of Caddo, DeSoto, Cameron, and Calcasieu all border Texas and might also profit marginally from out-of-state consumers. Due to their relatively high establishment in truck stops, Louisiana undoubtedly also profits from cross-state truckers who drive along any of the major interstates in the state. Revenue figures from VGDs generated from out-of-state residents are not available, however. As of 2013, Louisiana was one of seven states that permitted the use of VGDs. All other states are nonregional competitors.

RIVERBOAT GAMING

Riverboat gaming came on line in October of 1993.[8] Boats were added and relocated for the next several years, and full-time dockside gaming began in 2001. Gaming revenue earned by all boats settled into a monthly average of around $135 million by 2001. Currently, fifteen boats operate out of a maximum allowed of fifteen, thus making the riverboat market in Louisiana "complete." These riverboats are primarily in the metro areas of Shreveport-Bossier City, Lake Charles, Baton Rouge, and New Orleans. Since 2001, various additional boat relocations have occurred, as have major events such as two national recessions and four major hurricane landfalls in the state. Yet, until late 2014, the monthly average gaming revenue earned by all boats hovered around $135 million. That monthly average has stepped up to around $170 million with the opening of the fifteenth boat in the Lake Charles area in December 2014. The state issues a tax of 21.5 percent of these boat revenues plus various other fees paid by operators, totaling $410 million in fiscal year 2015, the largest gaming sector contributor to the state budget revenue mix. A discussion among the Louisiana and Mississippi riverboat markets is provided later in the chapter.

NEW ORLEANS'S LAND-BASED CASINO

The land-based casino in downtown New Orleans first opened in a temporary facility in May of 1995. That facility closed in November of that year as the construction on a new permanent facility was halted and the operating entity filed for bankruptcy. The casino emerged under a new ownership structure and began operating at its present location in October 1999. Initially, when it was fully operational, gaming revenue earned by the casino averaged about $22.5 million per month. Monthly revenue began trending up in late 2003, except for a five-month shutdown after Hurricane Katrina in August of 2005, peaking in mid-2008 at around $38 million per month. Since mid-2009, though, monthly gaming revenue has stepped down to average about $28 million. The state receives a fixed daily payment from the casino, and then an annual true-up payment is made in March of each year to provide tax receipts that are 21.5 percent of gaming revenue earned. In fiscal year 2015 gaming tax payments to the state were $71.4 million; they were the fourth largest gaming sector contributor to the state budget revenue mix.

SLOT MACHINES AT LIVE RACING FACILITIES

Slot machines at the live racing facility Delta Downs in Calcasieu Parish began operating in February of 2002. By May of 2003 slot machines were operating at Louisiana Downs in Bossier Parish, and then at Evangeline Downs, now located in St. Landry Parish, in December 2003. The New Orleans Fairgrounds began operating slot machines in September of 2007. Slot machine gaming revenue earned by the facilities in total has stepped up with the opening of each venue, and typically has continued to climb somewhat as each new venue settled into its market. Overall, the sector has remained essentially flat for a number of years, although this reflects a slight upward trend in the largest facility (Delta Downs), while the second and third largest facilities (Evangeline Downs and Louisiana Downs) have experienced slow downward trends in terms of gaming revenue earned. The state receives an effective tax of 15.17 percent of these revenues plus various other fees paid by operators, totaling $57.6 million from slot machine gaming in fiscal year 2015, which is the fifth largest gaming sector contributor to the state budget revenue mix.

Discussion of Mississippi's Gaming Industry

Mississippi remains the main regional competitor with Louisiana when it comes to gaming activities. Both Texas and Arkansas permit the lottery, though they ban all other forms of gaming. If residents in these states wish to engage in taxable gaming, they must cross their state's borders and enter a state that does permit taxable gaming. It comes as no surprise, then, that large portions of Louisiana's gaming industry are situated along the border of these states. Both Lake Charles and Shreveport have large riverboat markets and inevitably capture out-of-state consumers.

On the other hand, Mississippi does not permit a lottery, so residents there who wish to play must enter a state which allows it. Conveniently, Alabama does not currently permit lotteries, so residents in Mississippi might view Louisiana as an attractive marketplace. Unlike both Texas and Arkansas, Mississippi has a robust riverboat market. Here we examine varying rates between Louisiana and Mississippi and offer thoughts on Louisiana's competitiveness regarding gaming activities.

The effective tax rate on riverboats is an important factor to consider, both from the standpoint of the producer and the consumer. Louisiana has an effective tax rate of 21.5 percent on riverboats, which are distributed throughout the state in Shreveport/Bossier City, Lake Charles, Baton Rouge, and New Orleans. The one land-based casino in New Orleans also operates under the 21.5 percent effective tax rate. The effective tax rate of land-based and riverboat casinos in Mississippi is 12 percent, roughly half that of Louisiana's rate. Because both Texas and Arkansas prohibit casino gaming in their states, Mississippi remains the only pertinent regional state with which to compare.

The distribution of casinos in Louisiana is shown in Map 12.2. The majority of locations fall along the Shreveport–New Orleans line, with a few falling in the Lake Charles region within proximity of Interstate 10. Six riverboat licenses are held in the Shreveport/Bossier area, three in the Baton Rouge area, three in the New Orleans MSA, and three in the Lake Charles area. The one land-based casino in Louisiana in located in New Orleans, and all of these establishments are taxed at the 21.5 percent rate, with the majority of the revenue going to the General Fund.

Mississippi's thirty casinos are primarily located along the Gulf Coast regions of Biloxi, Gulf Port, and Bay St. Louis along Interstate 10, and along

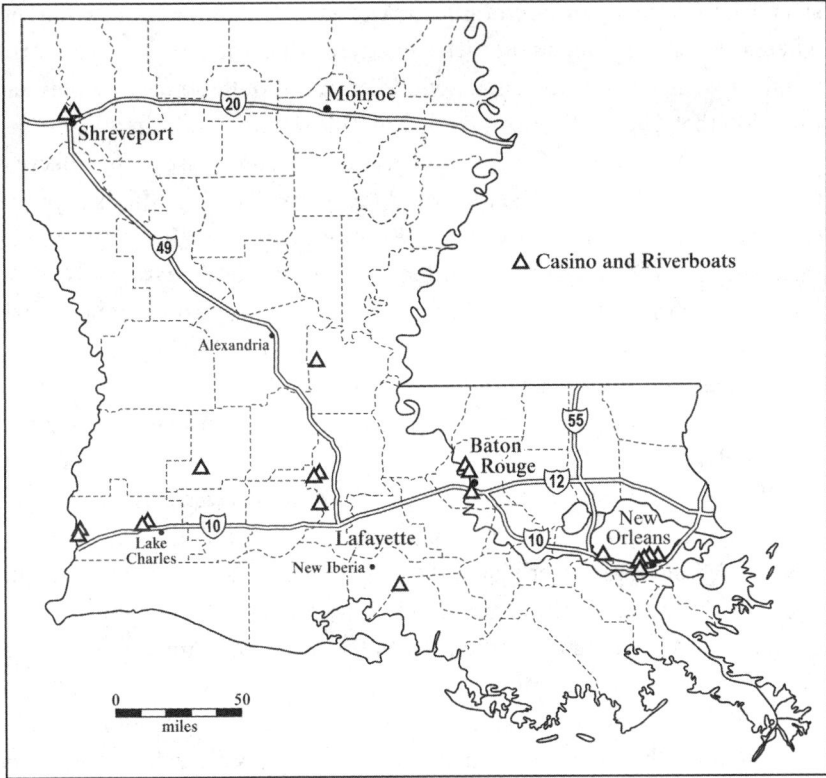

MAP 12.2. Casino and Riverboats in Louisiana

the Louisiana-Mississippi border near East Carroll, Madison, Tensas, and Concordia Parishes. This makes the Mississippi market accessible to Louisiana consumers, as well as to Arkansas consumers in the southern part of the state.

Louisiana has a substantially higher riverboat tax than does Mississippi—nearly double that of the neighboring state. In the face of other forms of gaming in Louisiana, namely, video gaming devices, racetracks, and a lottery, in addition to the competition of riverboats and casinos in neighboring Mississippi, it is important to understand the dynamics of such a rate. Nationwide, Louisiana's 21.5 percent tax on riverboat revenues is higher than average, but when accounted for license and operating fees, it appears slightly lower than the national average. In comparison, neighboring Mississippi has one of the lowest rates in the country. One of the major differences for a divergence of riverboat rates is the restriction of licenses. Louisiana permits the operation of fifteen riverboats through a license market, whereas Mississippi offers no such cap; there is an "unrestricted" supply of riverboats and casinos in Mississippi. In 2011, out of the thirteen states nationwide that offered licensing, only four allowed for unlimited licensing. These were Mississippi, Colorado, Nevada, and New Jersey. The effective tax rate among these four states was 8.8 percent, making Mississippi the state with the highest effective tax rate out of the group.[9] The difference in rates between the two groups—limited and unlimited licensing—is stark. Rates among the states with unlimited licensing observe, on average, much lower state-imposed tax rates. Rates among the states with limited licensing, on average, have nearly double or sometimes triple the effective tax rate of states with unlimited licensing. This comes as no surprise: when supply is restricted, prices are higher.

Although Louisiana and Mississippi both employ riverboat gaming as a source of gaming revenue, they can be seen as two different marketplaces. Because Mississippi's riverboat and casino markets are more crowded, the need for diversification and premium setting is heightened. Mississippi's casinos are more luxury treatment–oriented than Louisiana's appear to be. When comparing the gaming resort product typical to Mississippi (hotel quality, food and beverage, amenities) to the resort products of limited license states with higher rates (such as Louisiana), it is clear that Mississippi may offer a premium.[10]

Moreover, Mississippi does not have as diversified a portfolio of taxable gaming revenue as Louisiana does. Mississippi does not offer a lottery, making it one of six states in the country (Nevada, Utah, Alaska, Hawaii, and Alabama also do not offer a lottery) that does not collect revenue from this gaming endeavor. Residents in Louisiana can choose from a variety of gaming options. Of course, one can debate whether having so many gaming opportunities is in the best interest of the state.

Summary

Louisiana is one of two states in the country that employs all types of taxable gaming, including a state lottery, video draw poker, riverboat gaming, slot machines, and (one) land-based casino. Only West Virginia is similar in this fashion. Most states receive revenue through some form of taxable gaming. In forty-four states, this source is the lottery. However, presently it is uncommon to offer such a wide variety of taxable gaming options. Louisiana benefits from a robust revenue component, balanced by several sources that, in sum, account for approximately 8 percent of total state revenues.

The taxing rates Louisiana uses on the forms of gaming it allows are not uncommon or outliers nationally; in fact in some instances they are below average. Using any tax, behavior can be nudged by increasing or decreasing the incentive to participate. Policy regarding gaming should strive to achieve what tax policy on other sources achieves: a predictable source of revenue with consequences that seem to have a small effect on the daily life of the consumer. Consumers want predictability in their spending decisions just as much as state governments want predictability in their revenue estimates.

Louisiana is well positioned among her neighbor states in terms of the gaming industry, and this offers a "home-field advantage" of sorts; out of the three adjacent states, two offer a lottery, just as Louisiana does, while the other does not, and one offers riverboat gaming, while the remaining two do not. No neighboring state offers video poker. Simply put, Louisiana is one-of-a-kind in regional comparisons. One can view this as an opportunity or as possibly a curse.

TABLE 12.1. State Gaming Activities

States	Lotter	Number of Land-based Casinos or Riverboats	Number of Racetracks	Number of Video Poker Machines	Number of Casinos
Alabama	No				3
Alaska	No				2
Arkansas	Yes				
Arizona	Yes				26
California	Yes				70
Colorado	Yes	41			2
Connecticut	Yes				2
Delaware	Yes		3		
District of Columbia	Yes				
Florida	Yes		6		8
Georgia	Yes				

TABLE 12.1. (*continued*)

States	Lotter	Number of Land-based Casinos or Riverboats	Number of Racetracks	Number of Video Poker Machines	Number of Casinos
Hawaii	No				
Idaho	Yes				7
Illinois	Yes	10		1194	
Indiana	Yes	11	2		
Iowa	Yes	15	3		3
Kansas	Yes	3			4
Kentucky	Yes				
Louisiana	Yes	15	4	2071	3
Maine	Yes	1	1		
Maryland	Yes	2	1		
Massachusetts	Yes				
Michigan	Yes	3			22
Minnesota	Yes				39
Mississippi	No	30			3
Missouri	Yes	13			
Montana	Yes			1503	14
Nebraska	Yes				7
Nevada	No	265		2003	3
New Hampshire	Yes				
New Jersey	Yes	12			
New Mexico	Yes		5		21
New York	Yes		9		8
North Carolina	Yes				2
North Dakota	Yes				11
Ohio	Yes	4	1		
Oklahoma	Yes		2		114
Oregon	Yes			2322	8
Pennsylvania	Yes	5	6		
Rhode Island	Yes		2		

South Dakota	Yes	35		1459	14
South Carolina	Yes				
Tennessee	Yes				
Texas	Yes				1
Utah	No				
Vermont	Yes				
Virginia	Yes				
Washington	Yes				34
West Virginia	Yes	1	4	1490	
Wisconsin	Yes				31
Wyoming	Yes				4

Source: American Gaming Association

Notes

1. State Lotteries and Consumer Behavior, *Journal of Public Economics,* Melissa Schettini Kearney.

2. The state also allows pari-mutuel gaming and charitable gaming, and has three Indian nation casinos operating in the state. These activities are not included in the state's tax revenue totals or in this discussion because they do not contribute to the general operating budget of the state, but essentially pay taxes and/or fees to the state only to cover the state's regulatory expenses associated with each form of gaming.

3. *History of Gambling in the United States,* Roger Dunstan (January 1997).

4. The lottery was authorized by a state constitutional amendment proposed in Act 1097 of 1990, which was approved by the voters of the state on October 6, 1990, and became effective on November 8, 1990.

5. *Comprehensive Annual Financial Report for the Fiscal Years ended June 30, 2014 and 2013,* Louisiana Lottery Corporation.

6. Video Draw Poker gaming was authorized by Act 1062 of 1991.

7. *Video Game Revenue Report July 2015,* Louisiana State Police.

8. Riverboat gaming was authorized by Act 753 of 1991.

9. *Mississippi Gaming Taxes: Why the Existing Regulatory Environment Works,* Gulf Coast Business Council Research Foundation.

10. *Mississippi Gaming Taxes: Why the Existing Regulatory Environment Works,* Gulf Coast Business Council Research Foundation.

13

RECOMMENDATIONS AND CONCLUSIONS

James A. Richardson, Steven M. Sheffrin, and James Alm

In 2014 the Speaker of the Louisiana House of Representatives and the President of the Louisiana Senate asked the authors to conduct a thorough analysis of the Louisiana tax structure and to make suggestions and recommendations about improving it. We completed the study for the state legislature and presented a summary of our recommendations and conclusions to them in March 2015. Since 2015 the state has developed even more serious fiscal problems and will face a "fiscal cliff" in fiscal year 2019. This is a cliff of the state's own making; the state in 2016 asked a special Task Force to provide recommendations with respect to structural changes in the state's budget and tax policy, and the governor and legislature are reviewing recommendations about improving the Louisiana tax structure as they prepare to confront the fiscal cliff in fiscal year 2019.

The authors served on the task force created by the legislature and suggested the same recommendations that were made in our 2014–2015 study. The task force, being made up of representatives from the business community, labor organizations, and state and local governments, brought different perspectives to the discussion, so some of our recommendations were tempered. This, of course, is the public policy forum in which recommendations have to be adjusted to deal with the political environment, but with the idea that each amended recommendation still serves the public in terms of good tax policy. The pure form of our recommendations, but knowing full well that once they get to the political arena, some of the recommendations will be adjusted. We also note that over this period of three years, some of our recommendations have been accepted by the state legislature.

What Should Any State Accomplish with Its Tax Structure?

Louisiana, like every other state, must *establish the appropriate level of public expenditures* in line with the political preferences of its electorate and a *tax structure capable of funding* these desired state expenditures. At the same time, this tax structure must *not deter economic development* of the state *nor impose a disproportionately large and possibly counterproductive tax burden* on any one segment of the community. The tax structure should also be as *simple and transparent as possible and compatible with the local tax structure.* From an economist's perspective, the guiding principles of constructing a state tax structure include *broad tax bases* (meaning minimizing exemptions, credits, and rebates) allowing for *low tax rates* that typically contribute to simplicity of the tax structure, equity among taxpayers, long-term stability of the tax system, and the adequacy of paying for the public services demanded by the electorate. As simple as it sounds, low tax rates and broad tax bases are not nearly as easy to accomplish as one might think.

Present Louisiana Tax Structure

Louisiana's present tax structure includes two major sources of revenues, with the sales tax and the personal income tax making up 60 percent of total collections, and mineral revenues about 4 percent of revenue collections, while gaming and others contribute over 8 percent of total tax collections. Gasoline and diesel taxes represent almost 6 percent of revenue collections, corporate income and franchise taxes account for just over 3 percent of collections, insurance taxes make up almost 5 percent of all collections, and excise taxes (alcoholic beverages, beer, and tobacco) make up almost 2 percent of collections.

These tax collections have varied over time, responding to changes in economic expansions, national recessions, legislative changes in the tax structure, and energy volatility, as illustrated in Figure 13.1. From 2008 through 2010, sales taxes, personal income taxes, corporate income and franchise taxes, and mineral revenues (or in total about 70 percent of the state's revenue sources) declined. Taxes, licenses, and fees declined from just over $12 billion in fiscal year 2008 to about $9 billion in fiscal year 2010, a decline of 25 percent. This substantial decline in revenues followed a decline in economic activity related to the national recession and the decline in Katrina-related spending in southeastern Louisiana, a drop in energy prices, and legislatively approved reductions in personal income taxes in 2007 and 2008.

Tax collections from the major taxes are also affected by exemptions, credits, and other tax provisions approved either constitutionally or legis-

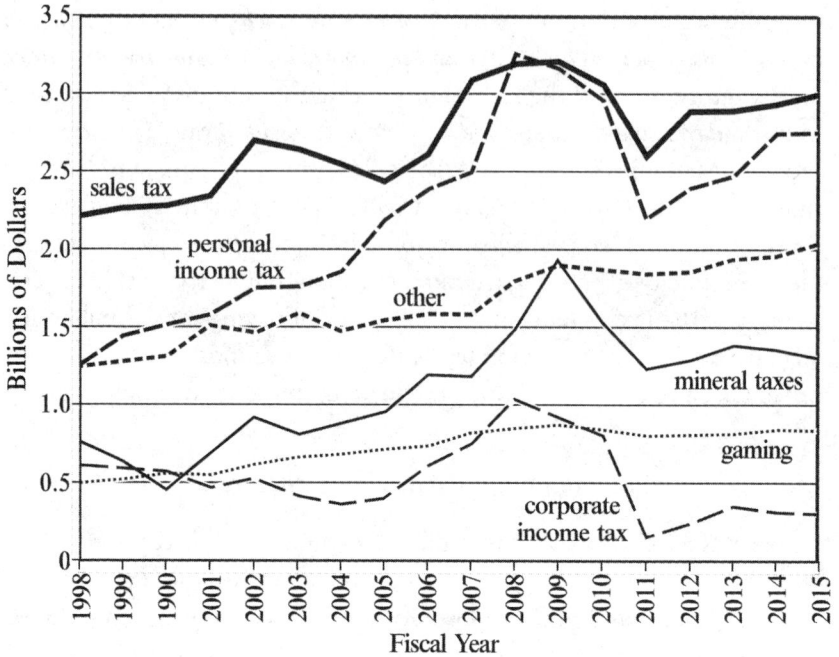

FIGURE 13.1. Louisiana Major Tax Sources

latively over a number of years. It is estimated that exemptions, exclusions, credits, and rebates amounted to over $7 billion in fiscal year 2010 and increased to approximately $7.7 billion in fiscal year 2014, an amount equal to about 70 percent of the actual collections. Tax exemptions reduce the tax base, thereby reducing the tax collections from a specific tax rate. Tax credits reduce directly the tax liability of a particular taxpayer. Together, exemptions and credits affect the major sources of revenue for the state—sales tax, personal income tax, corporate income and franchise tax, and the severance tax. Exemptions and credits must be carefully evaluated in any overall examination of a state's tax structure.

The sales tax is also a major source of local revenues along with the property tax. The state sales tax was 4 percent in 2014 and increased to 5 percent in 2016 to help solve a short-term budget shortfall, and the average local sales tax rate is 5 percent or higher. Together, the combined state and local sales tax rate is approximately 10 percent, the highest state and local sales tax rate in the nation, according to the Tax Foundation. Tennessee has a state and local sales tax rate of 9.45 percent, and Arkansas is third, with a state and local rate of 9.19 percent. Even as we focus on the state tax structure, we must address issues of local taxation as well. We also note that the local property tax base is diminished by several major exemptions—the homestead exemption for homeowners and the industrial tax exemption for manufacturing activities. Local tax capacity is constrained by constitutional mandates and legislative constraints.

Outside Review of Louisiana Tax Structure

In order to get a fresh perspective on the Louisiana tax structure as we initiated the study in 2014, we retained Professor George Zodrow, Rice University, and Professor William Fox, University of Tennessee, two noted tax experts, to give us their view of the strengths and weaknesses of Louisiana's tax structure. Fox and Zodrow saw the Louisiana tax structure as workable and sustainable but with a number of features that could be corrected. They gave a very *high priority* to the following changes in the Louisiana tax structure: (1) examine the sales tax base from the perspective of the many exemptions that have been enacted and from the perspective that services, the fastest growing area of the economy, have been for the most part excluded from the sales tax base; (2) coordinate the administration of the state and local sales tax collections, especially because of the Streamlined Sales and Use Tax Agreement (SSUTA); (3) lower significantly personal income tax rates by removing many exemptions from the tax law; (4) align basic excise taxes (including alcoholic beverages, beer, gasoline and diesel, and tobacco) with rates in other states; and (5) improve business taxes by lowering the high rates associated with the corporate income tax, reexamining the corporate franchise tax, and reviewing the method of apportioning corporate income for purposes of state taxation. Both Zodrow and Fox noted that local sales taxes were very significant since the other local tax base, the property tax, has been reduced substantially because of major exemptions. Zodrow felt the market would generate appropriate investment in oil and gas activities without the horizontal drilling incentive, since horizontal drilling is no longer an infant industry.

Making full use of the Fox/Zodrow reviews and suggestions, along with our own analysis of weaknesses in the Louisiana tax structure, we make the following suggestions for the state and local sales tax, the personal income tax, the corporate income and franchise tax, severance taxes, and excise taxes including alcoholic beverages, beer, tobacco, and gasoline and special fuels. These suggestions focus primarily on the *structure* of taxation in Louisiana. We are not suggesting an increase or decrease in the present *level* of state revenues or spending—this decision is properly the domain of elected officials. But we keep saying that state officials and the state's electorate have to decide on the appropriate level of state spending and then decide on the features of the state tax structure.

Sales and Use Tax

The state's sales and use tax has been levied since the 1930s. The state rate was increased to 4 percent in 1984 and then raised temporarily to 5 percent in 2016, and the average local rate has increased since 1984 from less than 4 percent to 5 percent presently. The state and local sales tax rate is now the highest combined state and local sales tax rate in the nation, based on sales tax data collected by the Tax Foundation. Also, it is estimated that current sales tax exemptions are almost $3 billion, an amount that roughly equals 80 percent of what the state sales tax actually generates. We do not believe that Louisiana should keep the state sales tax rate at 5 percent permanently. Instead, we suggest three major reforms of the sales and use tax: expand the sales tax base by examining existing exemptions, expand the base by adding services, and simplify the administration of the tax.

Sales Tax Exemptions

Our first major recommendation for the sales and use tax is to reconsider the many exemptions currently present in the sales and use tax. Nearly two-thirds of current sales tax exemptions, or approximately $1.7 billion, is embodied in seven exemptions, of which four are constitutionally mandated: food for preparation and consumption at home ($387 million); sales of electrical power, nonresidential ($319 million); gasoline sales ($301 million); prescription drugs ($289 million); purchases by state and local governments ($210 million); sale of electrical power for residential use ($176 million); and purchases of machinery and equipment ($60 million). Only seven states tax the purchase of machinery and equipment, and there are a variety of exemptions with respect to the sale of electrical power for nonresidential use across states.

Aside from these seven exemptions, there are over seventy other specific commodities exempted. These exemptions include ones for medical devices, agricultural purchases of seed and fuel, purchases of breastfeeding items, specialty Mardi Gras items purchased or sold by certain organizations, and tax holidays for back to school, hurricane preparedness, and Second Amendment rights. The tax holidays amount to about $4 million in reduced sales tax collections.

Each of these exemptions was passed with a specific purpose in mind. Exemptions, however, diminish the tax base. We suggest several reforms: first, a moratorium on any new sales tax exemptions; second, a removal of the sales tax holidays, since there is no evidence of any major gains to the state or to the citizens for this tax advantage; third, a sunset on all other tax exemptions over a five-year period; fourth, an analysis of the economic and social value of all exemptions; and, fifth, a requirement that any exemption shall be maintained only after approval by the state legislature and the governor.

Services

Our second major recommendation is to expand the sales and use tax to cover personal services. Given the high sales tax rate in Louisiana, expanding the sales tax base offers either strong revenue gains or possibly rate reductions. The taxation of services is likely to increase the progressivity of sales taxation, given the pattern of services consumption across income groups, and it would augment the sensitivity of the sales tax collections relative to overall economic growth, since services are becoming much more dominant in the mix of items that people purchase on a regular basis. Of course, expanding the sales tax to services could increase the administrative complexity of the Louisiana sales tax. There will certainly be a learning curve for state administrators who are collecting and monitoring the sales tax collections, but also for taxpayers who must record and remit taxes on services for the first time. The revenue potential ranges from $145 million of state revenues (using the personal services recommended by the 2013 Jindal plan) to $222 million (using services taxed by Texas but not by Louisiana) to almost $500 million (using personal and all other services included in the 2013 Jindal plan).

Administration

Our third major recommendation for the sales tax is to gradually and systematically work our way from the very decentralized system of sales tax administration that exists in Louisiana today to a more uniform system under which the state can apply for membership in the Streamlined Sales and Use Tax Agreement. We make this recommendation to align Louisiana with almost every other state in the union that has a state and local sales tax, and to enhance revenue collections at both the state and local level that might be lost due to internet transactions. The only other states that have a decentralized system of state and local sales tax collections are Colorado, a state that allows home-rule municipalities to collect their own sales taxes, and Arizona, which has just recently passed legislation to create a uniform method of collecting state and local sales taxes.

We propose the following steps in establishing a uniform method of collecting state and local sales taxes:

- As part of the tax reform effort, eliminate optional sales tax exemptions for any future legislative activity.
- Create a Local Sales Tax Commission (with members appointed by the Police Jury Association, the Louisiana Sheriffs Association, the Louisiana School Boards Association, the Louisiana Municipal Association, the Mayors Council, and the governor, Speaker of the House of Representatives, and President of the Senate) to initiate a process by which *local* taxes can be collected uniformly and appropriate auditing processes can be established.
- Once the Local Sales Tax Commission is working, have the state join the Local Sales Tax Commission to create a uniform process of state and local sales tax administration (collections and auditing).
- Initiate a Study Panel on State and Local Sales Tax Bases to estimate the variation in the tax bases among the state and localities and among the local governments themselves and to map out a reason-

able way to gradually eliminate the variation and minimize the cost of such changes. This study should be completed in two years.

Unifying the state and local sales tax base is an important challenge for Louisiana in meeting the criteria for the SSUTA. In making any changes, we must recognize that some local governments have issued bonds based on expected sales tax revenues, and that reducing or eliminating those revenue streams could unconstitutionally violate bond covenants. We recommend a series of steps to bring forth the desired uniformity. First, the SSUTA allows local governments to include food for home consumption and prescription drugs in the base even if they are exempt—as they are in Louisiana—at the state level. We would allow this practice to continue. Second, local optional exemptions from the sales tax should be eliminated by state legislation. Finally, legislation should eliminate other state exemptions to insure uniformity in tax bases.

The uniform collection of state and local sales taxes should be completed in a three-to-five-year window. The establishment of a uniform sales tax collection process is important to both the state and local governmental units. Current revenues are at stake, and even more future revenues are potentially at stake, especially if the sales tax is expanded (as recommended earlier).

This proposal is submitted with the greatest respect for local governments and with the understanding of the absolute importance of including local governments in every step of the process in establishing a uniform method of state and local sales tax collection. The administration of sales tax collections is not just a state issue; it is a state-local issue.

Personal Income Tax

Louisiana cannot eliminate the personal income tax as a method of paying for public services. This tax is very important to the state budget due to its absolute size, its share of total collections, its growth potential, its contribution to progressivity in the state's tax structure, and its broad reflection of economic activity. The state cannot make further extensive use of the sales tax since local governments in the state are also very reliant on the sales tax and since locals are very constrained by their use of the property tax. The

Louisiana personal income tax, as it is now structured, is competitive with the personal income tax in other southern states that have an income tax. Louisiana's lowest marginal tax rate applies to the first $25,000 of taxable income of joint filers, while most other states have the lowest rate apply from $5,000 to $10,000 of taxable income; Louisiana's highest rate is not effective until $100,000 of taxable income, while for most other states the highest marginal tax rate becomes effective on average at about $20,000. Three states in the South have higher top marginal tax rates, but no state has the highest rate becoming applicable at $100,000 of taxable income as Louisiana does. Kentucky's highest marginal tax rate becomes applicable at $75,000, and West Virginia's highest marginal tax rate becomes applicable at $60,000. There are ways, however, to reform the Louisiana personal income tax to improve the competitiveness of Louisiana relative to other states with an income tax.

We suggest the following changes to the personal income tax: (1) eliminate the federal income tax deduction, excess itemized deductions, and the net capital gains exclusion (all together about $1.1 billion of tax exemptions) and reduce the rates to 1 percent, 3 percent, and 5 percent; (2) maintain but decouple the earned income tax credit from the federal EITC; (3) place a moratorium on any new tax credits applying to the personal income tax and sunset all existing tax credits applying to the personal income tax; (4) limit credits for taxes paid to other states to Louisiana tax liability; and (5) examine and evaluate other major exemptions in the personal income tax, including those exemptions dealing with retirement income and social security income. Alternatively, if the electorate does not want to eliminate the federal tax deductions, we suggest a return to the Stelly Alternative—that is, narrow the brackets and eliminate excess itemized deductions as an exemption.

The proposal to eliminate the federal income tax deduction reduces the volatility and uncertainty of personal income tax revenues attributable to changes made in Washington, DC. Federal deductibility has allowed the state to reap the benefits if taxes are being cut at the federal level, such as in 2001 and 2003, but it has also meant a loss of state income tax collections if the federal government is raising taxes. Changes in itemized deductions by the federal government or changes in the federal earned income tax credit all affect state income tax collections. For this reason we propose restricting the connection of the Louisiana personal income tax structure to the federal system to the definition of adjusted gross income. We suggested the net capital gains exclusion as part of our reform package since this was a tax advantage that primarily affected high income taxpayers, and since it was initiated in 2009, it had been broadened by use to include almost any major capital gains associated with business transactions. This exemption was not eliminated but it was structured by legislative changes in the special session of the legislature in 2016, limiting the exemption to a certain percentage based on the number of years in which the capital had been held. To get 100 percent of the capital gains exemption, the property had to be held for thirty years or longer.

Presently, the state generates an estimated $3 billion from the personal income tax. The proposed 1 percent/3 percent/5 percent rate structure will generate roughly $3.4 billion. Households making less than $120,000 per year would pay slightly less than they are now paying under the present structure (about 1.6 million households fit into this category); households making more than $120,000 annually would pay slightly more, with those making over $1 million per year paying on average about $30,000 more per year (the average income for the above $1 million category is $2.8 million). This change would have to be approved by a vote of the people since the federal tax deduction is a constitutional restriction.

An alternative income tax proposal is to return to the Stelly Plan as implemented in 2002 and then reversed in 2007 and 2008. The brackets would be approximately cut in half, so the highest marginal tax rate would go into effect at $50,000 for joint filers as opposed to $100,000. This alternative would raise close to $800 million and would affect all taxpayers, though it would affect higher income taxpayers more than lower income taxpayers.

We also examined a flat tax since it has been discussed nationally, and North Carolina just recently passed a flat tax of 5.75 percent. We found that households in the middle to higher middle-income brackets would pay more in state taxes under virtually any version of a flat tax that did not raise taxes on lower income households. It is very difficult to protect middle-income taxpayers with only a single tax rate. Our recommendation of a 1 percent/3 percent/5 percent rate structure adds desired progressivity to the overall tax structure, progressivity that is simply not possible with a flat rate.

Also, it is important in interstate comparisons for the top marginal rate to be attractive, and Louisiana will be in an excellent position relative to other states, with the highest marginal tax rate being 5 percent and becoming effective at $100,000.

Corporate Income and Franchise Taxes

Louisiana last changed its corporate income tax structure in 1977, when the state increased its corporate tax rates from 4 percent to a graduated rate schedule of 4 percent on the first $25,000 of net income, 5 percent on the next $25,000, 6 percent on the next $50,000, 7 percent on the next $100,000, and 8 percent on net income in excess of $200,000. The state increased its corporate franchise tax in 1984 from $1.50 per $1,000 of equity and debt to $3.00 per $1,000. However, borrowed capital has been completely phased out of the tax base for taxable periods beginning on or after January 1, 2011, by the state legislature, and an adverse legal ruling in 2011 (*Utelcom, Inc. and Ucom, Inc. v. Bridges*) eliminating the tax for limited partnerships operating in Louisiana. These changes have substantially reduced the revenues from the tax. Additionally, the state has not fundamentally changed the tax law, but even so the state has changed the tax liability of corporations by creating refundable tax credits or special exemptions, such as the inventory tax credit or the net operating loss (NOL) carryback and carry forward. These credits substantially affect corporate tax liability.

In fiscal year 2008 corporate taxes surpassed the $1 billion mark, but revenues fell to less than $200 million in just two years, and presently revenues are hovering between $300 and $400 million. The corporate tax structure must be addressed for several reasons. First, corporate taxes are paid by corporations that cross state lines or are global companies. These corporations have a fiduciary obligation to their stockholders to assign their revenues and costs in the most advantageous places for tax minimization. The state has an obligation, not to tax the corporations unfairly, but to tax them consistent with their operations within the state of Louisiana and in line with companies based only in Louisiana. Second, the state wants to be business-friendly, and an 8 percent top marginal tax rate means Louisiana has the highest marginal tax rate in the South. The 8 percent top marginal tax rate is sometimes a company's first impression of Louisiana business climate. Mississippi has a top rate of 5 percent; Arkansas, 6.5 percent; Tennessee, 6.5 percent; Georgia, 6 percent; North Carolina, 6 percent; South Carolina, 5 percent; Florida, 5.5 percent; and Virginia, 6 percent; Texas does not have a corporate income tax but does have a gross margins tax. Third, the state incurs unnecessary volatility in corporate tax collections due to changes in federal tax policies, since Louisiana's corporate collections are tied to federal tax liability.

We recommend a major reduction in the corporate tax rate from the rate structure of 4 percent to 8 percent to a single rate of 5 percent without the deductibility of federal tax liability if the revenues are consistent with the current collections. We also suggest other changes in tax credits and tax exemptions that will allow the state to collect approximately the same amount of money.

We also recommended a more fundamental reform of the corporate income tax by making use of "addback statutes" as a means of addressing issues arising from intercompany transactions attributable to passive income. Addbacks are statutes that essentially eliminate certain intercompany transactions as deductions from the corporate tax base within a state. The most intensive addbacks include royalties for trademarks and other such services, intangible-related interest, intercompany interest, and management fees. Virtually all states that tax businesses on a separate-entity basis have addback statutes; specifically, twelve states have statutes defining these addbacks, including Alabama. The major reason for accepting the addback model is that it will provide stability and certainty for companies since they will now know the rules regarding what royalty income can or cannot be transmitted to another state as an expense. This modification can be easily administered by the Louisiana Department of Revenue. Louisiana has accepted this recommendation.

In the longer run, we also suggest that Louisiana should consider combined reporting. Under combined reporting statutes, corporations are taxed based on their apportioned share of income of their "unitary group." Corporations are combined into a unitary group under a variety of criteria, including common ownership, common management, and operating in the same line of business. The primary advantage of moving toward combined reporting is that it automatically handles the issues addressed in addback statutes without having to anticipate them in specific situations. It is generally acknowledged as the best method for safeguarding a state against corporate tax strategies to shift income to other locations. However, combined reporting does take time to implement, to properly administer, and to train a state's auditing staff to carry out. This is why we think it is prudent to start with the addback process and consider adopting combined reporting at a later date.

We also recommended several changes to how Louisiana apportions income for multistate businesses that were adopted in 2016. These were important to make sure that Louisiana taxes its fair share of the income from multistate businesses. We made two major recommendations: first, we believed that the state should increase the scope of apportioning income from multistate businesses using "single sales factor apportionment." Louisiana previously utilized this method for manufacturing and merchandising firms, but we believed it should be expanded without restrictions to most firms except for some specialized industries. Second, we recommended a new method called "market sourcing of services" for apportioning income from multistate firms that provide services. This method apportions income based on where a service is used, not where it is produced. This allow Louisiana, for example, to tax the income of large financial firms that operate outside the state but that have customers within the state. The legislature made these changes in 2016, and they are in line with those now being made in other states.

The net operating loss carryback and carryforward deduction allows the averaging of income for businesses that have fluctuations in their earnings. We recommend that the carryback be eliminated or, at least, be reduced to two years, consistent with the practice in most other states, while the carryforward be maintained at fifteen years. Eliminating the carryback and allowing for a fifteen-year carryforward would be very representative of practices in other states. The state made reforms in the net operating loss carryback and carryforward deduction in 2015, in line with our recommendation.

Finally, we recommend phasing out the franchise tax. As we discussed, as a result of legislative changes and adverse court decisions, the tax applies only to equity in corporate entities, and the base of the tax is narrowing over time. It is also not an economically sound tax. An alternative to its total elimination that could be considered would be to cap the tax at a relatively low level, but to restructure the tax to have it apply to all business entities, not just corporations.

Property Tax

In most of the country, local governments rely primarily on property tax revenues to finance their activities, along with some use of local sales and use taxes. In Louisiana, there is a much stronger reliance on local sales taxes. Local governments have little choice but to rely on the sales tax, as their property tax base is limited by two very large state-controlled exemptions: the homestead (or homeowners) exemption and the industrial property tax exemption.

Since 1982, homeowners have been able to exempt the first $7,500 from the assessed value of their property before any property tax is incurred. Since this type of property is assessed at 10 percent of fair market value, this is equivalent to exempting the first $75,000 of market value. By national standards, this is an extremely generous exemption, and it allows Louisiana to have one of the lowest average effective tax rates on homeowner property in the country, and one that is lower than other southern states have. Since the homestead exemption has not been changed since 1982, its effects on the tax base have eroded over time as property values have increased. In 1990, the homestead exemption reduced the taxable base by approximately 28 percent; in 2013, the taxable base was reduced by only 16 percent. Our recommendation is not to change the nominal value of the homestead exemption but to keep this nominal value from rising, thereby reducing the real value of the homestead exemption over time.

The industrial tax exemption is a program operated by the Louisiana Economic Development and the State Board of Commerce and Industry. The exemption offers full property tax abatement on new manufacturing investment for up to ten years (an initial five years with a five-year renewal). It includes taxable equipment but excludes land and inventories. While other states have similar exemptions, most states are not as generous, limiting their exemption period to five years. In addition, in other states, local governments must first request the exemption, while in Louisiana the exemptions are determined at the state level, and the local parishes have no say in the process. Our estimates suggest that the reduction of the property tax base from the industrial tax exemption program is approximately the same size as the homestead exemption in terms of reducing the tax base, although the differences vary sharply across parishes.

Unlike the homestead exemption (which is naturally reduced by increases in property values over time as long as the exemption is not increased), there are no mechanisms to decrease the industrial property tax exemption. Our proposal is to limit the amount of the exemption to 80 percent and to limit it to one seven-year period. This is a still a generous incentive for manufacturing, but our proposal would put a partial brake on the expansion of this exemption. Local parishes would then regularly assess and tax the other 20 percent. An important additional change would be to require approval by the local parish before approving any exemptions. The governor of Louisiana made a sweeping executive order in the summer of 2016, in line with our recommendations.

Exemptions and Tax Credits

Louisiana has, over a long period of time, added numerous exemptions and tax credits to the tax law. An exemption reduces the tax base; a tax credit reduces directly the tax liability. As noted earlier, it is estimated that all exemptions and credits amount to $7.7 billion, an amount that has grown by about 10 percent since 2010. Even aside from the already discussed exemptions and tax credits for the sales, personal income, and corporate income taxes, we believe that the various economic development incentives must be reconsidered. For all development incentive programs, we recommend that each incentive program must be specifically justified, designed with a sunset provision, limited in its magnitude, and evaluated regularly with rigorous and impartial analysis to determine whether its stated benefits exceed its costs. We also believe that certain tax credits need clarification and improvement. These tax credits are the inventory tax credit, the Motion Picture Investor Tax Credit, the Quality Jobs Program, and the Enterprise Zone Program, in addition to the homestead exemption and industrial tax exemption, as previously discussed.

INVENTORY TAX CREDIT

The inventory tax credit is a product of the 1990s, and it was an attempt to eliminate the Louisiana inventory ad valorem tax, a property tax that was not levied in most states. The tax credit was used since property taxes are local revenues; the state did not want to eliminate local revenues so it essentially said that it would repay companies for local property taxes on inventories via tax credit. Presently, nine states tax inventories with an ad valorem tax. The tax credit was phased in over seven years. It has grown rather quickly in the last decade, and it is now the third-largest tax credit/exemption, just behind the Subchapter S Corporation tax exemption and the federal tax liability deduction (both individual and corporate).

Taxing inventories is not a productive economic development policy. However, some changes are needed in the current method of providing this tax credit. The assessor values a company's inventories; the company pays the tax bill; and the company then submits its tax bill to the state government to lower the company's tax liability or to receive a refund, since this credit is refundable. The company has no incentive to question the assessment of its inventories, since the state is fully obligated to the payment. We recommend that the inventory tax credit be changed to 75 percent of the value of the assessment, thereby giving the company some "skin in the game." Over time we believe that the inventory ad valorem tax should be eliminated and replaced with other local revenues. However, this long-run change cannot be done quickly, since local governments currently rely on property tax revenues.

MOTION PICTURE INVESTOR TAX CREDIT

Louisiana's motion picture investor tax credit (film credit) provides a 30 percent transferable tax credit on total in-state expenditures, including resident and nonresident labor, with no cap, subject to a $300,000 minimum expenditure. The credits can offset personal or corporate tax liability, can be sold or transferred to third parties, or can be sold back to the state for 85 percent of face value. For productions using in-state labor, there is an additional 5 percent payroll tax credit. In the last year, Louisiana awarded approximately $250 million in credits. There have been a number of formal and informal analyses of the motion picture investment tax credit, including those commissioned by the Louisiana Economic Development Agency. A fair reading of this literature suggests the following four points:

1. The credit has been successful in attracting production of films to Louisiana and generating local economic activity.

2. The credit has cost the state considerable revenue, even after allowing for offsets due to the generation of new economic activity. The most recent study from the Louisiana Economic Development Agency pegged the budgetary cost for 2012 at approximately $170 million, while allowing for roughly a 33 percent offset from increased activity.
3. There is no natural ending point to the subsidization of the film industry. While there has been some infrastructure development, most observers believe that the level of film production we have witnessed in Louisiana is contingent upon the program continuing.
4. Although the program is structured as providing tax credits, it really has nothing to do with taxes and is effectively a subsidy program to the industry.

These four points can be summarized simply: the film tax credit should be viewed as an ongoing spending program that provides some benefits to the state.

As such, we recommend that the firm tax credit should be treated by the legislature on par with other spending programs. We also recommend that caps should be placed on the expenditures for the program, so that it is not an open-ended entitlement. We believe that current practice is an irresponsible budgeting practice for the state. In setting a cap, the legislature can determine how much activity it wants to subsidize and, if resources become limited, what types of activity it wishes to subsidize. Reconfiguring the film tax credit as an explicit expenditure program will require careful thought to structure a program that the state can afford and that meets the broader needs of its residents. This is an appropriate role for the legislature. The state has taken steps to put limits on the motion picture tax credit and to control it via a front-end cap which makes it essentially a spending program and not a tax program.

ENTERPRISE ZONE PROGRAM

Louisiana's Enterprise Zone (EZ) program is a jobs incentive program that provides income and franchise tax credits to a new or existing business located in Louisiana creating permanent net new full-time jobs and hiring at least 50 percent of those net new jobs from targeted groups. The benefits include a one-time $2,500 job tax credit for each net new job created; the benefits also provide either a 4 percent rebate of sales and use taxes paid on qualifying materials, machinery, furniture, and/or equipment purchased, or a 1.5 percent refundable investment tax credit on the total capital investment, excluding tax-exempted items. The intent of the EZ program is to encourage economic development in areas with high unemployment and/or low income, especially in areas with high concentrations of individuals on public assistance. The Louisiana Department of Revenue estimates that the EZ program led to a loss of $50.9 million in 2013, of which $8.0 million is due to the sales tax rebate, $11.6 million is due to the jobs credit, and $31.3 million is due to the investment tax credit. The estimated annual revenue loss has averaged $61.0 million over the last three years.

Enterprise zone programs have been extensively studied. The general conclusion from these many studies is that enterprise zone programs have been largely ineffective in encouraging targeted economic development, despite their considerable revenue cost.

Accordingly, we recommend that the enterprise zone incentives be eliminated. However, if lawmakers wish to preserve the credits, the credits should be restricted to firms that actually operate in designated low-income areas, to firms that actually create new jobs, and to nonretail firms. Incentives should also be limited, either by designing the incentive program as an explicit expenditure program or by capping the magnitude of the tax credit or exemption and limiting its transferability. The program should be evaluated regularly, with rigorous and impartial analysis, to determine whether it has achieved its stated justification, and at what cost. Louisiana has taken several steps in making the enterprise zone program more effective over the past several years.

QUALITY JOBS PROGRAM

Louisiana's Quality Jobs (QJ) program provides a cash rebate to companies in order to encourage the creation of well-paid jobs and promote economic development. The incentives include up to a 6 percent cash rebate of annual gross payroll for new, direct jobs for up to ten years; the incentives also provide either a 4 percent sales and use tax rebate on capital expenditures or a 1.5 percent investment tax credit for qualified expenses. The intent of the QJ program is to give an incentive to firms to locate or to expand their operations in the state.

Job creation programs like the QJ program have been extensively studied. The general conclusions from these studies are that (1) job incentive programs have been at best only modestly successful in encouraging net new job creation, (2) seldom is there solid evidence that the job incentive programs encourage economic development that would not have occurred anyway, in the absence of the programs, (3) the main beneficiaries of the job incentive programs have not been "mobile" workers but instead "immobile" factors of production, especially owners of land and commercial real estate, and (4) the job incentive programs have cost the government considerable tax revenue, even after allowing for offsets due to the possible generation of new economic activity.

The Louisiana Department of Revenue estimates that the QJ program has led to a loss of $51 million in revenues in 2013. The estimated annual revenue loss has averaged $44 million over the last three years, an average that is somewhat lower than in previous years. To make up these outlays, the economic development projects would have to create over $600 million of net new personal income that would not have otherwise been created in the Louisiana economy, or over 15,000 net new jobs.

We believe that the long-run goal should be to gradually eliminate the QJ program. However, a more immediate set of recommendations recognizes that complete elimination may not be feasible or even desirable in the short run. Our main short-run recommendations for the quality jobs program are therefore the following:

1. Limit the magnitude of the quality jobs program tax incentives, either by designing the program as an explicit expenditure program or by capping the magnitude of the rebate/tax credit.
2. Evaluate the quality jobs program regularly with rigorous and impartial analysis to determine whether it has achieved its stated justification, and at what cost.

Mineral Taxes

Louisiana has a long history of taxing oil and gas. In the 1970s the state changed its taxation of oil from a tax rate of 26 cents per barrel to 12.5 percent of value with lower rates for incapable wells and stripper wells. The timing of this legislative action to change the method of taxing oil was significant, since oil prices quadrupled and then doubled from 1973 to 1981

Louisiana enjoyed the additional revenues associated with higher oil prices.

The state also raised the tax rate on natural gas from 3.3 cents per Mcf to 7 cents per Mcf. Natural gas is taxed on a volume basis. The reason for not taxing natural gas on value related to market conditions. Namely, in the 1970s natural gas was subject to interstate price controls, so natural gas produced in Louisiana but shipped across state lines was subject to price controls, while natural gas produced in Louisiana and used in Louisiana as either heating fuel or a feedstock was not subject to price controls. Taxes from oil and natural gas provided well over 40 percent of the state's revenues through 1982, and then fell dramatically during the 1980s as oil prices plunged. Mineral revenues now make up about 12 to 15 percent of the state's revenues, depending on the price of oil. A major tax provision was introduced in 1994, providing a special tax advantage for horizontal drilling, a technique that in the 1990s could be classified as an "infant industry." This tax provision was then used in 2008 in conjunction with the Haynesville Shale and is applicable in the Tuscaloosa Marine Shale and the Brown Dense. The horizontal drilling tax break amounted to almost $240 million in fiscal year 2014.

We have two major recommendations regarding the taxation of oil and gas. Our first recommendation is to eliminate or scale back substantially the horizontal drilling exemption. This exemption was created in an entirely different market and technology environment than at present. The market provides the most effective incentive for oil and gas operators and producers to initiate investments. Oil and gas prices, along with cost considerations, will then drive investments, not tax policy.

Our second recommendation is to initiate a major study of the appropriate taxation of oil and gas. Our tax structure was created in the 1970s, a time in which the market environment was very different from at present. Most states tax oil and gas at about the same rate. Texas taxes natural gas more prominently than oil. Louisiana taxes oil more substantially than natural gas. This would be a good time to work through the overall tax structure regarding oil and gas taxation. We recommend an updated analysis of overall oil and gas taxation to be completed by March 2019 or sooner.

Our final comment is that mineral revenues will never carry the state from a revenue perspective again. The state has to accept the fact that the oil and gas industry will provide jobs in the state but it will not produce the lion's share of the state's revenues.

USE OF MINERAL REVENUES

Mineral revenues are being generated by the depletion of finite resources. It may be prudent for the state to discuss the appropriate use of mineral revenues in the operating budget of the state. In 1973 when Louisiana made significant and economically appropriate changes in the taxation of oil and gas, the state also made decisions to use the revenues from oil and gas to offset reductions in the sales tax (by eliminating food and drugs from the sales tax base) and in the personal income tax (by adopting federal tax liability as a deduction from adjusted gross income in calculating Louisiana taxable income). In other words, oil and gas revenues were paying for operating expenses of the state, even though oil and gas are finite resources.

We have a new opportunity to reevaluate our use of oil and gas revenues. The Tuscaloosa Marine Shale (TMS) has been projected to have as many as 9 billion barrels of oil, with about 7 percent of this oil being recoverable with current technology. Although production is in the early stages and there is still uncertainty about what prices will be needed to support sustained production in this play, the dollars associated with TMS production have not been absorbed into the operating budget of the state. We believe that this provides a unique opportunity for the state to create a "permanent trust fund." Even with only 7 percent being recoverable and assuming an average price of $80 per barrel, the permanent trust fund could accumulate as much as $6.3 billion, a fund that could be used for major projects deemed important by the state such as infrastructure improvements or other long-run state commitments. By designating severance tax revenues associated with TMS towards principal in a permanent trust fund, the state would create a financial asset for future generations of Louisianans. Not only would this be beneficial to the state in the long run, it has the opportunity to mitigate intergenerational equity concerns associated with extraction of a finite resource. Alaska has a permanent dividend fund established in 1976, and Texas has a permanent fund that was initiated in 1876.

Excise Taxes

Louisiana, like most other states, collects a number of taxes based on volume of consumption, including alcoholic beverages ($25 million), beer ($33 million), tobacco ($142 million), and gasoline and special fuels ($625 million). The gasoline and special fuels tax is dedicated to the Transportation Trust Fund. Together these taxes contribute $825 million to the state's budget, or almost 8 percent of the state's budget. When we began our study, Louisiana excise taxes were lower, and in some cases significantly lower, than regional or national average excise taxes. We recommended to the legislature that in all cases the Louisiana excise taxes be aligned to national or regional averages. In 2016, the legislature raised taxes on beer and alcoholic beverages and cigarettes.

BEER AND ALCOHOLIC BEVERAGES

Louisiana taxes alcoholic beverages on a volumetric basis at the wholesale level. The tax is organized into a low alcohol content beverage tax (beer and malts) and a high alcohol content beverage tax (liquor and wine). In fiscal year 2013, receipts from alcoholic beverages totaled approximately $57 million, a slight increase from the previous year. Beer and malts are taxed at a rate of $10.00 per 31-gallon barrel, or $0.32/gallon. This rate is relatively low compared to that in states in the southern region; nevertheless, it is slightly higher than the national average of $0.28/gallon. The average beer tax in Alabama, Georgia, Kentucky, Mississippi, North Carolina, South Carolina, and Tennessee averaged 83 cents per gallon, or over 2.5 times the Louisiana rate. Texas has a beer tax of 20 cents per gallon. If we compare Louisiana to its neighboring states, the average beer tax is 32.3 cents per gallon, or just about the Louisiana rate. At $34.9 million, beer receipts in Louisiana account for a majority of total alcoholic beverage revenue despite their leveling growth patterns.

Growth in alcohol revenue can be attributed to liquor and wine sales. Liquor and wine are taxed at a rate of $0.66/liter ($2.50/gallon) and $0.03/liter ($0.11/gallon), respectively. Louisiana's liquor excise rate falls well below the national average, while the wine excise is the lowest in the United States. In addition, the state imposes a graduated tax on wine of higher alcohol content. Just as a comparison, the average liquor tax is $8.78 per gallon for Alabama, Georgia, Kentucky, North Carolina, South Carolina, and Tennessee, an average rate that is 3.6 times the Louisiana tax rate. Using comparable rates in Texas, Arkansas, and Mississippi, the average liquor rate is $5.46 per gallon. Regardless of what average we use, the liquor rate in Louisiana is extremely low compared to the rate in other states.

Based on regional comparisons, these taxes can be raised in an overall attempt to update the tax structure and produce a certain amount of revenues for the state general fund. Louisiana has raised the tax on beer and the tax on alcoholic beverages in the last few years and did so again in 2016. But we may also want to index the taxes so that the tax rates will grow with inflation. The tax will still be a volume tax, but the rate will change from year to year.

TOBACCO

The tobacco tax in Louisiana was 36 cents per pack when we initiated our studies; it has now been increased to $1.08 per pack. The average tobacco tax in Texas, Arkansas, and Mississippi is $1.08 per pack, while the average for Alabama, Georgia, Kentucky, North Carolina, South Carolina, and Tennessee is 53 cents per pack. According to the Tax Foundation, Louisiana was the forty-eighth state in the country in terms of the tobacco tax. Tobacco taxes can be increased with a minimal impact on revenue collections, unless the rates are increased in order to deter smoking. Very high tax rates can create activity on the part of citizens to avoid the tax entirely by purchasing tobacco in other venues, so any increase in tobacco taxes must recognize that there are limits on any tax increase by the state. However, the evidence suggests that Louisiana could implement a substantial increase in the tobacco tax without encouraging persons to find alternative venues for purchasing tobacco.

GASOLINE

The gasoline tax is a tax that is used to pay for the Department of Transportation and Development, highway maintenance, and other highway improvements in Louisiana. The gasoline tax is a tax related to the volume of gasoline purchased. The amount of gasoline required to drive on the state highways and roads depends on the gas mileage relating to the fleet of cars and trucks that are on the road. The method of paying for roads and highway maintenance has not changed over many years, but the relationship between driving, gasoline mileage, and miles driven has changed over time. In comparing Louisiana to other states, Louisiana imposes a relatively similar tax burden. The average gasoline tax for Alabama, Georgia, Kentucky, Mississippi, North Carolina, South Carolina, and Tennessee is 22 cents per gallon; the average gasoline tax for Texas, Arkansas, and Mississippi is 20.2 cents per gallon. In both cases the average gasoline tax in these two groups of states is very close to Louisiana's rate of 20 cents per gallon. However, nationwide the average tax rates are slightly higher, at 24 cents per gallon.

An increase in the gasoline tax from 20 cents per gallon to 24 cents per gallon would be compatible with good tax policy, since the tax is similar to a user's fee. It would not drive many people from the market; it would provide additional revenues of $120 million; and it would be assigned to those persons using the streets. Given that the gasoline tax is dedicated to the transportation trust fund, it is appropriate to connect any changes in the gasoline tax to any suggestions for highway maintenance and additional infrastructure.

It would also be appropriate to initiate a study connecting the demand for highway maintenance with the appropriate method of funding such maintenance if the current tax sources cannot provide sufficient revenues. This would be the time to rethink the way in which we pay for the use of roads and highways in Louisiana, given that fuel efficiency is improving steadily and the gasoline tax does not account for inflationary trends.

Summary of Recommendations

Our recommendations are summarized in Table 13.1. These recommendations are made in concert with the tax study that we completed for the state legislature starting in 2014 and finishing with a presentation to the legislature in 2015 and the report of the Task Force on Structural Changes in Budget and Tax Policy completed as of November 2016. These recommendations have already begun part of the dialogue in discussing the fiscal issues facing the state of Louisiana. We make these recommendations as professional economists, and we fully appreciate the pressure that public officials face as they vote on a variety of tax alternatives. However, we believe that the state, in the long run, will benefit from the stability, the fairness, and the economic competitiveness of the suggestions from our report to the legislature, the recommendations of the Task Force, and the recommendations and suggestions outlined in this book.

TABLE 13.1. Recommendations and Suggestions, Tax Reform for Louisiana

Tax	Recommendations
Sales and use tax	Lower the sales tax rate from 5% to 4% if at all possible.
	Expand the sales tax base to include additional personal services, and review and sunset sales tax exemptions classified as "other."
	Move toward a single collector and single audit authority through a joint state and local authority to be consistent with the Streamlined Sales and Use Tax Agreement.
	Move towards a unified sales tax base for state and local governments, allowing local jurisdictions to continue to tax food for home consumption and prescription drugs. This unification should be accomplished by eliminating optional local exemptions and limiting state exemptions, as determined by a new Local Sales Tax Commission in consultation with the state.
Personal income tax	Lower tax rates while preserving the distribution of tax burdens.
	Eliminate federal deductibility and excess itemized deductions.
	Limit tax credits allowed to other states to potential tax liability in Louisiana.
	Repeal the net capital gains exclusion.
	Examine and review other major exclusions, including those for retirement, social security, and others.
	Place a moratorium on new tax credits.
	Maintain but allow the state EITC to be decoupled from the federal EITC.
	Establish a sunset date for all others to be eliminated unless reenacted.
Corporate and franchise taxes	Lower the top corporate tax rate.
	Eliminate federal tax deductibility.
	Enact an addback statute for the corporate tax. (Adopted) In the long run, move to a system of combined reporting.
	Move to single sales apportionment for most business entities except for specialized industries where it is not appropriate. (Adopted)
	Move to market sourcing for services for apportioning business income. (Adopted)
	Eliminate the corporate franchise tax or cap it at a low level and have it apply to all business entities.
	Reduce or eliminate carryback period. Maintain carryforwards.
Property taxes	Maintain but not increase the homestead exemption.
	Reduce the industrial property tax exemption from 100% to 80%, and limit the exemption to one seven-year period. Require parish endorsement for any exemptions.

Exemptions and tax credits	Limit the inventory credit to 75%.
	Work toward phasing out the property tax on inventories, with appropriate revenue replacement.
	Convert the motion picture tax credit to an expenditure program subject to annual appropriation.
	Eliminate the Enterprise Zones program and limit and reform the Quality Jobs programs.
Mineral taxes	Eliminate the horizontal drilling exemption.
	Designate revenues from the Tuscaloosa Marine Shale field for a permanent trust fund.
	Examine and review the relative taxation of oil and natural gas, with a goal of realigning relative tax rates as appropriate. Review other exemptions.
Excise tax	Align the excise taxes on alcohol, tobacco, and motor fuels to national or regional averages. (Partly Adopted)

APPENDIX

Summary of Recommendations by the Task Force on Structural Changes in Budget and Tax Policy

Preface

The Louisiana legislature created the Task Force on Structural Changes in Budget and Tax Policy during the First Extraordinary Session of 2016. The purpose was to look beyond the recent temporary revenue fixes and recommend permanent solutions for the growing and possibly intractable imbalance between annual state revenues and spending levels. Led by Rep. John Schroder and supported by House Speaker Taylor Barras and Senate President John Alario, House Concurrent Resolution No. 11 (HCR 11 can be found in Appendix A) directed the Task Force "to make recommendations of changes to the state's tax laws in an effort to modernize and enhance the efficiency and fairness of the state's tax policies for individuals and businesses, to examine the structure and design of the state budget and make recommendations for long-term budgeting reforms." The members of the legislature and the office of the governor are fully aware that this imbalance between state spending and revenues collected will not solve itself.

Public meetings commenced March 18, 2016, and continued on an almost weekly basis through October 2016.[1] The resolution called upon the Task Force to report to the legislature and to urge and request the governor to support and implement initiatives for structural change. The key component would be a "specific plan for long-term tax policy that may be used to introduce legislation no later than the 2017 Regular Session of the Legislature." The Task Force, in concurrence with House and Senate leaders, lengthened the original September 1 report deadline to November 1. On that date, the Task Force submitted its Outlook and Recommendations to the legislature and the governor.

This final report, which begins with a Summary of Task Force Recommendations, is larger in scope and includes additional perspectives, background information, charts, and tables offered by the Task Force for a fuller account of its work during the year. The report outlines the basic principles of a good tax and fiscal system, identifies the problems with the current system in Louisiana, and recommends a package of solutions. These recommendations are designed to be holistic in impact. As a practical matter, we have to focus on one tax at a time when assessing an entire fiscal structure, but the changes in the entire tax structure that we recommend should be examined globally in relation to one another. We strongly caution against a piecemeal approach, since one tax change by itself may appear to be focusing on taxing one sector of the economy or one group of taxpayers, while examining all of the proposed tax changes will allow the overall impact of the proposed tax changes on all income categories, on individuals versus businesses, and on state obligations versus local activities, to be fully appreciated. Equally important, once reforms are in place, the legislature and the governor must resist the temptation to begin carving out exceptions or diluting the impact of the new structure.

A failure to act is not an option. Most of the temporary revenue fixes in 2015 and 2016, valued at well more than $1 billion, will expire in 2018. Realistic spending cuts of this magnitude are not expected to be found. A massive budget shortfall and deeply damaging instability would ensue. Neither does the Task Force see a good solution in simply extending all of the temporary revenue measures. In that scenario, the state would be doubling down on a broken and inefficient tax system, thereby inviting poor credit ratings, greater uncertainty in both the private and public sectors, and an inevitable return to the drawing board. It is the fervent desire of the Task Force to see Louisiana graduate to a more mature and stable form of taxation and spending. All of the recommendations posted here are well within our grasp if we decide to choose them.

The Task Force has thirteen members supported by the staff of the Louisiana Department of Revenue. The members of the Task Force are as follows:

- Kimberly Robinson, Secretary of the Louisiana Department of Revenue, Co-Chair of the Task Force (LDR Secretary)
- Dr. James Richardson, Co-Chair of the Task Force. He is the John Rhea Alumni Professor of Economics and Public Administration in the Public Administration Institute in the E. J. Ourso College of Business Administration at Louisiana State University. (principal on the Revenue Estimating Conference)

- Dr. James Alm, Professor and the Chair of Economics at Tulane University (one economist or tax specialist appointed by the Speaker of the House of Representatives from a list of nominees submitted by public or private universities in the state, including the Louisiana State University AgCenter and the Southern University AgCenter)
- Tom Clark, a partner with the Adams & Reese law firm and Chairman of the Committee of 100 (a member appointed by the governor)
- Jay Dardenne, Commissioner of Administration (Division of Administration Commissioner or designee)
- Jason DeCuir, Director of Public Relations for the tax service firm Ryan (one member of the business community appointed by the Speaker of the House from a list of nominees submitted from Blueprint Louisiana, Committee of 100 for Economic Development, and the Louisiana Association of Business and Industry)
- Barry Erwin, President of the Council for a Better Louisiana (a member appointed by CABL)
- William Potter, Senior Tax Director at Postlewaite & Netterville (a member appointed by the Society of Louisiana Certified Public Accountants)
- Sean Reilly, Chief Executive Officer for Lamar Advertising (one member of the business community appointed by the President of the Senate from a list of nominees submitted from Blueprint Louisiana, Committee of 100 for Economic Development, and the Louisiana Association of Business and Industry)
- Louis Reine, President of the Louisiana AFL-CIO (a member appointed by the President of the Senate from a list submitted by the Louisiana School Boards Association, the Louisiana Budget Project, and the Louisiana AFL-CIO)
- Randy Roach, Mayor of Lake Charles (a member appointed by the Speaker of the House of Representatives from a list submitted by the Louisiana Sheriffs' Association, the Louisiana Assessors' Association, the Police Jury Association of Louisiana, and the Louisiana Municipal Association)
- Robert Travis Scott, President of the Public Affairs Research Council of Louisiana (A member appointed by PAR)
- Dr. Steven M. Sheffrin, Professor of Economics and the Director of the Murphy Institute at Tulane University (One economist or tax spe-

cialist appointed by the President of the Senate from a list of nominees submitted by public or private universities in the state, including
the Louisiana State University AgCenter and the Southern University
AgCenter)

The Task Force would like to thank the substitutes who sat in for members at some meetings. They included Steven Procopio, Policy Director for
PAR; Scott Richard, President of the Louisiana School Boards Association;
Ed Parker, Louisiana AFL-CIO; Camille Conaway, Vice President for Policy
and Research at the Louisiana Association of Business and Industry; Bar-
bara Goodson, Deputy Commissioner of Administration; Ron Gitz, CEO
of the Society of Louisiana CPAs; Brandon Lagarde, a Director in the Pos-
tlethwaite & Netterville Tax Services Group; and Bryan Beam, Calcasieu
Parish Administrator.

Additional and profound thanks are owed to the many individuals, government officials, and interest groups that provided valuable information
and testimony to the Task Force. Their input was vital to the process. Due
to the engagement and support of employees of multiple state agencies, including in particular the staffs of the Division of Administration, the Department of Revenue, and the Legislative Fiscal Office, the Task Force was
able to request queries and multiple analyses of fiscal data. For these efforts,
the Task Force is most appreciative and forever indebted, as it would have
been impossible to conduct the Task Force's work without their substantial
knowledge, experience, and support through this process.

Summary of Task Force Recommendations

The Task Force on Structural Changes in Budget and Tax Policy started
with the premise that a tax structure should generate sufficient revenues to
fund legitimate and necessary government expenses. In so doing, the tax
structure should be fair, simple, competitive with other states, as well as
stable over the short and long term. These qualities are best achieved with
taxes that are broad-based with low rates and that do not play favorites for
or against a particular constituency. The Task Force viewed economic competitiveness and comparisons to other states as fundamentally relevant factors in its decision making, while attempting to assure that compliance with

a new structure would be easy and clear. The Task Force also believes that exceptions should be minimal and done for clearly established reasons that serve our state's needs.

The Task Force acknowledges that much of what the state spends each year is constitutionally and statutorily obligated before the legislature begins the budget debate and is primarily required to meet fundamental state obligations. The legislature is limited in its ability to alter the spending obligations, and there are few clearly identifiable areas that can easily be eliminated to materially reduce overall state spending. Additionally, a substantial portion of the state budget is derived from federal matching funds that cannot be used for anything other than the designated purpose. However, there are areas that should be addressed to provide for better budgeting practices and to prevent overspending, that would mitigate the potential for midyear deficits, allow for better long-term planning, and potentially free up revenues to address long-standing accumulated state obligations.

The Task Force offers the following recommendations, which should be considered as a package. Although the changes will require separate pieces of legislation, they should be considered in their entirety and not in isolation, because of their interactions with one another in establishing a balanced and fair tax system. With that in mind, the Task Force—after more than six months of information gathering and deliberations—makes the following recommendations:

BUDGET AND SPENDING RECOMMENDATIONS:

1. Avoid budgeting practices that allow for spending beyond available recurring revenues.
2. Implement and adhere to improved revenue-needs forecasting, particularly with regard to the MFP, Medicaid, and TOPS, that more closely predicts actual utilization. The state should strengthen current law, which provides for estimating conferences in various major spending areas, to provide a formal multiyear spending forecast for such things as Medicaid, the MFP, TOPS, and Corrections.
3. Continue the ongoing review of state contracts to identify opportunities for consolidation, renegotiation, or elimination.
4. Examine individual constitutional dedications to determine if they remain a state policy priority.

5. Conduct a holistic review of state trust funds for possible revision, elimination, or merger of funds.

6. Continue to implement fiscal structures that will help protect the state budget from swings in volatile state revenue streams, such as mineral revenues and corporate taxes.

7. Implement staggered sunsets on all statutory dedications to see if they can be adjusted, eliminated, or combined with others.

8. Continue payments to state pension systems on the initial Unfunded Accrued Liability under the current timeline to avoid increasing debt, while looking for ways to accelerate payments toward an earlier debt retirement.

9. Examine expected rates of return on pension investments to make proper adjustments to ensure that the retirement systems are not creating another new and costly unfunded accrued liability in the future.

10. Continue review of various tax credits, rebates, deductions, and exemptions to state taxes to determine whether they can be eliminated, curtailed, or more closely regulated.

SALES TAX RECOMMENDATIONS:

1. Expand the sales tax base and reduce the sales tax rate from its current 5 percent to no more than 4 percent. To do so, the Task Force recommends: (1) retaining, with a few modifications, the expanded state sales tax base adopted in Act 26 of the first special session of 2016 and amended by Act 12 in the second special session, which would continue the tax on such things as custom software, business utilities, and storm shutter devices; and (2) making certain services, such as those taxed in Texas and digital transactions, subject to sales tax. Some of the taxable services include cable and satellite television services, repairs to nonresidential commercial property, web hosting, and security services.

2. The state should take meaningful steps to establish a more uniform sales tax base by bringing exemptions and exclusions in line on both the state and local levels.

3. State and local governments should work to create a uniform system of tax administration, collection, and audit that respects and protects local revenue streams from any overlap with state revenues.

4. Give local governments the authority to increase their sales tax rates without a vote of the state legislature, but still require a vote of the people in the area being taxed. Sales tax and property tax reform are essential if local governments are to have the tax capacity to independently provide their own funding.

5. In order to provide greater clarity and ease of compliance, the Task Force recommends a recodification of sales tax law.

INCOME TAX RECOMMENDATIONS:

1. Eliminate the state deduction for federal income taxes paid, accompanied by appropriate state income tax rate reductions. This change would decouple Louisiana's income tax base from federal tax changes. Eliminating federal tax liability as a deduction for the income tax will break the connection between federal changes in tax policy and state income tax collections. The state should not be rewarded when the federal government decides to lower taxes nor penalized when the federal government decides to raise federal taxes. The only way to lower the individual income tax rates is to get rid of the federal tax liability exemption. The Task Force also recommends limiting the excess itemized deduction for personal income to 50 percent. These two deductions account for a reduction of $1.225 billion in income tax collections in Louisiana at the current rate structure. These exemptions provide a much larger tax break to higher income groups, both absolutely and proportionally. If the excess itemized deduction were limited to 50 percent, mortgage interest and charitable giving would still be deductible. This proposal, along with the state's reliance on the sales tax, will balance the overall tax structure among various income categories in terms of who is paying for state services.

2. Two options for changes to the individual income tax law—one constitutional and the other statutory. A constitutional option allows Louisiana to expand the income tax base, narrow the brackets, and lower all rates by 25 percent. A statutory option only allows base expansion and narrowing of the brackets.

• Under the constitutional option, the Task Force recommends allowing voters to approve the elimination of the federal income tax deduction that decouples the Louisiana tax base from federal tax changes. This option would include scaling back excess itemized deductions to 50 percent. A new three-bracket structure would be used, and rates of taxation lowered—1.5 percent on the first $25,000 ($12,500 single), 3 percent on $25,000 through $50,000 ($12,500 through $25,000 single), and 4.5 percent above $50,000 (above $25,000 single). Not only would rates be lowered by 25 percent, but they would also apply more fairly and evenly to all taxpayers because of the proposed elimination of many deductions and exemptions.

- Under the statutory option, the excess itemized deduction would be fully eliminated. This would be coupled with the elimination of other deductions and exemptions proposed by the Task Force. The statutory option would use the new compressed three-bracket structure, but tax rates would remain at the current 2 percent, 4 percent, and 6 percent levels.

3. Eliminate many income tax exemptions and credits and impose a moratorium on any new tax credits or exemptions applied to the individual income tax. The Task Force recommends keeping (1) the standard and dependent deductions, (2) the exclusion for military pay for active duty personnel, (3) the credit for taxes paid to another state, (4) the earned income tax credit (because it allows the state to enhance the progressivity of its income tax and reduce the regressive nature of the overall state tax structure), (5) the exclusions for social security and retirement income for public employees, and (6) credits related to child care and early childhood education (in part because these programs help all families and improve educational outcomes, and in part because they leverage federal money).

CORPORATE TAX RECOMMENDATIONS:

1. Eliminate the deduction for federal taxes paid for the corporate income tax. A constitutional amendment included on the statewide ballot on November 8, 2016, failed, with 44 percent of voters favoring the amendment. The reform would have decoupled the Louisiana tax base from federal tax changes and would have set the corpo-

rate tax rate at a flat 6.5 percent. The upper bracket rate for Louisiana currently is 8 percent. This approach would have better aligned Louisiana with its competitor states, potentially provided for a more stable source of revenue than the current corporate income tax structure, and eliminated instability in state corporate tax collections due to actions in Washington, DC. The Task Force believes this proposal should be considered again since it will be impossible to lower the marginal corporate tax rate, a very important ingredient in long-term tax reform, without eliminating a major exemption such as federal tax liability. Also, at this stage, it will be combined as part of an overall tax reform package and hopefully will be backed by political leaders with a strong constituency of support. A convincing public education effort will be needed.

2. Direct the Department of Revenue, with the Louisiana Tax Institute, to study moving from single-entity taxation on the corporate level to a system of combined reporting with findings due by January 2019. Under combined reporting, corporations are taxed based on their apportioned share of income of their "unitary group," which includes a variety of criteria, including common ownership, common management, and common lines of business. Combined reporting solves the profit-shifting incentive because related companies are part of a unitary group in which intercompany transactions are eliminated. Instead a state will apportion the entire unitary group, using a combined return to determine its share of its tax base.

3. Restructure, phase out, or eliminate the corporate franchise tax, provided the state identifies replacement revenue that coincides with changes in the tax. The analysis of the restructuring, elimination, or phaseout, along with the identification of the replacement revenue source, is to be conducted by the Department of Revenue with the Louisiana Tax Institute. The findings are to be presented to the legislature by January 2019.

AD VALOREM TAX RECOMMENDATIONS:

1. Amend the Louisiana Constitution to provide local governmental authorities with a role in granting industrial tax exemptions and create

a statutory framework to establish the extent of this role for local involvement, as well as defined policies for use of the exemption as an economic development tool that favors job growth.

2. Expand the use of payment in lieu of tax arrangements for local governments considering property tax exemptions to attract economic development. Such arrangements should require the coordinated approval of the elected officials in the impacted taxing jurisdiction.

3. Amend the Louisiana Constitution to allow for a gradual elimination of locally imposed inventory taxes over a ten-year period, accompanied by the elimination over a five-year period of the state income and franchise tax credit paid on inventory. To offset local governments' reduction in revenues, the Task Force suggests several options, including a constitutional change to allow a roll-up in existing property tax millages, enhanced local revenues resulting from expansion of the sales tax base, and changes to the industrial tax exemption, and creation of a temporary revenue sharing fund to bridge the gap as the inventory tax goes away.

4. Amend the Louisiana Constitution to limit the property tax exemption on property owned by nonprofits to that used exclusively for the tax-exempt purposes of the nonprofit.

ECONOMIC DEVELOPMENT INCENTIVE RECOMMENDATIONS:

1. Require the Louisiana Department of Economic Development (LED) and the legislature to establish sunset review periods for all incentive programs and eliminate underutilized or inactive programs.

2. Require LED to continue to monitor and regularly report on the performance of all its incentive programs. The reporting must include information on the return on investment for each program and be conducted by independent third parties in accordance with the legislatively established objectives for these programs.

3. Retain the Motion Picture Investor Tax Credit as a nonappropriated, nonrefundable tax credit incentive with both discounted redemption and transferability as alternative options for use. The legislature should implement a modified front-end cap to control the number of credits issued from inception and implement other mechanisms

to encourage reasonably timely use to avoid the creation of another backlog of credits that would put a drain on the state budget. The implementation of the front-end cap should coincide with the elimination of the back-end cap.

Note

1. Presentation materials, supporting documents, and video archives are available on the LDR website, http://www.revenue.louisiana.gov/LawsAndPolicies/TaskForceOnStructuralChangesBudgetTaxPolicy.

CONTRIBUTORS

Bibek Adhikari is an Assistant Professor of Economics at Illinois State University. He received his PhD in Economic Analysis and Policy from Tulane University in 2016.

Gregory V. Albrecht is the Chief Economist for the Louisiana Legislative Fiscal Office. He received his MA in Economics from Louisiana State University in 1983.

James Alm is Professor and Chair of the Department of Economics at Tulane University. He was formerly editor of *Public Finance Review,* and has worked on tax compliance and tax evasion, tax and expenditure limitations, taxpayer responses to tax reforms, and the determinants of state economic growth. He has also worked on state tax reforms, as well as on international projects supported by the World Bank, the US Agency for International Development, the UN Development Program, and the International Monetary Fund. He received his PhD in Economics from the University of Wisconsin–Madison.

Nathan Babb graduated from Louisiana State University with a Bachelor's degree in Economics in 2016. He has worked for the Louisiana Department of Revenue, the Board of Governors of the Federal Reserve System, and the Bundestag in Germany.

Grant Driessen is an analyst in public finance at the Congressional Research Service in Washington, DC. He received his PhD in Economic Analysis and Policy from Tulane University in 2016.

James A. Richardson is Alumni Professor of Economics and Public Administration at Louisiana State University. In 1988 he coedited *Louisiana Fiscal Alternatives* and in 1999 *Handbook on Taxation.* He has served as a member of the Louisiana Revenue Estimating Conference since 1987. He has consulted with the US Department of State, the US Department of

Commerce, and the US Department of Justice. He worked with the Financial Services Roundtable regarding recovering from disasters after Hurricane Katrina. He received his PhD from the University of Michigan.

Steven M. Sheffrin is Professor of Economics and Director of the Murphy Institute at Tulane University. He previously was on the faculty at the University of California, Davis and has served as visiting professor at the London School of Economics and Political Science, Princeton University, and Nanyang Technological University in Singapore. He has served as a financial consultant to the Office of Tax Policy Analysis with the US Department of Treasury. He received his PhD from the Massachusetts Institute of Technology.

Dan Teles is a research associate in the Metropolitan Housing and Communities Policy Center at the Urban Institute. He has also worked on the Louisiana Hazard Mitigation Grant Program and the New Orleans Area Habitat for Humanity. He received his PhD in Economic Analysis and Policy from Tulane University.

Greg Upton is an assistant professor in the Center for Energy Studies at Louisiana State University, with his research areas being economic, environmental, and public policy issues in energy and regulated industries. He received his PhD in Economics from Louisiana State University.

INDEX

Page numbers in italics refer to figures, tables, and maps.